Myths and [Mis] Perceptions

U.S.–MEXICO CONTEMPORARY PERSPECTIVES SERIES, 11
CENTER FOR U.S.–MEXICAN STUDIES
UNIVERSITY OF CALIFORNIA, SAN DIEGO

Myths and [Mis] Perceptions

Changing U.S. Elite Visions of Mexico

SERGIO AGUAYO

//with content analysis assistance from Miguel Acosta V.//

Translated by Julián Brody

LA JOLLA

CENTER FOR U.S.–MEXICAN STUDIES
UNIVERSITY OF CALIFORNIA, SAN DIEGO
///
CENTRO DE ESTUDIOS INTERNACIONALES
EL COLEGIO DE MÉXICO

Printed in the United States of America

Library of Congress Cataloging-in-Publication Data

Aguayo, Sergio.
    [El panteón de los mitos. English]
    Myths and [mis] perceptions: changing U.S. elite visions of
Mexico / Sergio Aguayo Quezada: translated by Julián Brody.
      p. cm. -- (U.S.–Mexico contemporary perspectives series ; 10)
    Includes bibliographical references (p.) and index.
    ISBN 1-878367-36-6 (pbk.)
    1. United States--Foreign relations--Mexico. 2. Mexico--Foreign
relations--United States. 3. Mexico--Foreign public opinion,
American--History--20th century. 4. Elite (Social sciences)--United
States. 5. Mexico--Politics and government--1946–1970. 6. Mexico--
Politics and government--1970–1988. 7. Mexico--Politics and
government--1988–   I. Title. II. Series.
E183.8.M6A48 1998
327.73072--dc21
                                      97-51682
                                        CIP

For Eugenia Mazzucato, creator of space and determination. For everything she did—and was unable to do—so that Cristina, Andrés, this book, and so many other things could come into being.

Contents

List of Figures

Preface

Few neighboring countries are as diverse as Mexico and the United States. Their differences are not merely economic. The two countries also have widely divergent worldviews, the products of dramatically different histories. Following World War II, the United States emerged as a global superpower, the center of an unprecedented network of riches and influence. Mexico, meanwhile, remained virtually unchanged—an insular society locked in its own reality and dominated by an authoritarianism that regulated day-to-day existence and interpreted the past, present, and future to suit its own ends.

In line with Mexico's worldview, nationalism and the border served as barriers against encroaching foreigners who sought to exploit the country's natural and spiritual wealth. But more, they demarcated the arena outside of which Mexicans were not to air their country's many problems. The most dangerous foreign presence, of course, was the United States, with its long history of aggression against Mexico. But because there was little Mexico could do against such a powerful neighbor, the national attitude became one of entrenched indifference.

One of the many consequences of this state of affairs was that most Mexicans knew very little about the United States. For someone like myself, growing up in Jalisco, *"el Norte"* was a contradictory and mysterious territory, idealized by migrant workers returning laden with electronic equipment and exaggerated tales of the United States.

At the time I began my studies at the Colegio de México in the early 1970s, the first serious cracks were appearing in the political system Mexico had inherited from its revolution. A wide range of groups was struggling to shake off the mantle of authoritarianism, while President Luis Echeverría criss-crossed the country preaching his vision of an independent Mexico and reminding us of the inherently perfidious nature of foreign countries, especially the United States.

Realizing how profoundly ignorant Mexicans were of the United States and catalyzed by the teaching of Josefina Vázquez, Lorenzo Meyer, and Mario Ojeda, I determined to do postgraduate work on the exotic topic of the United States. My central question was how much Mexico's proximity to this superpower had conditioned its economy, its political system, and its relationship with other countries of the world. Although I was well aware of the United States' long history of aggressiveness toward Mexico, I wondered whether the nature of the U.S. threat to Mexican sovereignty had ever varied. That is, if the United States was engaged in a permanent conspiracy against Mexico, what was the nature and thrust of its instruments over time?

These questions took me to the School for Advanced International Studies (SAIS) at Johns Hopkins University, where I soon learned there were no quick and easy answers. Although some U.S. natives did fit the caricature of the arrogant gringo, many—far more than I would have imagined—did not. I was surprised to discover that most were relatively unconcerned about Mexico. All of their energies were absorbed by a collective psychodrama of mutual recrimination and self-doubt about their past and their future. This was the state of the United States after Vietnam, after Watergate, after waves of demonstrations by students and minorities, and after marijuana and acid rock had turned the new generation against this materialist industrial and interventionist society.

Against this backdrop, I wrote a doctoral thesis on how the U.S. elite perceived Mexico following World War II. My reasoning was that if I could understand how they viewed Mexico, I could also comprehend the nature of their hostility and perhaps help Mexico develop more effective lines of defense. I was still blissfully ignorant of the many pitfalls that bedevil anyone pretentious enough to think he or she can fully understand the ideas and consciousness of a society as complex as the United States.

Although I obtained my degree in 1984, thirteen years would pass before I considered this work ready for publication. During this time, I explored other fields of knowledge while the world, the United States, and Mexico were transformed. In 1990, Carlos Salinas de Gortari's administration informed the Mexican population that their country had shifted course: proximity to the United States would no longer be considered a misfortune, but rather a golden opportunity for Mexico to penetrate world markets, overcome its economic crisis, and advance toward social justice and (perhaps) democracy. Mexico duly entered the North American Free Trade Agreement (NAFTA).

But just as Mexico seemed poised to join the ranks of First World countries, a rebellion broke out in Chiapas in January 1994. And in December of that year, Mexico was plunged into a major economic crisis that only exacerbated its already dramatic dependence on the United States. Concurrent with these events, Mexican society—and Mexico's political system—began to change. The midterm elections of

July 1997 suggest that the conditions for an accelerated transition to a democratic regime may finally be in place.

Despite these transformations, gaining an enhanced understanding of how Mexico is perceived by the United States, and of the nature and extent of U.S. influence, remains fundamentally important to Mexico. And this fact created a dilemma I did not anticipate when I began my studies. Over the years I had developed friendships and close professional relationships with U.S. colleagues whose work I cite in this volume. Should I follow the course set by Raymond Vernon who, in *The Dilemmas of Mexican Development*, omitted the names of Mexicans whose ideas contributed to his work, because some of them might be "ashamed to find themselves associated with conclusions that they did not share"? Or should I follow the practice of Judith Hellman who, in her preface to *Mexico in Crisis*, stated that she would "report on things just as they were, . . . without fear of offending my very dear Mexican friends, because even they would want me to write about these matters in a manner as objective and revealing as possible"? I chose the latter option, and it is this spirit that informs the present volume: with all possible objectivity and rigor, I explore the manner in which government officials, scholars, and journalists have written about Mexico, pointing out success and failure, truth and myth.

This book goes beyond my original intentions. As I became increasingly aware of the evolution of U.S. perceptions and the impact of ideas on reality, I was also able to reinterpret certain aspects of Mexico's recent history. In this process, I confirmed, adjusted, or put to rest a number of myths about Mexico, Mexicans, and the role of the United States in Mexico's recent history. Despite the inherent difficulty of uprooting well-established beliefs, I am pleased with the accomplishment: nothing could be more harmful, particularly in the present period of redefinition and transition, than to continue misleading ourselves about what we were and what we are.

Over the years, I have incurred a series of debts, and I am at last able to express publicly my thanks to some of the people and institutions that have made this work possible. The book began as a doctoral thesis presented to SAIS at Johns Hopkins University, where my studies were financed by grants from Mexico's Consejo Nacional de Ciencia y Tecnología (CONACYT) and the Institute of International Education, which awards the "Lincoln-Juárez" scholarships—in addition to support from SAIS itself.

The process of transforming the dissertation into a book manuscript was eased by support from many individuals and institutions. The directors of the Center for International Studies at the Colegio de México have patiently witnessed the evolution of this book. They are, chronologically, Lorenzo Meyer, Rafael Segovia, Blanca Torres, Soledad Loaeza, Ilán Bizberg (whose enthusiasm and generosity were crucial through the final stage), and Celia Toro, all of whom were unfailingly generous in their support. The book also gained from input from colleagues and friends at the Colegio de México: Jorge Padua, Manuel García y Griego, Gustavo Vega, and the Academic Computing Services division. Special thanks are due to Bernardo Mabire and Lorenzo Meyer, who read the final draft and made many useful suggestions. I also benefited from the support of Diana and Mario Bronfman, Laura Mues, and Julio Sotelo.

An indirect though critical influence was my experience as a columnist for *La Jornada*. One of my most important sources was journalistic material, and my active participation in establishing this newspaper and continuing as a contributing writer for over twelve years gave me a better understanding of the sometimes neurotic but always creative passion involved in the elusive search for objectivity under the inexorable pressure of deadlines. My learning experiences in this vein continued when, in 1996, I moved to another great newspaper, *Reforma*, where I continue to write a weekly column that is carried by fifteen other Mexican dailies. Another extremely important influence, especially for certain chapters, was the ideas and the spirit of colleagues and friends at the Academia Mexicana de Derechos Humanos, Alianza Cívica, and many other organizations that have contributed to the unfinished adventure of building a just and democratic Mexico.

In the United States, I would like to acknowledge the encouragement I received from Riordan Roett, Bruce Bagley, Piero Gleijeses, and Ekkehart Kripendorff at John Hopkins University, as well as the support of Wayne Cornelius, who in 1981 provided me with a much needed tranquil space in which to work at the Center for U.S.–Mexican Studies at the University of California, San Diego, of which he was the founding director. Kevin Middlebrook, the Center's second director, gave the text a careful reading and provided a timely stimulus. And Ruth Adams, a dear friend, provided an example of vitality in the exploration of new ideas.

Vital financial support from a number of U.S. institutions allowed me to comb archives and carry out interviews, in addition to underwriting some of the book's costs. My deepest thanks to the Mexican office of the Ford Foundation and to two programs of the John T. and Catherine MacArthur Foundation: the Program on Peace and International Cooperation, administered by the Social Science Research Council, and the Research and Writing Program of the Program on Peace and International Cooperation. The William and Flora Hewlett Foundation also contributed, through the Colegio de México's Center for International Studies. The manuscript's final draft was begun at the New School for Social Research, where I received the support and encouragement of Judith Friedlander and Aristide Zolberg.

I would also like to thank those who participated directly in locating, organizing, and coding information: Mónica Guadalupe Mora, Betty Strom, Blanca María Jouliá, Noel Thomas, and particularly Yolanda Argüello and Laura Valverde. The proofing and correction of many drafts was deftly handled by Patricia Bourdon and Virginia Arellano. In the final stages, Doris Arnez Torrez and particularly Fernando Ramírez Rosales contributed much-valued enthusiasm and professionalism. Mrs. Antonia Fierro Mota gave me both affection and food throughout my months of isolation in Tepec, Morelos, and became the confidante of my silences. Cristina Antúnez gave me support in resolving some computer problems. The book's swift publication in English is due to the professionalism of Sandra del Castillo. Julián Brody Pellicer contributed the passion and intelligence of an artist-translator.

But I have reserved my most special acknowledgments for four individuals. The first is Miguel Acosta, who carried out one of the most arduous—though fascinating—aspects of this research with enormous diligence, responsibility, and cheerfulness. Together we mastered the methods of content analysis. And to the others I dedicate this book—to my wife, Eugenia, and to my very dear children, Cristina and Andrés, whose long-running skepticism and good humor are now finally rewarded with this publication. To them, at last, I can say, "believe it or not, it's finally finished."

1

Methods and Objectives

IN BROAD OUTLINE

The initial objective of this work was to describe the evolution of the U.S. intellectual and political elite's vision of Mexico from the end of World War II onward. While this remains a key objective, as the research progressed it became increasingly clear that the underlying causes for the transformation of the elite's vision itself called for explanation, leading to a second research focus: how ideas have influenced, and continue to influence, the relationship between Mexico and the United States. Once on this path, an evaluation of the United States' positive and negative impacts on Mexico, and especially on that country's political system, became inevitable. Looking back over the completed work, one realizes that in many ways it constitutes a reinterpretation of several aspects of Mexico's contemporary history.

Following certain historical antecedents, the analysis begins with 1946, a year that signaled a new era in global history, in which the United States was to be the dominant force. This nation began creating the institutions and fine-tuning the mechanisms it needed to exert its new-found power, and in the evolution of this grand U.S. strategy Mexico has played a fundamental role.

The features of Mexico's political system, economy, and international relations were clearly delineated during the presidency of Miguel Alemán (1946–1952). His term in office, which reaffirmed Mexico's corporatist, authoritarian, and centralized presidentialism, produced an eclectic combination of private and social economies regulated by a powerful State. It also gave rise to a peculiarly bi-dimensional style of international relations, the product of an independent diplomacy combined with close geographic proximity to the United States.

The analysis runs chronologically to early July 1997. It includes President Carlos Salinas de Gortari's six years in office, the first half of the Ernesto Zedillo administration, and the economic and political crises that have slowed Mexico's passage through this recent period of (as yet unfinished) transition, which reached an apex in the mid-term elections of July 6, 1997. Special attention is given to 1986, the year in which Mexico's ruling classes decided to dismantle the prevalent economic model. Their efforts were aided by the United States, and this cooperation led to the gradual abandonment of Mexico's independent diplomacy. One underlying factor in the relationship that held constant, both before and after 1986, was Washington's unconditional support for the Mexican government elites. The first indication that such support could ever waiver did not appear until May 1997.

Although this book deals with diverse aspects of Mexican reality, the emphasis is on Mexico–United States relations and the Mexican political system, especially the Mexican regime's capacity to control society through a skillful combination of hegemony and coercion, and the persistent efforts of a number of groups to struggle against the government's grip.

Little or nothing is known about what weight the "external factor" had during this historical period (and continues to have) in the political system, and its inclusion here is somewhat groundbreaking. With only a few exceptions, the literature on transitions to democracy rarely considers the external factor;[1] further, the Mexican transition itself is largely ignored.

This research will demonstrate that the characteristics, evolution, and perseverance of Mexican authoritarianism can best be understood if we incorporate what the U.S. elite does, or fails to do. To go one step further, one might assert that the single most important factor underlying the permanence of the Mexican regime—or its slow rate of degradation and decay—has been the backing of the U.S. elite. This is one of the reasons why understanding how Mexico has been perceived through the prism of global visions, and the myths and ideologies of the United States, has now become a project of some urgency.

The methodology used and the interpretation offered here carry a caveat: new approaches are often unsettling, and hopefully the reader will show patience with this approach to an extremely complex and multidimensional problem, guided by a reflection of Lucien Goldmann's: "there is no general or universal rule for research, save for adaptation to the concrete realities of the studied object" (1969).

---

[1]Exceptions include Huntington 1991 and Lowenthal 1991.

IDEAS AND PERCEPTIONS

How did Americans perceive Mexico between 1946 and 1996? How were these perceptions transformed, and why? How objectively or truthfully did these perceptions portray Mexican reality? How did they affect other aspects of reality? What is the importance of these issues for current-day Mexico? To answer these questions, one must begin at the beginning, with the raw material, the perceptions themselves, and a central thesis: no concept emerges from nowhere; each has a reason for being, an explanation.

Trying to capture in words the meaning of "ideas," "perceptions," or "consciousness" is to venture into inhospitable realms of knowledge, a journey traced and retraced by philosophers, psychologists, and biologists without a hint of conclusive success.[2] Extensive bibliographies cover the topic of ideologies, but here, too, we often find "several meanings, sometimes difficult to distinguish from one another" (Plamenatz 1970: 27). Nor will we find any apparent consensus regarding the importance of ideas for social transformation. Despite these obstacles, how these terms are understood here must be clarified in order to define this volume's theoretical scope and methodology, to create a systematic framework for information, and to establish a continuity of approach throughout the various stages of the research.

Ideas are human beings' mental representations of concrete objects as perceived through the senses, or of abstractions, based on other ideas and expressed as words, the "instruments of thought" (Aldous Huxley, in Humphrey 1993: 117). Ideas can be expressed as words or as visual images (in caricatures, for example), with language or drawing serving as the instruments of thought.

Through ideas (which may rest on rigorously established facts or on unsubstantiated subjective judgments), individuals, groups, and societies gradually develop explanations—both true and false—concerning themselves and their surroundings, which can then serve as guidelines for action. Through our examination of the ideas held by U.S. elites, or of the Mexican regime's control over the ideas that reach Mexican society, we will find that there is an inescapable relationship between what we do and what we think and feel—as considered in the following discussion of four capital concepts: worldview, myth, consciousness, and relationships of domination.

---

[2] A brilliant analysis of the current state of the debate appears in Humphrey 1993.

WORLDVIEW AND IDEOLOGIES

Worldview is understood here as it was used by Lucien Goldmann: a society or social group's general interpretation of reality (Goldmann 1969: 103).[3] A worldview takes form and expression in foundational documents (such as constitutions or other writings considered pivotal); in aesthetic, ethical, and philosophical values; and in a pantheon of heroes and mythologies. Its function is to explain reality and, in so doing, to provide guidelines for the organization of the social groups that adopt it and for the direction these groups must go. Some societies hold a more scientific worldview than others, for example.

When we speak of worldviews, we are usually referring to those of nation-states; however, Plamenatz has pointed out that worldviews can also emerge from geographic regions encompassing a number of countries, or from "diminutive sects found only in one small corner of the world" (1970: 15). This is a crucial point, because it will enable us to conceptualize a complex map of ideas that transcends national borders.

As represented in this volume, ideologies are closely related to a global optic, although they occupy a lesser category, because, in providing but a partial notion of reality, they hold a reduced explanatory capacity (Goldmann 1969: 103). From this perspective, a number of ideologies can coexist within any specific collectivity. Relationships will be fluid and harmonious to the extent that the fundamental postulates of a worldview are shared or charged with tension when one ideology seeks to supplant the dominant worldview—as sometimes occurs.

MYTH

One of the most important criteria in evaluating worldviews and ideologies is how faithfully they reflect reality. In order to apply this criterion, analysts often employ the concept of myth, with its two meanings. The first, which is the most prevalent, associates myths with lies or false explanations of reality. Frazer, for example, suggests that myths are "mistaken explanations of phenomena, whether of human life or of external nature. . . . [B]eing founded on ignorance and misunderstanding, they are always false, for were they true, they would cease to be myths" (in Murray 1960: 309). One might say, then, that the explanatory validity of worldviews and ideologies is determined by the number of falsehoods contained within their myths. An accepted procedure for separating truth from falsehood involves

---

[3]Goldmann is known for his insights into literature and society; see Goldmann 1969, 1976a, 1976b, 1977.

employing the scientific method, which requires that all statements be supported by verifiable facts. In other words, science serves as the critic of mythologies (Levin 1960: 114).

The second meaning associates myths with the aspirations of an individual or a social group. For Henry Murray, a myth is a "collective dream" expressing future goals that make sense of action and life. A great many myths have been founded upon the belief that the installation of a political regime with specific characteristics can solve the problems that ail a particular society, or even the world. This is of fundamental transcendence for social transformation: "collective dreams" form the basis for imagining better futures. They can motivate members of groups to make enormous sacrifices, radically transforming their surroundings (Murray 1960: 316). Although only after installing a given political regime are we able to evaluate the veracity of their asseverations, imagining diverse futures is in itself a fundamental factor for change.

In sum, worldviews and ideologies combine objective, incontrovertible facts with myths, endowed with shifting and diverse combinations of truth and falsehood, of aspirations and frustrations. This volume outlines the U.S. elite's perception of Mexico and examines the truthfulness of its central tenets.

CONSCIOUSNESS

Consciousness, both "real" and "potential," is one of the most important concepts in the study of ideas, and its interpretation has provoked extensive, often acrimonious debate (see, especially, Humphrey 1993: chap. 16). For Goldmann, "real consciousness" is a sort of instant snapshot of the beliefs held by a nation, an individual, or a group of individuals, regarding a diverse range of subjects at a specific point in time. According to this definition, huge amounts of information can be reduced to quantifiable (and often believable) indicators by means of public opinion polls, which can ascertain the beliefs of specific groups at a particular moment.

One of the most serious shortcomings of opinion polls is that, although they can discern changes in ideas, they cannot explain how and why such transformations take place. For such an explanation, we must introduce other elements and concepts, such as "potential consciousness," the maximum horizon for a person's or group's capacity for understanding.[4] Evidently a person's or group's real margins of consciousness can be either broadened or reduced. According to Goldmann:

---

[4] One disconcerting question is whether there are any limits to what the human mind is able to comprehend.

> Every group tends to have an adequate knowledge of reality; but its knowledge can extend only up to a maximum horizon which is compatible with its existence. Beyond this horizon, information can only be received if the group's structure is transformed; just as in the case of individual obstacles, where information can be received only if the individual's psychic structure is transformed (1976a: 34).

In other words, some information cannot be received, because "it transcends the group's maximum potential consciousness." Consequently, history is sometimes envisioned as a battle between knowledge and ignorance. This book will explore the changing frontiers of consciousness in Mexico and the United States and the obstacles to consciousness that exist in intelligence, in the state of knowledge, and in created interests. When created interests come into play, ignorance is frequently deliberate and pretended.

Bernard Lonergan has referred to the phenomenon that leads individuals to ignore "relevant questions" that could provide them with a "balanced and complete opinion" concerning a certain topic as *scotosis* (1970: 191–93). But how can we know if this inattention is voluntary or involuntary? What role do political and economic interests play? What is the importance of individual, as opposed to group, history?

A psychoanalyst's role is to enhance his patients' capacity for introspection and perception, so that they can understand and overcome impediments to adequate processes of thought and function. Societies as a whole have no psychoanalyst; perhaps social scientists, intellectuals, or journalists fulfill this function somewhat by formulating the questions that generate and popularize knowledge and ideas, ultimately expanding a society's consciousness. These individuals— whose function it is to produce ideas—interact permanently with their reference groups and with society.

RELATIONSHIPS OF DOMINATION

The notion of relationships of domination can link the concepts in the preceding sections with political realities. Inequalities permeate both society and the international system, and it is natural that the established order, imperfect thought it may be, will be supported by those who benefit from it. What is less evident is why the established order should also be accepted by those who are dominated, those who derive little or no benefit from it. The answer encompasses two concepts: coercion and hegemony.

When a member of a group violates one of the group's explicit or implicit rules, those who dominate, who govern, can select coercion as an option to force this individual to adhere to the norms that sustain the established order. In an oft-quoted phrase, Max Weber wrote that "the State is an association that claims a monopoly upon *the legitimate use of violence*" (1946: 334, emphasis added). Methods of coercion, as well as their legality or legitimacy, vary through time and space: in Europe, barely two centuries ago the myth of the ruler's divine right was sufficient justification for the physical elimination of anyone who questioned it; torture was a legitimate procedure, and its application was regulated in legal codes (one of the most terrifying instances is the Austrian *Constitutio Criminalis Theresiana* of 1769). Torture is still practiced today, although it is legally forbidden and enjoys no legitimacy.

Coercion need not be applied at all times. In general, all that is required is that the members of a given society internalize the possibility of potential punishment (public tortures and executions clearly obey a pedagogical motivation). As pointed out by Michel Foucault, "The role of disciplinary punishment must be to reduce deviations. It must, therefore, be essentially *corrective*" (1976: 184).

The notion of hegemony has a different logic and intent: dominators incorporate into their conceptualizations the idea that relationships of inequality and domination are natural, inevitable, even desirable. This turns upon a number of factors, which usually appear in combination: ignorance on the part of the dominated, the guarded and subtle nature of the domination, the deep internalization of feelings of inferiority or impotence, the advantages enjoyed by the established order, and, finally, the fact that rebellion is frequently considered to be unrealistic, farfetched, or fraught with risk (O'Donnell 1978: 1158–59).

Hegemony depends on ideas that can legitimate it on the basis of reason or tradition. Once formulated, these ideas must be disseminated, a process in which policies for communication and propaganda are fundamental. In this propagandizing process, the role of the State varies according to the regime. In an authoritarian or totalitarian nation, a great deal of the government's energy is expended in controlling ideas, especially those that run contrary to its vision. The incarceration, elimination, or demotion of opposition members has frequently been justified by labeling them as heretics, Communists, or capitalists.

In modern democratic countries, the State also seeks to control ideas and use coercion, but its ability to do so is limited because the relationships of domination are operating under different rules. For example, it is society's aim that the State (the central agent for the implementation of relationships of domination) be an impartial power, regulating social conflicts and relationships as a representative of society's interests (Bartra 1978: 32–33). In this kind of regime, a social contract is renewed periodically by the citizenry through elections. Government behavior is monitored by an extremely broad range of academic, media, and citizens' groups, leading to more legitimate and stable political "structures" (Milliband 1978: 175–76; Poulantzas 1975: 255–56). Consequently, the restraints on the use of coercion are tightened, and relationships of domination become less visible, or more tolerable.

Even a glance at history from this point of view will reveal that State coercion has not disappeared, although the brutality of its application has been limited and even in authoritarian or totalitarian regimes there are constraints on its use. Over the last two centuries, as restrictions on coercion have increased, the importance of hegemony as a form of domination has grown, and increasingly it must be justified with rational arguments. Even in nations like Mexico, hegemony is more important than coercion.

The specific combination of hegemony and coercion differs by country, and it changes across time according to culture, history, geopolitical standing, the solidity of society and/or the State, and so on. The nature of this combination will determine the profile and weight of the instruments used to preserve the relationships of domination: ideological, economic, political, diplomatic, or military (O'Donnell 1978: 1158–73). It is even possible to analyze a society by examining how its ruling classes use and justify coercion and hegemony, and what types of resistance emerge within the society.

IDEAS AND HISTORICAL CHANGE

Coercion and hegemony are justified and applied through ideas, ordered into worldviews and ideologies, whose contents, whether myth or reality, are determined by potential consciousness. During the peak of Nazi power and influence, broad sectors of German society, and many in other countries, were convinced of (or forced to agree with) the validity of the fascist worldview, even though it included many myths whose content was fallacious and unsupported by the scientific method but were premised on the assumption that the future would be better. This and many other instances forcefully demonstrate that the importance of certain ideas depends on the level of power behind them, and not only on their internal coherence. There are also ideas that are supported by the intellectual or moral authority of those who pronounce them.

This leads to a complex issue: the relationship between ideas and economic structure, politics, culture, military power, or the determinants of social change (see, especially, Gramsci 1975: 64–66). Of particular interest is the importance of ideas for a regime's permanence or transformation. Nicos Poulantzas summarized a key criterion: although "economic factors" are determinant in the long run, this "does not mean that [they] always hold the dominant role in the structure" (1975: 14). Ideas, therefore, have a certain autonomy and can even become the determinant factor.

Every regime seeks to maintain its hold on power through the use of violence or hegemony. Yet history has demonstrated time and again that transformation is inevitable. Social change may be controlled or postponed, but never eliminated. Dissatisfied groups or individuals will appear, disagreeing either totally or partially with the established order, with the dominant ideas. Peaceful or violent attempts to "correct" the problem will soon follow, potentially effecting change at one or several levels of society or in the regime as a whole.

To be successful, the dissatisfied person or group must offer an alternative ideology; and for this ideology to be transformed into a worldview, it must have sufficient intellectual capacity to develop a proposal for the future that could win wide acceptance. During this gestation period, the myth as "collective dream" is fundamentally important, as it extends the promise of a more attractive future for those who are dominated or dissatisfied, in exchange for certain sacrifices on their part. In his *Reflections on Violence*, Georges Sorel put forward the concept of "total strike" as a method for achieving socialism. He suggested that the "total strike" is a "myth within which socialism is compressed" (1961: 127). Years later, Mohandas Gandhi postulated *satyagraha* (passive resistance, civil disobedience) as the weapon with which the weak can, through an act of internal conversion, modify unfair laws and improve their situation (1993: 318). These are but two perspectives, two different methods, in the perennial struggle to transform relationships of domination.

Another event of enormous transcendence among the revolutions and social transformations taking place in recent centuries was the French Revolution. It obliterated the institutions of the ancien régime and revolutionized social relationships and the nature of thought by establishing equality as the criterion for all social relations and rationality as the ingredient of all legitimacy. As Hegel summarized in his *Encyklopadie*, "in this reasoning and reflexive era, no one will get far if he cannot adduce a founded reason for everything, no matter how wrong or mistaken it may be" (1817).

THE USE OF CONCEPTS

Inter-American relations, the understanding that exists between Mexico and the United States, and the Mexican political system can all be explained within the theoretical framework outlined above. For example, the nature of inter-American relations is irrevocably stamped by the might of the United States, which uses diverse combinations of coercion and hegemony to maintain an order that is in line with its best interests. In the summer of 1953, for example, Washington concluded that the Guatemalan regime of Jacobo Arbenz was headed toward Communism and that it must be overthrown. Following a sophisticated campaign of destabilization and isolation, U.S. forces invaded Guatemala in 1954 and forced Arbenz to resign the presidency. There was no public outcry in the United States; the overwhelming majority of those who had an interest in Guatemalan affairs accepted and supported the U.S. government's actions.

Three decades later, President Ronald Reagan's National Security Council admitted in an internal document that its Central America policy—which pursued the overthrow of Nicaragua's Sandinistas and the containment and destruction of insurgents in El Salvador—posed "serious problems for public opinion and Congress," creating difficulties for the "maintenance of its orientation" (*New York Times*, April 7, 1984). Society's consciousness had broadened, and limits had been imposed upon its government's will.

U.S. public opinion regarding Mexico has undergone similar transformations. A 1960 internal White House memorandum quotes President Dwight Eisenhower as stating, "If communists were to come to power in Mexico, we would very probably go to war" (WH 1960). Almost thirty years later, in 1989, ex–CIA director William Colby commented in an interview that "were the new Mexican left, or Cuauhtémoc Cárdenas, to come to power, this would not pose a threat to the security of the United States" (author interview). Evidently a greater flexibility of opinion now prevails among members of the U.S. elite.

The viewpoints espoused by the hundreds of U.S. citizens writing about Mexico in tens of thousands of pages also underwent a similar transformation. Between 1946 and 1986, eleven *New York Times* correspondents wrote 1,328 articles, each of which expresses a moment of individual history but also demonstrates the influence exerted on these correspondents by their editors in New York, by officials of the U.S. Embassy in Mexico, by members of the Mexican government, and by Mexican society. These influences also acted on academics and functionaries, guiding their decisions about topics, emphasis, theoretical framework, methodology, and sources.

The opinions of U.S. elites regarding the best methods for exerting dominance over Latin America underwent extensive transformations. In general terms, the space for the use of coercion shrank, while that for persuasion or hegemony expanded. But how and why did these modifications take place? To provide an answer, we could focus on personal histories, detecting crucial points in education or work experience; we could even examine mystical revelations. However, the most fruitful approach may well be to focus on the collective consciousness, which frames the development of individual consciousness.

Edward Carr has pointed out that every historian—and, in fact, every social analyst—is a part of history: "The point in the procession at which he finds himself determines his angle of vision over the past." In other words, "before he begins to write history, [the historian] is a product of history." Our perceptions depend on our point of view or on that of the group or groups to which we belong. An academically rigorous social chronicler must be conscious of the role he plays, both as judge of and participant in the studied society. In this way, one can achieve a certain intellectual distance, affording a more objective appreciation of society. As Carr suggested, "Before you study the history, study the historian. . . . [B]efore you study the historian, study his historical and social environment. The historian, being an individual, is also a product of history and society" (1963: 43–48). And, according to Goldmann,

> Every manifestation of ideas is the work of its individual author and expresses his thought and way of feeling, but these ways of thinking and feeling are not independent entities with respect to the actions and behavior of other men. They exist and may be understood only in terms of their inter-subjective relations which give them their whole tenor and richness (1969: 128).

Forms of behavior—or written texts—can be expressions of a "collective consciousness to the extent that the structures" they express are not unique to their authors, but rather are shared by the "various members who form the social group" (Goldmann 1969: 129). Sociolinguistics also employs the notion that individuals are representatives—consciously or unconsciously—of the social group in which they are immersed; they are "collective speakers" (*locuteurs collectifs*) (see Marcellesi and Gardin 1974).

Because a collective consciousness, derived from a shared ideology or worldview, does in fact exist, different individuals who wrote about Mexico (many of whom never met) frequently expressed similar ideas in different media. This is not to say that individuals serve as megaphones, repeating the ideas of the groups from which they emerge. This would nullify the potential of the human mind and consciousness by implying that humans must repeat the same ideas again and again throughout eternity, not unlike the scratched record of a bygone technology.

The relationship between a person and his social group is dynamic and charged with tension; every collectivity seeks, in greater or lesser measure, to homogenize its members' thought processes. Nonetheless, individuals invariably appear who are willing to think differently, who are willing to imagine alternative futures, to take risks, and to transcend the confines established by the collectivity, in order to return as bearers of new perceptions of reality. A certain risk is always present; such individuals may on occasion formulate aberrations or confusions that can mislead others.

Every era has produced adventurers of thought and action, the sort of exceptional individual who, Hegel believed, "can put into words the will of his age, tell his age what his will is, and accomplish it" (1942: 295). In general, contributions are more modest and transformations more gradual. This examination of the U.S. elite's vision of Mexico spans an era rich in individuals who transcended the views of the majority and who, even under unfavorable circumstances, modified the perceptions of their groups and their countries as part of a consistent, though uneven, process. We should not forget that the reverse has more often been the case. Research by Foucault and others has amply demonstrated that the social group always seeks to sap and/or confine individual imagination, imposing controls and marginalizing anyone who thinks differently.

This is why we must differentiate between "individual time" and the "historical time" of groups, classes, or nations (Goldmann 1976b: 112). In the culture of the United States, for example, the individual generally plays the primary role, and it is not unusual for students of American journalism to focus on "individual time." Thus Walter Lippmann envisions the product that reaches the reader as the result of an entire series of individual decisions as to "what items shall be printed, how much space each shall occupy, and what emphasis each shall have" (1957: 354).

The value of "individual time" is undeniable. Nevertheless, a study with such a focus would require several lifetimes merely to outline the intellectual biographies of the academics, journalists, and functionaries whose words appear in this volume, though many of their individual histories are fascinating. The volume focuses instead on "group time"; therefore, the emphasis is on points of agreement and the individual contributions that have amplified consciousness. This work will also establish the validity of U.S. perceptions, the weight of various interests, the functional mechanisms of relationships of domination, and the effect of ideas upon other aspects of reality (in particular, the authoritarianism of the Mexican political system).

Because the interpretations and conclusions presented are mediated through the author's own ideas, myths, and interests, they may be questioned. The scientific method, which was used to gather, organize, and process the collected information, is also a mechanism that can detect and correct the limitations of one's individual consciousness.

HUNTING FOR IDEAS IN THE UNITED STATES

The complexity and heterogeneity of U.S. society soon dashed any early hopes to conduct a systematic study of the multiple ways in which Mexico and "what is Mexican" have been understood by diverse social groups in the United States. It would also have been impossible to cover every shade of perception in every group and specific region (California, for example, calls for special treatment). Therefore, all references from the worlds of literature, art, cinema, or television have been set aside, to concentrate instead on the perceptions held by public officials, academics, businessmen, and journalists with a specific interest in U.S. foreign policy (the so-called establishment).

This elite includes individuals at the peak of political, military, and economic power, easily able to realize their will, though others may be opposed, or to take important decisions that affect nations such as Mexico. Institutions that enjoy this power include the U.S. Congress, the Department of State, the armed forces and intelligence services, and the Departments of Justice and of the Treasury, as well as multilateral organizations such as the World Bank and the International Monetary Fund. This group also includes large transnational corporations and the private banking sector. These entities, clustered around Washington and New York, have a shared group consciousness, and they function and interact according to fairly elaborate formal and informal rules (Mills 1956).

Closely linked to this elite are the communications media and universities which, along with their other roles, must generate and reproduce ideas, information, and knowledge. These are not mere appendages to a larger structure; they are autonomous institutions in an intense, though nonantagonistic, relationship. As argued below, the journalist, the congressman, the CIA analyst, and the academic share the same set of values, although they may interpret and fight for them in different ways.

Another central actor is society, which influences and interacts with the elite in a number of ways. Because U.S. society has to a great extent turned inwards, participation in the development of foreign policy usually has been restricted to small groups. The half-century that I examine, however, included a fundamental break with this rule. The convulsions of the 1960s—especially those related to the Vietnam War—gave rise to relatively broad social groups determined to intervene in a range of foreign policy affairs. This phenomenon, which has not yet run itself out, now holds a wide range of implications for Mexico in the 1990s.

In order to retrieve the ideas of the "establishment" elite, the research included a review of official documents, reports of academic research, and journal articles, as well as hundreds of formal and informal interviews. One early finding was that the U.S. community of "Mexicanists" has a far more sophisticated and informed vision than that found in popular culture; even prejudices are expressed with greater subtlety. This community's members are in permanent communication through formal and informal relations; their interpretations frequently merge, diverge, and merge again within the framework of a shared worldview.

The research also included comparing Mexican and U.S. writings and the interpretation of certain key events by the Mexican press. The latter provided important insights into the mechanisms that the Mexican regime employed to control ideas. The full range of the Mexican research has not been incorporated, however, because the objectives in writing this book called for a heavier emphasis on the U.S. literature.

Also examined were both public and restricted-access official documents. Those that were once confidential or secret carry a special advantage: they are sometimes very explicit about the attitudes within the U.S. or Mexican bureaucracies, and about the strategies and policies these bureaucracies have developed to protect their interests. This research draws on extremely rich material from the U.S. Department of State, the U.S. Embassy in Mexico, the armed forces, the CIA, and the U.S. Federal Reserve. Although hundreds of documents were consulted, there is no way to tell how representative this sample really is; it is impossible to know how many similar documents remain classified.

Other valuable public documents were the memoirs of former U.S. presidents and high-ranking functionaries, as well as the reports on the human rights situation in Mexico and the world that the Department of State has presented to Congress on a yearly basis since 1976. Another relevant source was a collection of articles on Mexico— published in twenty-seven American military publications between 1949 and 1988[5]—that reveals the U.S. military's view of Mexico.

Books and articles by academics were of special interest, because the U.S. elite places a great deal of importance on knowledge and because the basic social function of academics is to generate knowledge. Their writings trace the development of U.S. knowledge concerning Mexico. In total, the present volume refers to the work of over one

---

[5]These were selected based on the *Air University Library Index to Military Periodicals* (Maxwell Air Force Base, Alabama), which covers seventy-nine publications.

hundred academics writing about Mexico after World War II.[6] It also covers the left flank of the U.S. academic spectrum and incorporates everything regarding Mexico that appeared in the magazine *NACLA Report on the Americas,* which began publication in 1967.

Only the most important works have been considered, and the various authors' trajectories through time were not traced. During the 1950s, for example, Robert Scott expressed great confidence in the Mexican political system, but by 1980 he had been forced to modify his views significantly (see Scott 1971, 1980). If one were to explain the motives for his individual trajectory, this work would edge into the biographical. And, as noted above, that is not the intention—for several important reasons.

The third important source was the articles on Mexico that appeared in U.S. daily newspapers. Because of the dailies' publication schedule, they can serve as a barometer for the transformation of U.S. perceptions and agendas into instant snapshots. Nearly 7,000 articles were examined; because of the importance of these materials, their representativeness and the methods and techniques employed in their analysis are outlined in the following sections.

One additional consideration lends confidence to the assumption that this work has captured the essence of the U.S. elite's view of Mexico: American political culture is more open than its Mexican counterpart (it is easier to gain access to information, for example). These journalistic and academic sources, official documents, and interviews provide a clear vision of the U.S. elite's way of thinking. They also serve as the basis for a coherent explanation of contemporary Mexico.

SOCIETY AND THE PRESS IN THE UNITED STATES

The press is a reflection of the society in which it operates. In order to fully understand the nature of newspapers, we must understand the societies within which they exist. Diversity, one of the most distinctive features of the U.S. press, is a clear reflection of this society's heterogeneity: 1,611 newspapers, including daily and evening editions, published in 1990, for a combined average daily circulation of 62,327,962 copies. None can be considered truly national; they all reflect the cities, regions, and/or social groups toward which they are aimed. This wide variety poses problems for any definitive affirmations regarding the representativeness of the U.S. press.

Yet despite this heterogeneity, U.S. newspapers share three characteristics (exceptions do exist but are of little significance). First, they

---

[6]For a panoramic overview of the academic bibliography produced through 1989, see Camp 1990a.

are private enterprises oriented toward profit through extensive circulation and the sale of advertising space. Second, they are guided by a "social responsibility" code, in which the media represent the public interest; their responsibility, therefore, is to inform and educate their readership with objectivity, to act as watchdogs over government action (assuming they are politically and economically independent), and to play a part in the identification of issues that should appear on an agenda of national debate (see Sigal 1973; Siebert, Peterson, and Schramm 1963; Carey 1974; Harrison 1974; Monteforte 1976; Jensen 1962). And third, and most important, they express the diverse values, beliefs, and mythologies of U.S. ideologies and worldviews.

For example, studies of journalism in the United States frequently focus on individual actors. Newspaper owners such as Robert McCormick of the *Chicago Tribune* or William Randolph Hearst, owner of the chain that bears his name, were famed for their total control over editorial policy, turning their editorial pages into a "megaphone or conduit for the transmission of their prejudices." They also manipulated the media to defend their own business interests, as the Hearst-based film character "Citizen Kane" so aptly portrayed. In stark contrast, the Ochs-Sulzbergers—current owners of the *New York Times*—are scrupulously careful not to influence the paper's editorial line.[7]

For practical reasons, a single newspaper was chosen as the focus of study; a comparative study covering a broad historical period was simply not feasible in the time available. The newspaper selected had to be as representative as possible of the U.S. elite's worldview. Those considered included the *Los Angeles Times*, the *Boston Globe*, the *Dallas Morning News*, the *Miami Herald*, the *New York Times*, *USA Today*, and the *Wall Street Journal*, looking at their circulation, influence, quality (as gauged by specialists in journalism and the press), the consistency of their international coverage, the existence of indexes facilitating the location of articles about Mexican affairs, and their deployment of Mexican correspondents.

THE *NEW YORK TIMES*

Ultimately the *New York Times* (henceforth NYT, or *Times*) was singled out as one of the newspapers that best represented the ideas on Mexico that circulated among the U.S. elite. An important reason underlying this choice was the paper's distribution. In 1991, the *Times* ran

---

[7]These cases are discussed, respectively, in Hulteng 1973: 33, and DOS 1925. See also Sigal 1973. Hulteng has demonstrated that, regardless of intent, the opinions of newspaper owners do influence editorial content through, for example, their reporters' and columnists' self-censorship.

1,209,225 copies of its daily edition and 1,762,015 copies on Sundays. Although these numbers may seem small against the backdrop of a total newspaper circulation of some 62 million copies daily in a nation of 249 million inhabitants, only two papers performed better: *USA Today* and the *Wall Street Journal* (the former is a relatively new publication, and the latter does not appear on weekends).

An even more important factor was the *Times*'s decision to adopt the norms of U.S. society. Its owners envision the *Times* as a "cathedral" of liberalism, pursuing the same aims as the nation as a whole: "the preservation of the democratic system and the established order." History has shown time and again that the United States and the *Times* are "equally committed to capitalism and democracy" and that what has been "bad for the nation" has often been "just as bad for the *Times*" (Talese 1969: 93). Based on these principles, the *Times*, and other communications media, aim to inform their readers in an objective and professional manner, perform a vigilant and ceaseless appraisal of society's leaders and businesses, and generate profits for their shareholders.

Published material is ruled by the same criteria for the generation of knowledge as those that apply in universities and government research centers. That is, at least in theory, in the United States producing a published work involves the objective handling of facts and the incorporation of diverse opinions. To guarantee their independence, the *Times* and other media expressly forbid gifts or subsidies from the organizations on which they report. According to a document outlining the paper's policy regarding conflict of interest, "the integrity of *The Times* requires that its staff avoid employment or any other undertaking, obligation, or relationship that creates or appears to create a conflict of interest . . . or otherwise compromises *The Times*'s independence and prestige." Those who write for or work in the newspaper's financial section are barred from both direct and indirect participation in the buying or selling of stocks and shares (NYT 1986a: 2, 5). These strict principles, and the unquestioned rigor with which the *Times* seeks to apply its professional criteria, have generated solid respect for a newspaper whose intellectual sophistication is well matched to the lifestyle of one of the most cosmopolitan cities in the world.

The respect that the *Times* has garnered is widely reflected in the specialized literature. Irving Kristol wrote that there has never been a paper "so dedicated to the public interest, so uncompromisingly committed to what it conceives to be the highest journalistic standard" (1967: 37). Another reason for the *Times*'s influence, according to John Ottinger and Patrick Mainess, is that "editors from Coast to Coast check the *Times* front page as a reference point, if not as a guide for their own news judgments" (1972: 1006).

The *Times* is also widely read in other countries. Ottinger and Mainess consider that there is no "head of government anywhere who is not a *Times* reader" (1972: 999). Although this affirmation seems exaggerated—many heads of government are unable to read in English, and some are hard-pressed to read at all—the *Times* clearly does enjoy an extensive global readership, largely as a result of the United States' great influence. That is, a newspaper's international presence depends on its quality and on the power of the nation in which it is published. When the United States displaced Great Britain as the leading world power, the *New York Times* acquired the preeminence that once accrued to the London *Times*.

Another aspect that made this newspaper particularly attractive was its internationalism (a typically New York characteristic). Although society in the United States is notoriously ignorant regarding the rest of the world, it does include a sophisticated elite that is specialized in foreign affairs. The foreign affairs establishment nourishes and feeds upon the *Times*; specialists like Bernard Cohen consider it the leading exponent of a "small and specialized foreign affairs press in the United States"; he adds that it "is read by virtually everyone in the government who has an interest or a responsibility in foreign affairs" (1963: 134, 231).

Even its critics acknowledge this fact. Vitalii Petrusenko—an old-fashioned Soviet academic whose prestige was built upon denunciations of Yankee imperialism—pointed out that the *Times* is "the best news source (especially foreign news) in the US" (1976: 56). In sum, the *Times* is a "prestige newspaper,"[8] the opinion source on foreign affairs for a nation's government elite. Thus this research follows Claire Selltiz's advice: "select the paper that is commonly quoted as the origin with the greatest authority or prestige in the nation concerned—for example, the *New York Times* in the United States" (Selltiz, Wrightsman, and Cook 1976: 394).

The *Times*, as the paper that prints "all the news that's fit to print," sees itself as a first draft of history. Its emphasis on facts, numbers, and declarations proved invaluable for this reinterpretation of Mexican history over the last five decades. After a detailed analysis of how the *Times* has treated Mexico and a comparison with the writings and analyses produced by both Mexican and U.S. academics, this author was able to confirm that praise of the *Times* is well deserved and that the *Times* is highly representative of the elite in the United States. Nonetheless, some shortcomings were also apparent: conservative thinking is not well represented in the *Times*, and there are certain aspects regarding Mexico that are insufficiently treated or totally ig-

---

[8]For a detailed discussion of the notion of "prestige newspapers," see De Sola Pool 1952.

nored. It is revealing that these shortcomings are mirrored in the writing of academics and functionaries, allowing us to detect a broader process of evolving consciousness. The following chapters will delve into the reasons for these transformations and limitations.

CONTENT ANALYSIS OF THE *TIMES*

Once the *Times* had been selected as the paper that best represents the U.S. elite, the next step was to decide which (and how many) Mexico-related articles to include in the study and what criteria to employ to guide the analysis of the paper's various sections (editorials, current events, news, etc.). The choice was made for complete coverage: every article on Mexico published between January 1, 1946, and December 31, 1986—a total of 6,903 articles, opinion pieces, informative notes, and editorials, dealing with politics, society, finance, and so on—located through the annual NYT *Index*. Based on a review of thirty-one categories of articles, the sample is believed to be representative of the total universe.

This information, recovered from microfilms, was subjected to content analysis, a procedure identified by Philip Stone as a "research technique for making inferences by systematically and objectively identifying specified characteristics within a text" (1966: 5). In other words, content analysis is a way of dissecting texts to reveal the ideas, intentions, and styles of their writers. Through content analysis, we can establish the relationship between different texts or evaluate the effect of a text on the "attitudes or acts of readers" (Berelson 1952: 5). This technique is extremely useful in detecting the frequency with which key issues (the variables) appear or fail to appear. With well-chosen variables, content analysis can provide an insight into the thought processes of a group or society.

The present study utilized 215 variables for the analysis of the 6,903 items on Mexico, including visible characteristics (page, size, section, etc.); the nature of the information source (functionaries, diplomats, the opposition); and the most revealing aspects of the economy, the political system, foreign policy, and the nature of Mexico and Mexicans. Each article was coded for the number of topics it examined and whether the ideas put forth were positive, negative, or informative (neutral). (The coder's objectivity was guaranteed through a technique described in appendix B, which also lists the variables used and provides a more technical discussion.) The information processing resulted in a rich and versatile data bank, allowing for a broad range of comparisons and conclusions regarding the evolution of ideas in the United States. (Appendix A presents this information in a series of figures.)

It became apparent early on that content analysis provides an excellent empirical basis for the study of the U.S. elite's perceptions of Mexico.[9] For example, it clearly reveals the distribution of *Times* sources. The 6,903 articles examined included the opinions of 10,524 individuals or institutions, of which 59 percent were public officials, 12 percent businessmen, 7 percent other newspapers, and only 4.5 percent members of the opposition (figure 8), confirming that between 1946 and 1986 the *Times*, and especially the daily edition, primarily quoted members of the elite.

Interestingly, a large percentage of these opinions came from Mexicans. However, even though Mexican opinions figure in this analysis of U.S. viewpoints, this does not alter the goal of the research, as it was U.S. nationals who decided whom to quote and which ideas to feature.

The most frequently quoted Mexicans were functionaries and businessmen, demonstrating a rarely documented but not uncommon proposition: that there are remarkable similarities between the thinking of elites in Mexico and in the United States, the result of an understanding that frames and conditions the bilateral relationship, Mexico's political system, and Mexican nationalism. Obviously, an exclusively journalistic and numerical view of reality has limitations, which have been compensated in part through the use of official documents, academic research, and interviews.

To summarize, this analysis covers multiple dimensions and is sustained by a wide range of information, ordered through an original methodology. Certainly not every question raised by the phenomenon of consciousness, by the evolution of U.S. perceptions of Mexico, by the bilateral relationship, or by the nature of the Mexican political system has been resolved. However, the abundance of material presented here can cast light in certain dark corners and can do much to help us reinterpret the last fifty years of Mexican history, including Mexico's relationship with the United States.

---

[9]Although this kind of analysis has gained popularity in recent decades, most content analyses seem to cover relatively brief time periods or are based on representative samples. None covers as extensive a period nor as broad a universe as that described here.

2

Ideas and Institutions in the United States

WORLDVIEW

U.S. society is extraordinarily complex, diverse, and in many ways contradictory (Hartz 1955: 52). Yet Americans share a worldview that has been consolidated through laws and institutions, and that has become a model for a large number of countries in this century. This worldview is founded on the U.S. version of economic capitalism, which exalts private property, market forces, individual initiative, and liberalism—and liberalism's goal of creating greater freedom for individuals, who, at least in theory, have equal rights and opportunities before the law (David Smith 1968). According to U.S. thought, the individual enjoys a privileged position. A pivotal notion here is the subordination of governmental institutions to the individual, whose responsibility and right it is to participate in the handling of public affairs. Because public power corrupts, the logic goes, government officials must be rigorously controlled.

Former U.S. president Harry Truman (1945–1950) declared that "the State exists for the benefit of man, not man for the benefit of the State" (NYT, March 4, 1947), reiterating a persisting theme in U.S. society, whose culture—films, literature, and theater—celebrates individual figures who confront, and usually vanquish, the powers of government as well as all manner of external threats. Complementing and reinforcing this worldview is the myth of the American Dream—the premise that anyone can go from rags to riches (or become president) in this land of opportunity and freedom, a promised land, at least for those who adhere to its prescribed lifestyle.

The individual's rights are upheld by a number of mechanisms, including a wide range of organizations, both large and small, that constitute an extensive and complex social fabric. A multiplicity of groups, representing the interests of the many communities that practice participatory or "direct" democracy or who supervise and control their government officials, have appeared on every level and are concerned with a vast range of issues.

These broad arenas for individual action are supported, but also limited, by stipulations in law and custom. For example, custom dictates that wealthy individuals should return some of their wealth to the community. These philanthropists are rewarded with tax deductions in the short term and renown in the long term as their names are preserved in foundations, plaques, and buildings.

This exaltation of the individual, allied to an innate mistrust of the State and a preference for intermediate organizations, has generated in the United States an abiding disdain for systems of political ideas that are formally structured as ideologies; these are associated with institutions that curtail or inhibit the individual's freedom of choice and action. This goes some way toward explaining the absence of militants or rigid, structured platforms in the U.S. political system. In the United States, as opposed to the rest of the world, political parties modify their programs according to the region, the election, the period, and/or the individual, with political debate focusing, therefore, on specific issues (Gabel 1974: 254).[1]

Despite the diversity and heterogeneity of their social fabric and their mistrust of ideologies, Americans have nonetheless created structured bodies of ideas to explain reality and also to serve as guidelines for action. The great majority of American society, including its most politically representative forces, shares a dominant worldview, even though specific groups or individuals may lean toward one or another variant of the conservative and liberal ideologies, generally converging on fundamental principles and diverging on the details.

Points of contention between conservatives and liberals have included the extent of the State's role in resolving social problems and the form that foreign assistance should take. In very general terms, conservatives tend to assign a greater responsibility to the individual, while liberals have a "greater awareness of the group, and of the community's responsibility for the maintenance of social welfare" (Marcus 1960: 224). Regarding foreign aid, conservatives have long held that the emphasis should be on private investment and trade; liberals, meanwhile, have stressed a greater role for government and multilateral resources.

---

[1] On this topic, also see Shils 1968 and Aron 1966.

Even though they may disagree within the political arena, Republicans and Democrats, independents and libertarians, are linked by an essential set of values. This diversity founded on unity, this extraordinarily developed capacity to generate peaceful consensus, lies at the very heart of the enduring strength of U.S. institutions.

Other characteristics of U.S. political culture are optimism, pragmatism, and impatience. Americans believe that humanity is in a state of perpetual progress, confirmed by continual technological advancement. This widespread faith in technology is largely a result of the importance that the United States has traditionally assigned to education and the development of knowledge. It forms an important part of the American belief that almost any problem can be solved with initiative and the right technology, as long as both are applied in a timely manner (Marcuse 1968: 221–39).

Thus the American worldview is predicated on the principles of equality, individual freedom, respect for private property and free market forces, and a belief in the exceptional character of the United States and the American people (to be discussed in the next chapter). Such ideas pervade Americans' very existence and define how they perceive themselves and other nations. These principles also inform American social science and journalism, whose exponents frequently seek to present facts in an objective manner and take a variety of perspectives into account.

"THE WORLD'S BEST HOPE"

Americans are absolutely convinced that they enjoy the best political, economic, and social system in history. As Stanley Hoffmann pointed out, Americans see themselves as the "favorites of history" (1968: 112).[2] Heightened self-esteem and self-praise are nothing new; these have always formed part of the history of the United States. Shortly after the United States gained its independence from Great Britain, Thomas Jefferson announced that this new nation was the "hope of the world." Some years later Abraham Lincoln added that the United States was the "last, and best hope on earth." And well into the twentieth century, Ronald Reagan assured Americans that "U.S. citizens are freer than any other people" and that "they have achieved more than any other people" (in Armstrong 1983: 31–32).

These beliefs have been fundamental in shaping U.S. foreign policy. Americans have often felt a messianic need to impose their system of democracy, free economy, and social organization on the rest

---

[2]Not so many years ago, the Soviets were quick to reply that it was they who enjoyed the chosen system, in a clash of national egos that nourished the long-standing conflict between the two superpowers.

of the world, usually justifying their actions by asserting that sharing American ideas benefits everyone, including Americans. Such actions would be unexceptional if they were founded on egoism alone. But there is a spiritual dimension to this view of foreign policy, evident in the fact that presidential initiatives are termed "doctrines," as though they were part of the canonical precepts of religion. This deeply ingrained belief in the exceptional character of the United States has been used to justify this country's acts of aggression toward weaker nations.

The United States' arrogance, as well as the country's continued success, has provoked a broad range of reactions throughout the world. Some applaud Americans for their ability to generate wealth, their scientific advancements, capacity for organization, common sense, the high level of freedom most U.S. citizens enjoy, the tight rein they maintain on their political leaders, and their generosity. In many international sectors, the American way of life is a model to be emulated.

However, others criticize their defects and incongruities. They point out the United States' pervasive racism, unrefined cuisine, and lack of taste; the infantile nature of Americans' sense of humor; the drug addiction, violence, and loneliness that characterize life in the big cities; and the proliferation of unbalanced individuals, who, obsessed with success, adopt extravagant forms of conduct, ranging from impersonating Elvis to founding religious cults or cannibalizing their neighbors. The hypocrisy of U.S. foreign policy, which preaches the values of democracy while supporting corrupt and repressive governments, is also a frequent target for critics.

Following chapters focus on Americans' innate belief in themselves as an exceptional people, using this as a doorway to a more general exploration of the history of the United States and its relationship with Mexico.

WHY AMERICANS BELIEVE THEY ARE EXCEPTIONAL

The American system encompasses a number of valuable features, among them the solidity of U.S. institutions and the clear-sightedness of the country's leadership at key historical moments. However, other factors have also played an important role in the history of the United States, and one of these is luck. In the United States' struggle for independence, the absence of feudal institutions and the meager opposition from the colonial British government meant that the country had no need to create a new central power in order to destroy the old order (Hartz 1955: 5, 16, 42). The human cost of independence was fairly minor: after eight years at war, the American forces had suffered only 4,435 battleground fatalities. This, together with the infant nation's able leadership, allowed a system to emerge that guaranteed ample margins of freedom for its citizens.

This lucky star continued to shine into the nineteenth century, when, isolated from the mainstream of European intrigue, the United States annexed extensive territories formerly belonging to its weaker neighbors. The U.S. invasion of Mexico in 1846, in which Mexico lost half of its national territory, cost the United States the lives of 1,733 combatants and some $170 million (in 1972 dollars) (Handleman 1973: 28–29). In 1867, the United States purchased Alaska from Russia, and in 1898, after an easy victory over an exhausted Spanish empire, it occupied Cuba, the Philippines, and Puerto Rico.

This expansion brought with it vast material resources, which were exploited with foresight and diligence. The expanding American experiment also served as a magnet, attracting an influx of dynamic and enterprising immigrants from all over the world. Once arrived, these immigrants had greatly varied experiences, with Africans, Chinese, and Mexicans, along with Native Americans, bearing the brunt of the heavy social costs of this ambitious experiment.

This period was followed by a schism between two opposing worldviews—the northern and the southern. The Civil War (1861–1865) inflicted lasting scars on the American social panorama. Its fatalities, numbering in the hundreds of thousands, make it the United States' most costly conflict in terms of casualties as a proportion of the nation's total population. In the realm of ideas, this conflict largely suppressed the southern worldview (although the "Jim Crow" laws extended the life of segregation).

Following the Civil War, the United States embarked on a redefinition and consolidation of its worldview. The "progressive" era that covers the late nineteenth and early twentieth centuries eliminated many of capitalism's most glaring defects, thus preempting the active and vocal Left that was engaged in vigorous political planning for an alternative, socialist worldview (LaFeber and Polenberg 1975: 316–17).

In 1917, the United States entered World War I, just as the Bolsheviks came to power in Russia, initiating the global confrontation between two diametrically opposed worldviews that was to dominate the twentieth century. Within the United States, the ruling elites unleashed a ferocious campaign against the Left in the "Red Scare" of the 1920s, which effectively eliminated it as a viable alternative.

During capitalism's most serious crisis—the Great Depression of 1929—Fascism and Nazism played havoc with the European democracies, but in the United States even the most agitated of political protesters dared not overstep the system's rules.

By the end of World War II, the United States had attained a level of power unprecedented in human history. The wars of the first half of the century had stimulated unparalleled economic growth in the United States, while the costs of war—in matériel and human lives— was shouldered primarily by other nations. In World War I, for example, the United States lost 116,516 soldiers in combat, compared to Russia's total of 1,700,000; and in World War II, the United States suffered 291,557 casualties, while the Soviet Union reported total losses of 6,115,000.

UNITY AND DISSENT IN THE POSTWAR PERIOD

The second half of the twentieth century can be subdivided into three periods. The first two were summed up by Henry Kissinger: "after the Second World War, the American people were united in the firm belief that our cause was just, our purposes benign. . . . [After] Vietnam, we became a nation divided, full of doubt, and with little confidence in the kindness of destiny" (DOS 1975). The third period began in the 1980s and continues to the present.

World War II confirmed that the United States' participation was indispensable in global affairs, thus resolving a long-standing struggle for dominance between the country's internationalists and isolationists. Fighting under the liberal standards of individual freedom, free trade, and self-determination, the United States confirmed its exceptional character on the battlegrounds of World War II; it remained to be tested in the conflict with the Soviet Union.

During the Cold War, the United States was able to demolish every trace of left-wing organizations within its own territory, reaffirming the unity and consensus underlying the country's worldview, fine-tuning their instruments, and imposing relationships of domination. Although coercion was used (in the witch-hunts of McCarthyism), in the main the majority view was imposed by means of hegemony, with the government and the media constantly reiterating the principles of the dominant worldview. In a society predisposed to believe any government statement, these ends were easily achieved.

A consequence of this process was the homogenization of society and the weakening of the cultural diversity introduced by the steady immigration stream. Paul Piccone noted that "Taylorization, capital-intensive technology, the culture industry, and consumerism, combined within a productive system that was based on the automobile and military expenditures, and this facilitated the penetration of capitalist relations into all crevices of everyday life" (1978: xxi).

Herbert Marcuse has suggested that American culture fell into a certain "unidimensionality" during the 1950s. Most Americans opted to adapt to the established order and abandoned all imaginings of alternate futures which, by questioning the intellectual validity and legitimacy of the present, might support a different worldview. Drawing on terminology presented in the preceding chapter, Americans' capacity to create "collective dreams" was diluted. Marcuse maintains that perhaps "the most singular achievement of advanced industrial society" was that critical theory no longer had "the rationale for transcending this society" (1968: xii). Quashed in the arenas of politics and of ideas, critical theory's ties to any significant social group or social class were severed. Alternative worldviews persisted only as intellectual proposals, relegated to library collections or to clandestine radical groups in the ghettos of political marginalization.

This unidimensionality of American society, this gathering lethargy, came to an end during the 1960s and 1970s, when the established order was shaken by a series of protests against ethnic, political, economic, and gender inequalities, against the many vices (real and imagined) of industrialized society, and against the Vietnam War and the Watergate scandal. The greatest blow in terms of foreign affairs was surely the intervention in Vietnam, where the United States suffered 58,135 dead and a serious political defeat. This debacle was catastrophic for a people that had, so far, never lost a conflict on foreign soil (Hoffmann 1968). These years brought the exceptional character of the United States into question. U.S. society's enduring faith in its leadership crumbled, and public interest in foreign affairs began to rise. A majority of the population had concluded that their leaders needed permanent oversight, and this included their activities in other countries.

The 1980s went some way toward restoring confidence in the exceptional nature of the American system, but society's mistrust of its leadership, bred during the 1960s and 1970s, was not dispelled. In the sphere of foreign policy, this heightened awareness was reflected in an effort to understand and tolerate the differences of other societies and in a marked reticence to use military force to impose the United States' will on other nations. This attitude persisted even after the Cold War's demise. An important change taking place during the 1980s was that domination abroad came to be exerted through economic instruments and multilateral institutions that enjoy the support of most world governments and in which the most important member is the United States. Democracy and peace are now enforced mainly through the United Nations or through economic adjustment programs imposed by the International Monetary Fund.

A THEORETICAL FRAMEWORK FOR INTERNATIONAL RELATIONS

Relationships of domination, hegemony, and coercion are useful concepts when analyzing events within a nation-state whose government holds a monopoly on the use of violence. To apply these concepts to the study of international relations may seem somewhat unconventional; the international system lacks a supranational authority able to exert coercion. Nonetheless, these concepts are useful in the study of an international system that includes strong and weak nations, and in which powerful countries can resort to force or hegemony in order to impose their will.

The goals of U.S. foreign policy have always been to defend America's interests, to combat threats to its integrity, and to promote (sometimes to impose) its lifestyle and forms of political or economic organization. What has evolved is the manner in which these goals are pursued and adapted to the moment, the region, and the country. Although during the nineteenth century Washington rarely hesitated to dispatch marines or gunships to impose its will by force, by the turn of the century a transition was under way. This era witnessed significant European expansion into Africa and Asia, while the United States merely demanded that these lands open their doors to U.S. trade and capital in a "anticolonial imperialism" that sought to dominate without actually occupying territory (and facilitated the Morrow-Calles understanding of 1927).

The United States' self-perception, the nature of its political system, and certain changes in the international community's agenda all made persuasion an increasingly important tool. A National Security Council report dated March 1953 reflects the alternative policies regarding Latin America that received consideration in the postwar era (NSC 1953a). The report was based on the notion that the "salient political feature" in the Western Hemisphere was the "United States' predominant status" (NSC 1953a: annex, p. 1). The NSC's intelligence analysts confirmed a widely shared idea: that the Soviets could potentially project their power into the region, and that "Communism in the Americas" was a "potential threat" (JSPC 1947: 20; NSC 1948: 2). Three options were suggested:

- A "policy of compulsion," defined as a return to "military force, economic sanctions, and political pressures to compel Latin American countries to act in accordance" with the United States' best interests. It was concluded that, at that time, this option would prove "disastrous."

- A "policy of detachment," which would rely on "occasional favors, and the occasional display of military force in urgent circumstances, to keep the situation under control." This option was rejected: given the ongoing global confrontation with the Communist countries, such a policy might facilitate the "rise to predominance in Latin America of forces inimical to United States interests."

- A "policy of cooperation," which would accentuate the "community of interests, the close interdependence both in peace and in war, and the similarity of goals of all Western Hemisphere countries, including Canada." It was felt that this would be the policy that could "best serve the interests of the United States" in both the short and the long term.

An important aspect of this NSC document is that it states the manner in which this goal is to be achieved: the best method would be to convince Latin Americans that it is in their interest to "collaborate" with the United States, with whom they share a "similarity of objectives." The U.S. Department of State also emphasized that the goal for American foreign policy should be to persuade Latin Americans that "their own best interest requires an orientation of . . . policies to our objectives" and that the United States was treating them fairly and respecting their economic and social aspirations (DOS 1952: 34–36).

To pursue this objective, U.S. policy makers implemented a number of procedures. Intelligence systems produced extensive reports on the situation in Latin American countries and on the views of their elites. Opinion polls, meanwhile, provided "snapshots" of public opinion; in 1947, public opinion polls carried out by American intelligence indicated that Latin American "majority opinion is not only Catholic and patriotic, and thus inherently anti-Communist, but it is also strongly pro-democratic and reformist" within a "predominantly capitalist framework" (CIG 1947). Some of these opinion polls cast doubt on the accepted myth of Mexico's anti-American stance. The United States Information Agency reported that "in no other countries . . . does the US rank higher in the opinion of the general public than it does [in Mexico and Brazil]. A large majority [of Mexicans and Brazilians] found US economic policies generally helpful [and were favorable toward] private foreign investment" (USIA 1956: iii–iv).

The United States' preference for hegemony does not mean that it has renounced the use of coercion. To the contrary, a wide range of military, economic, and diplomatic instruments for coercion remained, and a multitude of arguments were developed to justify their use. An internal State Department document from 1952 notes that the principle of nonintervention was "not a United States doctrine: it was imposed . . . by the unanimous will of the Latin American states as the price for their participation in the inter-American system" and was directed "solely against [the United States]" (DOS 1952: 22). According to another document, an important U.S. goal in Latin America should be to "prevent the spread of irresponsibility, of extreme nationalism, and of the belief that [this region] can ever be immune from the exercise of American power" (NSC 1952: annex, p. 11).

Following chapters include explanations of the different ways that hegemony and coercion were combined, as well as the justifications that were presented for their use.

3

The Understanding between Mexico and the United States

Experts who explore the relationship between Mexico and the United States cannot ignore the marked contrasts between the two nations. Although the two countries share an extended border and important interests, their ethnic, religious, and cultural origins, models of political and economic organization, and historical evolution are all profoundly different.

Although the relationship has been studied extensively, many aspects remain unclear and paradoxes unresolved. Of particular interest is the fact that, after the Mexican Revolution of 1910–17, Mexico followed policies that diverged from the paradigms set down by the United States. That is, Mexico pursued an independent foreign policy in which the United States was viewed as a potential threat; its economic model was a mixed property regime in which the State played an active, clearly protectionist role; and its one-party, authoritarian, corporatist, and presidentialist political system bore no resemblance to the liberal paradigms that prevailed in the United States.

Given Mexico's importance for the United States[1] and the United States' intolerance toward divergent tendencies, especially during the Cold War, how can we account for the U.S. strategists' indifference, even cordiality, rather than hostility or alarm, toward the Mexican elite? How was the Mexican leadership able to develop and implement such a divergent model in the very shadow of the United States? We may be able to answer these questions by approaching the relationship from another perspective.

---

[1]Underlined by the fact that only Mexico and Canada fall under the jurisdiction of the Joint Chiefs of Staff, while other nations in the hemisphere are assigned to the Southern Command.

THE HISTORICAL LEGACY

Different cultural and political systems and marked asymmetries in power have created a legacy of stereotypes and a jumble of love and hate, admiration and fear, attraction and disdain between these two frequently nationalistic and racist societies, forced to coexist in geographic contiguity. In the early centuries of the two nations' common history, the colonies that would become the United States were the weaker party and New Spain was the regional power, but their respective population centers were so distant from one another that this power inequality left virtually no mark. Mexican and U.S. histories began to clash only after both nations had won independence.

After independence, the United States established a highly novel form of political organization that was widely copied by groups wishing to transform their own societies. These emulators included the leaders of the Mexican independence movement. Because the U.S. elite's interests in Mexico were limited to its material resources, the U.S. reaction to the Mexican struggle was largely one of indifference, almost certainly symptomatic of a deep U.S. contempt toward Mexicans, who inherited the stereotypes originally applied to the colonizing Spaniards: cruel, lazy, "corrupt, and effeminate" (Vázquez 1984). This was the basis for a widespread belief that Latin Americans are incapable of developing viable democratic governments. For John Adams, "democracy [could not be established] amongst the birds, the beasts, the fish, or the peoples of Hispanic America" (in Vázquez 1984). Such reasoning was frequently used to justify the exploitation of an inferior nation (Mexico) by an exceptional people (the United States), who believed that in dominating a weak population they were fulfilling their historic duty.

There is an interesting parallel between the United States' concept of "manifest destiny" and the Communist Manifesto. Underpinning both views of history is an innate belief in the respective actors' exceptional character and predestined role as mankind's redeemer. These ideas would ignite a smoldering confrontation between two opposed worldviews; they would also be used to justify widespread atrocities.

In 1848, Mexico, weakened by internal conflict and defeated on the battleground, was forced to cede half of its territory to the United States,[2] inflicting enduring scars on the Mexican consciousness and modifying Mexican attitudes toward the United States. Although Mexico had lauded the American experiment during the early decades of the nineteenth century, after its defeat in the Mexican War, the country turned inward and did its best to ignore its northern neigh-

---

[2]It was long held that the Mexican government was responsible for the war of 1846–47. See U.S. Army 1963.

bor. One consequence was Mexico's failure to study the United States, a shortcoming that persisted well into the 1970s (Cosío Villegas 1968; Vázquez 1985). This was an unwise course of action, because it meant that Mexico also failed to develop appropriate instruments with which to defend its interests.

Moreover, ignoring the United States did not make that country disappear. It continued to figure in the calculations and obsessions of Mexico's ruling elite, who have always had to negotiate and strike agreements with this dominant power more accustomed to taking unilateral action.

THE UNITED STATES AND TWO REVOLUTIONS

Early twentieth-century Mexico posed no serious concern for the United States. Although it was ravaged by dramatic social problems, Mexico enjoyed economic growth under dictator Porfirio Díaz, who governed hand-in-glove with foreign interests. The U.S. elite saw this as the ideal regime for a people incapable of governing themselves.

The Mexican Revolution elicited a different, though not enduring, attitude in the United States. President Woodrow Wilson sympathized with the revolutionaries and believed that they would demonstrate the viability of democracy for the Hispanic American nations. To aid Venustiano Carranza in his struggle against Victoriano Huerta, Wilson invaded Veracruz, manipulated weapons deliveries, and played the trump card of diplomatic recognition. However, Wilson's experiment in support of democracy faltered when the United States began gearing up in 1917 to enter World War I. The Bolsheviks' triumph in Russia that same year completely reversed U.S. opinion concerning the Mexican Revolution.

The nearly simultaneous revolutions in Mexico and Russia show certain parallels. After the Bolsheviks' October revolution, the United States expressed its distaste for revolutionary democracy or dramatic transformations, always preferring gradual, peaceful change within a formal democracy where economic growth is encouraged by means of an absolute respect for private property, the private sector, and contractual agreements (especially those signed by the nation's citizens).

In the late 1920s, the United States finally came to terms with the Mexican Revolution, although it continued to condemn the Soviets. This two-dimensional outlook reflected the differences between the two social transformations. Not only did the Bolsheviks do everything in their power to eliminate private property from the means of production and to eradicate class differences and liberal democracy, they also sought to export their model around the world, leading them to a head-on collision with the United States and other Western powers.

In the case of the Mexican Revolution, the United States' initial hostility was largely a result of the economic nationalism espoused in Article 27 of the Mexican Constitution, as well as the foreign policy principles embodied in the Carranza Doctrine: juridical equality among all nations, nonintervention, self-determination, and domestic control over natural resources. The factors that ultimately led London and Washington to accept the Mexican Revolution are key to the understanding that still regulates the U.S.–Mexico relationship.[3]

One factor was the moderation and pragmatism of Mexico's victorious "Sonora dynasty." Unlike the Bolsheviks, their economic policies did not contemplate doing away with private property. Although they did not seek to establish a democratic system, this was of marginal concern to the majority of the U.S. elite, who still believed—as did U.S. Ambassador to Mexico James Sheffield—that the Mexicans were "Latin Indians," incapable of understanding "any argument save brute force" (in L. Meyer 1985: 22).

The Mexican Revolution mined a prominent vein of nationalistic feeling fed by abuses inflicted by foreigners, especially Americans. This nationalism, a source of cohesiveness among the Mexican population, was embodied in statements such as the Carranza Doctrine. As Arnaldo Córdoba has argued, Carranza's "aim was to recover Mexican wealth from foreign hands, providing the nation with an independent model for development and the world with an image of the 'real' Mexican society," composed of "peasants and workers" (in L. Meyer 1972: 203–12). The revolutionaries did not seek to break with any of the powerful nations of the time, including the United States; they merely hoped for the respect they felt they deserved.

Although the Mexican revolutionaries were certainly nationalistic, they were also pragmatic men of power who hoped to consolidate and maintain their positions and implement their political programs. To this end, they had to take the needs and concerns of Washington and other powers into account. In order to implement their agrarian reform program or to recover at least some measure of control over the nation's natural resources, the revolutionaries desperately needed diplomatic recognition, and they were prepared to make concessions to win it. In the Bucareli Agreements of 1923, certain points of Article 27 were dropped, and the government of Álvaro Obregón made concessions regarding repayment of the nation's external debt and regarding another thorny issue: legal claims stemming from American losses during the conflict. In return, Washington recognized the revolutionary government, allowing Obregón to stand for reelection

---

[3]Key texts on this topic are L. Meyer 1985, 1991. The author's conversations with Lorenzo Meyer also proved extremely enlightening.

the following year (L. Meyer 1985: 17). Even so, the Bucareli Agreements did not resolve the differences between the two countries.

TOWARD AN UNDERSTANDING

Plutarco Elías Calles, president of Mexico from 1924 to 1928, initially mined the radical vein of the Revolution, creating serious tensions with the United States. By mid–1925, Mexico–U.S. relations were badly deteriorated, to the point that the Department of State asserted "the Mexican government was on trial before the rest of the world" and Ambassador Sheffield called Calles a "murderer, a thief, and a man who has broken his word of honor" (in L. Meyer 1972: 223). As for U.S. opinion on the other revolutionaries, a cable stated that the only thing differentiating government officials from bandits was "the line between success and failure" (in Melzer 1987: 6). This hostility stemmed from U.S. uneasiness with instability, a deep nostalgia for the days of Porfirio Díaz, and irritation with Mexico's economic nationalism, embodied in a series of agrarian and oil industry–related legislation.

While Washington debated the possibility of intervening militarily, Great Britain was moving in a different direction. In December 1925, London took an important step toward normalizing diplomatic relations with Mexico by naming Esmond Ovey as its first plenipotentiary minister. Ovey offered a fresh view of the Revolution, laying the conceptual foundations for an understanding between Mexico and the United States; his dispatches to the Foreign Office amounted to a reinterpretation of the Revolution. Ovey felt that the dictatorship of Porfirio Díaz had inherent structural weaknesses that made the Revolution inevitable. He also pointed out that the Revolution was now in a process of consolidation and that its leadership (the Sonora dynasty) was not as radical as it first appeared. The British ambassador called on his countrymen and others to respect the new Mexican leadership, which, though perhaps less refined than the government of Porfirio Díaz, was nonetheless prepared to reach agreements with foreign powers. To sum up, he recommended that Mexico be readmitted to the community of nations.[4]

These ideas gathered momentum in Washington, fostered by sectors of U.S. society that did not want war with Mexico, and by a reevaluation of Mexico's importance in a broader context. Following the Revolution, the United States had been forced to deploy half of its armed forces along the U.S.–Mexico border, just as the nation was mustering for World War I (Dziedzic 1996: 67). U.S. strategists' fears

---

[4]See, especially, Ovey to Chamberlain, January 25, 1926, and Ovey to Chamberlain, November 4, 1926, in Bourne and Watt 1989: 156–57, 270–73.

of instability in Mexico would play a pivotal role in their security considerations from this point on. We should bear in mind that history has accustomed the United States to an extremely broad security margin, and even *potential* threats provoke heightened reactions.

As the situation evolved, Washington adopted a new stance. Sheffield was retired in 1927 and replaced by Dwight Morrow, instructed by President Calvin Coolidge to "keep the United States out of a war with Mexico" (Melzer 1987: 6). Coolidge defined his new policy as "a firm commitment with our rights, and scrupulous respect for Mexican sovereignty . . . accompanied by patience and tolerance" (Rippy 1931: 377). Ovey's position had been adopted by the United States, providing a clear example of how changing perceptions can produce political effects.

A CONGENIAL AMBASSADOR

Dwight Morrow's years as ambassador to Mexico would prove crucial for the history of relations between the two nations—and for the longevity of Mexican authoritarianism. When he arrived in Mexico City by train in October 1927, he received a welcome "the likes of which had never been provided for any diplomat in Mexican history" (Melzer 1987: 1).[5] Two days later, Morrow had already begun to establish direct communication with Mexico's most important functionaries. Although Morrow never learned to speak Spanish—and persisted in addressing ladies (*señoras*) as "Sonoras," to the amusement of the revolutionary generals—he became a specialist on Mexico. To foster goodwill, he agreed to replace the name "American Embassy" with "Embassy of the United States" and arranged for Charles Lindbergh to fly the *Spirit of St. Louis* nonstop from Washington to Mexico.

There were less congenial sides to Morrow, such as his indifference toward violations of Mexicans' rights. Soon after his arrival in Mexico, the government summarily executed Jesuit priest Miguel Agustín Pro Juárez and three others accused of conspiring against Álvaro Obregón (no evidence was produced to substantiate the charges and no trial was held). Although this was in flagrant violation of Mexican law, Morrow nonetheless agreed to accompany Calles in his subsequent travels through northern Mexico, claiming that the executions were a "domestic matter" and that offending Calles would undermine his hopes of having an impact in Mexico.

Lorenzo Meyer has suggested that Morrow's achievements were "spectacular." Moreover, the manner in which Morrow handled the

---

[5]In Mexico's political culture, the government has traditionally used rapturous multitudes as an instrument to earn the goodwill of visiting U.S. or other foreign dignitaries.

ongoing dispute surrounding foreign-owned oil companies in Mexico set a pattern, foreshadowed in the Bucareli Agreements, a pattern that still prevails. Calles made important concessions to the oil companies, all the while preserving his regime's nationalistic image. At Morrow's suggestion, Calles ordered the "Mexican Supreme Court to declare the nationalistic oil legislation which threatened foreign investments as anticonstitutional; the new legislation [approved by Congress] reflected the efforts of Morrow and the Minister of Trade, Commerce, and Labor" (L. Meyer 1985: 31; see also L. Meyer 1972: 266–81). These and other agreements were made possible through the conservative pragmatism of Mexico's ruling elite (James 1963: chap. 10).

This arrangement constituted a guarantee of mutual support between the elites of the two countries that has not wavered since its inception. When president-elect Álvaro Obregón was assassinated in July 1928, Morrow did everything he could to support Calles. He was present, for example, at the famous State of the Nation Address in which Calles said that the days of the caudillos had come to an end and an era of institutions had begun; Morrow was the first to applaud the Mexican president, a gesture charged with symbolism. When a rebellion headed by General Gonzalo Escobar broke out in March 1929, the United States implemented a rigorous arms embargo and froze the rebels' U.S. bank accounts. The government, in contrast, received ammunition and technical assistance (Lindbergh was an adviser) and the backing of a series of warships along the Mexican coastline, which clearly denoted who Washington's favorites really were. In the November 1929 presidential election, Morrow backed Pascual Ortiz Rubio, who used both official resources and violence to defeat José Vasconcelos in the first electoral fraud of the postrevolutionary era.

When Morrow left Mexico in 1930, President Ortiz Rubio stated that relations between the two nations had reached a "peak of cordiality" (in Rippy 1931: 381). During the 1950s another Mexican president, Emilio Portes Gil, wrote that a "neighborly policy had been set in place by a great ambassador, a Republican, in fact, *señor* Morrow. He was able to dissolve away the grave conflicts that threatened to plunge our nations into war" (Portes Gil 1954).

PIECES OF THE UNDERSTANDING

The level of understanding between Dwight Morrow and Plutarco Elías Calles set a precedent that has governed the relationship ever since. To summarize, the U.S. ambassador, in an informal, personal, discreet, and effective conversation with the president of Mexico, suggested a practical procedure for resolving the dispute over the vital issue of Mexico's oil industry. The Mexican president, who needed an agreement with Washington, quietly accepted Morrow's proposal for instructing the Supreme Court to declare any conflicting laws unconstitutional. His action simultaneously demonstrated the vigor of Mexican presidentialism, the malleable nature of nationalism, the lack of respect for Mexico's legal system, and the increasingly conservative character of the Calles regime.

As a result of this diplomatic maneuvering, U.S. oil companies were able to retain much of their privileged status, and the Mexican government earned Washington's support in preserving the Calles regime's nationalistic image. On March 28, 1928, the U.S. State Department declared that "the measures *voluntarily* implemented by the Mexican Government will, it seems, bring discussions which began ten years ago to a practical conclusion" (in Rippy 1931: 379, emphasis added). Washington also aided the Mexican government by ignoring human rights violations and by funneling economic, military, and political assistance to the regime as needed. The Mexican government's tight hold on the domestic media served to bolster further its efforts to maintain a nationalistic image.

In sum, this arrangement between politicians accustomed to exercising power gradually evolved into a flexible and adaptable framework, capable of ensuring continued benefits for the elites of both nations. Regarding the motivations of Plutarco Elías Calles and his group of revolutionaries, it appears that the margins for action afforded by this informal understanding provided the space for a series of Mexican governments to conduct experiments in economic development and social politics, while simultaneously pursuing a progressive and independent foreign policy. In this sense, the arrangement was a positive outcome, made inevitable by the asymmetry of power between the two countries. It follows, then, that bilateral relations have been driven by a dose of authentic nationalism tempered by a desire to maintain personal power and privilege.

If we accept that this is a case of well-intentioned pragmatism, we must also admit that the Mexican government in fact manipulated both its nationalistic image and its relationship with the United States in order to enhance its control over the population. It promoted an incomplete and distorted view of reality in which the United States' malevolent intentions justified the regime's demands for unity and obedience on the part of the Mexican people. Contact with the United States was allowed only through official channels, thus imposing a sort of double seal: Mexicans rarely traveled to foreign countries to discuss what was happening in Mexico, and the international community turned its back on Mexican affairs. This level of manipulation, which obscured the complex and ambiguous nature of the true relationship, was possible only because of the Mexican population's almost total ignorance of U.S. affairs.

The U.S. elite also found the understanding to their advantage. Their economic interests had been respected, stability along their nation's southern flank was guaranteed, and, in crisis situations, they felt assured of Mexican support.[6] Some arrangement of this nature was essential, because geographic contiguity limits viable options for action (for example, an extensive intervention can have negative repercussions upon a nation's own territory). Mexico's isolation from the rest of the world posed no problems for the United States, a nation uninterested in any intimacy with its southern neighbor.

The bilateral understanding was tested a number of times between 1927 and 1946. The expropriation of the oil industry and collaboration during World War II are the two clearest examples. In 1938, General Lázaro Cárdenas finally curtailed the high-handed international oil-companies by nationalizing the oil industry. Remarkably, U.S. Ambassador to Mexico Josephus Daniels and Washington, sensitized by the international context, responded by working to maintain the cordial relationship with Mexico, against the backdrop of veiled U.S. preparations for war in Europe.

This response confirms that, although the oil industry expropriation was a high point for Mexican nationalism, Lázaro Cárdenas was very careful not to overstep the unwritten rules established by U.S. interests. For example, he never attempted to nationalize the second great enclave of foreign investment: the mining industry. He also took advantage of every opportunity to show support for the Morrow doctrine. The choice of moderate Manuel Ávila Camacho as his successor is perhaps the clearest evidence of Cárdenas's pragmatism.

The U.S. strategists' decision to be flexible proved to be sound: during World War II, Mexico cooperated with the United States by surveilling foreigners potentially hostile to the Allies; providing workers through the *bracero* agreements; creating the Joint Mexican–U.S. Defense Commission (JMUSDC); increasing exports of raw materials; and declaring war against the Axis powers—giving Washington clear evidence of Mexico's trustworthiness as a neighbor (Vázquez and Meyer 1982: chaps. 7–8).

Following chapters explore the development of this extraordinarily solid understanding, based since the end of the war on a commitment of mutual support established around shared interests. Although this understanding is not formalized in treaties or complex

---

[6]A number of academic texts and documents confirm the importance of Mexico's stability for U.S. security. See WD 1942; SDN 1945; JIS 1946; CIA 1951; DOS 1951. The pivotal nature of this link is reiterated in more recent texts: see Deagle 1981; Linn 1984; Moorer and Fauriol 1984; H. Douglas 1985; Sanders 1987. Neuchterlein (1985) provides the most systematic overview.

protocols,[7] it has nonetheless become an indispensable tool for the discreet resolution of differences.

The understanding has undergone a gradual process of modification. Mexico's isolation began to give way to economic imperatives and increasing contact between political parties, intellectuals, and nongovernmental organizations in the two countries. Although Washington was never truly satisfied with the Mexican experiment and would have preferred a neighbor who embraced capitalism, installed a liberal regime, and became a close ally in the international system, patience prevailed—until Mexico's accelerating economic deterioration in the 1980s finally allowed Washington to force an overhaul of that country's economic model. The political system, however, was only slightly transformed, partly because the U.S. elite, obsessed with stability, decided to persevere in its support for the ruling Institutional Revolutionary Party (PRI).

These transformations blurred the goals and the essence of Mexican nationalism. What had once been a mechanism to extend the margins for development and foreign policy now became a shield, isolating and safeguarding the Mexican president and his power group. Following chapters will show how this blurring led to a new, transitional phase, still in progress, both for nationalism and for the United States' role in Mexico's national history.

---

[7]There are a number of formal agreements between Mexico and the United States, governing a variety of issues. However, they were inspired by the informal "Morrow Doctrine."

4

Mexico and the United States during the Cold War

FROM EUPHORIA TO PARANOIA

In order to appreciate fully the nature of U.S. perceptions of Mexico during the Cold War, we must bear in mind an idea that permeated the United States following World War II: that the United States had become the "most powerful nation in the world, in economic, military, and moral terms"(JIC 1946: 1). Although the claim of primacy in moral terms has been challenged by analysts from a wide range of ideologies, the United States was unquestionably the world leader both economically and militarily.

At the end of the war and for the first time in history, there was a single truly global power. In 1945, the United States produced 40 percent of the world's goods and held a monopoly on atomic power, at a time when most traditional powers were prostrate. Woodrow Wilson's vision of an international order wholly favorable to the United States, able to stave off another Great Depression, appeared to be at last within reach.[1] It is not surprising that the notion of an imminent "American Century" enjoyed widespread popularity.

According to this vision, the majority of nations should embrace a capitalist economy and a liberal political system; international conflicts should be resolved by the newly created United Nations; and the United States should play a key role in international affairs in order to preclude the emergence of hostile powers that could potentially dominate Europe, because any change in the balance of world power would be to the detriment of the United States.

---

[1]This vision informed President Roosevelt's Atlantic Charter.

Then came the disintegration of the United States' relationship with the Soviet Union, and U.S. euphoria turned to anxiety. The process was swift. As late as July 1945, the Soviet Union was favorably portrayed in *Life* magazine; a few months later, the Soviets had become the foremost threat to the United States and to the values that sustained its worldview. Driving this change in attitude were the deteriorating situation in Central Europe, where Communist allies of the Soviet Union had seized power; the civil war in Greece; gathering tensions in Turkey and Iran; and the possibility of Communist parties coming to power in France and Italy. The Soviet Union's first nuclear tests, in August 1949—closely followed by the Chinese Communists' occupation of Peking in October—did nothing to alleviate the mounting tension.

The mood of the times was captured in a number of documents—reports by presidential adviser Averell Harriman, a series of telegrams from Moscow drafted by a young diplomat named George Kennan, and an article by Kennan (signing as "Mr. X") published in *Foreign Affairs*—maintaining that Russia had always harbored expansionist tendencies and that the Soviet Union was perpetuating this tradition by exporting its ideology and dictatorial system to Eastern Europe and other parts of the world. The expansion of Communism was viewed as a serious threat by the United States, whose security depended on a world favorable to liberal institutions and capitalist economies. The solution, according to Kennan (1947), was to "contain" Communism and the Soviet Union, and this was to be a guiding principle in U.S. foreign policy over the next forty years (LaFeber 1976).

Under this policy of containment, the world was divided into good and evil, locked in merciless conflict without limits or frontiers. To contain Communism, and to extend U.S. power and influence around the world, new institutions were created and old ones were adapted to fit the way that international relations would be organized in the second half of the twentieth century. Mechanisms dating from this era include the Central Intelligence Agency, the North Atlantic Treaty Organization, the Organization of American States, the Inter-American Treaty of Reciprocal Assistance, the International Monetary Fund, and the World Bank.

Most of the principles guiding U.S. actions throughout this period were set down on paper. In April 1950, the Departments of State and Defense prepared a report for the National Security Council that elaborated upon the dualistic Manichean logic of containment: the world's nations must choose freedom or slavery. Slavery was represented, of course, by the Soviet Union, which, according to this same document, sought to "impose its absolute authority over the rest of the world." As the main defense against Soviet designs, the United

States must act on every front and in every way to oppose the threat (NSC 1954: 54).

In true Hollywood style, good and evil faced off in a deadly struggle that could end only with the destruction of one or the other adversary. Although the Communists certainly were hostile to the United States and its espoused system, Americans amplified the magnitude of the Soviet threat, nourishing a state of paranoia in which analyses combined truth and fantasy.

In the resulting climate of anxiety, fear, and hatred, politicians vied with one another to produce the most apocalyptic version of the Soviet and Communist "problem" (Freeland 1975). Joseph McCarthy dedicated his meteoric career to denouncing the "monstrous conspiracy" that had infiltrated America's institutions. The senator from Wisconsin reasoned that, given the United States' awesome might and exceptional character, Communist advances could only be explained by treasonous betrayals on the part of U.S. intellectuals and government officials. A true patriot's duty lay in exposing these traitors and expelling them from their institutions.

McCarthy's proposals had far-reaching impacts on the producers and transmitters of ideas. The McCarthyite witch-hunts proved devastating for the production of knowledge and for fundamental civil rights. Tolerance waned while conservative ideologies triumphed over liberalism, leading worldviews to the right (LaFeber and Polenberg 1975: 316–17). The fact that the hysteria of McCarthyism prevailed as a global worldview was almost wholly attributable to society's continued acceptance of its leaders' interpretation of reality. The people of the United States, believing that their nation's security was truly at risk, willingly left foreign relations in the hands of the established elite, who, in turn, were free to act without restraint, secure in the knowledge that few would question their decisions.

JOURNALISM DURING THE COLD WAR

The U.S. media adopted the era's schematic notion of reality, either through true conviction or from fear of conservative coercion. It was an era of "intense collaboration between the press and the government, which led the former to ignore its social responsibility: to keep watch on the latter." The media avoided any "searching examination [of U.S.] foreign policy and the basic assumptions that underlie it" (Abrams 1981). Containing Communism was given priority over individual guarantees and objectivity. When Allen Dulles was named director of the CIA in 1953, "one of his first steps was to explore the possibilities for a close working partnership with the press [because] the news media could help the intelligence community in two important ways: intelligence collection, and propaganda." Dulles believed that "cooperation with the government was, for the journalists like any other citizen, the patriotic thing to do" (Loch Johnson 1989: 183–84). And the press cooperated: the call of government authority proved stronger than the call of social responsibility.

The United States' attempts to overthrow Guatemalan president Jacobo Arbenz exemplify the obsessions and understandings that linked the government and the press. With few exceptions, the U.S. media backed the campaign against the Guatemalan government, accepting the official argument that this was a Communist regime and that it threatened the security of the United States (NYT, June 5, 1955; Galloway 1953). The *Times* was no exception; its editors acquiesced to a petition from the Department of State and withdrew Sidney Gruson, a correspondent covering the Guatemalan affair, at a crucial moment in the CIA–coordinated campaign against Arbenz (Salisbury 1980: 478–82; author interview with Gruson, 1983). In effect, the media contributed to the overthrow of a legitimate government and to the installation of a military regime that was to become one of Latin America's gravest violators of human rights (Loory 1974).

Although a solid consensus prevailed in the field of foreign policy, internal issues received different treatments in the conservative and liberal media. The conservative press was a staunch defender of anti-Communist dogma and saw the need to combat the enemy free of distracting moral considerations. This is apparent in Henry R. Luce's *Time-Life* or the *Chicago Tribune*, which supported Senator McCarthy's crusade against Communist infiltration in the United States, publishing a series of anti-Communist articles written by Willard Edwards in 1950. The *Los Angeles Times* also adopted a hard-line conservatism, harshly criticizing "foreign influences . . . socialism and labor unions and Communism and public housing" (Halberstam 1980: 76, 113, 138–57; Wendt 1979: 691–94).

The liberal press, which also backed government efforts to construct a "credible bulwark in Western Europe against the Soviet Union and Communism," nonetheless preserved a liberal attitude regarding internal affairs (Bray 1980: 8; Halberstam 1980: 182–201). The *New York Times* defended Americans' right to think differently and protested the violations of "individual civil liberties and freedoms that the newspaper had so clearly espoused for years on its editorial page" (Halberstam 1980: 239). Even so, the *Times* community, according to one of its chroniclers, lived through a "strange, awkward, embarrassing time . . . one of suspicion and conflict, anger and compassion" (Talese 1969: 237). This atmosphere would significantly color U.S. notions of Mexico during the Cold War.

MEXICO AND THE UNITED STATES' LOGIC

The United States' traditional aspirations for Mexico—stability, progress, and friendship—have changed little during the twentieth century. But the circumstances of the Cold War significantly decreased the amount of attention that the U.S. elite paid to Mexico and changed perceptions of that country as well. Mexico scarcely figures in the period's key U.S. security documents regarding Latin America (see, for example, NSC 1949, 1953a; DOS 1952). The United States Continental Defense Plan of 1949—a very important military document—comprises fifty typed pages; Mexico, tightly controlled by an authoritarian, well-entrenched government with strong nationalistic tendencies, merits only seven lines in those pages.[2] No more than twenty articles on Mexico appeared in U.S. military publications during the Cold War era; all dealt with historical issues. Interest in Mexican affairs within the U.S. military usually focused on histories or anecdotes from the Mexican War of 1846–1848. In modern Mexico, only Guadalajara, considered a "paradise" for retired American military personnel, proved to be of any interest.[3]

This indifference was also reflected in academic publications on Mexico, which were scarce, confused, discontinuous, and of poor quality. The two most important texts from the late 1950s (Tucker 1957; Scott 1959) suffered from seriously flawed theoretical underpinnings, even if—as Roderic Camp believes—they led to a transition from an "essentially descriptive literature, to more critical analytical interpretations of political functions and their consequences" (1990a: 25). Travel guides, of which there were few, largely served to perpetuate an image of an enigmatic, unknown Mexico and did little to change U.S. attitudes (see Crow 1957; Rodman 1958).

Although Mexico was not a priority topic in *Times* articles, this did not imply a lack of interest. The *Times* maintained a permanent correspondent in Mexico, although most published pieces were brief and opinion pieces or major stories were very rare. Between 1946 and 1986 the *Times* published 3,080 short pieces (measuring less that 10 cm in column length), of which 44 percent (1,433) appeared between 1946 and 1959. Only six of the 114 opinion pieces on Mexico appearing during the forty-year period were published between 1946 and 1959 (see figure 7); these peaks of interest were related to the oil situation (1946–1947 and 1951–1954), Guatemala, and the Korean War.

This lack of interest reflected the United States' general satisfaction with the situation in Mexico: a stable regime in full control of the country, and a weak opposition. Although the Mexican government was authoritarian, centralized, and independent in foreign policy,

---

[2]It is mentioned in another eight lines, but in association with Canada.
[3]For a more detailed analysis of the military literature, see Aguayo 1991.

Mexico was enjoying the benefits of stability and economic growth and that was good enough for the United States (SDN 1945; Cunningham 1984; Jordan and Taylor 1984; Ronfeldt 1983).[4] Furthermore, the U.S. elite were convinced that Mexico would support the United States in any serious development. This certainty informs the Continental Defense Plan, for example. Two of the seven lines concerning Mexico reiterate a fundamental thesis, that "in case of war [or in any other critical situation] . . . Mexico would be an ally of the United States" (DA 1949: 1, 6).

This notion, which will figure largely in the present analysis, reappears in a number of documents that reflect the United States' logic. John Foster Dulles, secretary of state during the Eisenhower administration, stated that "there is no room for doubt: in any crisis, Mexico would be on our side" (in Whitehead 1991: 330). In 1955, Ambassador Francis White observed, "if the Communists should force a showdown with us, Mexico would definitely be on our side" (DOS 1955: 2). An editorial in the *Times* concurred: "when a crisis arises we will stand side by side" (NYT 1953). In brief, the U.S. elite accepted Mexico as it was because, once the pros and cons had been taken into account, the status quo was favorable to U.S. interests.[5]

Although the bilateral relationship has proved stable, the United States at the time had a number of concrete suggestions for Mexico. A military memorandum from 1955 reflects typical U.S. concerns; the memo's priorities included: (1) persuading the Mexican elite to remove Communists from high-level government posts; (2) protecting strategic U.S. interests, ideally through further investment in Mexico's oil industry; (3) discouraging the Mexican government from tendencies leading to "the nationalization of industries and State socialism"; and (4) establishing a close "relationship of cooperation between the two governments." Persuasion continued to be the tool of choice: the U.S. elite believed that their "objectives could more readily be achieved by recognition by the Mexican government and people that Mexico's national interests are best served by close military, economic, political, scientific and cultural cooperation with the United States" (DOS 1956: 5).

These ideas were the very foundation of U.S. perceptions of Mexico, which served to justify U.S. policies. As argued in following discussion of the different facets of the understanding, the relationship was not crafted solely by the United States. Mexico contributed as well.

---

[4]In 1951 the CIA stated that "The Mexican government [was] stable and in control over the political machinery" (CIA 1951: 63).

[5]This has been explicitly acknowledged by the CIA (CIA 1977: 8).

5

Presidential Summits

Presidential summits serve as a starting point for this discussion for two reasons: first, because the meetings between presidents of Mexico and the United States became regular events after World War II, and second, because the president is by far the most important element in the Mexican political system. An analysis of this presidential summitry will help uncover the relationship from the United States' point of view, the distinct styles and personalities of the diverse actors involved, and the characteristics of the two nations' respective political systems.

A CONGENIAL PRESIDENT

The U.S. elite has never underestimated the centrality of the Mexican president (whom Robert Scott identified as the "patron of the entire political system" (1959: 147). It is not surprising, therefore, that considerable U.S. efforts are expended to ascertain each Mexican president's ideological orientation, personality, and feelings toward the United States.[1]

President Miguel Alemán (1946–1952) was one of the more popular Mexican presidents in the United States. He was praised 166 times—and criticized only once—in the pages of the *Times* during his six years in office. No other Mexican president has aroused such enthusiasm, although Carlos Salinas de Gortari also attained immense popularity in the United States. (The Salinas presidency has not been subjected to a content analysis as rigorous as Alemán's.) There are certain obvious parallels between these two presidents' regimes: both

---

[1]The biographical and psychological profiles that U.S. intelligence services prepare on Mexico's presidents confirm the richness of Washington's information.

were praised by the United States for their policy orientation, and both excelled in deciphering the codes of American political culture.

Alemán's desire for friendly relations with U.S. elites was readily apparent; as a candidate, he visited the U.S. embassy to assure diplomats there of his ideological position.[2] Not content with an improved private understanding, he also fed the voracious American ego (an unusual gesture for a Mexican politician); in an interview with the *Times*, then-candidate Alemán suggested that Mexican history would have been much smoother if our "first President had been a statesman of George Washington's caliber"—that is, if Mexico had been more like the United States. This comment was especially flattering in the early years of the Cold War, when the United States and the Soviet Union were promoting divergent socioeconomic models.

Unlike their U.S. counterparts, Mexican politicians rarely allow the public a glimpse into their private lives. In his interview with the *Times*, Alemán broke with this tradition and discussed with journalist Anita Brenner some details of his rocky life history (his revolutionary father, who had been executed, and his impoverished childhood). His candor—combined with his acknowledged personal charm—captivated Brenner, who stated that the "rise of Miguel Alemán is the all-American legend: from newsboy to President, Mexican style." Alemán, paraded as an example of the American Dream, was described as honest, pragmatic, moderate, charming, and a true friend of the United States (Brenner 1946).

Americans are fond of reducing the history of societies to individual biographies. Thus Alemán became the young president who would transform Mexico into a "modern" country—prosperous, democratic, and friendly toward the United States. The United States wholeheartedly supported his project for the reorientation of Mexican life. (Later discussion will address how the U.S. elite chose to ignore all facts that contradicted the image they had concocted for Alemán.) Alemán's meetings with Truman (which were not unlike the warm exchanges between Carlos Salinas and George Bush that began in November 1988) were also crucial in shaping this image.

TWO HISTORIC ENCOUNTERS

A few months after being sworn in as president of Mexico, Miguel Alemán held two presidential summits whose real importance has yet to be fully appreciated. Hoping to cement the goodwill of the United States (an indispensable ingredient for his industrialization project), Alemán welcomed Harry Truman to Mexico in 1947 with a tumultu-

---

[2]This finding is part of Medina's (1979) analysis of the Alemán regime.

ous and enthusiastic reception. Alemán praised Truman as the "new champion of solidarity and understanding among the American peoples," a noble leader, striving for the "cause of continued unity, independence, and justice . . . the greatest statesman produced so far by the United States" (NYT, Mar. 5, 7, and Apr. 30, 1947). Alemán's words adhered to an unwritten rule of official Mexican nationalism (which still prevails): it is politically correct to praise a U.S. envoy but not his country or his institutions—that is, the individual, but not the system of which he forms a part.

Truman showed that he, too, was a master of words: he responded that he had "never had such a welcome" in his life and that if the inter-American system were to resemble Mexico–U.S. relations, the hemisphere would be "the happiest place in the world." He added that Alemán was "a gentleman of whom I have become very fond, who is doing a great piece of work for his country, and who is a friend [of the United States]" (NYT, Mar. 4, 6, and Apr. 30, 1947). As far as can be determined, it was from this moment that certain sectors within the U.S. elite began to refer to Alemán as "Mister Amigo."

Toward late April and early May of 1947, Alemán made a nine-day visit to the United States. He met with an extraordinarily warm welcome, unparalleled in the history of relations between the two nations. Even by the *Times*'s conservative estimates, between 600,000 and 800,000 Washingtonians turned out to welcome the Mexican president, and this in a city well accustomed to visits by world figures. Truman declared a national holiday for schoolchildren and the federal bureaucracy, in order to further swell the enthusiastic multitudes, in an Anglo-Saxon version of the *acarreo*[3] (NYT, Apr. 30, 1947). Congress opened its doors to Alemán, the first Mexican (or Latin American) president to address the joint houses of Congress, clear evidence of the "warm friendship with which the American people see Alemán and his nation" (NYT 1947).

Alemán's reception in New York was even more spectacular. Published estimates of the crowd range from one million (NYT, May 3, 1947) to two million (*New York Mirror*) and even 2.5 million (*Excélsior*, May 3, 1947), again including children, who were given a school holiday. Alemán was showered with honors and distinctions, incidentally reinforcing a close friendship between the Mexican president and New York mayor William O'Dwyer, which was to develop an interesting trajectory.

Throughout his visit, Alemán stressed that, in his opinion, the two neighbors were allies and that Mexico was more than willing to support the United States, satisfying the conservative ideology that con-

---

[3]*Translator's note*: This is the practice, traditional in Mexican politics, of cajoling multitudes into attending political rallies or events through bribes or coercion.

trolled the United States' dominant worldview. He declared that
Mexico and the United States had "similarity of institutions and a
common love of freedom" and that they were marching together
down the path of democracy. He reiterated his "absolute faith in democracy" (NYT, April 30 and May 3, 1947). And in order to make it
absolutely clear that his version of democracy was the same as the
U.S. version, Alemán added that "when the State curtails individual
freedom in order to impose its will or that of a political party, civili-
zation is on the wane" (NYT, May 2, 8, 1947).

One of the U.S. elite's priorities during this era was to redirect
"Latin American political and military policy toward regional collaboration in hemispheric defense" (NSC 1949: 3). Alemán touched on
this topic on a number of occasions. In his speech before Congress, he
declared that "democracy, if not backed by force, whets the appetites
of dictators." Before another audience, he emphasized the "interdependence of the American nations" and warned that "the weakness
of one of them could jeopardize the security of all, and of the world."
He was even clearer when speaking at the United States Military
Academy at West Point: "You belong," he cautioned the cadets, "to
the generation in whose hands destiny has placed the imperative necessity of bolstering collective security." He added that Mexico would
contribute to the common effort, sending workers to the United States
and providing a warm welcome for foreign investors (NYT, May 1–3,
6, 1947).

American reactions were enthusiastic, and press accounts over-
flowed with praise for Alemán and the relationship between the two
countries. *Times* coverage of the two presidential summits included 52
positive, 12 informative, and only one negative comment (figures 54–
55), making them the best covered of all presidential encounters.

MEANINGS OF THE 1947 SUMMITS

The presidential summits shed a great deal of light on the state of the
relationship and on the influences that have shaped it over time. In
1947, both heads of state were clearly willing to provide mutual support. During Alemán's visit to the United States, Washington announced a $100 million loan to Mexico for the construction of roads
linking the two countries (Truman 1955: 219–21, 1956: 104). This set
an enduring precedent: with few exceptions, U.S.–Mexican presidential summits have all resulted in the announcement of loans for Mexico. This was motive for some celebration in 1947; it would gradually
turn into a cause for concern, and eventually into a nightmare as
Mexico's foreign debt mounted uncontrollably. (This spiraling debt
reflects a schizophrenic tendency in Mexico's foreign policy: despite

all attempts to adopt an autonomous development model, the economic relationship with the United States has imposed a gradual integration of the two national economies.)

From a historical perspective, the summits were yet another indication of the power asymmetry between the two nations. An entire chapter in Miguel Alemán's memoirs explores the significance of his visit to the United States (Alemán 1987: 263–72). Truman, on the other hand, considered his meetings with Alemán to be of little import. Despite the speeches and the crowds, Alemán's visit (or Alemán himself) is not mentioned in Truman's memoirs, while Truman's visit to Mexico is recalled in a single cold phrase (NYT, May 14, 1947). Truman's attitude was not unusual: except for Jimmy Carter, whose focus on Mexico intensified as a result of his bitterness toward José López Portillo, not a single U.S. president has penned more than a few lines concerning Mexico.

The summit also illuminated some darker aspects of the relationship. Mayor O'Dwyer of New York, who had struck up a close relationship with Alemán, was named ambassador to Mexico in 1950. Unfortunately (for O'Dwyer), his appointment coincided with the establishment in the U.S. Senate of the Special Committee to Investigate Organized Crime in Interstate Commerce, which concluded that "the problem of organized crime can be summed up in the parallel lives [of gangster Frank Costello and Ambassador to Mexico William O'Dwyer]." According to the Committee's findings, Costello committed crimes, and O'Dwyer then covered them up, thereby contributing "directly or indirectly to the spread of organized crime" (Dwight Smith 1975: 132).[4] O'Dwyer resigned from his post in 1952, at the end of Alemán's six-year term. He stayed on in Mexico, however, where he established a prosperous law firm.

Certain aspects of this facet of the relationship invite closer examination. For example, could there be a pattern in the not uncommon custom among diplomats of staying on to do business in Mexico? And could there be collaboration among members of the government elites in the creation of binational criminal organizations? During his stay in Mexico, for example, did O'Dwyer establish a relationship with Colonel Antonio Serrano, founder of the feared Federal Security Directorate (Dirección Federal de Seguridad, or DFS) created by Miguel Alemán? According to the CIA, Serrano "abused his considerable power by tolerating, and even participating in, illegal activities including drug trafficking" (CIA 1953). Could O'Dwyer's links with the Mafia be the origins of some binational network to promote the trade of illegal narcotics between Mexico and the United States?

---

[4]Every study of organized crime since 1950 mentions O'Dwyer (see Albini 1971; Ianni 1972; Talese 1971).

ENTHUSIASM OF MEXICAN POLITICIANS AND MEDIA

The reaction of the Mexican press demonstrates the free rein that journalists have when it comes to *laudatory* coverage of the Mexican president—and the close ties between the media and the Mexican government. The Mexican media competed to see which could produce the most flattering portrayal of Alemán. The following comes from a front-page article in *Excélsior*:

> ALEMÁN, TRUMAN . . . such smiles of optimism! Smiles that augur a noble, firm, and sincere friendship between two people who understand and admire one another, who seem to see the road of their progressive futures growing broader and more luminous, a road which, premised on democracy, will follow a clear and magnificent course. Geographical destiny has determined that the lives of these nations will be forever closely joined (May 1, 1947).

The following day, *El Nacional* reported on Alemán's speech before the U.S. Congress under the headline, "SENSATIONAL SPEECH . . . LOUDLY ACCLAIMED." The opening sentences of the article blend readily with the political rhetoric of postrevolutionary Mexico: "The Mexican people's scheme of ideas [was] laid bare before Congress with transparency and frankness by the president, *licenciado* Miguel Alemán. In his gallant statement, we discern certain 'essential concepts'" (*El Nacional*, May 2, 1947).

The special envoys who accompanied Alemán also waxed eloquent. In a front-page story, legendary journalist Luis Spota stated that "one of the greatest days in the life of Miguel Alemán [came when] he spoke before the United States Congress, harvesting the greatest ovation ever heard in this hall of historic decisions." No-less-famous journalist Carlos Denegri added, "A few hours after a solemn session in Congress, the President of Mexico was brilliantly undergoing . . . the test of a lifetime: facing the world's press, which bombarded him with questions and flashbulbs, with no aid save his own inspiration" (*Excélsior*, May 2, 1947).

Alemán returned to a welcome that rivaled a national holiday. According to journalist Luis Ochoa, "people who know about our national fiestas cannot help but draw comparisons. And they feel that the welcome accorded to Francisco I. Madero in Mexico City, after the triumph of the Revolution in 1910, could not compare with the homecoming for President Alemán on his return from an extremely fruitful trip to the United States" (*Excélsior*, May 8, 1947). Because Truman's aircraft (the *Sacred Cow*), in which Alemán had traveled, landed to this reception late at night, Mexico City authorities declared the following day a holiday so that the many thousands who had poured out to greet Alemán could rest.

Press coverage included Alemán's speeches in full, as well as countless articles exploring the most trivial aspects of the experience with saccharine obsequiousness. Although Alemán undoubtedly received an unparalleled reception in the United States, the excessive response among the Mexican media suggests a possible point of origin for the delusions of omnipotence that frequently grip Mexican presidents.

There was an almost total lack of even remotely serious analyses regarding the significance of the summit for both nations or for Mexican society. No one pointed out the patently superficial nature of Mexican nationalism: based merely on a warm U.S. welcome for its president, Mexico's traditional suspicions of its northern neighbor virtually melted away. This raises certain question—and leads to a closer examination of the myth of Mexican nationalism.

THE CONTRASTING STYLE OF RUIZ CORTINES

The discretion that characterized President Adolfo Ruiz Cortines's six years in power (1952–1958) was very much in evidence during his two summit meetings with President Dwight Eisenhower.[5] These two leaders' first meeting was to inaugurate a dam on the U.S.–Mexico border. Eisenhower spoke about how agreeable it was to have a neighbor like Mexico and attacked "totalitarianism, its gaudy promise and grim practice." Ruiz Cortines replied by emphasizing the Mexican people's "inherent aversion to all injustice" as well as "their intense devotion to the cause of peace and, above all . . . their great love of liberty." He defended the principle of self-determination, as well as the right of all peoples to choose a government and economic system to their own liking (NYT, Oct. 20, 1953).

Ruiz Cortines's comments underscored the independent image of his nation's foreign policy—especially significant in view of the fact that only a few months earlier Eisenhower had approved the overthrow of Arbenz in Guatemala. If this was the subtext of Ruiz Cortines's speech, Eisenhower apparently remained unaware of it. His memoirs merely state that "a gratifying friendship" grew from his meeting "with the Mexican President, which allowed the establishment of effective lines of communication" to settle problems approaching on the horizon (Eisenhower 1963: 240).

At the second summit, held in West Virginia in 1956, Canadian prime minister Louis St. Laurent was also in attendance, making this

---

[5]Alemán's summits merited 64 mentions in the *Times*, Ruiz Cortines's, 26; see figures 54–57.

the first summit of heads of state from the three nations of North America. A confidential document reveals that Ruiz Cortines brought up the issues of migratory workers (which had already provoked confrontations with Washington), cotton exports, and a fisheries dispute. Eisenhower, on the other hand, was more interested in halting Communist subversion and in obtaining landing rights in Mexican airports for U.S. airlines (WH 1956). The *Times* quoted the Mexican chief executive as stating that "the question of continental security had not been discussed" (NYT, Mar. 30, 1956). Minutes of these discussions confirm Ruiz Cortines's declaration.

Thus Alemán and Ruiz Cortines sent similar messages to the people of the United States. They differed only in tone. Mexico wished to preserve the relationship within the framework of an understanding struck decades earlier: Mexico's presidents would support a pragmatic and functional relationship with their northern neighbor in order to guarantee the maneuvering space they needed to promote a mixed economy and keep themselves in power. The United States felt that, even if Mexico failed to endorse military agreements, open its oil industry to foreign investment, or openly oppose Arbenz, the problem was not the president's lack of will; rather, it was a result of his need to maintain stability by pacifying nationalists and Communists (NYT 1956a). A 1958 *Times* editorial suggested that problems in the relationship were minor, and that "except among a few thousand professional Mexican Communists the old hatreds are dead" (NYT 1958a). As we shall see, this view of Mexican reality was being encouraged by events in other areas of the relationship.

6

Four Facets of the Relationship

The relationship between Mexico and the United States encompasses several facets, all interconnected through the tacit understanding that the two governments would provide mutual support in times of need. In some areas of the relationship, the Mexican government has acceded to Washington's dictates. In others it has established significant levels of autonomy and independence, a remarkable achievement in light of the marked power asymmetry between the two nations. This chapter explores several aspects of the bilateral relationship and begins to establish their connections with Mexico's political system. The chapter draws heavily on the findings of prior research. What is new is the approach, which attempts to bring together a broad array of materials, both published and unpublished within a theoretical framework that permits a more precise and integrated understanding.

Mexico's foreign policy is not unusual. It tends to reflect the interests of the nation or its governing elite. In general terms, its goal is to extend Mexico's margins of autonomy as much as possible within the shadow of a neighbor accustomed to having its own way. Sometimes Mexico has succeeded, sometimes not. But regardless of foreign policy outcomes, Mexican discourse exalting the myth of independence has remained constant, preserving an image of a sovereign Mexico. The Mexican government has used such discourse to placate the nationalist Left as well as the progressive international sector, and in this it generally has succeeded.

Results have varied by issue area. This chapter explores four of these areas, reflecting four facets of the relationship. They are the overthrow of Jacobo Arbenz in 1954; Mexico's refusal to enter into a military alliance with the United States; the petroleum industry's rejection of foreign investment; and Mexican migration to the United States. These widely diverging issues reflect a kaleidoscopic relation-

ship, founded upon a basic understanding between the two government elites.

AN INDEPENDENT DIPLOMACY?

Does the United States impose limits on Mexico's foreign policy? The
answer, for revolutionary Mexico, is emphatically negative. An established myth holds that Mexico's foreign policy is guided by the principles of self-determination, nonintervention, and peaceful resolution
of conflicts. The U.S. elite was never bothered by the independence of
Mexican diplomacy. The reason for this is outlined in part in a military document from 1946:

> Mexican foreign policy has always evinced a clear under-
> standing of the weakness, in fact the indefensibility, of its
> position should the United States decide to use military
> force, or exert serious economic or political pressure over
> an extended period. Mexico seeks to consolidate its posi-
> tion as an independent power in international affairs,
> within the limits imposed by this understanding. In conse-
> quence, we can expect Mexico to frequently be at odds
> with the United States, in matters *of secondary importance*
> (JIC 1946: 31, emphasis added).

This view of Mexican foreign policy is complemented by the certainty, cited earlier, that "in case of war . . . [or in any other critical
situation] Mexico would be an ally of the United States" (DA 1949: 6).
The Guatemalan revolution which took place in the 1950s will allow
us to compare these notions with reality.

When Jacobo Arbenz became president of Guatemala in 1950, he
stepped up the pace of his country's reform process. Although the
changes were fairly modest, by the summer of 1953 Washington had
decided to oust Arbenz, arguing that his regime was dominated by
Communists who posed a threat to U.S. security. This decision entailed the implementation of a complex strategy, combining instruments of hegemony and coercion (see, especially, Gleijeses 1991).

The U.S. strategy also called for the diplomatic isolation of Guatemala, which required the support of the hemisphere's other nations.
During the tenth Inter-American Meeting of the Organization of
American States in Caracas in March 1954, the United States proposed a resolution issuing a "simple, clear, and direct" warning for
international Communism: stay out of the hemisphere. Clearly, this
message was directed specifically at Arbenz's Guatemala. Throughout this meeting Mexico voiced support for Guatemala, defending the
principles of nonintervention and self-determination, and suggesting

a series of amendments to Washington's resolution which, according to the *Times*, sought to "cripple" the American position (NYT, Mar. 12, 1954). The U.S. government was so annoyed by these proposed amendments that it publicly labeled the Mexican position "vague, legalistic, unacceptable" (SRE 1958: 69–76). In any event, Mexico's diplomatic objections were no more than an irritant: the U.S.– proposed resolution passed, with seventeen votes in favor, one against (Guatemala), and two abstentions (Mexico and Argentina) (Pellicer and Mancilla 1978: 100).

Ample documentary evidence indicates that Mexican diplomats gallantly defended the principles of their country's foreign policy. Mexico's minister of foreign affairs during this era, Luis Padilla Nervo, held a conversation with his counterpart in the United States, John Foster Dulles, in which he recalled "the days when Mexico was alone; the times when we were carrying out economic and social reforms, the days of the Revolution. If a panel of American nations had sat in judgment upon Mexico during that era, surely they would not have found us to be free from foreign influences." For Dulles, Padilla Nervo's point of view was not based on principles; it reflected "no less than a true Communist infiltration, or its equivalent, into the Mexican government" (in Whitehead 1991: 331).

This statement reflects a prevalent idea among conservatives in the United States—that Mexico's Ministry of Foreign Affairs is a nest of leftists. The Ministry's activism has always been seen as part of a balancing act, which only rarely affects U.S. interests. For the Americans, what truly counts are the statements and actions of the president, because it is he who determines the course of Mexico's foreign policy.

The apex in negative references to Mexican foreign policy appearing in the *Times* came between 1953 and 1954, against the backdrop of a generally optimistic view of Mexico. Distrust of Mexico was common during this period; *Times* correspondent Sidney Gruson openly labeled the Ruiz Cortines government "anti-Yankee" (NYT, May 17, 1954). However, as the covert operation against Arbenz proceeded undeterred, U.S. annoyance with Mexico, as expressed in the *Times*, abated. The numbers speak for themselves: in 1953, the variable that registers bilateral relations contains 14 negative mentions but only 4 for 1954 (figure 49).

The reason behind this turnabout was that the Mexican president and administration had modified their position. According to the *Times*, Mexico executed "a complete reversal in its position on Guatemala" on June 10, 1954, when Minister of Foreign Affairs José Gorostiza announced that Mexico favored a "new meeting of the American republics, to discuss the question of Communism in Guatemala" (NYT, June 11, 14, 1954). Pellicer and Mancilla confirm that a few days later, with the CIA–organized invasion of Guatemala well under way, the Mexican government "failed to live up to its vaunted support for the principle of nonintervention"; on the contrary, it maintained total silence, turning a deaf ear on Arbenz's increasingly desperate pleas for assistance (1978: 102).

Times correspondent Sidney Gruson's interpretation of this about-face confirms the pragmatic nature of Mexican foreign policy. The government abandoned Guatemala at this key juncture for three fundamental reasons. First, President Ruiz Cortines hoped to "overcome the impression held by many foreign observers and Mexicans" that his was a "pro-Communist, anti–United States government." Second, the Mexican president was swayed by information received from the United States that established the existence of close ties between the Guatemalan Communists and Moscow leaders. And third, the peso had suffered a recent devaluation (in April 1954) and, as Gruson himself was quick to point out, "Mexico's economic progress or economic stagnation might well depend on the quality of its official relations with the United States" (NYT, July 26 and Sept. 1, 1954).

After Arbenz's overthrow, Mexico's collaboration with the United States proceeded apace. On June 27, 1954, Arbenz resigned the Guatemalan presidency and sought asylum in the Mexican Embassy in Guatemala City. After seventy-three days, he and his family obtained a safe-conduct and traveled to Mexico City, where Arbenz vowed to continue the struggle against the new Guatemalan government. He then left for Europe, in December 1954. Although he had been officially promised he could return to Mexico (most likely by the Ministry of Government), once he reached Paris his application for a return visa was rejected by the Mexican Embassy there, which stated that this was not a "suitable moment." Arbenz, who hoped to live out his remaining years close to Guatemala, persisted in his application, which was consistently denied until 1970, when he was finally allowed to return to Mexico. He died a few months later, in January 1971 (Gleijeses 1991: 390–92).[1]

The Guatemalan case exemplifies the changes that were taking place in Mexico's foreign policy. In Caracas, Mexico espoused a diplomacy of principles. However, as soon as Mexico's relations with the United States began to fray, principles were abandoned. This adjustment likely resulted from Mexico's official pragmatism, interacting with pressure that the United States brought to bear. Because this episode has not been subjected to detailed analysis, we cannot establish the magnitude or intensity of U.S. pressure. We can state, however, that Guatemala was a good example of the Mexican govern-

---

[1]These events, incidentally, reveal that the myth of Mexico as a country open to asylum seekers does not always prove true.

ment's ability to preserve the image of pursuing an independent foreign policy even when such an image does not coincide with reality.

THE PETROLEUM INDUSTRY

U.S. attitudes toward the Mexican petroleum industry reveal a great deal about the bilateral relationship. The history and evolution of this sector also reflect Mexico's capacity to resist pressure from the United States, whose interest in oil was even greater than its mistrust of state-managed enterprises.[2]

A 1948 congressional report noted that the United States required "adequate supplies, especially of petroleum, for any threat to our security" (in Krock 1948). The State Department, therefore, encouraged the U.S. oil industry to "expand operations into all areas where there were prospects of tapping additional oil sources for the purpose of aiding national defense." Evidently the development of Mexico's petroleum industry was an integral part of the "defense of the Western Hemisphere" (NYT, June 13, 1948; Sept. 14, 1954). In Mexico, however, where the petroleum industry was entirely in the hands of a state-managed company created through the nationalization of foreign-owned assets, foreign investments were prohibited by law.

Washington abhorred all forms of nationalism—except, of course, American nationalism. The Department of State defined Latin America's nationalism as "an emotional rationalization of [Latin Americans'] political, economic, and social failures" (DOS 1952: 9). The U.S. elite viewed nationalizations as identical to expropriations and, as pointed out in the *Times*, the "word 'expropriation' is like a red cape to a bull" for the U.S. oil community (NYT, Apr. 11, 1947). Americans' reactions to the "expropriation" of the Mexican oil industry were also reflected in their attitude toward Lázaro Cárdenas, the *Times*'s least favorite president (figures 19–20).

A 1951 *Times* editorial bemoaning Iran's nationalization of its petroleum industry asked whether "the Iranians took the trouble to study what oil nationalization has meant to Mexico," a nation that could have become an important producer of crude oil, but instead had "not turned up a single new rich field in thirteen years" (NYT 1951a). A further editorial noted criticisms from "Communists and others who dislike us," who maintained that U.S. companies all too frequently exploited "the countries in which they do business," usually leaving "nothing behind them but a hole in the ground." The *Times* countered these criticisms with examples like Venezuela's Creole Petroleum which, the paper argued, "'exploits' Venezuelan oil,

---

[2]For a broad overview, see L. Meyer 1973, 1978; Grayson 1980.

not its people or its government; it puts into Venezuela far more than it takes out" (NYT 1959a).

Ideas like these led the United States to pressure Mexico and PEMEX (Petróleos Mexicanos, the state-run oil company) into increasing production and opening the petroleum sector to foreign investment. Washington also refused to authorize loans or any other form of support for the Mexican oil company. However, these attitudes changed on par with changing circumstances. A U.S. Defense Department memorandum from 1950 considered that in "the development of Mexican oil production no strong military interest is evident at present or likely in the near future" (DOD 1950). But when Iran nationalized its oil industry in 1951, U.S. Secretary of the Interior Oscar Chapman visited Mexico, where he declared that the United States now wanted "new oil sources discovered and exploited in our hemisphere" (NYT, July 22, 26, 27, 1951).

At this juncture, Mexico was hoping to obtain loans with which to purchase needed capital goods from the United States. Negotiations for these loans demonstrated once again the inconsistent nationalism of certain Mexican government officials and the U.S. elite's willingness to help them maintain their nationalistic image. A game now began in which a number of Mexicans made secret overtures to the United States, confirming their willingness to offer concessions (they immediately reversed themselves when their maneuverings became public). A U.S. State Department memorandum from 1952 explained the situation thus: "the conditions laid down by our government for an oil loan were received with understanding when expressed orally"; but "when the same conditions were explained in an aide-mémoire, the Mexicans felt obliged to react strongly for the record and to terminate the negotiations" (DOS 1952: 26).

The U.S. elite accepted these inconsistencies, which were seen as a mechanism designed to calm Mexican nationalists and ensure stability. Nationalism, however, even that espoused by former president Lázaro Cárdenas, concerned them, although the reasons for such concern are not apparent in any available documents.

This "image game" produced tangible results for both governments. The Mexican elite was able to curtail U.S. ambition somewhat, while Washington earned a number of concessions. The first U.S. investment in the Mexican oil sector dates from 1948, ten years after the oil "expropriation" (NYT, Mar. 23, 1948); it was followed by a number of small contracts in 1949, whose questionable legality, however, was a source of continuing unease in the United States. According to influential columnist Arthur Krock, many of these contracts had to skirt Mexican law in order to avoid political problems (Krock 1949). Such comments serve to explain the increased coverage of Mexican corruption during the 1940s and mid–1950s (figure 93). Of greater relevance for the United States, however, was the fact that the Mexican president was willing to guarantee privately that, in any critical circumstance, the United States would have access to Mexican crude.[3]

This state of affairs, while not completely satisfactory to the United States, was the only arrangement possible within the rules of the established understanding. The United States would have preferred an explicit alliance, or total financial opening of the oil industry, rather than verbal commitments or concessions based on varying interpretations of the law. But they accepted Mexico's conditions, a clear coup for that government.

THE MILITARY RELATIONSHIP

Within the framework of the bilateral relationship, Mexico's greatest level of independence was in the military arena. After World War II, the United States began to incorporate the Latin American nations into the Inter-American Treaty of Reciprocal Assistance, complemented over time with bilateral military accords as part of a broader global strategy (B. Smith 1982: 262–300). The Mexican government disagreed with this strategy and suggested that security might better be enhanced by channeling economic aid to the region, given that "economically weak nations [are unable to act] decisively and effectively against aggressors" (NYT, Aug. 16, 1947). This was not the only difference; Mexico also refused to sign the Inter-American Treaty or any bilateral military accord with Washington.

Mexico's new attitude contrasted sharply with the close military cooperation that had prevailed during the war. The United States had hoped to extend this cooperation into the postwar era, and there are signs that the Mexican army was amenable. A meeting of the Joint Chiefs of Staff of both nations took place in Mexico in March 1945, for which Mexico's National Defense Ministry prepared a secret report documenting the Mexican military's willingness to play a more active international role—and to enter into a close relationship with the United States. The military stated that they were "prepared to assume any international obligations which may be agreed upon at the upcoming San Francisco Conference" (SDN 1945: 5).[4]

But Mexico's civilian leaders thought differently, and they prevailed, curtailing the relationship between the Mexican military and the United States. Nonetheless, for a number of years the Pentagon,

---

[3]U.S. government documents reveal that in January 1947 President Miguel Alemán informed the U.S. ambassador that "in any emergency that might threaten the United States or this hemisphere, Mexico's oil resources will be at its immediate disposal" (in Whitehead 1991: 327).

[4]It was at this conference that the United Nations was created.

hoping to establish a bilateral accord, continued to strive for a closer relationship with Mexico's armed forces.[5] These efforts were doubled during Miguel Alemán's presidency (NSC 1949).

At this point the Mexico–United States military relationship was the most important issue on the U.S. agenda, as reflected in the *Times* coverage. Its primacy was largely the result of the two nations' proximity and of the Korean War, which broke out in 1951. The United States sought to pressure Mexico into making a "concrete gesture of solidarity by sending a token force to fight in Korea" (NYT, Feb. 5, 1952). Mexico refused, despite the United States' continued insistence. In 1952, a U.S. military mission arrived in Mexico, hoping that newly installed President Adolfo Ruiz Cortines would display a different attitude. Their talks proved fruitless, and by mid–1953 the White House had "about given up hope of obtaining Mexico's agreement" (NYT, July 8, 1953). These events sorely vexed the U.S. elite, and 8 of the 9 negative references concerning the military relationship between Mexico and the United States that appeared over a span of four decades following World War II were published between 1953 and 1954. The latter year also witnessed the greatest number of references to Mexico's nationalistic tendencies, which were equated with anti-American sentiment (figure 94).

The Mexican government justified its stance in terms of a basic principle—the peaceful resolution of conflicts—which precluded their military intervention in foreign affairs. The Americans did not blame Ruiz Cortines; they blamed "the Communist Party and its left-wing allies, who played upon the anti-American feelings of many Mexicans" (NYT, Sept. 14, 1954). However, there is a more likely explanation: the Mexican civilian government's parade of principles also served, not coincidentally, to distance their military from the Pentagon and from foreign ideas and doctrines, in line with the general objective of keeping Mexico isolated. This may well have been a wise move, because, as Laurence Whitehead noted, "subsequent events have shown that the price paid in the long term for [military support from] the Pentagon proved very steep for the political authority and the stability of the Latin American governments" (1991: 331).

We should consider what motive prompted the United States to tolerate Mexico's continuing rejection of any form of military accord. There are two likely candidates. First, the Mexican expeditionary force that Washington hoped would travel to Korea had, in fact, no genuine military role to play and was merely a piece of political symbolism; exerting further pressure on Mexico in this matter might have threatened the country's internal political equilibrium, which was the

---

[5]For an overview of the military affair, see Wager 1992. Mexican authors who have explored this issue include Piñeyro (1987) and Benítez (1994).

top priority. Second, any disaccord between Mexico's and the United States' respective armed forces did not extend to other security-related areas, where close cooperation was very much in evidence. The FBI maintained an office in Mexico, and U.S. intelligence services exchanged information with Mexico's Ministry of Government and its Federal Security Directorate.

In any case, Mexico was able to preserve a remarkable degree of autonomy in military affairs into the 1980s, at which point increasing contact between the U.S. and Mexican governments affected this and all aspects of the relationship.

MEXICAN MIGRATION

The phenomenon of Mexico–U.S. migration sheds light on the American consciousness, on the Mexican government's tight controls over the dissemination of information, and on the nature of coercion as an instrument of domination.[6] In the eyes of the U.S. government, migration to the United States from Mexico is an internal, domestic issue, to be dealt with unilaterally by the United States, without input from or consultation with Mexico. During the 1950s, migration was the only issue area in which the United States successfully employed coercion and Mexico was forced to accept the conditions set down by the United States.

Mexican migration gained importance during World War II, when the demand for military goods, along with a shortage of workers in the United States, led the two countries to sign the first "Bracero" accord in 1942. After the war, migration persisted: the U.S. economy had come to depend on the Mexican workforce, and the Mexican economy was having increasing difficulty absorbing all of the would-be entrants into its labor market. During the Bracero period (1942–1964), U.S. opinion was divided into two camps. The first camp, which included the great majority of Americans, had little interest in the Mexican workers who were employed, largely invisibly, in U.S. agriculture. Among the individuals who did care (the second camp) were those who were in favor, because they profited economically from Mexican labor; those opposed, because they felt they were being hurt by migration; and those who viewed migration as an issue of principles (such as public safety, national security, and/or humanitarian considerations) and favored or opposed it on those grounds.

Those who defended migration for economic reasons included the growers, who argued that they required large numbers of cheap, temporary workers because U.S. workers were insufficient and ex-

---

[6]This section benefited from the suggestions of Dr. Manuel García y Griego, of the University of California, Irvine.

pensive (NYT, Jan. 15, 1950). Migration, they suggested, benefited both societies: Mexicans obtained a better wage, and Americans paid less for agricultural products. This sector proved sufficiently powerful—in both economic and political terms—to keep the border open to migratory labor. The U.S. agricultural sector flexed its muscle on other migration-related issues as well. In 1951, the state of Arizona proposed a sanitation code to improve working conditions for Mexican field laborers. The code was rejected after growers' associations claimed that it would force them into bankruptcy (NYT, July 16, 1951). In Washington, farmers' organizations pressured Congress to reject "amendments"—such as fines on employers of migrant workers, or increased allocations for the Immigration and Naturalization Service (INS)—designed to penalize or curtail the migratory flow (NYT, June 28, 1951). All the amendments were defeated by a significant margin (NYT, Feb. 14, 1952). Further, the Texas Proviso, adopted in March 1952, exempted all employers from any form of punishment for hiring undocumented workers.

Foremost among those who opposed migration for economic reasons were U.S. labor unions, which argued that the problem was not a shortage of American labor, but rather the poor working conditions and low salaries that were on offer. They added that the Mexican migrant workers were exploited and that they took jobs from local day laborers, increased unemployment, and posed serious problems for the organization of agricultural workers' unions (NYT, Oct. 17, 21, 26, 1948; Aug. 13, 1950). Therefore, they called upon Congress to establish "adequate sanctions" for those who hired Mexicans and to approve additional resources for the INS (NYT, Feb. 7, 1947).

Other sectors that opposed migration predicated their opposition on a variety of grounds, which changed over time. Some believed that migration led to an increase in crime (NYT, Mar. 26, 1951). Others linked migration to the opium and marijuana trade (NYT, Apr. 12, 1951). And still others cited sanitary or racial arguments: Representative Emanuel Celler, of New York, expressed concern for the migrants' working conditions, but he also suggested that their presence carried negative moral and sanitary implications. He criticized farmers for closing the border to diseased cattle while allowing "Mexican humans to come in without examination of their health and morals. What of the contagion of trachoma, leprosy and smallpox?" Convinced that Europeans were innately healthier, Celler suggested that Italian farmworkers be hired "as permanent residents, instead of temporary Mexican migrant workers" (NYT, Apr. 12, 1951; Jan. 29, 1952).

Finally, some opponents felt that migration threatened the United States' national security. In 1953, the "possibility that Communists [could be] infiltrating their agents" into the United States disguised as

Mexican peasants was taken quite seriously. Walter Reuther noted that "wetbacks" often participated in "fifth-column activities of subversion and sabotage," and in 1954 a member of the Immigration and Naturalization Service suggested that "approximately 100 present and past members of the Communist Party" were entering the United States from Mexico every day (NYT, Jan. 27, 1953; Feb. 9–10, 1954). This statement was patently tainted by the paranoia that typified the era. At the time, the Mexican Communist Party had some five thousand members; had the INS member's assertion been true, all would have found themselves in the United States in less than two months.

THE *TIMES*, CONSCIOUSNESS, AND CONTENT ANALYSIS

The information that the *Times* published concerning migration, as well as the preferential treatment the topic received, are quite extraordinary (figure 58). The paper's editorial line was to oppose the presence of migrant workers but to support the migrants' right to receive decent treatment. In an editorial from March 27, 1951, the paper supported tighter controls on migration, which, it claimed, was having a negative effect upon the labor market. However, it also called for an end to "the merciless exploitation" of the braceros. In another editorial from 1951, the *Times* backed the allocation of more resources for agencies charged with enforcing immigration regulations and the implementation of penalties against employers who hired migrant workers (respectively, NYT 1951b, 1951c, 1951d).

One extraordinary aspect of the *Times* coverage of this phenomenon was its genuine effort to portray the many aspects of migration. By so doing, the paper contributed to a heightened awareness of this issue's inherent complexity. Gladwin Hill—the best journalist to cover Mexican affairs during this era and a pioneer of Mexico–United States migratory studies—provided extensive detail regarding the appalling conditions endured by the Mexican workers, the extortion to which they were subjected by Mexican functionaries, and the exploitation they suffered once in the United States. He also demonstrated that American labor unions had a sound basis for their criticisms of migration.[7]

One way to evaluate an individual's, group's, or society's progress in terms of consciousness is to observe what they do *not* discuss or take into consideration. During the Cold War, neither the causes of migration nor the Mexican government's viewpoint were taken into consideration in the United States. Nonetheless, some ideas that would later come to the fore—during the 1970s and 1980s—

---

[7]Of the many articles that Hill published on this issue, see especially the series that ran from March 24 to 29, 1951, which resulted in a number of congressional hearings.

occasionally surfaced, generated by individuals who were transcending the boundaries of the group's maximum consciousness. In a
lengthy article from 1950, for example, Albert Steinberg stated that
"the sudden invasion [of braceros] stems from the serious depression
and general inflation" prevailing in Mexico. His conclusion was remarkable, especially for the time: "whether the answer to the
'wetbacks' can be found without a general solution to Mexico's economic ailments is hard to tell" (Steinberg 1950).

Another early glimmer of an idea that would spread in later years
appeared in an editorial which suggested that what motivated Mexicans to leave their country was "the low living standards and wages
that can be found in Mexico."[8] Yet another nascent concern was the
idea that migration would cause the United States to lose control over
its border. In 1953, a front-page article in the *Times* warned that "there
is nothing to stop the entire Mexican nation from entering the United
States" (NYT, May 10, 1953).

It is important at this point to note that content analysis is extremely useful in establishing how often a specific idea or fact is mentioned, but subtleties are sometimes lost. For example, while negative
references to migration outnumbered positive ones (figure 58), content analysis fails to indicate the extent to which the *Times* also stood
up for migrants' rights. Another limitation of content analysis is that
it cannot measure a newspaper's or an article's true impact. We know
that the U.S. elite reads the *Times*, but establishing the extent to which
its articles influence their decisions is difficult. For this, other techniques are needed—such as tallying the frequency with which the
Times is quoted in the Congressional Record and then observing
whether Congress's decisions coincide with the *Times*'s recommendations.

FRICTION AND COERCION

If we adopt a different perspective, we find that American indifference toward Mexico's views on migration was due partly to the fact
that there were no Mexicans in a position (or determined enough) to
make themselves heard in U.S. debates. The migrants themselves
were disorganized and without resources. Mexican academics were
not studying migration—nor the broader field of U.S. affairs (an important exception was Daniel Cosío Villegas). Although the Mexican
Left criticized the aspects of Mexican society that underlay the exploitation and discrimination that migratory workers suffered in the
United States, its influence in Mexico was limited and its credibility in

---

[8] For an article by Hill that includes the Mexican perspective, see NYT, Jan. 18, 1953.

the United States was nil. The Mexican press explored the issue only superficially, rarely straying from official guidelines. The Mexican government, meanwhile, had found in migration a perfect solution to the shortage of jobs in Mexico, as well as a source of income to support the country's industrialization project and a captive population on which avaricious functionaries and politicians could feast (by using a wide range of methods to systematically extort monies from peasants traveling to the United States).

Although some in government (including President Ruiz Cortines) sought to protect migratory workers from exploitation, extortion, and discrimination, they made little headway. It seemed that the only way to improve working conditions for braceros in the United States, the only way to bring pressure to bear, was to cut off the flow of labor. Mexico's attempts to take this decisive step produced negligible results, demonstrating both the weakness of Mexico's position and the United States' brazenness and unilateralism.

In 1947, the Mexican government tried to hold up the legal migration of braceros, hoping to secure better economic and working conditions for them through an accord then being negotiated. Washington's response was swift. The El Paso office of the Border Patrol "[opened] the border to thousands of *braceros*, and turned them over to [American agricultural employers]" without prior authorization from Washington (NYT, Oct. 17, 1948). Angered Mexican authorities renounced the accord, but after they received a diplomatic apology from the Department of State, the accord went forward and was approved less than a year later.

A much more serious situation arose a few years later, when the United States was obviously using coercive tactics. Negotiations relating to labor migration had stalled, but U.S. employers desperately needed their Mexican workforce. At this juncture, in January 1954, the Departments of State, Labor, and Justice began hiring Mexicans unilaterally. Because the executive branch had no legal authority to act in this way, hiring was interrupted for a few weeks until the House of Representatives passed legislation empowering employers to hire Mexican workers directly, "with or without the consent of the Mexican government" (NYT, Mar. 3, 1954).[9]

An infuriated President Ruiz Cortines deployed Mexican immigration agents and army units along the border to prevent peasants from traveling to the United States. The only result was a series of embarrassing confrontations between angry peasants who wished to work in the United States and the confused soldiers who had been ordered to stop them (NYT, Jan. 24, 27, 28 and Feb. 2, 1954).

---

[9]Antecedents can be found in NYT, Nov. 8 and Dec. 22, 1953.

These incidents clearly illustrate the Mexican authorities' tight grip on the dissemination of information. An analysis of the coverage of these events for January and February 1954 in three Mexico City dailies (*Excélsior*, *El Nacional*, and *El Universal*) revealed that all three painted reassuring pictures of events on the border, widely at odds with coverage in the U.S. press. The Mexican media's techniques (still in use today) included running as front-page headlines statements by key functionaries or celebrities favorable to the regime. For example, *El Universal* ran an eight-column front-page headline announcing that "The Bracero Problem Is Minor and Unimportant," quoting Gustavo Díaz Ordaz, then an upper-echelon government official under Ruiz Cortines and later president of Mexico (1964–1970). According to Díaz Ordaz, "a great deal of information concerning the braceros in northern Mexico has been exaggerated. . . . Truth has been sacrificed to sensationalism, magnifying a problem that is basically minor and unimportant. Such information is worthless" (*El Universal*, Jan. 30, 1954). Of course, his opinion, though interesting, was not supported by the facts.

Another editorial, this one from *El Nacional*, used a different technique, also employed to downplay the confrontations taking place along the border. "The nation patriotically applauds and supports President Ruiz Cortines," it stated; according to an "official statement [it continued], hundreds of 'wetbacks' who had entered the United States illegally have now turned back into Mexico, into the nation that values them and does not want to see them despised abroad, confirming that the appeals of the authorities and the brotherly wishes of the Mexican people are being heeded by the would-be braceros" (*El Nacional* 1954).

The Mexican press also abstained from publishing photographs (which did appear, however, in the *Times*) of the clashes taking place in Mexicali and other border areas. Another curious aspect of the coverage was that two dailies, *Excélsior* and *El Universal*, also published cables from international news agencies that belied the official declarations appearing on their front pages. Although these cables were buried in the back pages, the contradiction was immediately apparent to any careful reader (see, for example, *Excélsior*, Jan. 24–30, 1954).

A few months later, economic and political considerations led Washington to reverse its policy, and all illegal workers were expelled from the United States in "Operation Wetback" in the summer of 1954. This vast operation transported Mexicans via specially chartered planes, trains, and buses to deep within Mexican territory (NYT, June 21 and Aug. 7, 1951). By this time, the Mexican government had also changed its mind, and it acquiesced to the repatriation of illegal migrants. In exchange, the United States agreed to hire greater numbers of the legal braceros.

LATER DEVELOPMENTS

The migration of Mexican workers into the United States highlighted the weaknesses in the economic model adopted by the Mexican elite as well as the United States' dependency on imported labor, leading both parties to seek a structural solution. Proposals that failed to address both the problems characterizing Mexico's development and the United States' economic dependency upon Mexican workers proved hopelessly inadequate.

The migration issue reemerged with some intensity during the early 1960s, when renewal of the Bracero agreement was being debated. The agreement was ultimately terminated, in December 1964, but migration did not stop; it simply became undocumented. Whether legal or illegal, according to the U.S. perspective, Mexican labor migration remained purely an internal matter. Lobbyists for the agricultural sector continued to win important legislative victories in Congress (so much so that one secretary of labor referred to them as the toughest pressure group he had ever come across (NYT, July 29, 1960), while other sectors became increasingly critical of the migrants' poor living and working conditions (letters to the editor, NYT, July 21, 23, 1960). The Mexican government continued to call for respect for the migrants' human and workers' rights, although after 1954 it would never again directly oppose American will on this issue.

The *Times* frequently criticized growers for their lack of respect for migrant workers' rights, although the paper did recognize that these migrants were competing with domestic workers for jobs during an economic recession, which, the *Times* maintained, was reason enough to tighten controls on their presence (NYT 1960a–c, 1961a, 1963a–b, 1964a). In any case, the number of negative references to migration fell sharply, while the number of informative references rose (figures 63–64), reflecting a growing awareness of migration's true nature. An article from 1961 (whose author surely took the Cuban Revolution into consideration) suggested that suspending the Bracero agreement would have "a serious impact upon Mexico" (NYT, Oct. 5, 1961).

The realization that any changes in the migratory flow would affect both Mexico and the United States began to gain currency and was widespread by the 1970s. Although this was some acknowledgment of the two nations' interdependence, the United States would continue to act unilaterally in migration-related matters, using coercion "when necessary."

CONCLUSION

The four issue areas discussed in this chapter clearly speak to the complexity of the bilateral relationship. Although each case would seem to be ruled by a different logic, all in fact pivot around an implicit accord to provide mutual support in times of need.

Another aspect that comes through very clearly is the marked pragmatism of Mexico's foreign policy. The Mexican elite abandoned both Arbenz and the migrant workers, but they succeeding in isolating the Mexican army from the United States and in preserving State control over the petroleum industry. Given the asymmetrical power relations between the two countries, the Mexican side came out quite well. Their strategy may have been the best available for expanding Mexico's room for maneuver, especially in light of the unilateralism that characterized U.S. foreign policy throughout the Cold War, for, as the migration question demonstrates, when the United States decided to employ coercion, Mexico had little defense.

7

The Myth of Mexican Democracy

Throughout the Cold War, most Americans believed that the Mexican system was (almost) a democracy. This was an exaggeration, a myth, brought about by lacunas in knowledge. Understanding this myth will help us comprehend how the U.S. elite managed information, molding it to fit preconceived ideas while simultaneously maintaining a self-image of objectivity. This chapter also explores the effects of U.S. perceptions on Mexican authoritarianism.

THE INGREDIENTS OF MEXICAN AUTHORITARIANISM

The Mexican political system reached maturity during the 1940s. The country was ruled by a group that governed through an effective combination of coercion and hegemony, flexible enough to adapt to changing circumstances. It had created a convincing democratic facade, holding elections and tolerating the existence of opposition parties—although these were rigorously controlled. The opposition was weak and disorganized, and international interest in Mexico was scant. Washington's priorities for Mexico were economic growth and political stability, along with a friendly relationship between the Mexican regime and the United States. The U.S. elite cared little about how these objectives were to be achieved.

One reason for Mexico's political stability was the cohesiveness of the group in power, whose members shared a flexible worldview inherited from the Mexican Revolution. They were a disciplined group, adhering unquestioningly to a set of ambiguous rules (interpreted by the president and his party) that frequently diverged from both the letter and the spirit of the law. This cohesion was also nourished by a more mundane element: the "Mexican Dream"—the belief that the elite have an innate right to enrich themselves through public office.

The regime's solidity also derived from the (passive or active) support of organized sectors of the population that took part in the nation's public life. Economic growth enabled the government to distribute benefits widely, silencing some of these organized groups' complaints. Although the distribution of power was profoundly unequal, the population as a whole looked forward to an ever brighter future, part of the mythology of the Mexican Revolution. The revolutionary governments of this era—which used repression with great caution (a lesson learned from the Revolution) and relied more on hegemony—skillfully controlled the flow of information and knowledge. This was achieved through complex webs of legal and illegal mechanisms: these governments monopolized the production and sale of newsprint, awarded radio and television station concessions to individuals or groups close to the PRI,[1] and established an efficient system to co-opt and/or corrupt journalists and intellectuals, thereby allowing the government to regulate which stories reached the public.

Despite such controls, Mexico continued to beget its share of skeptics, including journalists, intellectuals, and popular and peasant leaders. The government traditionally took sophisticated steps to restrain such individuals and the groups that coalesced around them. When opposition opinions surfaced, the government's first reaction was calculated indifference, accompanied by close scrutiny of their proponents' intentions and capabilities. Individuals or groups who showed signs of becoming a potential threat were subjected to even closer scrutiny. The regime was known for studying its opponents with great care (the limits of what level of opposition is permissible varied by regime). The government's customary response was to meet some of a group's demands while quietly trying to co-opt its leadership, playing to any uncovered weaknesses. They enticed a leader with symbols of prestige or invited him to join in the "Mexican Dream"—that is, to feed at the public trough. If these enticements were ineffective, the government activated its strategy of suffocation and containment. It tried to splinter the group and/or to establish parallel groups with similar goals, thereby creating confusion. The media, tightly controlled by the regime, played a central role in this part of the strategy.

If an opposition group continued to gain strength, the government deployed a wide variety of harassing tactics: tax audits, loss of employment, incarceration, death threats, and so on. Pressure intensified in proportion to the threat's perceived magnitude until, in extreme cases, the government physically removed the threat, usually through murder or "disappearance" and, in some cases, through indiscriminate repression. These stages varied from state to state. A comparison

---

[1]These concessions are renewed periodically.

of some of the best known instances of state violence indicated that workers or peasants were more frequently repressed than were the professional, middle classes.[2]

The government includes institutions that have specialized in coercion. Until the 1970s, the army was frequently used in rural areas and against large public demonstrations. Selective repression (ranging from harassment to murder) was carried out by the feared Federal Security Directorate created by Miguel Alemán in 1947 and disbanded in 1985. The DFS was followed in importance by federal, state, and municipal police forces and a number of paramilitary groups.

This combination of hegemony and coercion peaked in the 1950s and 1960s. In later years the government's efficacy in this area was curtailed as independent media and organizations gained strength and experience, and especially after the severe blow that the July 1997 elections inflicted to the government's structure of control.[3] The United States has played a central role in the history of Mexican authoritarianism, as can be seen if we explore the U.S. elite's changing perceptions of Mexico between 1946 and 1960.

THE UNITED STATES' LOGIC

The U.S. State Department had clear goals for Latin America: it sought to "propel an orderly evolution toward democracy throughout the hemisphere," thus establishing a continent where "everybody accepts and practices . . . the same political, social, and economic principles [as the United States]" (DOS 1952: 24). Scholars and journalists agreed with this objective. *Times* editorials advised the U.S. government to guide Latin Americans, to help them acquire "as much insight as they can get into the 'political and philosophical' forces that the world's most fortunate nation relies on" (NYT 1956b). According to Robert Scott (1959) and others, the United States should serve as a "political prototype" for other nations. Democracy, it was argued, entailed adopting a "political system along the lines of the United States and the United Kingdom" (Lagos 1977: 27), the logic being that these Anglo-Saxon nations had developed the "institutions of partici-

---

[2] The cases examined include the repression in León (1946), Guerrero (1960 and 1967), and San Luis Potosí (1961), among others. Also studied were the railroad workers' strike of 1958 and the physicians' movement of 1964–65. The single exception to this generalization was the student movement of 1968.

[3] The increased openness that resulted is a dual phenomenon, which can be both economic and political: external groups' increased attention on Mexican affairs and an increased number of Mexican actors who are willing to establish contact with their foreign counterparts. This presupposes, of course, not only their willingness to establish contact but also the existence of laws that allow them to do so.

pating" (such as voting) that make democracy work (Lerner 1958: 60). The enemies of democracy were readily identifiable: nationalists like Juan Domingo Perón, or the Communists who were, according to the State Department, exploiting "instabilities, deficiencies, and demagogy" (DOS 1952: 3).

Proceeding from these ideas, Americans arrived at certain remarkable conclusions. As a *Times* correspondent noted in 1952, "very few, if any, are willing to pretend that democracy actually exists [in Mexico]" (NYT, Feb. 2, 1952). A 1958 editorial acknowledged that the Mexican political system "is not quite like ours" (NYT 1958a). However, such warnings went unheeded, and optimism prevailed. During this period, the "general political balance" variable registered 107 positive references, versus 24 negative; the "political democratization" variable received 65 approvals against 7 condemnations (figures 35–37). In fact, Mexico was even paraded as a role model for other countries (NYT 1957a).

Such optimism grew out of the U.S. elite's belief that Mexico was gradually coming to resemble the United States. Scott suggested that Mexico was becoming "systematized into a working political culture in the Western sense";[4] he concluded that even if Mexico did not yet "have a 'perfect' political system," the country had nonetheless "fulfilled the most basic requirements for a Western political system" (1959: 17, 32). His diagnosis was founded on a number of observations. One was the existence of a Mexican middle class, which provided the "broad basis required for moderate or center-weighted parties." The U.S. elite felt that class differences "would gradually diminish until, as is the case in the United States, almost everyone belongs emotionally, albeit not economically, to the middle classes."[5] Enthusiasm for the middle classes and their social role grew, nourished by the notion that, as suggested by Seymour Lipset, a "large middle class [that] tempers conflict by rewarding moderate and democratic parties and penalizing extremist ones" could serve as a solid buffer against political radicalism (1963: 51).

The existence of political parties and elections also contributed to U.S. optimism. A *Times* correspondent felt that political parties were "all to the good in the opinion [of those] interested in seeing the country evolve toward political democracy, as the term is understood in the United States" (NYT, Feb. 2, 1952). For Scott, the existence of elections made "Mexico's political process a great deal more like that of the United States than appears on the surface" (1959: 29).

---

[4]That is, with a separation of powers, regular rotation of government officials via free and transparent elections, political parties, and so on.

[5]American investors claimed at least partial credit for the expansion of Mexico's middle class. Sears Roebuck, for example, was congratulated for helping to improve "social and economic conditions" in Mexico.

PRESIDENTS AND EVASIVE STRATEGIES

Neither Mexico's middle classes, nor its political parties, nor its elections have the pivotal quality of the presidency, and Americans are
well aware of this fact. During the four decades covered by the content analysis, Mexican presidents were mentioned on 2,360 occasions,
while members of the docile legislature were mentioned 348 times,
and the judiciary only 80 times (figure 18). For the United States, the
first and foremost concern regarding an incoming Mexican president
is his ideological orientation. With each succeeding PRI nomination, a
question resurfaces that was posed as follows in 1946 by *Times* correspondent Milton Bracker: "Will Ávila Camacho's successor [Miguel
Alemán] lead a return to the era of Cárdenas, sweeping the nation
toward the left, or will his policies be center-oriented?" (see figure 19
for the answer). Of Mexico's seven presidents in office between 1946
and 1986, the four most praised—and least criticized—in the *Times*
were Alemán, Ruiz Cortines, Díaz Ordaz, and López Mateos, in that
order. Together, these four administrations cover the years from 1946
to 1970.

From 1946 to 1960, Americans had the opportunity to evaluate
three Mexican presidents.[6] Miguel Alemán they viewed as having
"moderate right-wing tendencies." Adolfo Ruiz Cortines was believed to be "a moderate . . . who has always expressed an unequivo-
cal friendship towards the United States" (NYT, Nov. 17, 1957). And
López Mateos, "despite his close trade union ties, personifies the rising middle classes," according to Daniel James. James went on to
predict that López Mateos would "probably keep to the Center already well furrowed by Ruiz Cortines" (James 1958; see also NYT,
Nov. 17, 1956).

Based on these diagnoses, the U.S. elite treated these four presidents well, even though such treatment was not always deserved.
When discrepancies appeared between the U.S. vision and events on
the ground in Mexico, the American elites merely resorted to a number of evasive mechanisms: disassociation, the manipulation of time
distinctions, an enduring faith in the perfectibility of Mexican politicians, selective criticism, and silence about the role played by the
United States.

Disassociation came into play in media coverage of electoral processes. Mexico's official party has rarely hesitated to use fraud to win
closely contested elections. In the 1946 and 1952 presidential elections,
when the ruling Institutional Revolutionary Party faced stiff competition, the regime resorted to a variety of irregular practices in order to
ensure its candidates' success. Despite the electoral irregularities, the

---

[6]For an analysis of this era, see Medina 1979.

Times legitimated the winners. One way to smooth over this contradiction was to disassociate the PRI candidates from the elections' more negative elements, blaming the long-vilified caciques for the irregularities. The United States has always condemned Mexico's caciques (figures 40, 44), whom Paul Kennedy described as holding "life-and-death power, [ruling by] the power of their own pistols and those of their followers." Another correspondent stated that caciques had been "notably evil for centuries." By asserting that the caciques had no "particular loyalty toward the PRI or its candidate Alemán" and that if they appeared to support him, this was for purely "personal reasons" (NYT, Jan. 19, 1946; Oct. 26, 1958), the journalists could isolate the candidate from certain of his supporters. This logic has been adapted to present-day circumstances by observers who viewed presidents from Echeverría to Zedillo as reformers struggling against political "dinosaurs" [entrenched old-timers], without realizing that presidents and caciques, technocrats and dinosaurs, are all part of a single system, although they fulfill different functions within it.

Another technique commonly employed to mitigate discrepancies between perception and reality has been to adjust time distinctions: the present is always better than the past, and there is always hope for the future. (When a commentator wishes to *condemn* something, the order is reversed.) During Mexico's 1946 presidential election, Virginia Lee Warren indignantly described the "tricks that have been *used in the past* in order to violate the will of the people" (emphasis added). She noted that there were "good reasons to believe" that the 1946 elections would be different (NYT, June 30, 1946).

In an editorial examining the 1952 election, the *Times* predicted that if Mexico did not swerve from its present course, it could become "even more democratic," and that "six or twelve years from now" Mexicans would have "a real electoral choice to make for President" (NYT 1952a). Another editorial added the following: Mexico is on a "long, hard, and slow climb toward true democracy. . . . It would be naive to expect a nation that knew nothing but chaos, bloodshed and revolutions throughout a century, to become a democracy in Anglo-Saxon style overnight" (NYT 1952b). This belief is premised on an almost religious faith in the perfectibility of Mexican politicians, who need only promise major reforms or carry out some symbolic action and they are believed, or at least granted the benefit of the doubt. The U.S. elite is notable for its willingness to believe official Mexican interpretations without running a reality check, as they would in their own public arena.

One of the clearest examples of this can be seen in the media's extremely selective coverage and treatment of corruption. Between 1946 and 1947, there were 33 references in the *Times* to corruption in Mexico. Between 1948 and 1951 there were only 6, and in 1952 and 1953 the number of references soared again, to a total of 36 (figures 91, 93). That is, during the peak of Miguel Alemán's power and influence (1948–1951), the *Times* maintained a discreet silence regarding the blatant corruption that characterized this regime. As Alemán's presidency drew to a close, this discretion vanished and criticism reappeared. In an editorial from 1952, the *Times* declared that "it would be dishonest to turn a blind eye on the extraordinary degree of corruption in high circles [in Mexico]" (NYT 1952c). A year later, correspondent Sidney Gruson explored the "former President's practice of enriching his personal cronies" (Mar. 24, 1953). That same year, an editorial voiced the perception that would become widespread during the 1980s: "graft and corruption [have become] a part of the Mexican system" (NYT 1953). That is, corruption was a structural, and no longer an incidental, phenomenon.

The differential treatment of corruption was also evident in the coverage of the Mexican presidents' periodic, though ineffectual, campaigns against it. When Ruiz Cortines initiated one such program, a *Times* correspondent announced the birth of "promising new era . . . for Mexico," adding that Ruiz Cortines was a "wise man" carrying out a clean-up campaign "without recrimination for past regimes, and without trying to bring to justice all those guilty of bribery and corruption." An in-depth cleanup of the system, he added, would have been "an impossible task [which] would have sent asunder the governing party" (NYT, Dec. 29, 1952). A further editorial, which acknowledged that the Alemán regime had been guilty of "some corruption and some abuses of power," nonetheless concluded with a call for patience, suggesting that the system would advance "toward liberal policies" of its own accord (NYT 1957b). Clearly the American elite deplored corruption—but only to the point where efforts to curtail it might threaten Mexico's stability.

These evasive strategies would come into play in the future to deal with a variety of problems, such as abstentionism, popular demonstrations, and so on (see figures 35–38, 40–44). Tracing how these variables evolved will allow us to detect changes in U.S. perceptions of Mexico.

THREATS TO THE SYSTEM

The manner in which U.S. elites responded to threats against the Mexican political system confirms their support for Mexican authoritarianism and allows us to appreciate the relevance of observing how sources are handled. Given its worldview, it comes as no surprise that the United States has always firmly opposed leftist politics. Between

1940 and 1960, criticism of the Mexican Left rose very sharply: the Mexican Communist Party (PCM) had 154 negative and only 2 positive references; the Popular Party (PP) had 57 references against and none in favor; and the left-wing opposition overall garnered 145 negative references versus 4 positive. Cold War paranoia greatly magnified the Left's importance: between 1946 and 1960, the PCM received more mentions than any other party, including the PRI (figures 28–33). This level of attention was hardly justified; the number of registered Communists in Mexico did not exceed 5,000 (Schmitt 1965: 33), and their political presence was minimal, although the Left was undoubtedly seeking to expand its popular support.

Attention to the Left was due to the extremely broad margins of security that the United States sought to establish. Although the National Security Council acknowledged that Communism in Latin America was "not seriously dangerous at the present time," in a more disquieting vein the State Department reasoned that Communism could become a "force which exploits and makes articulate nationalistic aspirations and which supplies organizational and directive guidance to all [anti–U.S.] elements" (NSC 1948a: part 2; DOS 1952: 10).

Nebulous or potential threats can serve to justify all sorts of excesses. During this era Communist conspiracies were seen at the root of an astonishingly broad range of ills (mirrored on the Left by a tendency to blame Yankee imperialism for most of the world's problems). For example, after a screening in Mexico of a film about racism in the United States, a demonstration ensued outside the theater. Correspondent Paul Kennedy's (unsubstantiated) interpretation was that the event revealed an "organized plan . . . to turn the showing of the film into political paths" (NYT, Oct. 20, 1958). He later added that it was "generally conceded" that Mexican criticism of the United States' racist policies was "the work of an organized clique" (NYT, Nov. 2, 1958).

The subtle nuances that can preserve objectivity dissipated in this extremist atmosphere, and this resulted in remarkably poor analytical treatment of certain Mexican opposition leaders. Vicente Lombardo Toledano was an archetypal nationalistic, leftist politician. As a union leader, he backed Miguel Alemán for the presidency. Later, after he was expelled from the official Confederation of Mexican Workers (CTM), he founded the Popular Party upon a bizarre mix of Marxist and nationalist theses. Both the still-extant Popular Party and its heir, the Socialist Popular Party (PPS), viewed U.S. imperialism as the greatest threat to Mexico and elected, therefore, to support the party in power, which was nationalistic (and which was subsidizing them). Lombardo Toledano and the PPS symbolize a domesticated, beholden

Left, which is as much a part of the Mexican political sys the caciques.

Nonetheless, in 1947 U.S. intelligence services observed if Lombardo Toledano was not a self-avowed Communi: "regarded throughout the area as the Communists' spokes......... ... ia- bor affairs" (CIG 1947: 4). The *Times* agreed, pointing out that Lombardo Toledano's distinction between Communism and Marxism was "a differentiation that hardly anyone in Mexican politics takes seriously." The Americans were convinced that he was the "mentor of organized labor in Guatemala," whose goal was "to organize a Latin American trade union federation tied to the Soviet leadership" (NYT, Feb. 17, 1952).[7] Scott also considered Lombardo Toledano a Marxist (1959: 141).

The absence of shadings in the U.S. elite's view of some Mexicans' political orientation also affected General Miguel Henríquez Guzmán, a member of the PRI who struck out on his own to challenge Ruiz Cortines in the 1952 presidential election (NYT, July 30, 1951). Henríquez was a right-winger, described initially, and fairly accurately, by the *Times* as a "good bourgeois conservative." However, to win popular support for his candidacy—and demonstrating the ideological malleability that has characterized many Mexican politicians—he began to maneuver for an alliance with the Left in a move which, according to a *Times* correspondent, "had been inspired by Cominform." The *Times*'s verdict continued to shift as Henríquez drifted through the political geometry in pursuit of the presidency, until he was ultimately classified as a leftist (NYT 1951e; Feb. 17, 1952).

The U.S. elite's support for the established order was also reflected in Americans' poor opinion of labor movements—which received 62 negative references and no positive mentions in the *Times*—and demonstrations, which were condemned on 25 occasions and approved in 7 instances. Government repression was covered 88 times but was censored on only 13 occasions—11 times by correspondent Camille Cianfarra, who reported on the January 1946 massacre in León (figures 40–43).

The government and media employed a number of techniques to condemn these independent movements. One, utilized in both Mexico and the United States, was to maintain silence regarding cases of repression. Another involved the handling of sources: official sources were quoted frequently, while opposition spokespersons were ignored or branded as Communists or instruments of Communists, usually without evidence. It would be absurd to deny the existence of a political Left in Mexico, or that it was hostile to the United States, or that it was present in certain opposition movements. However, this

[7]On this subject, also see NYT, June 5, 1951; June 9, 1952; Jan. 1, 1953; Jan. 29, 1954.

does not justify the bias of U.S. journalists and academics who refused to recognize that popular discontent could also be a response to poverty, electoral fraud, or corruption.[8]

The U.S. press either ignored the opposition or, in some cases, justified its repression by the regime in power. The *Times* Mexico correspondent accepted the thesis that the Mexican oil workers who went on strike in 1947 were infiltrated by Communists, and he approved of Miguel Alemán's harsh handling of the situation. He considered that bringing the full weight of "the law down upon the problematic oil-workers' union" was a healthy move, and concluded that this could be "a culminating moment in Mexico's handling of its oil-based resources" (NYT, Dec. 22, 1946). Shortly thereafter, Mexican banker Juan Monasterio boasted in the United States that, long before Truman's campaign against Communism, "the Mexican President had ejected all Communists from power" (NYT, Apr. 12, 1947). It is interesting to note that because Lombardo Toledano supported Alemán during the strike, criticism of him eased temporarily (NYT, Dec. 24–25, 1946).

Coverage of peasant movements followed a similar pattern. Because the situation in the Mexican countryside was not a priority for the United States, and because foreign correspondents rarely left the capital, peasant movements received little attention during the 1940s and 1950s. Despite the correspondents' lack of knowledge about the rural sector, they nevertheless condemned the peasant movements out of hand.

Most noteworthy was an article from 1954, which purported to cover Rubén Jaramillo, a peasant leader from the state of Morelos. Jaramillo had run for the state governorship during General Henríquez's failed bid for the presidency, and he had organized a guerrilla movement in Morelos during the 1950s. He was described by the *Times* as a "hard-riding pistol-packing bandit in the old style who had been terrorizing the state of Morelos." Jaramillo, stated the newspaper, was the leader of "a group of about 80 desperadoes" who wandered through the countryside as though "Pancho Villa had burst out of a movie screen back on to the Mexican landscape." A "self-avowed revolutionary," he was on some occasions "disguised as a priest, on others as a Protestant pastor." He sometimes traveled on "a mule cart loaded with produce," and at other times he "moved from place to place, along dusty lanes, in a long and shining Cadillac" (NYT, Mar. 13, 1954). This article, dense in adjectives and unfounded attacks, was completely lacking in objectivity though replete with historical inaccuracies. It perpetuated some of the most time-worn cowboy-thriller

---

[8]For an examination of how some of these movements were reported, see NYT, May 17, Dec. 13, 1950; Oct. 1, 1954; Apr. 1, 18, 1956.

stereotypes of Mexican peasants as malevolent, violent, dirty, shabby, and dishonest, spending their days in lascivious contemplation of blond-haired, blue-eyed American beauties.[9] Given the close collaboration between the CIA and the American press during this era, this may well have been a case of propaganda masquerading as news.

Fifteen years later, in 1969, as the anti-Communist hysteria that had gripped the United States was abating, a U.S. writer published a piece in the *Times* stating that "in 1962, a popular peasant leader, Rubén Jaramillo, his wife, and his three foster children were brutally slaughtered by the authorities" (Jellinek 1969). Such dissimilar treatments of a single individual foreshadow some of the changes in store regarding Mexico's place within the consciousness of the U.S. elite.

THE WORKERS' PROTESTS OF 1958–1959

Given such antecedents, the meager and rarely objective coverage of the popular and union movements of 1958–59 should come as no surprise. Protests were sparked by the telegraph workers in 1958. They were soon followed by a group of railroad workers, headed by Demetrio Vallejo, whose legitimacy the *Times* summarily dismissed. Toeing official guidelines, the *Times* declared that the agitators were leftists disowned by "the majority of workers," that their strike was illegal, and that Vallejo was "close to Communist-infiltrated labor sectors."[10]

The specter of conspiracy, nourished through a skillful, engineered handling of sources, was a constant in *Times* dispatches. "Leftist elements," it suggested, "are following the classic pattern of capitalizing on the culmination of unrest that has been boiling beneath the surface for years" (curiously, the *Times* had never noted or reported on this "boiling unrest"). As the movement gathered momentum among oil workers, professors, and students, the *Times* went on to affirm that this was "a coordinated action," part of "a Leftist offensive" seeking to control the communications and transport sectors. The paper also criticized President López Mateos for capitulating to "the demands of the dissident forces led by Leftist organizers."

One month after the railroad workers went on strike, the government, invoking national security, jailed the movement's leaders and thousands of workers, filling their jobs with army recruits. *Times* correspondent Paul Kennedy applauded this move, stating that "the

---

[9]This kind of stereotype has been examined in at least three doctoral dissertations: W. Anderson 1977, Paredes 1973, and Zelman 1969.

[10]The discussion of the railroad workers' movement is based on articles appearing in the *Times* on Aug. 3–7, 26, 31, Sept. 2, 3, 7, 11, 19, and Nov. 11, 1958; and Apr. 2, 4, 7, 10, 12, 14, Oct. 4, and Nov. 8, 1959.

wildcat strike was a Communist plot," that Vallejo was linked to the Soviets (the Mexican government proceeded to expel a number of Soviet diplomats in a move designed to give credence to the conspiracy theory), and that the railroad leaders had attacked federal communication lines, corrupted authorities, hurt the national economy, and, in general, betrayed the nation.

After hundreds of workers had been incarcerated, Kennedy finally acknowledged that perhaps they had "[rebelled] against their leaders . . . after the national leadership announced that it would defer wage raise demands," that there was "serious contention among the rank and file union members over the legality" of the government-imposed Directive Committee, and that there were "indications that the government received unreliable information regarding the loyalty of the rank and file toward the leadership." Media efforts to describe these movements with some measure of objectivity were too little too late. In total, the railroad movement received 36 negative references in the *Times*, 17 informative references, and no positive ones (figure 41). The Mexican press employed similar tactics, although in a more overt manner, to undermine the workers and their movement (see Stevens 1974).

Robert Scott condemned the 1958 railroad movement as well, though from a different angle, stating that "the *majority* of Mexicans approve the *apparent* harshness of the President's relationship" with the railroad workers (Scott 1971: 304, emphasis added). Karl Schmitt also minimized the protests' legitimacy, stating that the strike had failed because of Vallejos's "senseless demands," which merely "led to political conflict, and his own downfall" (1965: 164). Scott produced no evidence for his affirmation that the "majority" of Mexicans approved of the government's policy. He may have consulted the Mexican media—Schmitt did so—but the Mexican papers carried only the official story. It is astonishing that these two serious academics could have been so naive as to trust the Mexican media. Furthermore, the harshness that Scott mentions was more than just "apparent"; the army occupied workplaces, fired thousands of laborers, and jailed hundreds more, including the leadership, who would remain in prison for years.[11]

In the epilogue to the 1971 edition of his *Mexican Government in Transition*, Scott mentions that, after "being detained for a number of years, these men [the twenty-five leaders who were still incarcerated] went on trial. In 1963, they were found guilty of 'social dissolution', and condemned." This epilogue suffers from a lack of specifics. Scott fails to point out that the 1941 Law of Social Dissolution blatantly

---

[11]Stevens provides an excellent reconstruction of the railroad workers' strikes; see Stevens 1974, especially chapter 4.

violated the most fundamental rights. Article 145 of this law established prison sentences for any foreigner or Mexican who "verbally, in writing, or through any other medium disseminates political propaganda . . . containing ideas, programs, or forms of action . . . that might alter public order, or the sovereignty of the Mexican state" (in Stevens 1974: 253).

The *Times* also minimized the true nature of Mexican authoritarianism by quoting official sources almost exclusively. Between 1946 and 1960, the paper quoted 1,035 Mexican government officials and only 149 members of the opposition (figures 8–11). These data also contradict a prevalent American myth concerning Mexico. Although Vincent Padgett claimed that Mexicans were reticent about speaking to "foreigners, especially from the United States [and that] a good relationship with Mexican politicians is not easily established" (L.V. Padgett 1966: vii–viii), the figures attest to the fact that there was an ongoing dialogue between the two elites. This was confirmed by an anecdote from Miguel Alemán's trip to the United States. In New York, Alemán convinced Alejandro Carrillo (a Mexican politician and publisher of *El Popular* newspaper, and known in the United States as a Communist) to declare in a statement to the U.S. media that he was not, and never had been, a member of the Communist Party (NYT, May 4, 1947). Carrillo agreed to explain his political convictions to the American press, in the process demonstrating the open dialogue between national elites, the discipline among Mexican politicians, and the high degree of presidential control over the flow of ideas (and over the dignity of individual politicians).

The customary practice of ignoring protests and overlooking repression had a number of significant exceptions. Center or right-wing movements did garner attention. When some fifty peasants from the right-wing National Sinarchist Union (UNS) were murdered while protesting electoral fraud in León, Guanajuato, in 1946, a *Times* correspondent traveled to León and produced a fairly objective story, in sharp contrast to the coverage of Jaramillo's rebellion in Morelos.

The civic movement led by Dr. Salvador Nava in San Luis Potosí was also covered extensively and solicitously (see, for example, NYT, Dec. 8–9, 1958). A now somewhat more sympathetic Robert Scott pointed out that Nava's movement included "broad sectors of the population, who had joined in order to expel deeply entrenched political leaders. . . . Social development has finally reached the point where the general citizenry is no longer willing to tolerate the kind of strong government that is still in place in certain local units, when government on the national level is evolving into a more responsible authority" (1959: 303). That is, the local leadership was condemned and the national leadership was praised, despite the fact that both formed part of a single, cohesive political system.

CONCLUSION

In summary, the U.S. elite was well disposed toward the Mexican government during the 1940s and 1950s, at the same time that it ignored, and sometimes reviled, the opposition. Overall, the importance of the opposition was minimized. However, among the opposition, center-right groups tended to be somewhat favored, while nationalistic or left-wing groups came in for the worst kind of prejudicial coverage. Evidently, Americans were unwilling to expand their potential consciousness through events that conflicted with their interests or worldview. To preserve their outmoded perceptions without losing the semblance of objectivity, Americans employed a number of mechanisms that would resurface repeatedly in subsequent years.

These incomplete or tainted assessments raise an obvious question: how did this situation affect the Mexican political system? Although many of these movements have been defunct for decades, one cannot help but wonder where more objectivity in reporting might have led. Clearly, independent or opposition movements stagnate without media coverage. In 1957, when Herbert Matthews interviewed Fidel Castro in the Sierra Maestra for the *Times*, he breathed life into Castro's movement, which had been suffocating behind a wall of silence imposed by Cuba's authoritarian regime (Matthews 1969). Mexico's Rubén Jaramillo never caught the attention of the U.S. media. The thread of American indifference toward the struggles of Mexican society will reappear throughout this volume because it was one of the factors that sustained the myth of a well-consolidated Mexican regime in full control of a passive, resigned Mexican population.

The result was that the United States, the supposed champion of democracy and openness, became a jealous defender of an authoritarian regime, closed off from the outside world behind a barrier of nationalism. In exchange for its support of the Mexican regime, Washington gained a stable border on its southern flank. Thanks to a paucity of information, this situation prevailed in the United States throughout the 1940s and 1950s, but it would ultimately give way in the turbulent 1960s.

8

Economic Optimism

There have been three main stages in the evolution of U.S. thinking about economic development since 1945. Following World War II, it was generally agreed that the private sector should play the lead role in economic growth and that the best way for the U.S. government to stimulate development abroad was through its investors. During the turbulent 1960s, these assumptions underwent some modification, influenced by liberal thinkers who accepted the State's participation in the promotion of growth. At this point, Washington began channeling aid for economic development to a number of countries. Attitudes had come full circle by the 1980s, when the private sector was once again viewed as the central player, although with two permutations: heightened aggressiveness in pursuing economic development policies, and the use of international financial organizations as agents to impose the "policies of structural adjustment."

THE UNITED STATES' DEVELOPMENT PROPOSAL

During the early years of the Cold War, the U.S. proposal for economic development rested on an overwhelming consensus: government officials who developed the "doctrines," academics who postulated the "theories," and the press were all united in viewing underdevelopment as a serious threat, and they were in accord about the formulas that would generate prosperity (Packenham 1973: xi). Their notion of development was deeply influenced by the Cold War (Pratt 1973: 100). Capitalists and Communists were then competing in and for the Third World, and one arena in which they waged battle centered on their alternative proposals for development. On one side was the Soviet Union's state-dominated, centralized model; on the other was the United States and free market capitalism. In between were a number of experiments, such as Mexico and Yugoslavia, that combined elements from both models.

According to Cold War logic, the prosperity of a number of nations, including Mexico, was fundamental to the security of the United States because, should underdevelopment not be addressed, these countries could fall "into the hands of the Communists" (DOS 1948: 4). To promote development, the United States endorsed a formula that had proved its worth in the mature capitalist nations: respect for private property and market forces, industrialization, modernized agriculture, and the creation of a broad middle class, the basic instrument for the establishment of a liberal democracy (Sunkel 1977: 4, 10). Other nations' advances were also "defined in terms of growth of per capita product and other conventional measures" (Packenham 1973: 4).

Although Latin America's governments agreed with the U.S. proposal, at least in general terms, there was disagreement as to how it might be implemented. Washington asserted that development should be driven by the business sector rather than by government funds, and that each nation's government was responsible for creating attractive conditions for private investors (Packenham 1973: 4, 11). Latin Americans, however, influenced by ideas propounded by the United Nations Economic Commission for Latin America, maintained that state intervention was necessary to stimulate industrialization through import substitution (ISI), and they clamored for government aid.

OPTIMISM ABOUT THE MEXICAN ECONOMY

This was the backdrop against which the United States viewed the Mexican economy. Although Mexico's mixed economy diverged from U.S. prescriptions, the *Times* (and consequently the U.S. elite) had a very positive opinion of the Mexican economy between 1946 and the early 1960s. Between 1946 and 1959, the variable identified as "Mexico's general economic situation" had 115 positive references, versus 9 negative (figures 67–68), while the "general overview of industry" variable contained 69 positive and only 2 negative references.[1] In 1948, Anita Brenner awarded President Alemán "an 'A' for achievement" in economic policies (Brenner 1948). In 1951, Herbert Gaston, president of EXIMBANK, confessed that he was "frankly bullish on Mexico" (NYT, Jan. 3, 1951). Toward the end of Alemán's regime, Sidney Gruson insisted that, thanks to the Mexican president, this

---

[1] In some cases data deriving from content analysis techniques are presented without reference to specific figures. Space considerations make it impossible to provide the full set of figures, although the discussion draws on all of them.

nation was now "well launched in the development of a modern economy" (NYT, Nov. 25, 1952). And finally, in 1953, columnist Flora Lewis concluded that Mexico's portrait "should be removed from the section of the world gallery devoted to backwards areas and rehung in the middle, developing group" (F. Lewis 1953).

American optimism was in no way dispelled by certain features of the Mexican economy that contradicted the view held by U.S. elites, although the latter frequently criticized the Mexican state's excessive intrusion into the economy (figure 72) and the protectionism with which the Mexican government fostered industrialization. The *Times* dismissed the *ejido*—the traditional, semi-communal land-ownership system—as a "disappointment," incapable of "producing enough," and worse, as a "Socialist concept that was the basis of the Mexican Revolution" (respectively, NYT, Dec. 13, 1952; Mar. 19, 1954). Not surprisingly, the paper concluded that Mexico needed to "replace wasteful primitive cultivation methods with modern techniques" (NYT, Dec. 13, 1952; Jan. 7, 17, 1953).

A number of factors help explain why the U.S. elite continued to hold an overwhelmingly positive view of the Mexican economy. One was the basic moderation of the Mexican proposals. Despite the country's mixed economy, private enterprise had plenty of space to develop, and the regime kept a tight rein on the working sectors' tendencies toward economic or political radicalism. Furthermore, it was clear that the government was investing in areas where private capital had been "either reluctant or inadequate" (NYT, Jan. 7, 1953). However, the most conclusive factor arguing in favor of leaving Mexico alone was success through numbers; the steady rate of economic growth represented a "Mexican miracle" (NYT, Jan. 8, 1958).

Mexico's economic planners faced a long-term dilemma: all agreed that the axis of their country's economic policy was industrialization, which required capital goods, credit, and investment that could only come from the United States. But as economic links between the two nations tightened, Mexico was drawn into an increasingly dependent and subordinate relationship that would, in the long run, erode its thesis of economic nationalism (F. Cardoso 1973: 149–57). An uneasy balance held until the mid-1980s. Washington remained respectful of the Mexican experiment—as long as U.S. investments were not threatened. In fact, one of the most important variables for gauging U.S. opinion in this area is Mexico's policy toward foreign investment (Spengler 1965: 204–06).

According to a U.S. State Department document from 1952, American private investment develops, produces, and makes "strategic material" available to the United States. It also contributes to the "economic development of the Latin American nations" and promotes "American power and influence" (DOS 1952: 25). To achieve these aims, the United States had to persuade the governments of Latin America that it was in their best interest to create a "climate to attract private investment" (as the National Security Council advised; see NSC 1953a: 5).

As a point of departure, these ideas motivated Americans to be unusually careful to differentiate rhetoric from fact: the *Times* called, not for "kind words about foreign capital and private enterprise," but rather for "actions" (NYT, Sept. 20, 1954). Presidents Alemán and Ruiz Cortines were highly praised for supporting measures that favored U.S. investment which, in the paper's opinion, were helping to overcome the "psychology created by events of the Cárdenas regime" (a tacit reference to the expropriation of the oil industry, an event that still obsessed the American public) (NYT, Apr. 11, 1947).

This praise for the Mexican economy—centered on that nation's favorable climate for foreign investment (figures 77–78)—was somewhat unwarranted. Foreign investment was still regulated by a 1946 law that had a marked nationalist orientation. The implied contradiction was resolved through formulas introduced within the "understanding" reached between Ambassador Morrow and President Calles in 1927; according to a high-ranking official from the Truman administration, the Mexican legislation was "not followed in practice" during Alemán's administration because it comprised "merely protective devices to be used if needed" (NYT, June 11, 1947). The same appeared to be true of Ruiz Cortines's government, which continued the pattern of "flexibility" in "granting exemptions to the law" (NYT, Jan. 7, 1953; Jan. 4, 1954; Jan. 5, 1955; Jan. 5, 1956; Jan. 8, 1958).

FORMULAS TO FORESTALL PROBLEMS

A further reason for U.S. optimism was the fact that certain aspects of reality were simply ignored, possibly because they lay beyond the limits of consciousness. A key tenet of the worldview prevailing in the United States is that the private sector, the motor of development, is enterprising, inventive, and adventuresome. The Mexican private sector of the time, however, did not share these features; in fact, with few exceptions, it tended to be inefficient, corrupt, and highly dependent on the regime. The U.S. elite never submitted the Mexican business community to close scrutiny, and consequently they lacked insight into its failings.

The most interesting aspect of this apparent oversight is that it was deliberate; the shortcomings of the Mexican business community were certainly *not* overlooked when conflicts arose between U.S. and Mexican businesses (figures 72–76). For example, in 1959 a *Times* article quoted Mexican businessmen who were calling for the nationalization of U.S.–owned mining concerns. The article went on to chastise them, asserting that Mexicans were reluctant to invest because they had become accustomed "to a far swifter profit" than was usual in foreign concerns (NYT, Oct. 13, 1959).

Americans ignored or minimized other aspects of the Mexican economy as well. In 1953, a report by the International Bank for Reconstruction and Development alluded to the "poor distribution of the Mexican national income and the habit of those who got the income to spend it on luxury goods." The report concluded that this tendency needed to be "curbed in order to induce capital to go into development itself and to spread the national income" (NYT, Mar. 19, 1953).[2]

Marginalization and poverty, in urban and rural areas alike, were also ignored (figures 86–90). These problems only became a cause for concern during the 1960s; throughout the 1950s the emphasis was on industrialization and the need for steady capital accumulation in order to encourage the economy's rapid expansion. For example, Flora Lewis published an article in which she acknowledged that there were social costs in the Mexican model, but she argued that they were not a priority, adding that they were the "inevitable result of industrialization, more intense competition, and a larger and more demanding market." These conclusions reflected Lewis's conviction that "in the long run" this process would generate "better productivity and higher quality, and better distribution" (NYT, Jan. 6, 1954).

The U.S. attitude regarding Mexico's inflation rate was similar. Toward the end of a lengthy article from 1956, the *Times* noted Mexicans' "increasing resentment against rising living costs." However, this pronouncement did not fit with the basic thesis of the article as a whole, expressed in the opening paragraph: 1956 was an "exceptional year, which in many ways transcended anything in Mexico's past" (NYT, Jan. 5, 1956).

In summary, during the Cold War only a few aspects of Mexico's economic model posed any serious concern for U.S. elites, and their opinion of Mexico remained overwhelmingly positive. The Mexican economy was growing, and U.S. interests were not threatened. These were the golden years of the "Mexican miracle." Problems and shortcomings were ignored, downplayed, or presented as transitory, the inevitable toll that nations must pay on the road to development.

By juxtaposing these ideas with U.S. opinions regarding Mexico's political system, the diverse facets of the relationship, and the presidential summits, we begin to gain a panoramic view of the United

---

[2]Such observations were rare: from 1946 to 1959 the distribution of national income was mentioned on only twelve occasions, less than once a year; see figures 82–83.

States' consciousness, the Mexican political system, and the relationships of domination between the two countries. Having laid these foundations, we can move to the next stage, the 1960s, a decade of transition, of shake-ups, and of readjustments.

9

The United States in Transition

In both the United States and Mexico, the 1960s are associated irrevocably with the Cuban Revolution, the Vietnam War, assassinations of public figures, and student protests. These dramatic events were the outgrowth of intertwined circumstances and ideas, some of which were first apparent in the preceding decade.

During the Cold War, American society truly was convinced of its own exceptional character and the importance of remaining united around the established order and authorities. Cracks in this serene image as portrayed in the media—especially television—first appeared in the mid–1950s. In 1954, a landmark Supreme Court decision (Brown v. Board of Education) legitimated the African American community's battle against discrimination and marginalization. A segment of the white community responded with violence, and television cameras transmitted images around the world of whites blocking school entrances to keep out black children, in one blow fracturing the idyllic facade of U.S. society. The civil rights movement transformed the United States with an intensity unparalleled since the Civil War.

The ranks of civil rights protesters were swelled by members of other minorities and the women's rights movement. Broad sectors of America's affluent and well-educated youth also lashed out against the system's ills, both real and imagined. Distrust in authority spread like wildfire, and the consensus that had long sustained U.S. foreign policy crumbled. A perceptive chronicler described the 1960s as

> an explosive time. The old order was being challenged in every sense, racially, morally, culturally, spiritually. . . . It was as if all the social currents that had been bottled up for two or three decades . . . were exploding, and every element of the existing structure of authority was on the defensive (Halberstam 1980: 400).

The international system also underwent extensive transformation. In the Soviet Union, Stalin's intransigence was supplanted by Malenkov's and Khruschev's more conciliatory stance internationally as they focused on reducing Soviet military expenditures and resolving a growing number of domestic problems. Khruschev's "secret speech" before the XX Communist Party Congress in 1956, in which he denounced the "excesses" of Stalinism, coincided with a number of international initiatives. With the Soviet Union's cooperation, Austria was neutralized in 1955, the conciliatory "spirit of Geneva" was born, and an era of peaceful coexistence was inaugurated. Conflict did not disappear; it merely underwent a change of venue—to Africa and Latin America, and to Asia, where France's defeat in Indochina paved the way for the U.S. intervention in Vietnam.

By 1960, when John Kennedy, exemplar of the style and image of the 1960s, defeated Richard Nixon in the presidential race, the Cold War was abating. In the arena of ideas, Kennedy's victory allowed liberal theses to retake ground that had been lost to conservative ideologies. These were the early days of a golden age for a brand of liberalism shot through with an optimistic and messianic activism and unaccepting of any limitations, whether in the United States, around the world, or in space. Imbued with this spirit, the Kennedy administration set out to face threats—both concrete and fanciful—to the national security of the United States.

Not everything had changed. U.S. elites still held that both Communism and the Soviet Union were aggressive by nature. They also believed in the importance of exporting their political and economic system around the world. Kennedy—perturbed by the Soviets' apparent lead in the space race and their incursions into Asia, Africa, and Latin America (Vietnam, the Congo, and Cuba, respectively)— sought to revitalize the policies of containment. Under Kennedy, these policies took on extended breadth and force; and they were deployed with marked intensity. Recognizing that the old recipes no longer worked and had to be replaced, Americans were forced to extend the margins of their potential consciousness. Although this resulted from a vast array of shifting factors, the present discussion focuses on a select few: the conflict in Vietnam, the Cuban Revolution, inter-American relations, and the revolution of ideas.

THE VIETNAM WAR

Following Communism's triumph in China in 1949 and the outbreak of the Korean War, the Truman Doctrine—originally elaborated in 1947 and intended for Europe—was expanded to include Southeast Asia. In fact, the inclusion of Indochina was largely strategic and symbolic; Eisenhower never agreed to send troops into this region, even though the Pentagon had claimed in 1955 that a military solution to the conflict could be achieved with as few as sixteen military divisions.

When Kennedy assumed the presidency, he sent the United States into the conflict, justifying U.S. intervention on the following grounds: Vietnam had to remain part of the free world in order to safeguard Asia as a whole (John Foster Dulles's "domino theory"); and only by fully supporting the government of South Vietnam could the United States demonstrate to other nations the strength of its international commitments. (The latter argument and variations on it were the most frequently offered.)

As David Halberstam noted, Vietnam signaled "the end of an era, the end of a kind of innocence. No wonder the Vietnam War cut more sharply to the inner soul of American culture than anything else in this century. No wonder it has spawned an entire generation of revisionist film-making and historiography." He also noted that for the United States, perhaps the most important consequence of the war was that "it raised questions of who we were," thus signaling "the end of the myth that we were different, that we were better" (1980: 490–91).

The United States' defeat in Vietnam was not only military; it was also a political and moral upset. Vietnam became a central issue for civil rights activists, rebelling minorities, and America's youth, with devastating consequences. The very legitimacy of institutions was called into question, and the society's self-esteem was crushed. The 1960s shattered the country's dreams and battered the foundations of its worldview, deflating this superpower's robust ego—at least for a while. Another important consequence was that society became an active participant in the discussion and formulation of American foreign policy, permanently transforming the policy-making process.

The legitimation for society's incursion into foreign policy arose out of an intellectual current far removed from the traditional conceptions of analysts like George Kennan or Samuel Flagg Bemmis, who maintained that U.S. foreign policy was guided by morality and idealism. The new current comprised academics advocating a revision of the full range of American mythology. Critical revisionism was not new; William Appleman Williams published *The Tragedy of American Diplomacy* in the 1950s (although it had little impact at the time because it transcended the limits of social consciousness). However, during the 1960s and 1970s, the revisionist tendency, also known as the New Left, became widely influential. Its assault on America's most venerated myths coincided with an era of searching and social rebellion. The policies and motivations of Woodrow Wilson, Franklin Roosevelt, and Harry Truman all came into question.

Further—and the utmost sacrilege—revisionists concluded that the United States, having betrayed the guiding principles of its world-view, was largely to blame for the Cold War, the interventions in Vietnam and Chile, and a host of other tragedies. To avoid such disasters in the future, society would have to become an active participant in formulating and implementing foreign policy.

Although the revisionists' charges were extremely harsh, they were narrowly targeted; only a limited number of government officials and institutions were charged with betraying American traditions. Only individuals and particular laws—not the system's fundamentals—were condemned. This fact, and the absence of any political movement that could offer an alternative worldview, explains the system's permanence and the way it reappeared, redeemed itself, and reformed after the traumatic events of the 1960s and 1970s.

A METAMORPHOSIS IN U.S. JOURNALISM AND ACADEME

The media inevitably reflect society. During these years the media mirrored the social spirit of the time, serving as a forum for critical opinions and reasserting an autonomy that had been surrendered to the government in the name of national security. The press, in all its ideological diversity, was once again a vigilant watchdog monitoring the authorities and a representative of society's interests. Two contrasting events faithfully reflect this metamorphosis.

In 1961, the *Miami Herald*, *U.S. News and World Report*, and the *New Republic*, acceding to a government request, abstained from publishing reports on CIA operations against Cuba, which included preparations for the island's imminent invasion. The *Times* also dropped key paragraphs from an article by Tad Szulc on the same subject. One of the few publications to hold an independent and critical editorial line, in this instance and during the overthrow of Jacobo Arbenz, was the weekly *The Nation*.[1] Most dailies agreed to collaborate with Washington because they accepted the official interpretation of national security. But only a decade later, the script had changed completely. The *New York Times* published the "Pentagon papers," detailing exactly how the government had deceived the American people over Vietnam. The *Times* drafted its story without consulting the White House; and the Nixon administration responded by seeking a legal injunction to halt publication. During these events, the press not only enjoyed the support of the judiciary, it also reclaimed its capacity to determine independently what constitutes a matter of "national interest"

---

[1]Different aspects of this episode appear in Wyden 1979: 45–46, 142–43 ff.; Halberstam 1980: 447–48; Cohen 1963: 44–45; Talese 1969: 462–64.

(Abrams 1981). From that moment forward, the automatic consensus between the government and the media was in ruins.

Underlying this metamorphosis was the media's new level of consciousness, heightened by a number of factors. One was the changing profile of the journalist. Journalism called for a new professionalism and was no longer a field dominated by self-taught adventurers. Although its legendary aura suffered, its rigor gained. This critical journalistic spirit reestablished the investigative tradition for which the U.S. press was famed (Gottlieb and Wolf 1977: 327). The media were able to challenge government because American society was rediscovering and exerting a critical attitude. To be wary of government officials and their statements was no longer considered treason; it had, in fact, become a sign of individual responsibility and a symptom of public well-being.

For individual journalists to be able to express critical views meant that the papers' editorial policies had to turn away from conservatism and toward the liberal center, mirroring broader transformations on every level of society (Halberstam 1980: 599). When Otis Chandler took over as publisher of the *Los Angeles Times* in 1960, he transformed this previously conservative paper into a liberal publication. In 1961 it went so far as to publish a series of articles criticizing the right-wing, Orange County–based John Birch Society (Gottlieb and Wolf 1977: 335, 337). Media watchers agree that the *New York Times*, *Newsweek*, *Time* magazine, and the CBS and ABC television networks all underwent similar transformations, each at its own tempo.

A second factor was a growing public interest in international affairs. The U.S. media now covered events in other countries in greater detail and with a new and critical attitude, leading the public to question some government interpretations of "national interest." A chronicler of the era commented that "for the first time came a growth in our willingness to perceive different dimensions and gradations in our national interest" (Halberstam 1980: 244). Henry Giniger, *Times* correspondent in Mexico during the late 1960s, suggested that the American press had become far more "wary, questioning, and suspicious of government" (author interview, 1983).

The Vietnam conflict, in which thousands of journalists experienced the trauma of front-line warfare, was an important factor in this transformation. David Halberstam noted the irony of the situation: journalists arriving in Vietnam were upbeat, convinced that the United States could save the Vietnamese and that the latter would be forever grateful. During a second stage, generally about three months into their stay, they realized that the conflict was more complex than they had imagined. Six to nine months in, they blamed the Vietnamese (never the Americans) for every problem. Next came the realization that the United States was losing (or at least not winning) the war. And finally the journalists would accept that "it isn't working at all, we shouldn't be here, and we are doing more harm than good" (1980: 490–91).

The government had grown comfortably accustomed to an uncensorious press during the Cold War. When the media turned critical, the media-government relationship turned contentious, as during the administrations of Lyndon Johnson and Richard Nixon (the latter was well known for his inability to relate to the press). Nixon's vice president, Spiro Agnew, even suggested that the print media had fanned social protests during the 1960s and this made them "fellow travelers of the counterculture" (Halberstam 1980: 599). (During the Cold War, "fellow traveler" was synonymous with "Communist ally.")

The media's new-found independence reflected transformations under way in the American public. It also mirrored an increasingly critical attitude among certain government officials. It was Defense Department analyst Daniel Ellsberg who leaked the Pentagon papers to the press; and the anonymous "Deep Throat" supplied information to investigative reporters Bob Woodward and Carl Bernstein of the *Washington Post* from within the administration during the Watergate scandal.

As noted earlier, the *Times* was one of the few newspapers to maintain its liberal principles almost intact throughout the dark days of the Cold War. In combination with its inherent flexibility, this fact allowed the *Times* to adapt to changing circumstances. During the 1960s it featured the writings of a new generation of journalists. Tad Szulc and H.J. Maindenberg in Latin America, and David Halberstam in Vietnam covered international affairs with the open spirit of the 1960s (Talese 1969: 466–69), renewing a liberal tradition whose adherents in the 1950s had included Herbert Matthews, Harrison Salisbury, John Oakes, and James Reston.

Even though liberal ideologies permeated the media in the 1960s, certain conservative ideas lingered on. The result was a new equilibrium, based on the principles underlying the U.S. worldview, even as ideas about development, democracy, the role of the State, and hemispheric relations were changing.

LATIN AMERICA AND CUBA IN THE UNITED STATES

U.S. perceptions of Latin America and the nature of relationships of domination changed during the 1960s. One reason for this was that social networks took shape that would have important impacts on developments in the hemisphere. Consciousness began to expand during the 1950s, especially after then-vice president Richard Nixon's eventful trip to Latin America in 1958. The hostility he encountered caught Washington's attention. President Eisenhower soon dispatched his brother Milton to report on the situation, and in 1959 the latter recommended an in-depth review of the inter-American system. That same year, the U.S. House of Representatives Committee on Foreign Relations embarked on a similar process; its report filled seven volumes (USC 1959a).

Confirming changing perceptions and growing interest regarding Latin American affairs, in 1959 the Joint Chiefs of Staff prepared a memorandum criticizing the secretary of defense for perpetuating the United States' "negative perspective" toward the "Communist problem" and for "being against Communism for the sole reason that the United States has stated that Communism is evil." The Joint Chiefs suggested that the time was ripe for a "positive attitude" (JCS 1959). Clearly they were not speaking out in favor of Communism; they simply sought to redefine the strategies being used to combat it.

No twentieth-century event has irritated the U.S. government and affected its perceptions of and policies toward Latin America more profoundly than the Cuban Revolution. Washington's hostility toward Cuba runs deep: by 1995 the United States was ready to reestablish relations with Vietnam, yet its economic, political, and diplomatic blockade of Cuba is still in effect. Perhaps U.S. sentiments on this issue can be illustrated through a comparison of the Cuban and Mexican revolutions. Mexico's revolutionaries realized, as early as the 1920s, that some pragmatic agreement with the United States was both necessary and inevitable, and that the degrees of freedom for the Mexican experiment's independence were determined by the interests of the United States. Even Cárdenas accepted this. The Cubans, however, followed the reverse strategy, supporting guerrilla movements in a number of Latin American nations (though never in Mexico), sending troops to Africa to back anti-American groups, and doing so blatantly, without regard for U.S. sensibilities.

Cuba's chances for success were limited by the fact that it lay within a basically conservative hemisphere. A U.S. Information Agency poll taken in Buenos Aires, Rio de Janeiro, Mexico City, and Caracas in 1964 indicated that "the friendly regard which large majorities [held] for the United States stood in marked contrast to the antipathy [expressed toward] the Soviet Union, Communist China, and Castro's Cuba." These results were "broadly consistent with those of earlier Latin American surveys" (USIA 1964a: 1). Furthermore the Defense Department concluded that the Latin American military "as a whole" were "probably the least anti-American of any political group" in the region (DOD 1965: 35).

Even such positive polling results could not completely allay U.S. fears. In 1964, the CIA conceded that Cuba was "being watched closely" and that any signs that it was extending its revolution "could have an extensive impact on the statist trend elsewhere in the area" (CIA 1964: 7–8). In 1980, President Jimmy Carter confirmed that the real threat was that Cuba provided an alternative model that might be emulated by populations dissatisfied with the established order (Carter 1980).

To vanquish this threat, Washington resorted to the strategy it had used to good effect against Jacobo Arbenz's Guatemala; it made ready to crush the Cuban Revolution. The United States used economic blockades and diplomatic isolation against Cuba, encouraged Cubans to flee the island, organized an invasion, and plotted extensively against Castro (Wyden 1979; USC 1975: 71–198).[2] Cuba resisted, reining in American arrogance, but at an enormous cost. In order to survive, Cuba's system became excessively rigid and dependent on a single leader.

REFORMISM AND REVOLUTION

The United States—determined to rule out the possibility of "another Cuba" in the hemisphere and to curb the spread of Communism more generally—formulated two main strategies. The more conventional one was to reinforce Latin American security structures by increasing military aid and personnel in the region. To justify this new policy, the United States redefined the doctrine of national security, identifying internal subversion as the priority menace.

The second strategy was characteristic of the turbulent 1960s. Emphasizing social transformation, it was intended to preempt extremists from the Right (landed oligarchy and the military) or the Left (radicals and Communists). Its most sophisticated expression was an ambitious program for political and economic reform known as the Alliance for Progress, which sought to bring about in Latin America a *"middle class revolution,* where the processes of economic modernization carry the new urban middle class to power," as James Schlesinger, Jr. noted in a 1961 memorandum to President Kennedy (WH 1961: 1; emphasis added).

Economic development was the program's top priority. In fact, Kennedy called it "today's most critical challenge." To promote development, Kennedy proposed a "serious and long-term program" of government loans for productive activities in underdeveloped regions (in Schlesinger 1965: 590–92). Both the language and ideas surrounding political and economic development had changed, as reflected in an increased awareness of the unequal distribution of income in the

---

[2]Regarding the United States' migratory policy, see Zolberg, Suhrke, and Aguayo 1989: chap. 7.

region, an acknowledgment of the role played by the State, and a new desire for change (Huntington 1971: 283).

This newly broadened consciousness found multiple expressions. A 1961 *Times* editorial acknowledged that only after "many years, a frightening revolution in Cuba, and the entrance of the Cold War into the Western Hemisphere" did the United States realize that "economic growth without social progress keeps the great majority of the people in poverty, while a privileged few reap the benefits of growing abundance." The *Times* also noted that U.S. "policies for 150 years have been *with* the ruling classes, and not *for* the people of Latin America"—a mistake that had to be corrected (NYT 1961b).

The revisionist spirit became so widespread that some government officials even admitted that perhaps the United States was not the ideal role model for the region after all. In 1961, James Schlesinger, Jr. prepared a lengthy memorandum for President Kennedy in which he argued that the United States should no longer seek "to remake the other nations of the hemisphere in our own image" (WH 1961: 7). The Defense Department also considered that "although the traditional order [appeared to be] destined to disappear" from Latin America, there was "no warrant that constitutional democracy on the Anglo Saxon model will take its place, either in the short or long run" (DOD 1965: 10).

The fact that such opinions surfaced among high-ranking government officials and conservative institutions demonstrates how far-reaching the revision of old assumptions really was, as well as how far Washington was willing to go in order to avoid another Cuba. For Washington to make concessions was not easy; Under Secretary of State for Inter-American Affairs Chester Bowles noted that an increased level of independence "might be tougher to swallow in Latin America than elsewhere because of our tradition of relative unquestioned U.S. leadership" (DOS 1961a: 3).

Reformulating U.S. policy toward Latin America called for a new combination of coercion and hegemony. The Kennedy administration showed a preference for hegemony and made every effort to persuade the dominated nations of Latin America that the new U.S. proposal was both viable and desirable. For example, the State Department suggested that its diplomats present the U.S. viewpoint as "the fruit of our own experience, offered by us as background for consideration by the host government *in its own interests*," rather than as an attempt to intervene in another nation's internal affairs (DOS 1965a: 2; emphasis added). Nevertheless, the United States never renounced the use of coercion; an internal State Department communiqué emphasized that, according to President Kennedy, "the principle of noninterference in the affairs of other nations" did not bind the United States to non-action in instances where U.S. national interests called for action (DOS 1961b: 1). The attitude pioneered by Dwight Morrow in Mexico in 1927 had now permeated the United States and become the conventional wisdom of the era.

Kennedy's confident reformism suffered from an inherent weakness: the United States' allies, Latin America's ruling cadres, did not share his liberal fervor. In fact, they tended to favor repression, their mechanism of choice to keep malcontents in line. Reformism languished after Kennedy's assassination in 1963. Lyndon Johnson was more concerned with domestic issues and the war in Vietnam; the Alliance for Progress was relegated to the dusty files of forgotten projects. Not everything returned to the status quo ante, however; local power groups in Latin America were now better armed and provided with a security doctrine that viewed internal subversion as a fundamental threat. Guerrilla groups continued to arise; in combination with a steady deterioration in the region's economies, this resulted in a wave of qualitatively different coups d'état. Latin America's military now saw itself fulfilling a new mission: to reorganize whole societies (see Crahan 1982; Corradi, Fagen, and Garretón 1992; Schoultz 1987). And in pursuing this mission, they had full support from the U.S. elite who, by that time, were primarily concerned with stability at any price, and had consequently reactivated coercion.

Part of the United States' academic community fell in line behind their government and those of Latin America in their struggles against insurgency—including giving their support to the notable "project Camelot," funded by the U.S. army to detect potential revolutionary movements in Latin America. Of course, not everybody was willing to collaborate with Washington, and many academics fought to maintain the autonomy of their research (Horowitz 1967). This split within the intellectual community has since become a permanent feature in U.S. interpretations of Latin America.

UNEXPECTED CONSEQUENCES

Historical analyses all too frequently overemphasize the role played by elites, while ignoring that played by societies. In order to understand the nature of inter-American relations from the 1960s forward, our analyses must include the social networks created by three groups. The first was the Peace Corps, established by President Kennedy to encourage economic and social reforms abroad. It was made up of young volunteers who, according to Peace Corps director Derek Singer, sought to reverse "the feelings of uselessness and impotence among the masses of many underdeveloped nations." These volunteers hoped to instill "a consciousness of [the people's] own capacity to improve their lives" (DOS 1961b: 7). Tens of thousands of young

Americans volunteered to revolutionize the consciousness of the Third World's impoverished populations.

The second group was the academic community. Because knowledge is central in the culture of the United States, issues on the national agenda are generally accompanied by funds for research and education. The Cuban Revolution released a flood of resources—both private and public—for regional studies, leading to an important rise in the number of students and scholars working on Latin America, within the context of a generalized resurgence in international studies (Coatsworth 1987: 17). Because both university students and Peace Corps volunteers were exempt from military conscription, there was no shortage of candidates for the Peace Corps or graduate study programs.

The third group comprised the large numbers of Catholic missionaries who traveled to Latin America during the 1960s in what has been called a "twentieth-century crusade" to fight the three enemies of Catholicism there: the Protestant church, Marxism, and spiritism.[3] Mexico played a quiet role in this crusade as a waystation for linguistic and cultural training, primarily at a diocese in Cuernavaca, Morelos, home to the Intercultural Center for Documentation (CIDOC). Here, Americans and Europeans were trained in the languages and realities they would soon encounter in Latin America.

In combination, these three initiatives—unleashed, or at least accelerated, by the Cuban Revolution—motivated tens of thousands of young people, academics, and Christian missionaries to spend relatively long periods of time in Latin America. Their early enthusiasm had its roots in their belief in their own ability to shape society through faith, organization, and material resources; but they were also sensitized by the civil rights movement, antiwar protests, and the prevailing atmosphere of intellectual searching.

Unfortunately, what they found in Latin America had little correspondence with their expectations. Gerald Costello, writing about the Catholic experience, documented his growing awareness of the "specter of oppression," the tragic effects of rural-to-urban migration, and the rigidity of local power structures and their resistance to change (Costello 1979: ix, 5, 16). These groups were also in a position to observe the role Washington played in the intervention in the Dominican Republic and in the coups in Chile and Brazil, and they soon voiced open criticism of their government's actions.

---

[3]This crusade was born in 1961 as a result of Monsignor Agostino Casaroli's address, in the name of Pope John XXIII, before the Second Religious Congress of the United States at the University of Notre Dame. Casaroli called upon American Catholics to send 10 percent—a tithe—of their 225,000 priests, brothers, and sisters, as missionaries to Latin America (Casaroli 1961).

It is an accident of history that the Americans arrived in Latin America at a time of intellectual effervescence, when two important Latin American contributions to Western thought—dependency theory and liberation theology—were emerging. Notions of fair play and the free exchange of ideas—important in U.S. culture—meant that the Americans who had come to study and transform the region felt impelled to recognize and respond to Latin American viewpoints. Many of these tens of thousands of Americans established a dialogue with their Latin American counterparts, the first time in history that such balanced exchanges had taken place. As a result, many who had come to teach became students. In a parallel process, many Latin Americans modified their views of the United States: their consciousness was broadened, and this enabled them to distinguish between American government and American society.

Although the paths that ideas travel are not easily reconstructed, the evidence confirms that the Americans' sojourn in Latin America, as well as the Latin Americans' own intellectual contributions, affected the United States' worldview. Even a swift perusal of the dissertations and bibliographies produced by the revisionists who reinterpreted American history reveals that they were influenced by Latin American ideas, and in particular by dependency theory. One of the harshest—and most prestigious—critics of the dependency school of thought, Robert Packenham, pointed out in 1978 that during the 1960s dependency theory became "one of the most influential in analyses of Latin America and of development in the Third World [at American research centers]" (1978: 1).

This south-to-north flow of ideas was apparent in another area. For the first time, the *New York Times* published editorials written by Latin Americans, including Felipe Herrera and Jacques Chonchol, the latter a minister in Salvador Allende's Popular Unity government in Chile (NYT, Jan. 22, 1968; Jan. 5, 1971). This openness was not limited to the *Times*. The thirst for change was so strong among the U.S. elite that in 1961 a State Department memorandum recommended that a "positive effort [be made] to include 'leftist' intellectuals in exchange programs." The recommendation was highly unusual in view of the fact that, as acknowledged in this same document, the United States had "been very reluctant to do so in the past" (DOS 1961c: 6.)

Latin America also influenced Christian thinking in the United States. At least 70,000 copies of Gustavo Gutiérrez's *A Theology of Liberation* were sold in the United States, and the *Christian Weekly* chose it from more than 15,000 volumes as one of the twelve most important theological works to be published during the 1970s (*Time*, Nov. 26, 1979; author interview with John Eagleson, 1984).

In brief, a nucleus of bilingual, bicultural Americans formed during the 1960s. Its members understood Latin American complexities and broadened the margins of the United States' consciousness. They also formulated a more refined and less ethnocentric vision of Latin America that was clearly different from those that preceded it. This new vision gradually acquired political weight as the young volunteers, missionaries, and scholars returned to the United States and entered into politics, government, universities, foundations, or ecclesiastical hierarchies. Because many of them maintained their ties with individuals and groups in Latin America, they became channels for communication, as well as an important influence on the formulation of U.S. foreign policy.[4] A full understanding of the history of the Western Hemisphere over the last thirty years must, therefore, include the social networks that influenced the United States' worldview, the formulation of its foreign policy, and the nature of hemispheric relationships of domination.

U.S. Views of Mexico in the 1960s

Mexico was not a Washington priority during the 1960s. Mexico was stable, its economy was growing, and it supported the United States when needed. Nonetheless, Mexico's increasing international activism did cause some tension, and its economic and political problems prompted many scholars to modify the parameters they used to analyze the country, in the process laying the foundations for a shift in perceptions of Mexico. It is no coincidence that three seminal texts which appeared in the first half of the decade broke with the existing consensus.[5] Despite these changes, U.S. attention shifted away from Mexico, at least in quantitative terms. Our barometer, the *New York Times*, indicates that the low point for articles on Mexican affairs was between 1965 and 1973; there was no significant increase in front-page stories, editorials, opinion pieces, and so on (figures 1, 4, 6, 7).

A similar pattern appears in the military literature. Although views on Latin America were evolving rapidly, Mexico merited no more than historical essays or articles praising its low cost of living. Two such articles penned by military spouses—one in 1960, the second in 1969—share the frivolous, paternalistic tone toward "the Mexican" which is characteristic of a certain facet of U.S. perceptions. Both authors aimed to demonstrate that Guadalajara was a veritable

---

[4]This was reflected in the publication of the first *North American Congress on Latin America (NACLA) Report* in 1967. This publication—founded by American Christians, activists, and scholars—has since become a forum for leftist and progressive viewpoints on Latin America.

[5]Frank Brandenburg's *The Making of Modern Mexico* (1964), Raymond Vernon's *The Dilemma of Mexico's Development* (1964), and Oscar Lewis's *The Children of Sanchez* (1961).

Shangri-la for retired military personnel, due to its good communications, agreeable climate, beautiful surroundings, and, most of all, low prices. In Guadalajara, they stated, the cost of "room and board was a third or a fourth of what they are in the United States." The inconveniences—bad water, dubious hygiene, and the "horses, donkeys and cows" that roamed the streets and by-ways—were offset by the natives' inherent good nature. The Mexicans were "friendly, honest and courteous," and their culture, although diverse, had certain aspects—such as the siesta—that could be emulated (J. Douglas 1960; Brown 1969). The authors' enthusiasm is as evident as is their ignorance of Mexican history. Their mistakes were extensive. They suggested, for example, that "the Aztecs carried out millions of human sacrifices at the Temple of Quetzalcoatl" in Teotihuacan. In fact, the Aztecs inhabited Tenochtitlan, not Teotihuacan, and there is little evidence that "millions of sacrifices" were carried out at the latter site in any case.

Yet even though the United States did not notice, problems were brewing in Mexico. Rather than address them, the Mexican government postponed reforms and repressed all opposition. The results were acute stress for the economic model and a steady decline for the political regime. Although this was not apparent at the time, the problems that ailed Mexico in 1996 had their roots in the 1960s, a decade that witnessed the emergence of an active social resistance against authoritarianism which evolved along two main lines: a peaceful social and party-based opposition, and an armed opposition of small guerrilla movements.

CONCLUSION

Thus, although the United States paid Mexico scant attention during this period, there were fundamental changes in how it viewed its neighbor country. A review of written material produced in the Untied States during the 1960s uncovers an apparent willingness to acknowledge problems that previously had been ignored. Mexico's unequal distribution of income received only 10 negative references between 1946 and 1959; the number rose to 21 during the 1960s. Unemployment had a single negative reference during the earlier period, and 9 during the latter. Poverty went from 12 to 21 (figures 83, 84, 87–90). New problems, such as Mexico's population explosion, also became apparent during the 1960s (figure 81).

This subtle transformation emerged within the academic community, catalyzed by the Cuban Revolution. In 1966, historian Stanley Ross recognized that "when America's journalists and politicians were faced with the disagreeable alternative of a Castro-style uprising, they began presenting the Mexican Revolution as the preferred revolution" (1966: 5). They reinterpreted and reevaluated the system inherited from the Mexican Revolution; during the 1920s they had tolerated it reluctantly, but during the 1960s they praised it. If the Latin American nations would not follow the example set by the United States, Washington hoped that at least they might emulate Mexico, whose political cadres were outspoken yet disinclined to rock the boat. Following chapters explore these paradoxes of history.

10

Mexico's Two-Dimensional Foreign Policy

The 1960s are replete with clues for anyone seeking to understand Mexican foreign policy. During that decade, President Adolfo López Mateos (1958–1964) reoriented Mexican diplomacy through a major but controlled opening to the outside, coinciding with changes that were under way in inter-American and international relations. The understanding between Mexico and the United States was subjected to unusual tensions, yet these did not damage the cordiality underlying the relationship. The most noteworthy feature of this period was that priorities on the bilateral agenda shifted, making more evident than before the two-dimensional, even schizoid, nature of Mexico's relations with the rest of the world: independence and progressiveness on some matters, but conservatism and close alliance with Washington on others.

RELATIONS WITH CUBA

Observers who claim that Mexico's foreign policy traditionally has been based on principles often point to the Mexican government's decision to maintain relations with revolutionary Cuba and to support Cuba against the United States. Mexico's fortitude on this issue is unquestioned, as is the importance of its stance for Fidel Castro's Cuba. However, Mexico's position was always a mutually agreed part of the country's understanding with Washington. Explaining this seeming paradox will illuminate certain aspects of the relationship, as well as the dynamics of consciousness in the United States.

The Mexican government expressed its empathy with Cuba in many ways during the early days of that country's revolution. On a visit to Mexico in June 1960, Cuban president Osvaldo Dorticós received "the warmest welcome in many years [for] a visiting head of state," with crowds chanting "Cuba sí, Yankees no." In July 1960, López Mateos declared that his government would veer to the "extreme left within constitutional limits," a statement whose meaning was very clear given the hemispheric context. That same month, Emilio Sánchez Piedra, president of the Permanent Commission of the Mexican Congress, stated that Mexico was squarely "on Cuba's side" in the growing confrontation between the United States and Cuba (Pellicer 1972; NYT, June 10 and July 8, 10, 13, 1960; Apr. 19, 1961).

As relations between Cuba and the United States deteriorated, Sánchez Piedra went on the warpath, declaring in September 1960 that "the Cuban people are engaged in a revolution to free themselves from foreign influences, such as Nazism, Fascism, and Franco-ism." His statement particularly annoyed a parliamentary delegation from the United States, which suspected that Sánchez was implying that the foreign influence in the Cuban case was the United States. Even the slightest such hint infuriated the Americans because, as emphatically reported in the *Times*, "all freedom-loving people [know], of course, that this is not true" (NYT, Sept. 16, 1960). In 1962, Mexico's ambassador to the Organization of American States, Vicente Sánchez Gavito, declared that the Americans were guided by a cowboy movie psychology, in which the fair-haired protagonist is "the good guy," and all the evil deeds are attributable to foreigners (NYT, June 9, 1962).

Mexico's decision to maintain relations with Cuba riled public opinion in the United States. Between 1959 and 1970, the variable for opinions on Mexico's relationship with Cuba had 28 negative references in the *Times*, against a single positive one. Interestingly, neither the Mexican declarations nor the U.S. responses merited more than brief articles in the paper's inner pages. Given U.S. belligerence toward Cuba, why did the *Times* consider the relationship between Mexico and Cuba to be of such little importance, and why did Washington tolerate the friendliness between these two nations? Although the United States was vexed by Mexico's statements and actions, except for a brief period in the late 1970s the United States was not unduly concerned, because Mexican policies were not considered to be a threat to the security of the United States. (This key aspect of the relationship's internal mechanisms is examined in greater detail in the following chapter.)

During the Cuban Revolution's early years, Washington was certainly concerned regarding its possible effects on Mexican stability. James Reston went so far as to suggest that "Mexico, and not Cuba, is undoubtedly the main objective of Communist activity in the Hemisphere." Although Mexico was at peace, its "immense problems" (which were only then being acknowledged) might threaten its precious stability (Reston 1962). This concern was transitory, and the United States soon formulated a different interpretation: that the aim of Mexico's policy toward Cuba was not to harass or annoy the United States; it was to appease the Mexican Left. Mexico's progressive foreign policies were, in fact, an aid in maintaining the country's established authoritarian order.

The United States would refer frequently to this nexus between stability and diplomacy. In a 1962 memorandum, Ambassador Thomas Mann pondered why Mexico adopted such apparently incomprehensible policies and attitudes. He then stated that in his "attempts to analyze the sometimes unexplainable policies of the Mexican government," he had "concluded that the 'international and national' actions of the government were based on the overriding objective of holding the PRI together" (DOS 1962a: 1). According to a State Department document, "the policy of the Mexican government, on both the Cuban and Dominican issues [was intended to erode Mexican] leftist propaganda on these issues" (DOS 1965a: 3; see also CIA 1964: 3–4). These ideas informed U.S. policy toward Mexico as expressed in an internal White House communiqué from 1961: "we should not demand that Mexico take an out-and-out United States line on Cuba [because Mexico's] political stability is worth preserving in a world of ferment" (NYT, Dec. 2, 1964).

THE FACTS OF MEXICO'S CUBA POLICY

The U.S. elite had good reason to be at ease regarding Mexico's foreign policy. Extensive evidence confirms that the Mexican leadership frequently disavowed in private the radicalism it espoused in public. On February 18, 1959, weeks after Castro's entrance into Havana, Presidents Eisenhower and López Mateos met in Acapulco. In his memoirs, Eisenhower recalled the "spirit of friendship" that prevailed at the meeting, as well as his satisfaction when

> López Mateos suggested to me that we maintain the relationship, using my brother Milton as a traveling intermediary. This agreement proved very useful. When "Project Mercury" [the United States' man-in-space program] required a control station in Guaymas, Mexico, for its success, my brother carried out the delicate negotiations with President López Mateos. In the end, we obtained total Mexican cooperation (Eisenhower 1965: 344).

Around August 1960, the State Department was informed, "through informal channels, that Mexico feared Communist influence in Cuba more than did the United States" (NYT, Aug. 14, 1960). Regarding Sánchez Piedra's declarations, the *Times* noted, just one day after these statements were made, that visiting U.S. representatives received an "unusually warm welcome" from López Mateos. Moreover, the U.S. contingent at the parade commemorating Mexican Independence received a "warm ovation"; Washington declared itself to be "completely satisfied" (NYT, Sept. 18, 1960). And finally, Manuel Moreno Sánchez and Minister Manuel Tello reassured officials from the U.S. embassy that Sánchez Gavito's statements to the OAS were no more than "personal opinions" (NYT, July 10, 1960).

In November 1964, a month before being sworn in as president, Gustavo Díaz Ordaz stated—in a private conversation with Lyndon Johnson—that the United States could "rest assured that, in the moment of truth, Mexico will unequivocally be on the American side." He added that "there will be a considerable advantage [for both nations] if Mexico is able to continue demonstrating its political independence, disagreeing with the United States on relatively minor affairs." Although this might entail "temporary tensions, it will also prove that the United States of America is in favor of independence" (DOS 1964a).

Mexico's actions accorded with such statements. During the U.S. invasion of Cuba at the Bay of Pigs, Mexican authorities maintained a low profile; the only prominent member of the ruling elite to speak out in Cuba's favor was former president Lázaro Cárdenas (NYT, Oct. 28, 1962). The government, carefully distancing itself from Cárdenas's position, tightened controls over what was published in Mexico regarding Cuba. By July 5, 1961, the *Times* was able to suggest that López Mateos had shifted "from the left toward a middle-of-the-road policy."

President John Kennedy's visit to Mexico in July 1962 confirmed the sincerity of Mexico's expressions of goodwill. The *Times* rated the event as a total success (figures 55–57). Approximately one million Mexicans accorded Kennedy a "tumultuous reception," thought to be "the largest and most enthusiastic ever given to a visiting chief of state in Mexico's history." It may not have been the largest, but it almost certainly equaled Truman's welcome in 1947 and far exceeded the recent welcome for the Cuban president. According to the *Times*, the most widely accepted explanation for this rapturous welcome was that President and Mrs. Kennedy had "captured the imagination of the Mexicans" (NYT, June 30, 1962; 1962a). (While the Kennedys' charisma was undeniable, one must remember that enthusiastic throngs to welcome foreign dignitaries rarely gather spontaneously in Mexico. Such multitudes have traditionally been one of the instruments that the ruling elite employs in order to earn the goodwill of visiting notables.)

Kennedy appreciated Mexico's warm welcome, especially since it came close on the heels of his failed invasion of Cuba, which Kennedy himself called the "worst defeat of his career" (Wyden 1979: 310). He reciprocated in the usual manner, with lofty speeches reflecting the attitudes in vogue in Washington and with the traditional loan. Kennedy stated that the Mexican Revolution was a model to be emulated, and he acknowledged that government should play "an essential role in stimulating and supplementing the efforts of private enterprise" (NYT 1962b). However, this encounter, like most presidential summits, merits only a passing reference in the history of the Kennedy administration. Mexico was, after all, a low priority for the Kennedy White House.[1]

Nonetheless, the United States was pleased with the demonstrations of Mexican support. During Kennedy's visit, for example, López Mateos first expressed support for the Alliance for Progress. "The terms of his approval," according to a *Times* editorial, "were sound and encouraging." Of course, López Mateos also took advantage of the occasion to reaffirm that Mexico would pursue an independent policy direction and that it would maintain its relations with Cuba (NYT, July 1, 1962). That a Mexican president felt free to deviate publicly from Washington's view on so delicate a matter confirms that on this issue Mexico and the United States had "agreed to disagree" (NYT, Oct. 28, 1962).

Despite this divergence, Mexico stood squarely behind the United States throughout the Cuban missile crisis in October 1962. The Mexican government firmly supported "President Kennedy's determination to dislodge Soviet missile bases from Cuba"; the missile bases were considered to be "a threat to the peace and security of the Hemisphere" (NYT, Oct. 21, 1962). Although López Mateos was in the Philippines at the time, he declared—employing a prudent euphemism—that "Mexico would stand by the Organization of American States in meeting the Cuban situation" (NYT, Oct. 23, 1962). Some months later, in Punta del Este, Uruguay, Mexico's minister of foreign affairs, Manuel Tello, was more direct, attacking "the regime of Premier Fidel Castro" and stating that Cuba's actions were "totally divorced from the policies which have been the common denominator of institutions of all peoples of the New World" (NYT, Jan. 25, 1963).

By 1964, this combination of private reassurances and overt backing at key moments led the CIA to conclude that "Mexico will probably pursue its brand of 'independent' foreign policy on issues such as Cuba, disarmament, and international trade, which at times will be at odds with those of the United States." Even so, there was no need for

---

[1] Kennedy's untimely death precluded any memoirs. A closely equivalent source is the text by Arthur Schlesinger, Jr. (1965: 768).

concern: the Mexican government was "at heart pro-Western, friendly toward the United States, and fully aware that its economic and political interests are closely tied to this country" (CIA 1964: 152). Thus, despite the dynamics surrounding the Cuban Revolution, Washington was able to corroborate once again that in critical situations Mexico would always stand as an ally (see, for example, NYT, Nov. 18, 1962; Apr. 8, 1963; Sept. 2, 1963).

Because the appearance of cooperation with the United States conflicted with "Mexican nationalism," mechanisms were set in motion to shore up the Mexican government's image. One was the two governments' "agreement to disagree," which was open to any number of interpretations. It led many Mexicans to believe that their country differed with the United States on matters of substance, while in truth the disagreements were over issues of secondary importance. The White House tolerated Mexico's pronouncements, because it recognized that these statements helped the Mexican government to maintain stability, preempt the opposition on the Left, and curb Cuba's revolutionaries who, in exchange for Mexico's support in the international arena, refrained from intervening in Mexican affairs.

Both at its core and on the surface, the U.S.–Mexico relationship was still regulated by the informal understanding reached during the 1920s. The Mexican government continued to invoke principles as the basis of its policy decisions and often was at odds with Washington. In certain crucial areas, however, it never overstepped the boundaries that the United States marked out to protect its interests, even when these boundaries shifted in line with changes in the U.S. worldview.

No evidence has yet come to light that the two governments ever explicitly discussed or agreed to the rules of this understanding. Based on available documents, interviews with government officials from both nations, and actions taken by the two governments, one can deduce that the understanding is implemented on a case-by-case basis, and that it has proved flexible enough to adapt to changing circumstances. It has remained in force because it brings continuing benefits to both governments. The United States has benefited from having a stable, supportive neighbor, and Mexico has gained maneuvering space for its experiment in self-determination and the latitude for maintaining a vise-like grip on society.[2]

One probably inevitable consequence was that the U.S. elite sometimes failed to take seriously the independence of Mexico's foreign policy. Carl Sulzberger, a member of the family that owns the *Times*, penned a column in which he stated that, had the Bay of Pigs invasion succeeded, Mexico would likely have felt "a wave of simulated in-

---

[2]The problems that would later plague the Mexican economic model would transform all of this.

dignation, accompanied by vast relief" (Sulzberger 1961). This view is seconded by Daniel James, who noted that if American troops had invaded Cuba, Mexico's official reaction would have been to denounce the action, but only for about a week, after which time the Mexicans would have "applauded [the United States] for being macho" (James 1963). And, according to a *Times* editorial: "many Mexican politicians of recent decades have managed to accumulate fortunes; they are men of substance who talk revolution, but do not practice it or encourage it, either at home or in Cuba" (NYT 1964b).

It is certainly true that many Mexican government officials firmly believed that Mexico's defense of a sovereign foreign policy, based on principle and under constant siege from the United States, was a noble and patriotic pursuit. Unfortunately, both for these officials and for Mexico, the facts indicate that all pivotal foreign policy decisions were made in Los Pinos (the president's residence) and in the Ministry of Government, and were guided by crassly pragmatic considerations, the uppermost being to keep the ruling elite in power. Principles, though frequently invoked, were rarely a factor in fact.[3]

CHINA, TITO, AND DE GAULLE

There are many aspects of Adolfo López Mateos's intense international activities that confirm the arguments outlined above, including the establishment of trade relations between Mexico and the People's Republic of China and state visits to Mexico by Marshal Tito of Yugoslavia and President Charles de Gaulle of France.

The triumph of Mao Tse-tung and the Chinese Communists in October 1949 and the creation of the People's Republic of China distressed conservative sectors in the United States. A campaign to castigate those responsible for having "lost China" was soon under way. By the 1960s, feelings had cooled somewhat, although there was still opposition to the idea of normalized relations between Mexico and the People's Republic. When a Chinese exhibition hall was established in Mexico, the *Times* called it a "propaganda center" (NYT, Nov. 17, 1963). Although the State Department quietly acquiesced to "expanded Mexican trade in nonstrategic commodities with the China mainland," it emphasized the need to "urge the Mexican gov-

---

[3]Interestingly, such pragmatism finds a parallel in the strategy of the Cuban revolutionaries vis-à-vis Mexico. Their top priority was always to preserve an image of affinity with the Mexican government, and to this end they turned a blind eye to the regime's authoritarian nature. Paradoxically, over recent decades the most consistent point of agreement between Washington and Havana has been their shared indifference regarding Mexico's internal affairs and their tolerance of its authoritarian government.

ernment to insist on strict reciprocity" in the number of commercial attachés exchanged (DOS 1964b: 2–3). This example of U.S. flexibility toward Mexico's independent stand was largely due to an expanding potential consciousness: as the United States' worries eased, China and Communism were perceived with greater objectivity and less paranoia.

In 1963, Yugoslav leader Marshal Tito traveled to Mexico, where he received a "warm, at times tumultuous welcome" (approximately 750,000 people turned out to greet him) (NYT, Oct. 5, 1963). Bearing in mind Mexico City's recent welcome for President Kennedy, one cannot but marvel at the regime's capacity for mobilization. It is hard to imagine that the city's inhabitants could be genuinely gripped by sudden enthusiasm for such dissimilar heads of state. Washington was not unduly concerned by Tito's visit because, as noted in a State Department memorandum, the United States did not "regard the presence of Tito's representatives and missions as a threat comparable to that presented by other Communist regimes" (DOS 1962a: 3), reflecting an increasingly relaxed attitude with which certain U.S. sectors viewed Communism.

In 1964, however, serious concerns did arise in Washington, brought on by the visit to Mexico of a U.S. ally, President Charles de Gaulle. This event produced 4 negative references to Mexico's foreign policy in the *Times*, more than any other visit by a foreign head of state (figure 46). De Gaulle's visit was considered a threat because he "represented a policy of independence . . . an old dream for Mexico and many other Latin Americans" (NYT, Mar. 15, 1964). When the visit was announced, the *Times* editorialized that the United States would perceive it as a "challenge," although a limited one, because, "just like the Communist bloc, the West has never ceased to be unified" (NYT 1964c). In fact, both the *Times* and Washington had underestimated the importance that Mexico attached to de Gaulle's visit. The climax came when the French president addressed an audience of some 225,000 people from the balcony of the National Palace. De Gaulle was the first, and still the only, visiting head of state to have been granted the use of this highly symbolic space (NYT, Mar. 17, 1964). Furthermore, all living former presidents of Mexico attended the banquet hosted in his honor, a tribute not extended to President Kennedy (DOS 1964c). Such signs of esteem expressed Mexico's dreams of becoming a midsized power with broad margins of autonomy, very much in the mold of de Gaulle's France.

Washington reacted like a spurned mentor, jealous with the realization that a devoted and submissive pupil had in fact a will of his own and could potentially change allegiance. After de Gaulle visited Mexico's National Autonomous University, correspondent Paul Kennedy noted that "there was not even a small demonstration," even though the university was "known as a center for demonstrations over remote as well as immediate causes" (NYT, Mar. 19, 1964). Commenting on the throngs that welcomed de Gaulle, the U.S. correspondent stated that the crowd "did not approach in size or enthusiasm the reception for President and Mrs. Kennedy in 1962" (NYT, Mar. 17, 1964).

The United States' jealousy was expressed more explicitly in private. A U.S. diplomat's report to Washington deplored the Mexican tradition of carting crowds of people downtown to applaud and wave, adding that de Gaulle's reception lacked the "spontaneity" of the Kennedy welcome (DOS 1964c: 1). These observations on the custom of hauling impoverished Mexicans to public events were intended to minimize the attentions paid to de Gaulle; no official document made note of the fact that the welcomes for American dignitaries were orchestrated in the very same way. Consciousness can be selective.

Both the French and the Mexicans came to realize that the visit had upset Washington. Toward the end of de Gaulle's sojourn in Mexico, they tried to "dispel the persistent feeling that the de Gaulle visit [was a] challenge to the United States' supremacy in Mexico, and in all Latin America" (NYT, Mar. 15, 1964). A confidential State Department report reached a similar conclusion (DOS 1964d). A corollary came from James Reston, who called the visit "symbolic" and suggested that it had been "a pleasant ceremonial success, but . . . a side show" (1964).

In brief, the independent diplomacy of López Mateos was no more than a minor irritant in Washington and had little effect on the cordiality of the bilateral relationship. Meanwhile, it contributed to Mexico's stability, satisfied nationalist and leftist sectors, and enhanced the nation's prestige in an international community that was willing seemingly to ignore the absence of democracy in Mexico and the country's long list of human rights violations.

López Mateos's successor, Gustavo Díaz Ordaz (1964–1970), narrowed the government's focus to Mexico's domestic problems and its relationship with the United States, rather than trying to diversify Mexico's relations in the international arena. The discourse of international independence would not resume until 1970, when Luis Echeverría once again sought to pursue the old dream of Mexico as a widely involved and active player on the world stage.

CLOSE, CORDIAL RELATIONS BREED NEW PROBLEMS

Cordial relations between Mexico and the United States continued throughout most of Gustavo Díaz Ordaz's six-year term. It was Díaz

Ordaz who ratified the understanding for mutual support with Lyndon Johnson in November 1964. Throughout the 1960s, the "general overview of the relationship" variable garnered 122 positive and only 10 negative references (figures 48–49). However, by the end of the decade problems began to surface as priorities shifted on the bilateral agenda. Issues that receded in importance include the oil industry (which had 81 mentions between 1946 and 1959, and only 6 during the 1960s) and military relations (78 references during the first period, 18 during the second). Variables that acquired a higher priority were border relations and drug trafficking, and these two were beginning to meld into a single concern. The former had 46 references from 1946 to 1959, rising to 149 during the 1960s; references to drugs rose from 10 to 41 over the same period (figures 58–66).

The continuing cordiality can be attributed to events such as Lyndon Johnson's trip to Mexico in April 1966. His visit came at an important moment; Johnson had recently ordered the invasion of the Dominican Republic, and the United States was rocked by protests against the war in Vietnam. Johnson's visit, initially intended to be purely ceremonial, ended up providing Johnson with tangible benefits. The U.S. president—who hoped to demonstrate his "concern for Latin America without undertaking a trip to a country where his reception might be cool or even hostile"—chose Mexico for a "brief and informal" visit and met with a "popular welcome as great as was possible on such short notice" (NYT, Apr. 16, 1966). Although Mexican officials condemned the U.S. intervention in the Dominican Republic, this did not preclude them from showering Johnson with hospitality. The "wild, surging, and genuinely affectionate welcome [was] like a spring tonic for Johnson," who considered this the warmest reception he had ever been accorded (NYT, Apr. 16, 1966). His press secretary told a journalist, "to suggest that Johnson was pleased" fell far short of the mark (NYT 1966a). A year later, Johnson still fondly recalled "his triumphant visit" (NYT, May 12, 1967).[4] While in Mexico, LBJ posed two rhetorical questions: "Who said we could not go to Latin America? Who said the Dominican Republic disgraced us?" (NYT, Apr. 16, 1966). At the end of the day, it was the Dominicans who were disgraced, not the Americans.

According to *Times* editorials, LBJ's trip had been "a great success." Johnson received an "affectionate and gracious welcome by Latin America's most prosperous nation" (NYT 1966a). Media coverage was overwhelmingly positive (figures 54–57). An internal document from the U.S. Embassy in Mexico emphasized the "enthusiastic welcome accorded to the President" (DOS 1966a). The encounter's

---

[4]Despite his cordial reception, Johnson spared little thought to this visit in his memoirs (1971: 348). Most American presidents seem to have taken Mexican hospitality for granted.

success was due in no small measure to the two presidents' decision, documented in the minutes of their meeting, to make no reference to Cuba, the Dominican Republic, or the Organization of American States (DOS 1966b).

Johnson showed his gratitude in two ways. First, he delivered a bouquet of political rhetoric, describing Mexico as "great" and "beautiful" (NYT, Apr. 16, 1966).[5] Second, he announced a loan, the traditional follow-on to a reasonably successful summit. On this occasion, it was a loan from EXIMBANK to PEMEX which, incidentally, broke a long-standing Washington taboo against loans to nationalized oil companies (DOS 1966b).

The warmth of the relationship facilitated the United States' decision to return to Mexico a small strip of territory, "El Chamizal," that Mexico had lost when the Rio Grande changed its course early in the century. The *Times* had argued in 1963 that it was time to correct "the error" the United States had made when it decided to ignore an international arbitration award in 1911 that granted the area to Mexico (NYT 1963c). Kennedy and López Mateos had hoped to settle this matter, but it was Johnson and Díaz Ordaz who came up with a final resolution in 1967 (NYT, Feb. 20, 1963; Oct. 28, 1967). Of course, the two national media interpreted the settlement differently. The Mexican media reported that El Chamizal was recovered thanks to the efforts of the Mexican government, the inherent validity of Mexico's claim, and the firmness of the nation's principles. The *Times*, however, stated that the agreements on El Chamizal and on a scheme "to control the salinity of the Colorado River water . . . were made possible by American concessions" (NYT 1965).

The meeting between Johnson and Díaz Ordaz in 1967 was the final event in an era of extraordinarily untroubled relations and friendly presidential summits between the two nations. For different reasons, both nations were soon engulfed by internal turmoil. In 1968, bowing to widespread protests over his escalation of the U.S. presence in Vietnam, Johnson opted not to run for a second term in office. The Mexican government, meanwhile, was facing a host of problems that stemmed from its bloody repression of the democratic student movement at Tlatelolco in 1968. These internal conflicts were soon exacerbated by tensions in the bilateral relationship. In 1969, the U.S. government carried out "Operation Intercept" to halt drug trafficking in Mexico, in the process demonstrating some of the less obvious aspects of the prevailing relationship of domination.

---

[5]He managed to weave the term "great" into his brief speech no fewer than eleven times.

DRUGS, NATIONALISM, AND RELATIONSHIPS OF DOMINATION

The illegal drug trade erupted suddenly and violently in 1969. This phenomenon had the potential to affect the security of both nations as well as the bilateral relationship as a whole. The drug trade provides a good window on the nature of the United States' worldview, confirms the weak and malleable nature of Mexico's official nationalism, and reflects the role and importance of coercion among the mechanisms that dictate the relationship of domination between Mexico and the United States. It also illuminates a perverse facet of the relationship: Washington sometimes overlooked or downplayed the narcotrafficking problem so as not to annoy the Mexican government.

There were three peaks in the *Times*'s interest in drug trafficking within the Mexico–U.S. relationship: 1969–1970, 1976–1977, and 1985–1986 (figures 65–66). Also noteworthy was the rapid and intense fluctuation between positive and negative references. There were 12 negative references in 1969, and no positive ones. Only a year later, there were 10 positive and 2 negative. The two interrelated aspects to the problem of drug trafficking go far toward explaining these fluctuations in interest. The first is the enormous demand for narcotics within the United States, and the second is Mexico's demonstrated proficiency as a narcotics producer and middleman.

Narcotics production and distribution had become firmly established in Mexico long before the 1960s crisis, but Mexico's role in the drug trade had not previously been a cause for concern in Washington. In 1952, for example, the CIA noted that Colonel Antonio Serrano—one of President Alemán's closest advisers and the founder of the powerful Federal Security Directorate—"tolerates, and in fact carries out, illegal activities such as the smuggling of narcotics" (CIA 1951: 58). Although Washington was certainly aware of Serrano's involvement, this was not considered important. A former regional director for the Drug Enforcement Agency, Edward Allen Heath, acknowledged in 1981 that the United States "ignored the growing problem in Mexico, and seriously underestimated this nation's potential as a heroin producer" (Heath 1981: 4).

During the 1960s, however, this attitude—and the policies associated with it—changed, as the U.S. government began to hold the drug-producing nations responsible for the country's drug problem and posited that they should collaborate, by choice or by force, with the United States in finding a solution. In 1962, the sheriff of Yuma, Arizona, testified before Congress that there was a growing traffic in drugs cultivated by "ignorant Indians and Mexican farmers," and that this activity was being "financed, organized and directed by a small group of wealthy, intelligent, ruthless and dangerous Mexicans" (NYT, May 10, 1962). This testimony foreshadows what would become the central thesis in the United States until the mid–1980s: the problems caused by drug use and the drug trade within the United States resulted directly from the existence of an available supply, and the point of supply was where these problems should be solved.

These ideas were congruent with one of the fundamental underpinnings of Americans' worldview: because they believed in their own exceptional character, the responsibility for drug consumption must perforce lie with those who produced and sold narcotics. However, this view eventually evolved, and Americans came to acknowledge the importance of demand and to accept that drug users were part of the problem, although it took years for the United States to own up to its share of responsibility. During the 1960s marijuana and heroin trafficking increased in Mexico (although Mexico had not yet become a major transit corridor for South American cocaine), and the United States predictably laid the blame on Mexico. In August 1969, the Pentagon declared Tijuana off limits for all U.S. military personnel, in a two-pronged strategy designed to stop the troops from buying drugs and to pressure the Mexican government to take stronger steps against drug trafficking (NYT, Aug. 29, Sept. 6, 1969).

During a presidential summit in September 1969, Nixon informed Díaz Ordaz that his administration intended to do something about the drug problem (NYT, Sept. 9, 1969). Almost simultaneously, a special task force created by Nixon concluded that "the fundamental responsibility for the eradication of production and processing of opium and marijuana in Mexico" should be borne by the Mexican government and its enforcement agencies, and that "nothing should be done to lift this responsibility from it" (WH 1969). Later that month, without informing or consulting the Mexican government, Washington set "Operation Intercept" in motion, enforcing a detailed security check on every person and vehicle entering the United States from Mexico. At least for the period covered in this study, this was the first occasion on which the United States used coercion so openly and so forcefully.

Operation Intercept was in fact intended to apply "limited economic sanctions against Mexico" and to pressure the Mexican government to cooperate more fully in the war on drugs. Its success was undeniable, as trade and tourism ground "slowly to a halt" (NYT, Sept. 25, 1969). A U.S. Customs supervisor neatly summed up Washington's opinion: "Mexico was paying dearly for its failure this far to move against major marijuana suppliers." This individual went on to add that, in his nation's view, drug-related graft and corruption among Mexico's "police and politicians becomes United States business." Further, if Mexico refused to cooperate, Phase 2 of Operation Intercept would go into effect, in which Washington would publish "the names of about 20 Mexican major offenders" (NYT, Oct. 2, 1969).

Some sectors within the American elite opposed Washington's coercive measures. The *Times*, for example, was of the opinion that "from every conceivable standpoint [Operation Intercept was a] massive political blunder" [and further reduced] the Nixon Administration's meager store of political capital with the rest of Latin America." Coercive strategies attracted criticism primarily because they only addressed domestic concerns within the United States and ignored all international implications. According to the *Times*, Operation Intercept's true mission was to fulfill "in spectacular fashion the President's campaign promise on the 'law-and-order' theme" (NYT, Sept. 30, 1969; 1969a, 1969b).

Mexican authorities reacted with extraordinary (rhetorical) energy. An indignant Díaz Ordaz stated that Washington's actions "had raised a wall of suspicion in Mexico's relations with the United States" (NYT, Sept. 30, 1969). Mexican government officials, who preferred to remain anonymous, pointed out that Operation Intercept reinforced "the characterization of Mexico as the source of the U.S. drug problem" (NYT, Oct. 5, 1969), while in Mexico the opposite view has always prevailed: Mexico's problems with drug traffickers are driven virtually in their entirety by U.S. demand.

The United States was also criticized for trying to force third parties to adopt the policies that Washington wanted to see deployed against the illegal drug trade. For example, Washington wanted Mexico to bombard its fields of marijuana and opium poppies with chemical products (NYT, Oct. 3, 1969). Mexican authorities were disturbed by the unilateral nature of the U.S. policies, continuing the "old story of United States policy decisions that affect a Latin American country profoundly being taken for domestic political reasons without consultations or consideration" (NYT, Oct. 8, 1969). One element of Mexico's response was "Operation Dignity," organized by Francisco Cano Escalante, then head of the Federation of National Chambers of Commerce (CONCANACO). Operation Dignity proposed a Mexican boycott of U.S. commodities; it was openly supported by the president of Mexico (author interview with Cano Escalante, February 1996).

The two governments soon began to negotiate. In a "dramatic overnight reversal of opinion," Washington suspended Operation Intercept and shelved its threat to disclose the names of major Mexican offenders (NYT, Oct. 11, 1969). In return, Mexico signed several anti-narcotics accords with the United States, which were presented to public opinion as "Operation Cooperate." According to a *Times* editorial, "Mexico promised to intensify its campaign against the production and exportation of narcotics" (NYT 1970a).

Mexico was forced to accept greater DEA involvement in its domestic anti-drug campaign. It agreed to spray marijuana and opium plantations, and to intensify activities against producers, dealers, and users. A "permanent campaign" against drugs was established, which relied heavily on Mexico's internal security forces, including the army (Treverton 1988: 214). (It is worth noting that the U.S. armed forces refused for decades to participate in the war on drugs.)

In effect, the Mexican government was forced to acquiesce to the will of the United States. This interpretation is confirmed in the memoirs of G. Gordon Liddy, one of the individuals responsible for the new operation (and later jailed for his role in the Watergate affair). Liddy states that the operation was "intended to bend Mexico to our will. We figured Mexico could hold out for a month; in fact, they caved in after two weeks, and we got what we wanted." He also noted that it was an "exercise in international extortion, pure and simple and effective" (Del Villar 1988: 200). Washington confirmed the effectiveness of coercion: in 1970 Under Secretary of State Elliot Richardson declared that "the greatest success so far in [the United States'] bilateral efforts [to halt the flow of drugs] has been with Mexico" (NYT, Apr. 3, 1970).

Even a glimpse at the issue of drug trafficking reveals that coercion is an important element in Mexico–U.S. relations and that the general design of Mexico's anti-narcotics policy is decided in Washington. In return, the United States has done much to help perpetuate the impression that Mexico's foreign policy is guided by principles.

11

Economy, Consciousness, Nationalism, and Hegemony

AN AMBIVALENT BUT PRAGMATIC VIEW

The attitude of the U.S. elite regarding Mexico's economic situation began to change in the late 1950s and early 1960s. Although opinions were still predominantly favorable, the Mexican government was becoming the object of increasing, and often critical, scrutiny.[1] On the one hand, Mexico was viewed as a country offering "important lessons" for other "underdeveloped nations seeking to propel their stagnant societies into the twentieth century" (NYT 1959b). On the other, there was a new willingness to acknowledge Mexico's shortcomings and problems. A study prepared in 1959 by the Senate Committee on Foreign Relations noted that Mexico needed to "enhance the lifestyles of millions of peasants, and diminish illiteracy" (USC 1959b: 20).

The increasingly critical scrutiny of Mexican reality was a logical outgrowth of the openness that characterized this era, when previously ignored aspects of development—such as income disparities, poverty, and illiteracy—were gradually acknowledged.[2] In effect, the United States' concept of development was changing.

The U.S. elite never lost faith in private-sector initiatives and industrialization as the shortest route to development and democracy. However, they also called for measures to counter Communist attempts to exploit the Latin American economic crisis (DOS 1961d: 10). Their

---

[1]We should bear in mind that what the critics of the era sought was not a complete transformation of Mexico's development model, but just a more efficient mixed economy. A steady growth rate, it was felt, was the Mexican experiment's best defense.

[2]For examples of this new perspective, see Packenham 1973: 70–71; Pratt 1973: 89; Whines 1974: 89–107; Seers 1973.

stance fostered a willingness to entertain new ideas (Packenham 1973: 70–71) in an atmosphere that eventually produced the Kennedy administration's vision of "total development" which, among other things, called for a "reform of the Latin American nations" (WH 1961: 3).

This new concept of development led James Schlesinger, adviser to President Kennedy, to suggest that "life would be enormously complicated" if the U.S. government persisted in its view that private investment was "the only motor for economic development." He warned that "doctrinaire attitudes should be abandoned," including the beliefs that precluded "loans for State-owned companies" (WH 1961: 3).

Allowing the State to play an enhanced role required revising a key assumption of the prevailing liberal mind-set. In 1962, Carl Sulzberger wondered whether "socialism or a free-enterprise regime" would lead to swifter development. He argued that the answer was a combination of both and that the United States might be forced to "swallow many of its ideological preferences, and acknowledge that a modified version of socialism could be the most effective form of government for Latin Americans" (Sulzberger 1962; see also Sachs 1972: 37).

Accepting that socialism held any merit was an enormous ideological concession, and it could only have occurred during this turbulent era, shaped by a sense of emergency and the apparent collapse of the United States' prevalent assumptions and beliefs (Sandbrook 1976). Nonetheless, this shift was typically American in its pragmatism: socialism, it was now acknowledged, might be attractive to underdeveloped nations but only because capitalism had yet to fully resolve certain inherent problems. Consequently, the American system not only had to contain Communism; it now also had to compete with it by providing facts to confirm its own superiority. As the *Times* presented it, the West had to prove that its "democratic and free-enterprise system was better than any version of socialism" (1961b). Kennedy, meanwhile, was pointing out that the "as yet unfulfilled goal" of the United States was to "demonstrate, before the entire world, that it is easier to achieve human aspirations, such as economic progress and social justice, with free workers, within a framework of democratic institutions" (NYT 1961c).

A CRITICAL OPTIMISM

Many of the variables used to evaluate the Mexican economy continued to register positive throughout the 1960s. The *Times* mentioned "the general state of the economy" on 75 occasions: 63 positive, only 2 negative, and 10 informative. There were 23 positive references to

Mexico's financial situation, against a single negative reference. Mexico's industry was mentioned on 34 occasions, with but a single negative reference. This optimism reflected reality: Mexico still enjoyed significant economic growth and was well on the road to industrialization, then considered to be the "only answer to too many people on too little land" (NYT, May 5, 1966). Mexico, it seemed, was at the point of "transition from a static, largely primitive agricultural economy into modern industrialization" (NYT, Dec. 2, 1964). The *Times* suggested that the country was at a "take-off point toward self-sustained growth" (June 8, 1966).

The Mexican experience seemed particularly attractive when re-evaluated vis-à-vis the Cuban Revolution. In 1962, Daniel James wrote that Argentina was in a "permanent crisis," Brazil was "a sleeping giant, incapable of awakening," Castro was "ruining Cuba's possibilities for becoming a glowing example," and only Mexico seemed able to "lead the way" (James 1962). Twenty-four positive references to the "model created by the Mexican Revolution" appeared during the 1960s (figure 71; see also figure 13).

U.S. perceptions changed so dramatically that Mexico's mixed property system came to be seen in a generally positive light. Senator Jacob Javits suggested that Mexico could now "provide leadership and guidance in the means of successfully applying private and state sector activity for the promotion of national economic development" (NYT, Oct. 19, 1963). Even the CIA acknowledged that "the [Mexican] private sector had certain insufficiencies [such as] its unwillingness to risk serious capital, its low volume of production, and its persistent search for high profits"(CIA 1965a: 5). These views were clearly reflected in the media: criticism of protectionist attitudes and State intervention in the economy dropped sharply (figure 73).

Foreign investment was still welcome in Mexico, of course, and U.S. opinion remained strongly in favor of such investment: 46 of 48 references in the *Times* to the role played by foreign investment in Mexico were positive (figures 74–76). References to Mexican policies on foreign investment and to the general climate for U.S. investors were mostly favorable as well (figures 77–79). A CIA document from the mid–1960s concluded that Mexico remained attractive for foreign investment (1964: 6).

Mexico's position on foreign investment came into question on only three occasions during the 1960s. The first was when Mexican businessman Bruno Pagliai declared that many investors were reluctant to invest in Mexico because of the Mexican government's Cuba policy (NYT, Dec. 18, 1961; Jan. 11, 1962). This reluctance diminished over time as the Mexican government demonstrated its loyalty to the United States (NYT, Apr. 8, 1963).

The second occasion was in 1962, after the Mexican Congress passed legislation requiring Mexican and foreign businessmen to share profits with workers, a move that foreign investors criticized swiftly and harshly (NYT, Sept. 13, Nov. 18, and Dec. 22, 1962). This controversy soon resolved itself because, as Mexican banker Aníbal Iturbide noted, "after deductions, workers will receive a yearly payout of only about two weeks' wages under profit sharing" (NYT, Aug. 9, 1964). Iturbide's statement reflects the private sector's ability to erect obstacles to government decisions.[3]

The third occasion resulted when the Díaz Ordaz administration decided to encourage the Mexicanization of foreign investment. The government's aim was to convince foreign investors to sell some of their shares to Mexicans (NYT, Feb. 8, 1966). General Electric, for example, agreed to sell 10 percent of its shares to Mexican nationals (NYT, July 5, 1968). This expression of Mexican economic nationalism was short-lived, however, and it did not make Mexico any less attractive to foreign investors.

U.S. CONCERNS ABOUT MEXICO

The truly original aspect of U.S. analyses during the 1960s was the way in which the problems inherent in Mexico's economic model were perceived. Raymond Vernon's *The Dilemma of Mexico's Development*, departing from schematic comparisons with the United States, concluded that several potential bottlenecks lay along Mexico's development path, including a "recent drop in growth, which could reflect structural deficiencies, and serve as a warning for the future" (1963: 27). The *Times* added that Mexico's import substitution strategy "had reached a point where the most promising and reasonable possibilities were covered" (Jan. 1, 1964). These passages illustrate the beginning of an extremely important consensus: the Mexican economy was in serious need of reform.

Suggestions for reform were aimed at very specific problems. Income distribution was one area of concern (it was mentioned on 12 occasions between 1946 and 1959, and on 23 during the 1960s), as were unemployment (10 mentions during the former period, 16 during the latter), marginalization (which rose from 2 to 11 references), and the poverty that afflicted most of the rural population (mentioned on 19 occasions during the earlier period, and 39 times during the 1960s; figures 82–90). In contrast, references to corruption dropped during the 1960s (figure 93). Although many of the references to cor-

---

[3]In 1965, the CIA noted this adjustment in the distribution of power among Mexican actors and warned that an aggressive private sector now existed that could put the brake on official policies (CIA 1965a: 9).

ruption appeared prominently—including in editorials—they tended to be dismissed as anecdotes and were not taken as signs of a serious problem.

Concern over Mexico's social problems was voiced in a variety of ways. One example is Oscar Lewis's popular *The Children of Sanchez* (1963), a raw description of the "culture of poverty" that dominated the lives of millions of Mexicans excluded from the country's "economic miracle." Washington's concern is visible in a 1962 memorandum in which the U.S. Embassy in Mexico noted that "over half of the [Mexican] population still lives in semi-primitive conditions" (DOS 1962a).

A *Times* editorial from 1961 illustrates this new, critical attitude, asserting that the Mexican Revolution was nothing but "rhetoric produced by political leaders," because "in 1960, over 60% of the population are still ill fed, ill clothed, and ill housed; over 40% are illiterate, and some 45% of the nation's children are not being schooled. The national wealth has greatly increased since 1940, but the gap between rich and poor is even more striking than before, despite some rise in the general standard of living" (1961c).

Another problem that awakened concern during the 1960s was Mexico's demographic growth. References to the population issue began to appear during this decade, when columnist James Reston articulated America's fears. He was not alone. The president of the World Bank stated that Mexico's uncontrolled population growth threatened to "nullify all our efforts to raise living standards in many of the poorer countries" (NYT, Feb. 27, 1963). In 1964, the CIA affirmed that the uncontrolled growth of the Mexican population was at the root of the country's problems (CIA 1964: 5).

The United States felt that finding a solution to the population problem lay squarely with the Mexican government. In 1967, Henry Giniger wrote that "ordinary Mexicans" were far more "ready to accept a birth-control program than their government [was prepared to implement it]" (NYT, Apr. 30, 1967). Juan de Onis added that this had become "a serious obstacle for the improvement of the quality of life of Mexico's poor majorities" (NYT, Oct. 9, 1969). U.S. attention was focused especially on rural Mexico, which was considered to be the arena where political unrest was most likely to arise.

RURAL MEXICO AS A U.S. PRIORITY

Because the insurgencies in both Vietnam and Cuba garnered extensive support from rural populations, an influential school of thought held that impoverished agricultural populations were potential breeding grounds for revolution. In 1961, Under Secretary of State

Chester Bowles urged the Foreign Service to "pay special attention to the rural areas which in Latin America offer both explosive dangers and great opportunities" (DOS 1961b: 6) (figure 88).

During the 1960s, for the first time since 1946, the *Times* took an interest in Mexico's rural milieu. What its reporters found was alarming. After visiting Sonora in the mid–1960s, Giniger stated that the Mexican countryside had "returned to the old pre-Revolutionary system of vast properties, in which a tiny minority controlled the nation's agricultural wealth" (May 17, 1966). Following the publication of an extensive series of Giniger's articles, a *Times* editorial applauded "Mexico's achievements" but warned that "most of her population, uneducated peasants and still very poor, [had to work] their land by primitive, traditional methods" (1966b).

Such comments reflected the United States' long-standing and persisting uneasiness regarding Mexico's stability. Paul Kennedy suggested that "the nation's landless peasants represented its greatest problem" (NYT, Sept. 2, 1964). In a later article, he stated that they were "a constant threat to national equilibrium" (NYT, Jan. 22, 1965). In 1966 Giniger wondered "how long [Mexico] will be able to keep the peace" (NYT, June 11, 1966). These concerns were shared by the CIA. In 1964, the intelligence agency noted that Mexico's agricultural sector had "lagged behind" (CIA 1964: 154–55), and a year later the CIA concluded that "poverty and unrest among peasants [were] a latent threat to the stability" on which the Mexican leadership rested (CIA 1965a: 0–1; see also CIA 1967a: 1–2).

The underlying message, of course, was that the "extreme left" could be preparing to "make use of the plight of the *campesino* or peasant, who has been caught in the grinding process of industrialization" (NYT Book Review, Sept. 22, 1963). The U.S. State Department was in accord, having suggested in 1963 that the "harder line" adopted by Mexican Communists had "evident potential for mischief if agrarian discontent should continue to grow" (DOS 1963a: 3). The arguments were extended to apply to impoverished countries elsewhere in Latin America. Tad Szulc argued that "conditions for a revolutionary situation . . . were increasingly evident throughout the vast Brazilian North East, pervaded with poverty and afflicted by drought" (in Page 1972: 12–13).

When U.S. strategists detect a problem, they tend immediately to initiate a search for its solution. The CIA soon identified "economic and social reform" as the solution to the problem of potential political unrest in rural Mexico (CIA 1966a: 4). James Schlesinger made a similar observation in a 1961 memorandum to President Kennedy: "small scale agriculturists [can] achieve a social transformation" in Latin America (WH 1961: 2). The *Times* also shared this opinion and suggested that Mexico should favor the "small landowners, who, benefiting from far larger tracts of land, have shown greater efficiency than the *ejido* farmers" (June 9, 1966). Such reforms were not implemented, however, even though Mexico's ambassador to the United States concurred with the Americans' proposal.

Following the 1960s, the U.S. elite's view of the evolving Mexican economy became increasingly informed and sophisticated. They came to acknowledge that the public sector played a positive role, and they limited their suggestions to adjustments that they felt would ensure the permanence of the Mexican miracle. At the time, conditions in Mexico were propitious for implementing adjustments to the economic model and controlling the pace of change. However, the inherent rigidity of the Mexican system, especially the concentration of extensive powers in the hands of the president, ultimately choked off all attempted reforms, precipitating a series of periodic economic crises with catastrophic social costs, and increasing Mexico's vulnerability vis-à-vis the United States.

NATIONALISM, LOYALTY, AND HEGEMONY

The United States has always been a reference point for Mexican nationalism. In Mexico's postrevolutionary worldview, there is the belief—amply supported by historical fact—that U.S. interventionism is the foremost threat to Mexico's sovereignty. In light of this belief, the Mexican government, portraying itself as the staunch defender of national sovereignty, cast aspersions on anyone who sought dialogue with the United States. For example, Miguel Alemán's allies took steps to discredit opposition candidate Ezequiel Padilla after the latter agreed to an interview with the *New York Times* in 1946. The Mexican opposition used a similar strategy to discredit the government in 1952, when General Henríquez's followers accused Adolfo Ruiz Cortines of collaborating with U.S. forces during their occupation of Veracruz in 1914.

Such accusations have obscured the real picture. History and a number of opinion polls reveal a very different panorama. Many Mexicans admire everything American; others reject anything that appears to originate in the United States or reflect U.S. influences. And there is a full range of positions between these extremes. If we are to determine which, if any, of these positions represent actual instances of disloyalty, we must review events using a critical and rigorous approach, such as is applied below to examine the actions of Ambassador Antonio Carrillo Flores of Mexico.

Walter Rostow—an academic specializing in development-related issues who ventured into public life—traveled to Mexico in 1963 as head of the State Department's Policy Planning Council. When he returned to Washington, he drafted a master plan for reforming rural Mexico. Rostow suggested that the key challenge was to "widen the market and modernize the backward rural areas." By so doing, Mexico could expect to become "the Sweden of Latin America" within a decade. Rostow's recipe for transforming Mexicans into Swedes had to have been known to and approved by President López Mateos (DOS 1963b).

The way in which Rostow introduced his ideas to the Mexican president vividly demonstrates the nature of hegemonic relationships of domination (in which the dominated party readily accepts the dominator's suggestions as the wisest course of action), and the malleability of the nationalism espoused by many Mexican government officials. In a second memorandum that Rostow prepared for President Kennedy, he appended a letter from Ambassador Carrillo Flores to President López Mateos in which the ambassador praised Rostow's intelligence and expertise and outlined his proposal for Mexico to the Mexican president. (Carrillo Flores himself had sent a copy of his letter to Rostow.) This letter, Rostow stated, "delineates the strategies that I have developed . . . and suggests that they be considered by Mexico's incoming administration" (EMW 1963; DOS 1963c).

Rostow put no pressure upon Carrillo Flores (who would later serve as minister of foreign affairs under President Gustavo Díaz Ordaz). The Mexican ambassador voluntarily adopted ideas and policies developed by an American government representative and presented them as his own. How can we best understand his actions? First, we must recognize that foreign diplomats in the United States have to reconcile their respective governments' nationalism with the important objective of gaining access to Washington's power circles. To this end, they may appear to be convinced of American views as part of a diplomatic simulation designed to earn the trust of the U.S. government. Of course, they may also be sincerely convinced of the rightness of the U.S. position.

Other historical moments adhere to this pattern. Porfirio Díaz, described as "rabidly anti-clerical, a radical liberal, a xenophobic anti-imperialist" (Cosío Villegas 1956: 11), issued a number of decrees during his years in power that impacted heavily on U.S. interests, requiring some complex diplomatic maneuvering. In 1877, for example, José María Mata and John W. Foster met to "discuss the former's mission to Washington, and the latter's activities in Mexico." During this intimate meeting, Mata "disclosed that he had suggested to Under Secretary [William] Seward that Mexico should accede to a reciprocal military interchange accord." He also agreed with the U.S. interpretation of Article 29 of the Mexican Constitution, which Foster believed upheld U.S. claims that forced loans (funds that the Mexican government compelled Americans and other foreigners to contribute to the Mexican treasury) were unconstitutional (Cosío Villegas 1956: 196).

There are other instances in which Mexican diplomats have agreed wholeheartedly with their U.S. counterparts. Three days after the Mexican government's expropriation of the petroleum industry in March 1938, Ambassador Francisco Castillo Najera informed U.S. Under Secretary of State Sumner Welles that, in his opinion, "the expropriation should be rescinded, in favor of a general modification of Cárdenas's policies" (L. Meyer 1972: 381).

Alexander Haig, secretary of state under President Reagan, described another such incident. In 1981 he found himself seated next to Ambassador Hugo Margáin of Mexico during the annual Alfalfa Club dinner. The Mexican ambassador queried whether Washington might be interested in opening a discreet line of communication with the rebels in El Salvador. Haig recalls: "I exploded: 'no longer,' I said, 'would Washington deal secretly with insurgents who were attempting to overthrow legal governments in the Western Hemisphere.'" Haig states that the Mexican ambassador displayed enormous relief, and "gripped my hand warmly. 'For years' he said fervently, 'I have been waiting for an American to speak words such as these. Tonight I will go home and sleep well!'" (Haig 1984: 99).

There seems to be a pattern here that merits closer examination. These incidents may represent no more than a diplomatic stratagem, or they may reflect a genuine willingness on the part of many Mexicans to collaborate with the United States, whether out of conviction or self-interest. A stunning example occurred during the United States' invasion of Mexico in 1846–1848, when General Winfield Scott had under his command a "company of 2,000 Mexican spies, who served so faithfully throughout the war that many received a reward of 20 dollars and a trip to Texas" (Phillip Smith 1971: 23).

The motives that guided the many Mexicans who have established close ties with the United States—people like Carrillo Flores, Miguel Alemán, and Carlos Salinas de Gortari—are hard to gauge. The only sensible procedure is to document each instance in order to understand the dynamics that govern the clashes between nationalism and Mexico's relationship with the United States. In the case of Ambassador Carrillo Flores, documents indicate that he adopted ideas put forward by a U.S. official as his own and used them to influence official Mexican policy. This was not necessarily an act of disloyalty or treason; rather, it may be an example of hegemonic domination.

12

Reappraising Mexico's Political System

During the 1960s, newly developed methodological tools enabled scholars to embark on a detailed analysis of the Mexican political system, and this, in turn, produced a heightened and increasingly sophisticated awareness of Mexican affairs. Although the PRI was still generally considered to be the country's best political option, suggestions for reform were beginning to circulate and individuals in Mexico who had suffered under the regime were advised to be patient—change would come.

This outlook rested on the underlying assumption, shared by the U.S. elite, that a peaceful and gradual reform of the political system was by far the best alternative, both for Mexico and for the United States. This view prevailed despite the elite's awareness of the Mexican regime's frequent spells of brutality, and its inherent contradictions found expression in a classic analysis of the Mexican political system. Frank Brandenburg dedicated his work to the "revolutionary family," which, he asserted, "transformed Mexico into a glowing example for the Latin American nations," but he also criticized the "family's authoritarian attitudes and failures" (1964: xii). This and similar judgments have significantly influenced the academic literature on Mexican affairs and contributed to the glacial pace of political transition in Mexico.

REASSESSING MEXICO

In general terms, the United States' assessment of political events in Mexico in the 1960s was positive. Except for 1968, the variables measuring Mexico's political behavior as reported in the *Times* ("general political overview," "orientation of the federal government," and "democratization") received more positive than negative references during this decade (figures 16–17, 36–37).

As noted earlier, Cuba provided a critical point of comparison in the U.S. elite's appreciation for Mexico's stability, to the extent that they were willing to overlook the means that were often employed to preserve it. In the early years of the Cuban Revolution, Washington feared that Mexico might become the next target of international Communism (Reston 1962). When it became clear that the Cuban revolutionaries would not intervene to encourage opposition groups in Mexico, the U.S. government began to advance the Mexican system as the model to emulate (Womack 1969).

Brandenburg acknowledged that "in order to gain any influence upon the popular movements [in Latin America], we must present viable alternatives to Marxism-Leninism—and the example set by the United States has proved not to be applicable." Brandenburg believed that Mexico embodied "what we need to know in order to inject new life into our global policies" (1964: 2). The State Department agreed, stating that the Mexican Revolution was an "example of the great revolutionary transformation in Latin America" free from Communist solutions (DOS 1961d: 7). To summarize, "thanks to Cuba," the United States now understood the advantages of a "stable, demo-cratic and prosperous Mexico, closely linked to the United States in economic terms, friendly and yet entirely sovereign" (NYT 1963d, 1960d; Dec. 5, 1965).

Although the U.S. elite had denounced the Mexican Revolution throughout the 1920s, during the 1960s they praised it, even suggest-ing that Mexico could take pride in the fact that it had eradicated any "leanings toward Communism." In a fairly macabre metaphor—considering the bloodshed of the Revolution—Mexico was compared to a "fortunate person, who has suffered a disease and subsequently acquired immunity" (NYT 1963d). One result was that stability and the PRI were defined as one, and the official party was legitimized because it incorporated the full gamut of Mexican political tendencies (Vernon 1963: 189; Brandenburg 1964: 3, 341).

The notion that only the PRI shielded Mexico from total catastro-phe became consolidated. In 1962, the U.S. ambassador to Mexico suggested that "the destruction of the PRI will bring chaos" (DOS 1962a). Raymond Vernon agreed with many "intelligent and discreet Mexicans, who feared the possibility of a break with the PRI's hegem-ony [and who suspected that] a multi-party system could result in a bloody spectacle of force and repression" (1963: 192). This myth has been crucial for the development of Mexican politics, because if we accept that there can be no substitute for the PRI, then any alternation in power is extremely risky. The resulting outcome for the domestic political situation has been to invest the Mexican government with extensive powers, exacerbating its authoritarian tendencies and curtailing viable arenas for the opposition forces that began to take shape during the 1960s.

MEXICAN PRESIDENTS OF THE 1960s

An intense and unique relationship exists between Mexico's presidents and the U.S. elite. The elite concentrate their attention on the Mexican presidents because they are the most important players in the political system. Mexico's presidents, for their part, focus on the U.S. elite in hopes of identifying their hopes, fears, and weaknesses, and they exploit this knowledge for an extremely interesting form of blackmail. Although this peculiar interaction reached its apex during the presidency of Carlos Salinas de Gortari, many of its essential features were already apparent during the 1960s.

Adolfo López Mateos is perhaps the Mexican president who best exemplifies the intricacies of the Mexico–United States relationship. Although he voiced support for the extreme Left and defended Cuba and its international activism, he was the least criticized of the Mexican presidents in power between 1946 and 1986.[1] Only 2 of the 246 *Times* references to López Mateos were negative (figures 19–27). According to Paul Kennedy, despite López Mateos's radical declarations, Washington considered him to be "more conservative than left-wing" (NYT, Sept. 5, 1963). The U.S. elite believed that Mexico's radicalism was merely an exercise in rhetoric, basing their belief on private guarantees given by the presidents themselves (NYT, Jan. 10, 1962).[2]

Gustavo Díaz Ordaz also received very little criticism in the U.S. media, and his ideological orientation was rarely questioned (figure 19). According to the *Times*, foreign investors were awash in a "sea of euphoria" when they learned of Díaz Ordaz's nomination as the PRI's presidential candidate (NYT, Jan. 22, 1965). Under Díaz Ordaz, Mexico was expected to "inch a little further right of center" (NYT 1963e). The CIA offices in Mexico concurred with this assessment: "the financial and business community reacted favorably" to Díaz Ordaz's candidacy, because they hoped that his government would be "more conservative than that of his predecessor" (CIA 1964: 4). Enthusiasm intensified as the new president—who formerly, as head of the Ministry of Government, had dealt "harshly with pro-Communist demonstrations"—appointed a cabinet with a "pro-Western, and in particular pro-American" orientation (NYT, Oct. 10, Dec. 2, 1963).

---

[1] Alemán was the most highly praised.

[2] This view was shared by the Department of State. An official document noted that "López Mateos has adopted a middle-of-the-road position" (DOS 1962a).

The coverage that Lázaro Cárdenas received in the 1960s confirms the raising of U.S. consciousness. Although Cárdenas was still vilified in some circles, there was a growing number of positive assessments of his presidency, in clear contrast with reports in earlier decades (figure 19). In 1962, a *Times* editorial affirmed that, despite "widespread belief in the United States, Cárdenas was never anti-American, and certainly never was, or is, a Communist. His place in history is that of a patriotic Mexican, a defender of his people" (NYT 1961e).

This generalized approbation of Mexico's presidents required disassociating them from the darker aspects of the country's political system. For example, Vernon suggested that the president was constrained by a "political strait-jacket: against growing obstacles, he seeks to gain the loyalty of each power source in the country" (1963: 189). As long as the president could be seen as engineering political equilibrium in Mexico, the American elite could mentally separate him from the system. It seems very probable that some of Mexico's presidents spied new possibilities in these mental sleights of hand and made use of them, portraying themselves as warriors trying to reform a corrupt system. Simply by proclaiming democratic ideals, they could earn the goodwill of the United States—and broaden their maneuvering space for authoritarian action.

A NEW REALISM

Although the U.S. elite supported authoritarianism and embraced unsubstantiated assumptions such as the supposition that Mexico's presidents were democratically inclined, they were also open to more detailed and realistic analyses of the Mexican situation, so that eventually the antiquated and discredited notion of Mexico as a democracy was abandoned. For example, Brandenburg provided a clear and perceptive description of the mechanisms that governed the Mexican political system. His ideas would ultimately form part of a collective consciousness: Mexico was "ruled by an elite" centered around the executive, a "political sun" that rose and set in six-year cycles (Brandenburg 1964: 3, 141; see also Womack 1969).

The CIA's level of awareness was on the rise as well. In 1964, this agency suggested that Mexico had a "paternalistic . . . one party regime" that defied "conventional definition." And although the Mexican government was "speaking and spending vast sums in the development of the socialist principles of the Revolution," it was "in essence pragmatic" (CIA 1964: 152), maintaining only the "facade of adherence to the principle of multi-party, representative government" (CIA 1967a: 1).

The *Times* was also making efforts to come to terms with this unorthodox system. One columnist noted that Mexico was politically "fairly distant from our notion of democracy" (Sulzberger 1962). Mexico's 1964 elections were described as a "pretense of a Western Democracy," because the deciding factor was the candidate's "selection" by the president (NYT, Dec. 2, 1964). Unknowingly, academics, government officials, and journalists were laying the intellectual foundations that would, a few years hence, support a definitive break with the image of Mexico's political system that had prevailed in the 1940s and 1950s.

Not all components of this image were cast aside, however. Certain elements (such as the United States' endorsement of Mexico's rejection of Communism) were retained (NYT, Dec. 14, 1962). Even so, how the U.S. elite viewed the Mexican Left changed dramatically. During the 1950s, Mexican leftists were labeled "Reds"; by the 1960s they were "left-wingers." The *Times*'s attention shifted from traditional left-wing parties to independent leftist movements, such as the Independent Peasant Central (CCI) or the National Liberation Movement (figure 33).

This moderation of views resulted from an acknowledgment that the Mexican Left did not pose even the faintest threat to the established system. The U.S. Embassy in Mexico noted that the "extreme left is extremely divided, and incapable of competing effectively against the PRI's organization, might, and ideology." Moreover, this situation was deemed unlikely to change in the "near future" (DOS 1965b: 2). The CIA added that Mexican labor leader Vicente Lombardo Toledano had an agreement with the government, which "partially subsidized" him to "gather information on Communist activities, creating divisions among Communist groups" (CIA 1964: 153). Curiously, in other documents the CIA persevered in viewing Toledano as a "long-standing collaborator" with Communist organizations (CIA 1967b: 2). Both views were probably true. Many in Mexico in the 1960s harbored leftist views along with an allegiance to the revolutionary family.

SOCIAL REBELLION, STATE COERCION, INDIFFERENCE TO VIOLENCE

For the U.S. elite, the greatest concerns regarding Mexico during the 1960s were the pervasive poverty in rural areas, possible divisions within the "revolutionary family," and middle-class revolts, including the physicians' and students' movements. Reflecting the elite's priorities, both the number and prominence of articles on Mexico's rural population increased. Concern was growing because Mexico was a largely rural nation and Americans considered that the "country's peace and well-being are still largely based on conditions in the rural areas" (NYT, Jan. 17, 1964).[3]

The Independent Peasant Central, founded in 1963, was immediately described in the *Times* as "politically left-wing, and fundamentally opposed to the United States and the Mexican government" (NYT, Jan. 8, 1963). The *Times* never covered the origins or objectives of the new Central, and most references to it were negative. The CCI was frequently criticized for its links to former president Lázaro Cárdenas. Although, as noted above, U.S. opinion on Cárdenas had softened, Americans still worried that Cárdenas might head up some "anti-Yankee" organization, with "economic and political ideals of a radical nature, that would conflict with American policies and ideals" (NYT 1961d). Cárdenas was considered a potential risk precisely because he had "a broad following among the peasant and Indian populations," whom he could have used to "steer his political actions along extremely problematic channels" (NYT, June 11, 1961). Exacerbating this worry was the fact that Cárdenas was strongly sympathetic toward the Cuban Revolution.

One important aspect of the bilateral relationship has always been the U.S. elite's position on and reactions to the use of force. A pattern was set during the 1960s in which the media and academic communities in the United States completely ignored signs of serious popular discontent in Mexico and the Mexican government's brutal suppression of dissidents.[4] It was not uncommon for violations of human rights to be covered by the Mexico City press yet totally ignored by the U.S. media. For example, it appears that neither the *Times* nor any U.S. academic publication made reference to the slaughter of thirteen peasants in Chilpancingo, Guerrero, on December 30, 1960, despite the fact that this event made the front page of every Mexican newspaper (see *Excélsior*, *El Nacional*, and *El Universal* editions for December 31, 1960).

In another example of differential coverage, in 1961, in gubernatorial elections in San Luis Potosí, the PRI falsified the vote count to steal the election from popular civic leader Salvador Nava. Dr. Nava's supporters rallied to protest the fraud on September 15, 1961, but the demonstrators were soon violently dispersed by the army. Reports of these events in the Mexican press were aimed generally at discrediting the Navista movement. For example, an editorial in *El Universal* accused Nava of assuming "histrionic attitudes at odds with the decorum demanded of anyone in public life," and having "no other aim but to occupy, by any means possible, the chair of command." Nava's

---

[3] The terms used by the *Times* correspondent were almost identical to those used by the CIA. See Kennedy 1963.

[4] This confirms an important caveat regarding methodology: content analysis must be complemented with unpublished information.

behavior, continued this Mexican daily, "contrasts sharply with the ever-rich and ever-enriching program of a revolution in progress, implemented through legal institutions" (El Universal 1968). What is important here is not the bias of the coverage but the fact that these events were reported on the front pages of most Mexican newspapers; they were completely disregarded by the *Times* correspondent in Mexico.

In May 1962, the assassination of peasant leader Rubén Jaramillo and his family was covered by the Mexico City press, though only on inside pages. It received no mention at all in the *Times*, even though this same paper had published an article on Jaramillo during the 1950s (NYT, Mar. 13, 1954).[5] Then in 1967 more peasants were slaughtered in Guerrero. On May 17 of that year, *Excélsior* published a brief note, on an inside page, stating that "nine people were killed and more than twenty wounded during a skirmish between police and householders in Atoyac de Álvarez, on the Costa Grande." This assault sparked an armed movement in Guerrero, which—together with guerrilla movements in several other states—constitutes one dimension of Mexico's political evolution over the last thirty years.[6]

The physicians' movement of 1964–1965 is another case that received no attention in the United States but garnered extensive media coverage in Mexico, most of which was directed at discrediting it.

The National Action Party (PAN), meanwhile, continued to participate in elections. On June 2, 1968, the PAN won the mayoral and state congressional elections in Baja California, but the seated state congress overturned the results in an electoral fraud documented in the national media but ignored by the *Times* (Sauer 1974: 131–33).

The swelling wave of dissent in Mexico encompassed diverse populations and regions. Its adherents ranged from radical peasants in impoverished rural communities to conservative urban professionals. Their protests were either ignored or de-emphasized by the U.S. elite, although there was little doubt that the regime in Mexico was poised to stifle all forms of opposition through a combination of coercion and persuasion. This indifference was not uncalculated; Washington was well aware of the methods employed by the Mexican ruling classes. One CIA document explored the entrenched government's capacity to "suppress" threats to its stability (CIA 1965b: 0–1). Another report wryly noted that Mexico's security agencies carried out "missions" when "so ordered . . . without overmuch regard for legalities" (CIA 1966b: 2).

---

[5] It was extremely negative and poorly researched, far and away the worst piece of coverage on Mexico to appear in the *Times* over the period considered in this study.
[6] The history of Mexican guerrilla movements is explored in Montemayor 1991; Hirales 1982; Hodges 1995; Tello 1995.

During the 1960s, each negative reference in the *Times* to acts of repression carried out by the Mexican government was offset by three informative references (figures 40, 43). Yet as the decade wore on, there was a growing trend toward objective coverage of the abuses committed by the Mexican government. Washington's decision to turn a blind eye to certain practices in the Mexican political system probably expanded the maneuvering space for the Mexican government to act repressively,[7] using violence against its detractors and opponents while simultaneously denying them a platform from which to object. This lack of interest was not limited to the United States; Mexico was also ignored by Third World and socialist nations, which for one reason or another decided to neither criticize the Mexican government nor support its opponents. It seems likely that the stance these nations adopted significantly slowed the growth and consolidation of a viable opposition, contributing to the exasperatingly slow pace of political transition in Mexico.

THE STUDENT MOVEMENT OF 1968

The 1968 student movement was a watershed in Mexican history, marking the starting point of a long-awaited transition. The U.S. elite's reaction combined an improved understanding of Mexican reality with solid support for the established regime and an obsession for peaceable and controlled change. It has been suggested that the uprisings in 1968 surprised most analysts of Mexican political affairs. This is only partly true; the CIA had already sounded an alarm in 1967 when it pointed out that the success of Mexico's educational system had allowed the middle classes to achieve a "level of sophistication that can bring them into conflict with the Mexican system of paternalistic government" (CIA 1967a: 1).

Many Americans were clearly able to take the student movement in stride, a remarkable improvement over their response to the railroad workers' movement in 1958. Two-thirds of all *Times* references to the 1958 movement were negative; in 1968 only one-fourth of all references were critical of the Mexican students. The government was criticized only twice for its repressive tactics in 1958 but 16 times in 1968 (figure 43). The *Times*'s outlook regarding the opposition had also changed. The paper quoted 9 opposition members by name in 1958; this number rose to 20 in 1968. There were no quotes from unnamed members of the opposition published during 1958; in 1968, 20 anonymous sources were quoted on the student movement. Evidently the regime's detractors and opponents were finally gaining a voice.

---

[7]This supposition is based on subsequent events and comparisons with other nations.

One preeminent journalist of this new era of greater openness was the *Times*'s Henry Giniger. Despite his own disapproval of university-based radicalism, he provided excellent coverage of the 1968 student movement. His discerning analyses contrasted sharply with the reports filed by other international news agencies or the Mexican press,[8] and they earned him a National Press Club award. Giniger pointed out the Mexican government's tendency to portray "student violence as part of a subversive plot, abetted by foreign and Communist agitators" (NYT, Aug. 4, 1968). He believed that problems arose because "the police had overstepped the mark," a detail that received incomplete and biased coverage in the Mexican press. He emphasized the modest scope of the students' demands: to defend constitutional reforms, root out corruption, and encourage the development of democracy (NYT, Sept. 9, 1968). Some years later, he commented that although the Mexican students "sometimes exaggerated or made unfounded accusations," he considered that theirs had been "a liberal movement, whose aim was to open up the system" (author interview, 1983). Giniger's efforts to understand this movement led him to conclude that the reforms the students advocated were necessary in order to put Mexico on the path toward democracy, and that such an outcome would benefit both Mexico and the United States.[9]

Then on October 2, 1968, came the event that would forever symbolize the Mexican government's repression of dissidents: the brutal massacre at Tlatelolco. The official version of that day's events influenced an editorial appearing in the daily *Novedades*:

> Upon arriving in the square, the army was met with gunfire from snipers shooting from nearly buildings. . . . The aggressive insurgents, whose lack of patriotism was clearly evident, especially in light of Mexico's imminent international obligations [Mexico was about to host the 1968 Olympic Games], launched a premeditated attack on the army, whose toll was an as-yet-unknown number of dead soldiers, plus the wounds sustained by General José Hernández Toledo (*Novedades* 1968).

All of the blame for this horrendous event was laid on the students.

The story by Paul Montgomery, who was standing in for Giniger while the latter covered a coup in Panama, differed radically from the *Novedades* version. According to Montgomery, "Federal troops opened fire against the students . . . killing at least 20, and wounding

---

[8]See NYT, Aug. 1, 1968. An excellent journalistic anthology on the role played by the Mexican media is Cano 1993.

[9]We should bear in mind that Giniger was able to publish his views thanks to the support of his publishers in New York, reflecting the growing predominance of liberal ideologies throughout the 1960s.

over 100" (NYT, Oct. 3, 1968). He later provided a detailed description of events, and this account was substantiated by a number of other *Times* correspondents (NYT, Oct. 5, 1968; see also NYT, Oct. 13, 1968).

Curiously, the *Times* also published articles that adhered to press releases from the Mexican government. Openly contradicting Montgomery, Sidney Thomas Wise suggested that the students were controlled by a "group of left-wing agitators and would-be politicians [whose strategy] seems more concerned with ridiculing the government and creating chaos, than with finding a solution for student problems." Practically all their demands, Wise added, were "negative and destructive" (NYT, Jan. 9, 1969).

THE BILATERAL UNDERSTANDING'S CONTINUED RELEVANCE

The 1968 student movement demonstrated that the implicit pact of mutual support between Mexican and U.S. elites remained in force. When Mexicans close to the regime suggested that the student mobilization was the result of an international conspiracy fostered in part by the FBI and the CIA,[10] Washington maintained a discreet silence which, in political terms, constituted no less than full support for the Mexican regime.[11] The U.S. Embassy in Mexico, meanwhile, accepted the official version of events and criticized Giniger's coverage (author interview with Giniger, 1983).

Not everyone in the U.S. government thought the same way. A State Department study group on student unrest, created to look at student uprisings around the world, eventually accepted the Mexican government's assertion that the Tlatelolco massacre was the result of a "bloody confrontation" (DOS 1969a: 1–2). However, the study group disagreed with the Mexican government's theory regarding the involvement of foreign elements. The State Department believed that "even with the aid of foreigners [the Mexican students] would never have maintained their strike for such a long period of time, unless their dissatisfaction were extremely extended and widespread." It was also noted that the Communists' role within the student movement was mentioned "far more frequently than it is confirmed." The students, this document concluded, could simply have been "the

---

[10]Such claims appeared in Veraza 1968 and informed Alberto Beltrán's popular cartoon for *El Día*, Aug. 25, 1968. See Cano 1993 and also the coverage in *Excélsior* and *El Día*, Aug. 10, 1968.

[11]Washington's response is reminiscent of its reaction to the accusations of treason levied by the followers of Miguel Alemán against Ezequiel Padilla following his interview with the *Times*.

detonator of events that would have taken place anyway" (DOS 1969a, 1969b: 8).

Despite such differences of opinion, the U.S. elite (government, media, and intellectuals) persevered in their support for Mexico's ruling party, but they also began to suggest gradual and peaceful reforms, to be implemented from the top down (a position they hold to this day). According to the State Department study group's final report, "despite the PRI's profound dishonesty, the students had to be convinced that the party still is, or can again become, a vital force for political and social change, as well as economic development"(DOS 1969a). It is very revealing that it was the victims of authoritarianism who were charged with developing a more sensible and mature outlook in the future, a view that also still prevails.

The *Times* followed a similar editorial line: "if the [PRI] aims to maintain its position as the instrument of a permanent revolution, it must open spaces for the younger generations [and prove its] concern for social inequalities and corruption in Mexican life." The *Times* stated that "repression cannot [lead to] the revolutionary renovation that [the PRI] claims to represent" (NYT 1968).[12] The *Times* was, in effect, politely suggesting that the regime embark upon a peaceful, gradual, and voluntary reform process.

In summary, although the U.S. elite now had an improved grasp on Mexican reality, the majority of them simply adapted their consciousness to the point where they could countenance the support being provided to this repressive, corrupt, and antidemocratic government because, they argued, it was still capable of maintaining a much-valued stability and it was friendly toward the United States. Their stance seemed justified in light of Mexico's continued economic growth and the regime's apparent impregnability. The Americans continued to hope that the system would reform itself, gradually. Although we cannot divine what might have ensued if perceptions had been different, we can suggest that the elite's expectations may explain the wide latitude given to President Luis Echeverría (1970–1976) when he embarked upon a reform of the Mexican political system with all the grace and delicacy of a hurricane.

---

[12]Two years later, the *Times*'s interpretation remained the same. See NYT 1970b.

13

Journalists, Academics, and Graduate Students

GROWING INTEREST, CHANGING ATTITUDES

After the benchmark year of 1968, the U.S. government, media, and academic communities demonstrated growing interest in Mexico. A parallel increase in articles on Mexican affairs published by the *Times* demonstrated that, indeed, Mexico was now a higher priority. Over the forty-ones years covered in the content analysis, the *Times* published 441 articles measuring between 60 and 121 cm. in length. Of these, 344 (78 percent) appeared between 1970 and 1986. A third of all front-page articles appeared between 1980 and 1986. A similar pattern can be detected in correspondents' dispatches, editorials, op-ed pieces, and letters to the editor. Four hundred and fifty-six of the 1,328 articles by the *Times* Mexico correspondents appeared between 1980 and 1986 (figures 6–7). Not only did articles on Mexico become more numerous; they also became longer. Of the 158 stories on Mexico published after 1946 that ran to a half-page or more, 118 (75 percent) were published after 1970.

U.S. law prohibits the release of certain recent official memorandums or reports. However, one document that is publicly available attests unequivocally to Mexico's growing importance for Washington. In 1978, President Jimmy Carter ordered the first-ever presidential review memorandum (PRM) to evaluate the relationship between Mexico and the United States: Presidential Review Memorandum 41.

In the academic literature, approximately 80 percent of ninety-three texts on Mexican affairs published in the United States after World War II were published after 1970[1] and were written for a gen-

---

[1]Based on an excellent literature review conducted by Roderic Camp (1990a).

eration deeply influenced by the spirit of the 1960s and 1970s.[2] The
authors of these works were not alone in their interest in Mexico.
Over a thousand doctoral theses on Mexican affairs were submitted to
U.S. universities between 1975 and 1984. The *National Directory of
Latin Americanists* published by the Library of Congress in 1985 lists
4,915 researchers, 1,400 of whom specialize in Mexico; 518 of the 2,600
members of the Latin American Studies Association (LASA) identify
themselves as "Mexico specialists"; and there are 227 members of the
Committee on Mexican Studies within the Conference on Latin
American History (Coatsworth 1987: 17–18).

Discussion of Mexican affairs also surged in U.S. military magazines. Although there was no large numerical increase (of 35 articles
published between 1949 and 1988, 15 appeared between 1949 and
1969, and 20 between 1970 and 1988), there was a significant shift in
subject matter—as attention turned toward the problems of contemporary Mexico—and in the treatment of certain subjects that had been
issues of contention in the past, such as the Mexican War. The United
States had consistently blamed Mexico for the war, but by the 1960s
there was also a realization that it may well have been "one of the
most unjust wars waged by a stronger against a weaker nation"
(Taylor 1982: 67). In contrast to the 1950s and 1960s articles in military
magazines that touted the merits of Guadalajara and Chapala as retirement spots for military veterans, Fred Reed suggested in a 1979
article in the *Air Force Times* that Guadalajara was not an earthly
paradise after all and, further, that Americans were not necessarily an
exceptional people. In Guadalajara, he pointed out, officers could re-
tire comfortably on ample pensions that allowed them to live with
"distinctiveness, charm, elegance and servants." The pensions of
those who had served only as enlisted men, however, would restrict
them to the city's poor *barrios*.

In describing Guadalajara's community of approximately 7,000
American retirees, Reed noted that a portion pursued at least some
form of productive activity, but others were dedicated to drink.
"Night after night, in place after place," Reed recounts, "we ran into
boisterous drunks, maudlin drunks, tearful drunks." The community
was separated into "widows" and "soon-to-be-widows," for this was
a "geriatric community, and the old die." Reed criticized the Americans' "remarkable ability for living in a country without really being
in it, for spending three years in Germany without learning German.
And now, in retirement, for *being* in Mexico, without really *living* in
Mexico." Relationships with the Mexican community were not poor;
they were nonexistent. "The Mexicans seem to tolerate the Americans

---

[2]This was a common thread that emerged in the author's interviews with John Bailey,
Wayne Cornelius, and David Ronfeldt.

as being more silly than obnoxious." The American women obses-
sively recited mantras such as *"keep your hand on your wallet, your legs
crossed, and for God's sake don't-drink-the-water."* Their fear of preying
and malevolent Mexicans, Reed reported, bordered on paranoia
(Reed 1979: 4–10).

Like the "lost generation" of early-twentieth-century writers—
John Dos Pasos, Lincoln Stephens, and John Reed—Fred Reed used
Mexico as a pretext for his critical reflection on American culture.
What is extraordinary is that a publication produced by and for the
military would print such a severe self-analysis. But in the 1970s, every-
thing was suspect and anything was possible.

JOURNALISTS

During this period, the people responsible for producing and dis-
seminating ideas in the United States stopped blindly accepting official declarations as fact and recovered their role of watchdog over
government actions. This spirit touched journalists as well. Howard
Bray suggested that "social mobilizations and protest politics" resulted in a "new and revolutionary attitude towards government and
authority in general" (1980: 112). David Halberstam pointed out that
"a generation [of journalists] who covered Vietnam would never
again place much confidence in their government" (1980: 567), in a
twist that clearly altered Washington's relationship with the media. In
February 1976, George Bush, then director of the CIA, issued a directive to limit the occasions on which the intelligence agency would
collaborate with the press (Loch Johnson 1989: 5).

The new government-media relationship was not overtly antago-
nistic. The media were still willing to defend the United States' national security and other interests, but the government now had to
prove that national security was at risk and the media had to agree
with this evaluation. Such was the case in 1977, a year after the "Bush
directive," when the CIA managed to convince a number of newspapers to postpone reporting on the recovery of a Soviet submarine lost
in the Pacific (Bray 1980: 148ff). To this day the press remains willing
to collaborate with the government, as long as there is consensus that
a genuine threat to national security exists or that there is a need to
protect U.S. interests (Armstrong 1983: 23). In most instances, however, government and the press each goes its own way, fulfilling the
functions each is assigned in the social contract.

Over the course of the 1970s, U.S. society shifted toward the center
of the ideological spectrum. An increasingly educated and critical
readership was forcing many newspapers to revise their often con-
spicuously conservative bent. The owner of the *Los Angeles Times*

grudgingly conceded that "newspapers can only survive by adapting to their new readership," and this adjustment called for a new generation of knowledgeable, discerning journalists, willing to formulate "relevant questions" and able to "interpret and analyze, and not merely to 'report.'" These requisites were reflected in a professional code that demands objectivity, condemns ideological bias, and prohibits the deliberate defense of vested interests.[3] Analysts of the U.S. media agree that these transformations had their strongest impact on newspapers' international coverage (Gottlieb and Wolf 1977: 530, 438, 454–55, respectively).

ACADEMICS

Both the quantity and quality of research on Mexican affairs rose significantly beginning in the 1970s, building on a foundation laid down by a group of young U.S. scholars who conducted their dissertation research in Mexico during the 1960s. William D'Antonio and William Form studied the National Action Party and its supporters in Ciudad Juárez; Lawrence Graham analyzed political conditions in Guanajuato; Richard Fagen and William Tuohy conducted similar studies in Jalapa, Veracruz; and David Ronfeldt produced a sophisticated interpretation of authoritarian control mechanisms in Mexico's rural milieu. In addition, established scholar Karl Schmitt researched the Mexican Communist Party (D'Antonio and Form 1965; Graham 1968; Fagen and Tuohy 1972; Ronfeldt 1973; Schmitt 1965).

The range of research topics has continued to expand to include the burgeoning technocracy, the role of the business sector, the relationship between politics and the economy, the opposition, the bureaucracy, peasants, the armed forces, student politics, labor unions, urban movements, nongovernmental organizations; the list goes on.[4] Other topics were largely ignored, however, and many students of Mexico eventually abandoned the field. Nonetheless, the foundation laid down in the 1960s held firm for a new generation of Mexico specialists.

Of course, not all the new research was creditable. For example, James Dalessandro erroneously affirmed that the 1968 student movement sought to "overthrow or destroy the government" (1977–

---

[3]Of course, ideological preferences or defense of the media's own interests did not disappear. But when they influenced journalists' reporting, it was with much greater subtlety.

[4]On these topics, see Grindle 1977a; Camp 1980, 1982; Derossi 1971; Shafer 1973; Maxfield and Anzaldúa 1987; Bennett and Sharpe 1985; Stevens 1974; Bailey 1988; Peter Smith 1979; Steven Sanderson 1981; Ronfeldt 1973, 1984; Tuohy and Ames 1970; Mabry 1982; Roxborough 1986; Thorup and Ayres 1982.

78: 52–53). Rex Applegate offered another extraordinarily short-sighted analysis when he suggested that in 1985 Mexico "fulfilled most of the necessary conditions and elements for a Communist-inspired power take-over" because the Mexican economy was "virtually socialized" (1985: 85). This may be the kind of research that prompted Sol Sanders to suggest that in the United States the field of Latin American studies had become a refuge for "third-rate academics" (1987: 52).

In any case, the new generation of Mexico scholars generally brought with them a fresh and more open attitude. One important result was the gradual disappearance of unflattering, even insulting, comparisons of Mexico with the United States. These began to fade after Brandenburg noted the "insuperable differences" between the two nations and recommended that Mexico be analyzed as it was; any other approach would result in a "victory for irrationality, for partial truths and falsehoods" (1964: 142). Oscar Lewis also noted that when writing *The Children of Sanchez*, he had no desire to view Mexico through "the mental fabric of the American middle classes" (1963: xi). Those comparisons that remained, which were invariably flattering to the United States, were much toned down from portraits sketched out in earlier decades.

The Mexicanists' methodology also changed. Previous generations had relied largely on secondary sources. They rarely ventured outside of Mexico City, and they often seemed more interested in anecdotes than in rigorous analysis. But the 1968 student movement and the government's violent reaction to it forced observers of Mexican affairs to formulate new questions and pursue new research findings (author interview with Wayne Cornelius, February 1996).[5]

This new attitude also informed Evelyn Stevens's pioneering work on social protest in Mexico and the mechanisms the regime developed in order to control it beginning in 1965.[6] One of the myths shattered by Stevens's research was the idea that Mexicans will not open up to foreigners. Vincent Padgett, for example, held that "Mexican politicians are not easily cultivated. The Mexican politician must know the observer very well before silence is broken." Padgett suggested that "the large number of unknown aspects in Mexican politics" was a result of this fact (1966: viii). Padgett's observations date from 1965, the same year that Stevens began interviewing 203 "communicative" participants in social movements. According to Stevens, these individuals "seemed to be waiting for someone willing to share their experiences," and her status as a foreign academic proved to be of little

---

[5]This applied to both U.S. and Mexican researchers. Pablo González Casanova's influential *Democracy in Mexico*, for example, was published in its original Spanish-language version in 1965.

[6]The publication process delayed the appearance of her work until 1974.

or no importance (1974: 17). Susan Eckstein reported similar experiences when working with impoverished urban populations in Mexico (1977). Henry Giniger also found students involved in the 1968 movement to be cooperative and willing to talk.[7]

In brief, the Mexican population's traditional mistrust of foreigners was shown not to exist. Most Mexicans were (and are) more than willing to share their experiences. What had been missing were researchers and journalists able to formulate relevant questions and willing to listen to the answers.

In his *Mexican Democracy: A Critical View*, Kenneth Johnson states from the outset that his text is substantially based "on a type of literature which is not well represented in the annals of American academia, which is to say, clandestine protest literature" from both the Right and the Left.[8] Although his research is not universally applauded, Johnson made a number of important observations. One was that the Mexican government frequently went to great lengths to court U.S. scholars. Openly criticizing his teacher, Vincent Padgett, Johnson wrote that "much about Mexican politics goes unknown simply because scholars [prefer taking] the safe route of a 'sweetheart contract' with the PRI." "The Mexican political system," Johnson mused, "has a curious anomaly. It is that once the researcher is welcomed into the official family, he is not likely to be free to mingle openly with the unofficial congeries of 'out groups' that do not enjoy the PRI's favor" (1971: 3–4).

U.S. scholars on the Left also began to pay more attention to Mexico; one of the most prolific and rigorous was James Cockcroft (see, especially, 1983). Others convened to establish the North American Congress on Latin America (NACLA) in 1967. Although many organizations born during the 1960s disappeared once their founders' long hair thinned and rebellious spirits calmed, this group continues to produce its bimonthly periodical, *NACLA Report on the Americas*, which presents solid research from a leftist perspective. NACLA's thirty-year history traces the evolution of leftist ideas in the United States: the strident radicalism of the 1960s and 1970s (which led some of NACLA's founders to posit that "revolution was around the corner and so was repression") gradually gave way to increasingly reflective viewpoints, though NACLA members have not lost their critical edge.[9]

Mexico was not always a priority for NACLA members. They first focused on U.S. policies toward Latin America in general, and later on

---

[7]The results of the content analysis also demonstrate that the number of opposition members who spoke with *Times* correspondents increased between 1970 and 1986.

[8]Among other things, Johnson's groundbreaking research resulted in his deportation from Mexico a year after his book was published.

[9]For an overview of the first fifteen years of NACLA, see Shapiro 1981: 48.

Chile's Popular Unity government, the coup that ousted Allende, and the military regimes that soon took power in South America. During the 1980s, NACLA's attention turned to the conflicts in Central America. But despite the fact that Mexico received scant early attention from NACLA, this organization's few observations were remarkably original. For example, the *NACLA Report* published an interview with a Mexican guerrilla fighter and an analysis of American "colonies" in Mexico (NACLA 1972; Baird and McCaughan 1974).

Improved understanding of Mexico's political system, founded on refinements in political theory, was also apparent in mainstream research. In 1964, Spanish theorist Juan Linz shattered the dichotomy of democratic and totalitarian regimes by establishing a third category, authoritarian regimes. Susan Kaufman Purcell later drew on Linz's work to classify Mexico as an authoritarian regime, a usage that has become widespread (Purcell 1973).

Interestingly, the pace at which ideas changed differed from area to area within the field of Mexican studies in the United States. Although ideas about Mexico's economy were evolving rapidly, attitudes toward its political system proved more resistant to change. Regarding the former, Raymond Vernon offered some cautious suggestions for improving Mexico's economic model in the 1960s. In 1971, Roger Hansen upped the ante with an extremely critical analysis of Mexican development. During the 1980s, with the rise of neoliberal thinking, critiques of Mexico's economic structure became positively harsh, with Washington openly advocating a fundamental transformation in the country's development model. U.S. academics' stance regarding the Mexican political system, on the other hand, has been largely uncritical, tending toward excusing the regime's multiple flaws.

We should take note here of the gaps in knowledge about Mexico that signal the limits of possible or potential consciousness. Despite some exceptions, such as Roderic Camp's research on the relationship between businessmen and politicians in Mexico (Camp 1989; see also Maxfield and Anzaldúa 1987), U.S. perceptions of certain Mexican issues—the private sector, particular aspects of the political system, the state's use of coercion, and the negative impacts of U.S. policies—suffered from surprising and serious lacunas. The imperfect knowledge that resulted, and which was occasionally hard to understand, affected the work of Alan Riding, who wrote for the *Times* from Mexico between 1979 and 1983. The *Times* published 434 pieces by Riding, and these accounted for a third of all articles produced by eleven correspondents working in Mexico over the nearly five decades considered in the content analysis (figure 6). Soon after leaving Mexico, Riding published a well-researched and insightful best-seller on Mexican affairs (Riding 1985). While living in Mexico, Riding had enjoyed access to practically all levels of Mexican life. Nevertheless, his book mysteriously overlooks, or scarcely mentions, a number of important topics. Was this a conscious decision, or were these gaps in consciousness over which he had no control?

ACADEMICS AND SOCIETIES

One of the most interesting but least studied aspects of the bilateral relationship is the manner in which a dialogue has gradually been established between the two societies. This section describes the basic elements in this process, in which the U.S. and Mexican academic communities played a central role. This raises a difficult question: to what extent should outsiders take responsibility for understanding Mexico, and what is Mexico's own responsibility in this area?

Preceding discussions of the transformation of ideas included the suggestion that a number of events in Mexico received little attention from the United States largely because the Mexican government was able to redirect attention toward Mexico's independent stance in the foreign policy arena. Another contributing factor was Mexicans' apparent limited capacity to articulate an alternative vision or to present such a vision to other societies. This long-lived isolation has gradually given way to an increasing openness, nourishing a new relationship between the two societies. Neither inter-American relations nor the last thirty years of Mexico's history can be fully understood without getting a grasp on this little-understood social dialogue.[10]

As noted earlier, throughout the 1960s academics, missionaries, and Peace Corps volunteers played an active role in building social networks between the United States and the countries of Latin America. But Mexico, intent on isolating itself from external impacts, discouraged most missionary groups and refused entry to the Peace Corps. This meant that only the academic community was in a position to bridge the gap that had long existed between Mexico and the United States (and which had been exacerbated by Mexico's loss of territory to the United States during the first half of the nineteenth century). The ill will between the countries had also undermined Mexican interest in the United States as a focus of academic research.

After World War II, there was a resurgence of academic interest in the United States among pioneering Mexican academics such as Daniel Cosío Villegas, Josefina Vázquez, and José Luis Orozco, a trend that gathered momentum throughout the 1960s and 1970s. Consistent with Mexico's new international opening, international studies centers were created at Mexico's National Autonomous Uni-

---

[10]For recent studies of social networks, see Aguayo 1993a; Frederick 1993; Ronfeldt 1993; Thorup 1993.

versity (UNAM) and the Colegio de México, where Mario Ojeda, Olga Pellicer, and Lorenzo Meyer, among others, were advocating more research on the United States and U.S. affairs. This coincided with the American academic community's growing interest in Mexico.[11]

Dialogue increased slowly but steadily. One indicator of this was the practice of including both Mexican and U.S. authors in edited volumes, an apparent acknowledgment of the two groups' academic parity.[12] This initiative began in the United States in 1966 when Stanley Ross published *Is the Mexican Revolution Dead?*, which included contributions by Mexican authors. This project met with the Mexican government's approval, and in 1972 the Ministry of Education (SEP) published the book in Spanish translation, incorporating additional Mexican authors including, significantly, then president Luis Echeverría (Ross 1966, 1972).

Binational collaboration spread. In 1977 the first book coedited by a Mexican and an American appeared (Reyna and Weinert). By 1994, nineteen such coeditions had appeared. Other publications were written jointly by a Mexican and a U.S. academic, such as Daniel Levy and Gabriel Székely's *Mexico, Paradoxes of Stability and Change* (1983). Robert Pastor and Jorge Castañeda appeared as coauthors of *Limits to Friendship* (1988) (although most of its chapters were written by one or the other; only the preface and conclusion were written jointly).[13]

The increased level of communication between the two societies was reflected in the *Times* coverage of Mexican affairs and events. One aspect was the rising number of Mexican opposition members and U.S. officials willing to be interviewed (figures 10–11). In October 1986 the *Times* published a week-long series of highly critical articles on Mexico, prompting Mario Moya Palencia, Mexico's ambassador to the United Nations, to dub it a "week of infamy." The series quoted fifteen Americans by name: eight government officials, seven academics, and one businessman. The articles also quoted unnamed informants from the CIA, the army, the State Department, the U.S. Embassy in Mexico, the DEA, Customs, and the Census Bureau. Many Mexicans were quoted as well, all by name; they included eight gov-

---

[11]The Center for U.S.–Mexican Studies at the University of California, San Diego has played a fundamental role in the evolution of research and the establishment of a binational dialogue.

[12]For some of the Mexican authors, this also entailed some political risk; Mexican nationals with a research focus on the United States were viewed with suspicion until fairly recently and were often accused of being CIA informants.

[13]This new era of collaborative research presented new questions. Which author should appear first in texts where both contributed equally? In 1990, Sergio Aguayo and Bruce Bagley developed a simple formula that has become the standard: in the Spanish-language edition, the Mexican author appears first; in the English edition, the American researcher takes precedence.

ernment officials, five academics, five businessmen, and one communist leader. Although approximately as many Mexicans as Americans were quoted, the two groups differed in terms of their rank
within their respective national hierarchies, reflecting the power
asymmetry that exists between the two nations. The Mexicans quoted
in the series included Mexico's secretary of defense, attorney general,
minister of foreign affairs, high-ranking members of the PRI, presidential advisers, and the like. Porfirio Muñoz Ledo, then a member of
the Democratic Current of the PRI, Arnoldo Martínez Verdugo, from
the Mexican Left, members of the PAN, and a sprinkling of academics
also provided information for the series.

MEXICAN GRADUATE STUDENTS IN THE UNITED STATES

The heightened level of dialogue was facilitated by an increase in the
number of Mexican institutions and scholars interested in the United
States. President Echeverría nurtured this development, probably
without anticipating the wide-ranging consequences of the dynamic
he had unleashed. In the early 1970s, a U.S. studies program was
created at the Center for Economic Research and Teaching (CIDE) in
Mexico City. Similar programs were set up at the Colegio de México,
the UNAM, the Universidad de las Américas, and elsewhere in Mexico. Academic personnel to staff these programs were recruited from
among the thousands of Mexicans who had done graduate studies in
the United States with scholarship support from Mexico's National
Council for Science and Technology (CONACYT), created by Echeverría in 1970. These students not only increased dialogue between
the two academic communities; they also constituted the axis around
which a new elite would form that would eventually replace the old
political cadres.

About 66,950 Mexican students—some 5,500 per year—were en-
rolled at U.S. universities between 1975 and 1986 (Coatsworth 1987).[14]
Some of them would go on to change the profile of Mexico's ruling
elite in the 1980s. Both Carlos Salinas and Ernesto Zedillo, for example, studied economics as graduate students in the United States
during the 1970s. Upon their return to Mexico, they were able to implement their economic model for Mexico, rooted in a further revolution in economic thinking. Something that went unnoticed, however,
was that these sophisticated "technocrats" still retained the authoritarian disposition they had inherited from their populist predecessors.

---

[14]For the 1985–86 academic year, over half of the Mexican students were pursuing a
bachelor's degree; nearly a third were graduate students; and the rest were in English language programs.

14

Luis Echeverría: Hope, Then Crisis

Despite the glacial rate of transformation in Mexico's political system from 1968 onward, the country has undergone substantial changes, most of which fall into three categories:[1]

- The ruling group's capacity for maintaining its authoritarian relationships of domination has diminished. That is, the old blend of hegemony and coercion is no longer as effective as it once was. Evidence in support of this observation includes the dissolution of the main political police (the DFS) in 1985 and the exhaustion of the economic model inherited from the Mexican Revolution.

- Independent social forces have emerged or become consolidated and now operate across Mexico's entire sociopolitical spectrum. These include opposition parties, independent news media, social movements, and nongovernmental organizations.

- The importance of external factors—particularly the United States—for national affairs has increased. Although Washington's support for the established leadership continues unabated, new constraints on the Mexican state's use of coercion have hastened the regime's decline and the appearance and evolution of alternative forces.

For our examination of the importance of these variables and the interactions among them, rather than continue the analysis by dividing the study period into two main eras, from this point forward information will be organized chronologically by presidential administration, though the same subject areas will be examined: foreign

---

[1]These categories are adapted from Skocpol 1979.

policy, the economy, and politics. The thread that weaves the analysis together is also the same: U.S. perceptions of Mexico and the United States' importance for Mexico's way of life, and especially for its political system.

The first presidential administration that made a serious effort to correct the inherent flaws in Mexico's political regime—flaws that became painfully apparent in the government's response to the 1968 student movement—was that of Luis Echeverría Álvarez (1970–1976).[2] Echeverría displayed a tremendous zeal for reform, rarely hesitating to exploit the full force of presidential power to implement his ideas. Although some of the changes he introduced had important positive consequences, the balance on the whole was negative, and he ended his term in the midst of Mexico's first severe financial crisis of the modern era. The United States' support for the Mexican government did not waiver, however, establishing a pattern that would be repeated on numerous occasions in the future.

Once the United States detected weaknesses in the Mexican system in the late 1960s, the U.S. elite began cajoling the Mexican government into a gradual and peaceful process of reform, administered from the top. Successive Mexican presidents often turned this situation to their advantage by portraying themselves as "reformists," thereby establishing their pro-democratic credentials and winning an automatic entitlement to solid support from Washington. Echeverría was the first president to consciously—and successfully—exploit this self-image. In June 1971, *Times* correspondent Alan Riding stated that Echeverría had, in "a short time, from being an obscure bureaucrat . . . become the brightest political hope for Mexico in generations" because, despite all obstacles, he seemed willing to reform the Mexican system (NYT, June 20, 1971).[3]

A PRESIDENT OF HOPE

An expert on the U.S. intelligence community has suggested that the 1968 student movement and the emergence of guerrilla organizations in many parts of Mexico were deeply disturbing to the American

---

[2]Authors such as Whitehead (1980: 845) argue that Echeverría's whole strategy stems from the events of 1968.

[3]Of course, the same sentiments were repeated a quarter-century later regarding President Ernesto Zedillo. A *Times* editorial asserted that President Zedillo "has shown a greater commitment with political reform than any other recent Mexican leader" (NYT 1995). This suggests that with each new Mexican administration, the United States places great faith in the incoming president—and is ultimately proved wrong, over and over again. If democratic change consolidates following the July 1997 elections and if President Zedillo continues to support democratic change at crucial moments, the pattern will be broken.

elite. It was not so much the guerrillas' military or operational capabilities that caused concern as the fact that these groups had appeared in response to Mexico's increasingly harsh socioeconomic reality. If not addressed, the country's problems had the potential to spiral out of control, undermining stability and threatening the interests of the United States.

Both conservatives and liberals in the United States believed that Mexico needed to pursue a thorough-going reform process and recommended that the United States encourage the Mexican government to take steps in this direction—always with the caveat that such an undertaking would have to be conducted with great caution to avoid threatening system stability, still the United States' number one priority for Mexico. In Echeverría the Americans thought they had found their system reformer, although nothing in his past suggested a passion for democracy. In fact, he had been minister of government in 1968 and in this post had participated in the decision to violently suppress the student demonstrators.

Even so, the United States showered Echeverría with praise during his first three years in office. The *Times* published 40 positive references, and only 6 negative ones, to Echeverría between 1970 and 1973 (figures 24–25). This response came in reaction to Echeverría's surprising espousal of a strict reform program to revitalize the system created by the Mexican Revolution. The positive reaction also reflected a number of important parallels between Echeverría and the U.S. elite: although both were convinced that change was the key to the Mexican system's survival (NYT, Jan. 12, 1975), neither wanted anarchic change. To the contrary, both sought to modernize the existing system "from within" (NYT, June 29, 1971).

According to the *Times*, Echeverría stood for a "type of democracy . . . that accommodates the peculiarities of the system"—in other words, a gradual and peaceful process of reform, guided and controlled from the highest levels of power (NYT, Aug. 1, 1971). The Americans were satisfied because Echeverría, having concluded that it would be impossible to rule "a country of this dimension and complexity through authoritarian means" (NYT, June 23, 1974), appeared committed to maintaining stability without recourse to repression (*Financial Times*, Oct. 26, 1971; July 14, 1972). The United States welcomed the Mexican president's promises of democratization and applauded his calls for an open discussion of problems affecting Mexico and for constructive criticism of the government. The *Times* frequently reported on the fact that the Mexico City newspaper *Excélsior*, headed by Julio Scherer, encouraged its reporters to "denounce corruption and injustice" and gave its "columnists and editorial writers unlimited freedom to criticize" (NYT, June 23, 1974). This was groundbreaking in a nation where "for decades, dialogue between the government and the people" was "virtually non-existent" (NYT, Aug. 1, 1971). Alan Riding found even more to praise when Echeverría "showed his good faith" by releasing most of the political prisoners taken during the 1968 student uprising (*Financial Times*, Oct. 26, 1971; July 14, 1972).

The United States resuscitated its old tactic of disassociating a reform-minded president from Mexico's authoritarian political structure and applied it to Echeverría. In a representative article from 1971, Alan Riding suggested that the PRI had become "a monolithic and corrupt bureaucracy, largely unresponsive to the aspirations of the Mexican people." He simultaneously described Echeverría as a president "involved in a daring and difficult attempt to modernize his country" (NYT, Oct. 3, 1971). When progressives within the Catholic Church in Mexico published a document criticizing Echeverría's administration and its policies, Riding sided with the government and wrote that the Right was exploiting the "church controversy as a way of attacking [Echeverría's] progressive policies" (NYT, Oct. 31, 1971). The same pattern emerged in the *Times* coverage of events on June 10, 1971, when student marchers were violently attacked by a paramilitary group known as the Halcones. Riding argued that the attack had been orchestrated by the president's "conservative opponents," including Mexico City mayor Alfonso Martínez Domínguez, an interpretation supposedly confirmed by anonymous "government sources" (NYT, June 14, 1971). The paper gave little coverage to opposing points of view, although such perspectives did receive visibility through other outlets. For example, NACLA published a long interview with a Mexican guerrilla fighter who pointed out that the leader of the Halcones lived in Los Pinos, the presidential residence (NACLA 1972: 7).

The United States applauded Echeverría's attempts at liberalization and overlooked the iron fist with which he quelled some sectors of the opposition. They also believed him when he outlined in his fourth State of the Nation Address his government's policy to contain the guerrilla uprisings: "we shall respond to their provocations, always maintaining the peace, within the procedures and limitations laid down by the law" (Echeverría 1974: 17). There was little desire, at least during the early years of the Echeverría regime, to seek out accurate information on political events in Mexico. The only international organization to carry out an independent investigation was Amnesty International.

The U.S. media's treatment of the guerrilla movements in Mexico exemplified the United States' general attitude toward violence in that country. The armed opposition was rarely mentioned, and what few references appeared were usually critical rather than explanatory or analytical (figure 34). An exception was correspondent Richard

Severo, who made an effort to research the underlying causes of the guerrilla uprisings and to listen to a range of opinions. In his first dispatch from Mexico he quoted "observers outside the government" to the effect that "there has been a political basis in the turmoil in Guerrero" (NYT, Nov. 29, 1971). His stance changed, however, after a guerrilla group kidnapped the U.S. consul in Guadalajara in 1973, at which point he, too, accepted the official view of the guerrillas as "bank robbers and political terrorists" (NYT, May 7–8, 1973).

At the time, Riding was well into his crusade in support of Echeverría. The guerrillas, he suggested, were playing into the hands of "conservatives and the army," who were using this "adventurism of the extreme left" as an excuse to derail Echeverría's "experiment in democracy" (NYT, Oct. 3, 1971). Riding also suggested that the Left was resorting to violence out of fear that Echeverría's efforts "to democratize Mexico may win popular support for his administration" (NYT, Aug. 7, 1971). These portrayals enabled Echeverría to ignore both the causes for the guerrillas' appearance and the tactics his administration was using to suppress them.[4]

A closely parallel attitude prevailed among U.S. experts on Mexico. In 1975, Susan Kaufman Purcell concluded that the Mexican regime was an example of "an inclusive and essentially non-repressive political authoritarianism" (Purcell 1975: 8). The most interesting aspect about this statement is that there is no evidence substantiating Purcell's appraisal of the Mexican government as "non-repressive." In fact, her article was published during a peak in violent repression. The U.S. government, media, and intellectuals were clearly predisposed to accept official versions of events in Mexico, and the Mexican government encouraged this tendency by deliberately cultivating its image among foreign journalists and academics. Echeverría was the first Mexican president to implement a systematic policy to this end;[5] his success can be measured in the rising numbers of Mexican government officials quoted in the *Times* (figure 10).

FAILED ATTEMPTS AT ECONOMIC REFORM UNDER ECHEVERRÍA

For Echeverría, economic reform was the most pressing priority. Convinced that the Mexican Revolution had "brought nothing but poverty and unemployment to most Mexicans" and that its legacy now posed a threat to the viability of the political system (NYT, June 20, 1971), Echeverría proposed fiscal reform to prevent social revolution. He announced his chosen procedure—taxing the most affluent

---

[4]The seven references to repression published during 1971 concerned the Halcones' attack on student marchers on June 10 of that year.

[5]Miguel Alemán's prior efforts were more spontaneous and sporadic.

sectors of society to achieve a "greater equality of income"—in his inaugural address (NYT, Dec. 2, 1970). His plan to impose a 10 percent luxury tax and a new capital gains tax, and to implement additional fiscal reforms in the future in order to increase resources for social spending without steeping the nation in debt, did much to establish Echeverría's image as a fiscally responsible reformer.[6]

Echeverría's projects for income redistribution accorded with the liberal prescriptions for development prevailing among academics and journalists at the time. In 1970, a *Times* editorial suggested that "what is critically needed [in Mexico] is a better distribution of the country's expanding wealth."[7] U.S. media attention shifted to other variables such as "marginalization," which was mentioned on 12 occasions between 1946 and 1969 and 47 times between 1970 and 1979 (figure 89). During the 1970s, both Severo and Riding produced extensive and detailed articles on urban poverty in Mexico. Their attention was drawn to the intersection of poverty and consumerism, which combined "the worst aspects of overindustrialization and underdevelopment."[8] They also collected abundant information on rural poverty in Mexico, for which they largely blamed the traditional *ejido* system of collective land ownership (NYT, Dec. 13, 1977).

In certain issue areas, Echeverría embraced U.S. priorities. For example, although candidate Echeverría had favored a vigorous and expanding Mexican population, he later reversed himself to line up with Washington in viewing "the population explosion" as "Mexico's basic long-term problem" (NYT 1976a; see also Hansen 1971: 209; NYT, May 13, 1973; Reston 1975a; Sulzberger 1973), a problem that resulted in increased migration to the United States (figures 63–64) (Reston 1975b). By 1972, Echeverría was suggesting that "many of the nation's problems stem from an increase in population" (NYT, June 22, 1972), and the *Times* was describing some of his policies as a "valuable example of techniques for limiting the population explosion" (NYT 1972).

The private sector, meanwhile, was resisting "government efforts to reform the antiquated tax system" (NYT, Aug. 2, 1974). Characteristically, the *Times* sided with Echeverría in his struggle against Mexico's business sector which, the *Times* noted, enjoyed one of the "lowest tax rates in the world" (NYT, Jan. 28, 1972). In a surprising and unique, though short lived, turn of events, the *Times* even began underscoring the gross inefficiencies and widespread corruption within Mexico's private sector (this sector received 43 negative refer-

---

[6]NYT, Jan. 1, Dec. 20, 1970. See also *Comercio Exterior* 1971: 219.

[7]NYT 1970b. Correspondent Juan de Onis shared this opinion (NYT, Dec. 2, 1970). See also Hansen 1971: 71.

[8]For articles by Severo, see NYT, June 5, 1972; Feb. 19, 1973; Mar. 31, 1973. For Riding, see NYT, Aug. 22, 1971; July 1, 1976; Jan. 30, 1977, and Mar. 6, 1978.

ences between 1946 and 1986, 13 of them published between 1970 and 1974; figure 74).

According to Alan Riding, Mexico's business and landowning communities—accustomed to "privileged status"—were the "groups feeling most threatened by the reformist zeal of Echeverría" (NYT, June 20, 1971). However, such opinions did not extend to foreign business interests in Mexico (primarily because of limits to consciousness), and only 5 references critical of foreign business interests appeared between 1946 and 1979, out of a total of 140 (figures 72, 76).[9] This explains the U.S. elite's reaction to Echeverría's efforts to control foreign investment in Mexico. When, in September 1972, Echeverría drafted a number of legislative initiatives to regulate transfers of foreign technology and investment and to encourage domestic investment, U.S. Ambassador to Mexico Robert McBride queried publicly whether "the rules of the game had changed" for American companies (NYT, Oct. 13, 1971). American businessmen saw this as a threat not only to themselves but also to their Mexican partners and clients, whom they firmly believed were benefited by U.S. investments.

The business community's fears were soon allayed. Echeverría reversed his position, reflecting the fact (amply noted by the *Times* correspondent) that he was not a "doctrinaire left-winger but rather a pragmatic politician who does what he must to maintain his country" (NYT, Jan. 28, 1973). The private sector had flexed its muscle, in the process proving that it was able to halt reforms and defend its privileges. Nevertheless, Echeverría was not deflected from his determination to right a broad series of what he saw as blatant national injustices. He consequently increased the state's role in various economic activities, including the banking sector which, he argued, was plagued by "conservative" loans policies (NYT, Sept. 20, 1971; Feb. 15, 1976). One direct result of his activities was a sharp rise in federal deficit spending and public foreign debt.

A DIPLOMATIC FRENZY

Echeverría's early ambitions did not extend beyond Mexico's domestic sphere. But around 1972, when it became clear that he was either unable or unwilling to solve Mexico's internal problems, he turned to the international stage, embarking upon a meteoric (but pointless) career as a champion against imperialism—especially Yankee imperialism—and international injustice. He never managed to cure the

---

[9]Only certain leftist sectors, whose influence was very circumscribed, condemned the activities of multinational corporations from within the United States (see Baird and McCaughan 1975; McCaughan and Baird 1976).

world's ills but he did succeed in currying left-wing favor both in Mexico and around the world (NYT, Dec. 1, 1976).

Echeverría shook up Mexico's foreign policy. An active reformism placed Mexico in the lead among progressive Third World nations.[10] In 1972, he began drumming up support for "the position of developing countries on such matters as natural resources and control over multinational corporations" (NYT, Oct. 20, 1974). He fought for a 200–mile limit for Mexico's territorial waters (NYT, July 1, 1976). And in conjunction with his Venezuelan counterpart, Carlos Andrés Pérez, he promoted initiatives such as the creation of the Latin American Economic System (SELA) "to defend the price of raw materials and strengthen Latin America's hand with the United States" (NYT, Apr. 21, 1975).

Adding insult to injury, Washington's least favorite Latin American nation (Cuba) was invited to join SELA, and in 1974 Echeverría visited seven nations in the region in an effort to convince their governments to lift their economic blockade against Cuba (NYT, Aug. 30, 1975). A year later he visited that country, praising the "success" of the Cuban Revolution and its triumphs over "threats and pressures from abroad," a less-than-subtle dig at the United States (NYT, Aug. 18, 1975).

Echeverría also expressed support for the socialist government in Chile and "frequently reminded Washington of its role in the overthrow of the late President Salvador Allende." On Panama, Echeverría declared that "Latin America was impatient" for the United States to recognize Panamanian sovereignty over the canal (NYT, June 6, 1975). He also used political asylum policies as an "active instrument of foreign policy," enabling the Mexican government to cast its progressive and liberal stance against the contrasting backdrop of the brutal authoritarianism of many South American regimes (NYT, Apr. 28, 1976).

Ultimately, Latin America proved too small a stage for Echeverría, and he began traveling around the world, signing agreements and promoting initiatives, including the "new international economic order," which he saw both as an alternative to war and as a useful instrument for denouncing the unethical practices of multinational corporations (NYT, Jan. 25, 1976).

We should note that Echeverría's ideas coincided generally with prevailing liberal viewpoints. During the 1970s, the call for greater economic justice at the international level was widespread. In 1974, the Club of Rome reported that a global catastrophe could only be

---

[10]This provoked extremely interesting reactions from the United States. Mexican diplomacy received more criticism than ever before: over 50 percent of the negative references to Mexico's foreign policy that appeared in the *Times* after 1946 appeared over the 1975–1976 period (figure 46).

avoided by "narrowing the gap between rich and poor lands" (NYT, Oct. 17, 1974). Suggestions for tighter controls over multinational corporations were aired in many nations, and Echeverría's proposals were not viewed as radical or extravagant despite the frivolous and headlong, hence costly and inefficient, manner in which they were advanced.

ENTHUSIASM COOLS

Sentiments regarding Echeverría's policies suffered a downturn between 1975 and 1977, with 49 negative and 6 positive references in the *Times* during this period (figures 24–25). Even Alan Riding participated in this shift from praise to condemnation. His articles for the London *Financial Times*[11] show him gradually cooling toward Echeverría's administration. His disenchantment arose from Echeverría's incongruities and the fact that "the government's economic policy" was riddled with contradictions (author interview with Riding, 1983). In an article that was deeply upsetting for the regime, Riding stated that although the president's "public declarations point in one direction, his actions are oriented towards another" and that Echeverría "must take much of the blame for the present uncertainty."[12] As the regime's six-year term wore on, Riding's disenchantment grew.

Riding was not the only observer to disagree with Echeverría's policies. James Reston suggested that the Charter for Economic Rights and Duties being promoted by Mexico was unbalanced and that the United States correctly "opposed its terms on expropriation and commodity prices and its support of the producer cartels." Reston added that Echeverría's proposals were "one-sided in favor of the Soviet Union and the Third World" and that, should they be implemented, they would lead to an "economic revolution" (Reston 1975c). He also suggested that the president was less than candid about his motives, and that his role as a "traveling missionary" out to change the world was nothing but a thinly disguised campaign to position himself as a viable candidate for secretary general of the United Nations (Reston 1975a, 1975b).

When in 1975 General Franco of Spain executed five members of the Republican opposition, Echeverría urged the United Nations to impose a "political, diplomatic, economic, and communications boycott on Spain" (NYT, Sept. 30, 1975). The UN Security Council refused even to discuss his petition. This, according to the *Times*, was the right decision because Echeverría's radicalism was, in fact, only a thin ve-

---

[11]Riding only published two articles in the *Times* during 1972 and 1973 (figure 6).

[12]After 1972 these ideas became a central feature in Riding's articles; see NYT, Aug. 16, 1972, Dec. 4, 1974; *Financial Times*, May 30, 1973.

neer on his maneuverings to succeed UN Secretary General Kurt Waldheim (NYT 1975a). Incidentally, the *Times* also revisited Echeverría's role as minister of government during the 1968 Tlatelolco massacre, in effect admitting that it had always known about the Mexican government's human rights violations.

In 1975 as well, Echeverría ordered the Mexican delegation to the United Nations to support a General Assembly resolution defining Zionism as "a form of racism and racial discrimination" (NYT, Nov. 11, 1975). The *Times* described the resolution as a "defection from morality which dishonored the UN, reducing the General Assembly's authority to zero" (NYT 1975b). Mexico's support for it clearly angered the U.S. elite.

Alan Riding noted that Washington was incensed by Echeverría's "demagoguery" and irritated by his constant travels, on which he was surrounded "by sycophantic party officials" (NYT, Sept. 6, Oct. 6, Nov. 21, 1976). Another irritant was Echeverría's rhetoric, in which the United States was "the implicit target of the many . . . attacks on industrialized nations" (NYT, June 14, 1976; also, June 20, 1976). According to U.S. diplomats, Echeverría was stirring up "antagonisms toward the United States" (Nov. 20, 1975).

As on previous occasions, however, these criticisms of the Mexican president reflected annoyance but no real worry. The U.S. elite did not take either Echeverría or Mexico's official nationalism all that seriously. A 1976 *Times* editorial contains a very revealing phrase: Echeverría "rode the stormy waves of Mexican political life by appropriating as his own the symbols of radicalism" (NYT 1976a).

The shallowness of Echeverría's radicalism was evident on a number of occasions. Richard Nixon's memoirs briefly describe a visit by Echeverría in June 1972: "we had a long chat on the water-salinity problems, ending with an intense though friendly discussion on the treatment received by American companies in Latin America. He ended by stating that he believed that *my reelection was of vital importance for the planet*" (Nixon 1978: 624; emphasis added). There was Echeverría, radical reformer, heaping praise on a conservative. In 1976, Alan Riding recalled that in private conversations with correspondents, Echeverría sometimes suggested that they should interpret his radicalism as a "political necessity, exclusively for domestic consumption" (NYT, Sept. 6, 1976).

The facts continued to belie Mexico's "official" nationalism. Policies toward foreign investment, which had given Ambassador McBride pause, had been resolved satisfactorily by December 1974, and Mexico was once again wooing foreign investors. Riding noted that legislation on foreign direct investment had turned out to be "less hostile than was foreseen" and that, in practice, the Mexican government seemed "more willing to make exceptions" to the rule which, in theory, limited foreign holders to a ceiling of 49 percent ownership in a Mexican company. Of 103 requests for exemptions, 74 had been approved (figures 78–79) (NYT, Dec. 26, 1974).

Mexico's support for the UN resolution denouncing Zionism as racism provoked a boycott by Jewish organizations, which called on travelers to cancel trips to Mexico (NYT, Nov. 23, 1975). Echeverría, in the pose of "I'd rather die than apologize" (NYT, Dec. 1, 1975), never did retract his statements personally. Instead, he deputed a member of his cabinet. Minister of Foreign Affairs Emilio Rabasa, upon arriving in Israel, referred to the "land of Zion . . . created for a people who deserve our respect and admiration." Just so there could be no doubt about the purpose of his visit, he laid a wreath on "the tomb in Jerusalem of Dr. Theodore Herzl, the founder of the Zionist movement" (NYT, Dec. 6, 1975). Ten days after Rabasa's trip, Mexico declared in the United Nations that "Zionism and racism" were not comparable (NYT, Dec. 16, 1975). Rabasa resigned at the end of December 1975. A few months later Echeverría altered his Middle East policies 180 degrees and joined "the United States and its traditional allies" in opposing a General Assembly resolution that charged Israel, the United States, and other powers with collaborating with South Africa (NYT, Nov. 10, 1976).

COOPERATION IN THE WAR ON DRUGS

Drug-related issues took an unexpected turn during the 1970s. As U.S.–Mexico collaboration on the drug front become more routinized, Washington began to press Mexico on two related items: the arrest of U.S. citizens on drug-linked charges and their detention in Mexican jails, and the use of the herbicide paraquat on marijuana plantings, which was affecting the health of people who smoked marijuana.

In July 1970, correspondent Juan de Onis published the first in a series of articles on the fate of Americans in Mexican jails. He expressed indignation at the fact that U.S. citizens were forced to share with "Mexican criminals the personal insecurity, sexual abuse and corruption that characterize prison life here" (NYT, July 19, 1970).[13] The Mexican government was predictably displeased with the criticism of their prison system, in which growing numbers of foreigners

---

[13]It should be noted that Riding did not concur. In December 1977 he stated that conditions inside a prison in Hermosillo, Sonora, were "relatively good, and infinitely better than those experienced in state and county jails in the United States" (NYT, Dec. 4, 1977). However, few correspondents or analysts shared Riding's viewpoint. For opposing viewpoints, see NYT, Jan. 25, 1972; July 12, Oct. 21, 1974; Nov. 18, 1975; May 23, 1976.

were being incarcerated as a direct result of the anti-drug policies being imposed by Washington (NYT, July 19, 1970).

The altercation over the Mexican justice system climaxed when Dr. Sterling Blake Davis, a wealthy Texan, bankrolled a group of mercenaries to free fourteen U.S. citizens being held in a jail in northern Mexico, after "he had exhausted all other options of the Mexican extortion system." Despite Mexico's protests, U.S. authorities in Texas freed the fugitives, and State Department officials declared that "extradition in such a case is unlikely" (NYT, May 10, 1976). To avoid future incidents of this kind, Mexico and the United States explored the possibility of prisoner exchanges; they signed an accord on November 5, 1976, whose "almost exclusive objective was to address the problem posed by the Americans" (NYT, Nov. 3, 6, 1976). The following year, Mexico extradited sixty-one U.S. citizens, who arrived in San Diego to "banners, balloons, and cheers" (NYT, Dec. 10, 1977). The U.S. government contributed by "decking out the convicts in new uniforms of red, white and blue" (NYT, Dec. 11, 1977). The *Times* supported the prisoner exchanges, calling this a "humane treaty that allows this country to repatriate imprisoned" U.S. citizens and allow them to serve their sentences in their own country (NYT 1979a). In fact, very few exchanged prisoners served their full sentences; by 1979 the vast majority had been paroled (NYT, Nov. 11, 1979). This prisoner exchange issue would fade into the background until 1985, when it reemerged with unprecedented vigor.

Toward Economic Catastrophe

Echeverría's last two years in power proved to be extremely difficult for his administration, for the nation, for Mexico's relationship with the United States, and for Echeverría's own image. By 1975, Riding was reporting that Mexico's rural areas were rife with "repression as well as a steady loss of communal lands," that *ejidatarios* had no access to "credit, seeds, fertilizer and machinery," and that farmers and peasants were being repressed. He asserted that the Ministry of Agrarian Reform controlled the rural sector by means of a "strategy of rhetoric and repression" implemented by "a corrupt and confusing bureaucracy" that was a "monument to the [peasants'] patience." Their lot continued to be one of hopeless poverty, despite "the verbal commitments undertaken by successive governments." Riding added that "the assassination of peasants [was] routine" (NYT, Dec. 26, 1975; Dec. 13, 1977; Dec. 1, 1975, respectively). This was not a new situation in Mexico; what was new was the willingness of the media to report on it, after having ignored it since the 1960s.

As coverage of Mexican affairs become more independent and more critical of the government, Riding began to explore hitherto untouched subjects, such as what had motivated the emergence of guerrilla movements. After the death of Lucio Cabañas, Riding noted that the armed movement Cabañas had headed had been "an outgrowth of the extreme poverty and repression that have long existed in Guerrero, the most backward state in Mexico." The urban guerrillas, Riding wrote, arose from "the frustration and resentment bred among the middle class youth by the army's annihilation of anti-government protests in 1968" (NYT, Dec. 16, Dec. 4, 1974, respectively).[14] This was the first time that anyone had attempted to explain these movements, and the attempt at explanation hints at the manner in which liberal America would cover the upcoming wars in Central America (the Nicaraguan insurrection broke out in 1977).

And overshadowing even these severe social concerns was a growing uneasiness about Mexico's economic situation, which by the latter years of Echeverría's term had deteriorated to a level that would have been unimaginable in 1970. Although the factors underlying the crisis were multiple and complex, Americans held that the president bore the heaviest responsibility. He had seriously miscalculated when he ignored building pressures to devalue the currency and instead kept to the prevailing peso/dollar exchange rate. In 1973, Richard Severo reported that many Mexican government officials acknowledged privately that the peso was "overvalued in relation to the dollar" but that Echeverría had decided not to devalue (NYT, Nov. 20, 1973).

By August 1975 the question no longer was whether, but when, a devaluation would occur. Some analysts predicted that it would come before the July 1976 presidential elections (NYT, Aug. 23, 1975), and Riding wrote about the "persistent speculation" regarding the likelihood of a devaluation "during the next 12 to 18 months" (NYT, Jan. 25, 1976; Aug. 23, 1975). Throughout 1976, Echeverría doggedly sustained the peso at its old level, while the *Times* continued to assert that "a devaluation may be inevitable" (NYT, June 20, 1976).

In July 1976, in the midst of this economic upheaval, the government orchestrated a campaign to oust Julio Scherer García, editor of the Mexico City daily *Excélsior*, in an action that demonstrated the fragile nature of the regime's aspirations to democracy and elicited a response from the U.S. elite that is representative of their opinion of Echeverría and the Mexican political system (NYT, July 9, 1976). The *Times* noted that "the bully boys of Lenin in 1917 or of Hitler in 1933

---

[14]Despite such criticisms, the U.S. elite continued to support the cause of Mexican stability. In 1975 Riding himself acknowledged that Echeverría's reformism was the key to the survival of a system that, despite some flaws, preserved a reasonable level of political stability and encouraged economic development (NYT, Jan. 12, 1975).

could not have done a more efficient job of enslaving a once proud and free newspaper." It added that such an "act of totalitarian repression discredits those who now boast of Mexico's stability and democracy" (NYT 1976b).

During Echeverría's final weeks as president, there was no sympathy or respect for him in the United States. It was undeniably clear that he had stalled Mexico's democratization, failed to redistribute income or wealth, reduced the margins for national independence, and floundered in his efforts to bring about a new international economic order. The legacy of his administration was massive economic and political crisis, which could only be reversed by reestablishing a "climate for business expansion and capital investment." Mexico also now found herself at the mercy of the "willingness of the International Monetary Fund and the foreign bankers to continue making unconditional loans to sustain the Mexican economy" (NYT 1976c).

This outcome is not Echeverría's responsibility alone. Washington was clearly aware of his administration's rampant corruption, authoritarianism, and hypocrisy, yet it raised no outcry. In fact, the United States protected and nurtured the Mexican regime; as long as there was stability in Mexico, the United States would reap the associated benefits. Even so, Americans seem to have looked forward to the transfer of power. The *Times* ran an editorial welcoming José López Portillo to the Mexican presidency and urging him to reflect on the following: "I can defend myself against my enemies, but God protect me from my friends" (NYT 1976c). John Oakes noted that Echeverría had done "everything possible with his frenetic activity and Third World rhetoric to increase the traditional American mistrust of our southern neighbor as a turbulent land of revolution" (Oakes 1977).

The economic crisis that befell Mexico during Echeverría's presidency altered U.S. perceptions of corruption in that country. In prior Mexican administrations, U.S. references to corruption increased during the first year, as incoming presidents announced their respective anti-corruption campaigns, and in the last year, as their programs' failures became apparent, immediately prior to the next campaign (figure 93). But at the end of Echeverría's term the *Times* suggested that corruption was "ingrained . . . in Mexican life" (NYT, June 20, 1976). This was an important shift; corruption was now viewed as a way of life in Mexico, which would be almost impossible to eradicate (NYT, Dec. 22, 1974). This raised the corruption issue to a new level, as Americans became increasingly aware of its potentially negative effects on stability in Mexico and on the expanding illegal drug trade, with its concomitant and direct impacts on the United States.

A VIEW FROM WITHIN

The devaluation of the peso in 1976 by outgoing President Echeverría marked the Mexican economy's most difficult moment in decades. The United States, in an effort to protect U.S. investments in Mexico and to restore that country's economic and political stability, began firming up its support for its neighbor.[15] One of the central reasons for increased support from the U.S. Treasury and Federal Reserve was to demonstrate the United States' political interest in Mexico.[16] That is, the United States anticipated that the Mexican government would soon come under "intense internal political pressure," and aid would help maintain stability by calming the Mexican markets (ST 1976).

In a Federal Reserve Executive Council meeting on November 16, 1976, Federal Reserve chairman Arthur Burns laid out a number of additional reasons.[17] He began by acknowledging that a previous loan of U.S.$360 million to Mexico was not issued "with all due care and deliberation. We acted somewhat mechanically. . . . They asked for the money, we asked a few questions, grunted a little and accepted. . . . Mexico was close to bankruptcy, which could have entailed a moratorium. . . . This would have been extremely unfortunate, because our banks are heavily involved in Mexico and because, of course, this could unleash a global moratorium" (Mexico's debt to the U.S. private banking sector stood at $9 billion in November 1976). Burns added that the Federal Reserve did not wish to be held responsible for a default of such magnitude. He believed that the problem could be handled, although he did accept that his "faith in the operations of the Banco de México was somewhat limited" (FR 1976a: 1, 3, 17).

These were the motivations behind the United States' decision to increase the flow of funds sustaining the Mexican government, a decision necessarily premised on agreement with the International Monetary Fund. (Such an agreement was a prerequisite for all loans to Mexico from the Treasury, the Federal Reserve, or U.S. private banks.) The agreement with the IMF stipulated a number of financial and commercial constraints to which Mexico had to adhere (such as maintaining a minimum amount in reserves and limiting public-sector external debt and deficit spending). The IMF displayed extraordinary flexibility in working with Mexico. For example, although

---

[15]As recorded in classified information from the document collection of Arthur Burns. This collection is exceptional because the documents have not been as heavily censored as others from the same year (criteria on what to expunge appear to be influenced by individual librarians). The documents were provided by Kate Doyle, of the National Security Archives in Washington, D.C., who obtained them from the Gerald R. Ford Library.

[16]This was recorded in a memorandum from Secretary of the Treasury William E. Simon to President Gerald Ford.

[17]This discussion is based on minutes from that meeting.

the IMF signed its accord with Mexico in October 1976, this did not go into full force until January 1, 1977, allowing Echeverría to assume responsibility for the peso devaluation but to avoid blame for the new IMF–imposed austerity policies (see FR 1976b; DOS 1976).

Classified documents from the Federal Reserve and coverage in the *Times* concur generally on the origins of Mexico's economic problems, the need for a peso devaluation, and the logic behind the accords between the Mexican and U.S. governments. The only relevant differences lie in the naming of sources and in the level of detail about events in Mexico. While the *Times* employed conventions such as "a well-informed source," the Federal Reserve documents contain frequent references to interviews with Mexico's president and cabinet ministers and with the director of the Banco de México. And the information the Federal Reserve collected went beyond what was relevant for loan purposes. For example, the source cited in a secret CIA document from October 1976 was "López Portillo's private secretary, who insisted that his chief had no influence on Echeverría's economic policies" during the months of rumor, uncertainty, and devaluation (CIA 1976a: 2).

Another CIA cable from the same month gives precise details about López Portillo's forthcoming government program. Thirty-four days before López Portillo was sworn into office, the U.S. government already knew that his priority would be to "restore trust in the private sector and in the government" and that he was willing to control workers' demands "with all necessary force." They also knew that he would redirect the priorities of "Mexican foreign policy toward the United States and Latin America" and that Mexico's three most important embassies would be "the United States, Guatemala, and Cuba." The first two were important neighbors; López Portillo wanted to ensure that the third, Cuba, "did not meddle in Mexico" (CIA 1976b: 4–5). Clearly the Americans had all the information they needed to formulate adequate policies, and a great deal of this information came from Mexican government officials.

The contrast with the paucity of information supplied to the Mexican people could not be starker, a fact that did not escape the United States' attention. In October 1976, a Federal Reserve analyst acknowledged that "the total scope of the program, and the magnitude of the required adjustments, have not yet been explained to the general public" (FR 1976c: 3). Also in October 1976 the CIA's director of operations predicted that López Portillo's government would "centralize information, using it most of all for the promotion of its economic objectives" (CIA 1976b: 3). Clearly the Mexican government was providing far better information to a foreign government than to its own people.

None of these documents explicitly acknowledged the regime's authoritarian nature. Rather, the United States accepted Mexico's established order and identified as its own foremost priority the need to protect U.S. interests, which, in turn, were inexorably linked to the PRI's hold on power. The tacit understanding worked, and it established a pattern that would be repeated in the financial crises of 1982, 1985–86, and 1994–95. But although the basic policy remained unchanged over these various economic upheavals, the conditions that the United States imposed on Mexico varied from one crisis to the next.

FINDING A BALANCE

In a sense, Echeverría's frenzied reformism worked. He was able to bring many of the student leaders from 1968 into his government, while he simultaneously used coercion and repression to silence armed opposition to his regime, along with any media (such as *Excélsior*) that had shaken free of government controls. Although Echeverría did not always see eye to eye with Washington, at critical moments the United States did all in its power to protect the Mexican political system.[18]

On the other hand, Echeverría unleashed social forces whose ultimate impacts even he could not have foreseen. For example, he founded the National Council for Science and Technology. CONACYT grants allowed thousands of Mexican students to study abroad, and many of these foreign-educated Mexicans would eventually constitute the new cadres of the Mexican ruling elite, displacing traditional politicians from Echeverría's era. By the time of Miguel de la Madrid's administration (1982–1988), 63 percent of Mexico's cabinet members had studied at foreign universities (Peter Smith 1986: 109). The importance of the government elite's renovation is even more visible if we consider the following: Carlos Salinas studied at Harvard, Ernesto Zedillo at Yale, Pedro Aspe at MIT, and Manuel Camacho at Princeton. These academic institutions nurtured the neoliberal ideas that would transform Mexico's history.

---

[18]Despite the importance this support had for the bilateral relationship, it was rarely considered in U.S. analyses. Peter Smith, for example, ignores external influences as a factor in his discussion of Mexico's crisis. Sketching a general outline of Echeverría's regime, Smith stated that "in overcoming the problem of Presidential succession, and surviving the peculiar crisis of late 1976, the authoritarian Mexican system has once again proved its ability to adapt and change" (1979: 313). Smith makes no mention of the role played by the United States.

15

José López Portillo: Renewed Hope

U.S. perceptions of the José López Portillo presidency evolved along the same lines traced during the administration of Luis Echeverría. The U.S. media initially accorded López Portillo the by now traditional favorable coverage. Over the course of Mexico's 1976 elections, the *Times* published 30 positive and no negative references to Echeverría's designated successor. Six years later, in 1982, the order was reversed: the paper ran 31 negative and zero positive references (figures 22–23). These two years frame one of the most frustrating periods in Mexican history.

Discoveries of major oil fields during this administration offered the Mexican government an opportunity to carry out economic and political reforms that might have salvaged the country's ailing experiment in development. However, the administration was precluded from taking advantage of this opportunity by the system's inherent distortions (especially presidentialism), and by the end of López Portillo's presidency in 1982 the government faced a major financial debacle.

The United States came to Mexico's aid, despite the fact that the López Portillo administration had proved to be unlike any other in the history of the bilateral relationship. Thanks to its newly discovered oil deposits and the global context, Mexico had acquired unprecedented clout in its relationship with the United States, which it used to amend certain key aspects of the understanding. Even so, the Mexican president's failure to wield his power effectively and his almost total failure to understand the magnitude of the transformations that were taking place canceled out all possibility of shifting the relationship in Mexico's favor. For Mexico, these were the beginnings of an era of growing pressure from Washington to modify the country's economic model and of the stealthy ascent of a new technocracy that would gradually replace the established elite—and rewrite history.

The United States' interest in Mexico rose sharply after discovery of the petroleum deposits. In 1979, the *Times* published more than 250 Mexico-related articles, of which a high percentage were features (figures 1, 4, 6–7). The United States' understanding of Mexican realities was generally improved, although there were still trace misunderstandings to be resolved.

INITIAL OPTIMISM

López Portillo's predecessor—Luis Echeverría—had at one point been identified by the media as Mexico's "best hope in generations" because he sought to revitalize the system. The media presented his successor as the "president of hope," whose main task would be to restore the confidence that Echeverría had destroyed. The *Times* noted that what Mexico most desperately needed was trust. Only trust in the system would stabilize the peso and attract foreign investment and more tourism (NYT, Dec. 14, 1976).

Repeating the pattern of six years earlier, the U.S. elite hoped to find in the new president someone able to maintain Mexico's domestic stability while leading the country toward economic recovery. Early media assessments of López Portillo found him to be "more intellectual, less rhetorical, more pragmatic, less of a dreamer . . . and more pro-business" than Echeverría (NYT, Nov. 21, 1976; Nov. 14, 1975). Although Alan Riding had not fully overcome his disappointment with Echeverría, he was willing to place his trust in the new president, a man concerned with "efficiency, organization and productivity," a man with a "sense of humor" who "enjoyed good food and drink" and a good cigar—not unlike Riding himself. López Portillo, he predicted, would give only "secondary importance to cultivating his image through expensive publicity either in Mexico or elsewhere"; the new president represented the end of a "populist era" (NYT, Dec. 2, 1976). Riding's portrayal was to prove wildly off the mark.

Enthusiasm for López Portillo was intensified by the fact (mentioned in the preceding chapter) that he made his administration's program available to the United States a full month before his inauguration. True to his word, López Portillo departed from the previous government's rhetoric. His inaugural address contained no references to the Third World, and López Portillo's later pronouncements called for a "reasonable world order" (NYT, Feb. 16, 1977). Other measures that met with approval in Washington were the appointments of Santiago Roel as minister of foreign affairs and Hugo Margáin as ambassador to the United States; both were viewed as "admirers of America" (NYT, Feb. 14, 1977; Dec. 26, 1976).

Then in 1977 Mexico announced that it would not join the Organization of Petroleum Exporting Countries (OPEC), an important step for this fledgling oil power (NYT, Nov. 13, 1977). This was followed in 1978 by the administration's pledge to "supply Israel, on short notice, with all the oil it might need in an emergency" (NYT, Mar. 11, 1978). By this time, the new Mexican president was being hailed as "essen-tially pro-American" (NYT, Feb. 14, 1977; also Dec. 26, 1976).

These gestures were probably unavoidable; in the wake of the crisis left by Echeverría, Mexico's options were few. The incoming administration was initially almost wholly dependent on the "goodwill of the International Monetary Fund and the foreign banks," the only agencies able to provide the loan funds that could stave off collapse of the Mexican economy (NYT, Dec. 1, 1976). Not without irony, Riding noted that Mexico's "calls for independence [have been] replaced by calls for interdependence, a euphemism . . . for Mexican dependency on the United States" (NYT, Feb. 18, 1977).

Interestingly, the Mexican government's dependence on the United States, which Riding noted in passing, seems to have been overlooked by most members of the academic community. The approach taken by Peter Smith is representative: "in overcoming the problems of Presidential succession, and surviving the peculiar crisis of late 1976, the authoritarian Mexican system has once again proved its capacity to adapt and change" (1979: 313). Academics' general disregard for the role played by Washington distorted their analyses and exaggerated the prowess of the Mexican elite, whose survival was credited to their innate adaptability and resourcefulness. The fact that the Mexican elite's capacity for action was made possible by the United States was rarely taken into consideration.

Another facet of Mexico's political system that tended to be overlooked during the early days of the López Portillo administration was the gradual turnover in high-level positions. Top government jobs were going to younger politicians who had studied abroad, usually in the United States. This new elite was edging out Mexico's first generation of *"técnicos"* (defined by Peter Smith [1979: 298–313] as economists with a nationalist education) along with the old established cadres.

REFORMISM DURING THE EARLY MONTHS

During his first year in office López Portillo pushed through a number of moderate reforms, which were controlled from the highest tiers of government. On the political front, he granted amnesty to political prisoners and enacted a fairly limited electoral reform law. These steps, however modest, sufficed to establish his pro-democratic credentials with the United States.

On the economic front, López Portillo's foremost priority was to win the trust of "the conservative business community, alienated by Echeverría's reformist government" (NYT, Sept. 25, 1975; June 29, 1976). To this end, he carried out a number of reforms, some of which reflected commitments made to the International Monetary Fund (which have not yet been made public). One of his early measures was to support a federal judge's decision to return to "their rightful owners" lands that Echeverría had expropriated toward the end of his administration (NYT, Dec. 12, 1976). López Portillo also announced that he would encourage competitiveness and combat "corruption," which he labeled a cancer in Mexican society. To demonstrate his determination to hold all in public office to the highest moral standards, he had a former cabinet minister arrested on corruption charges (NYT, Sept. 25, 1975; June 29, 1976).

During his early days in power, López Portillo also pursued a plan to distribute wealth more evenly. His chosen mechanism, like Echeverría's, was fiscal reform. The outcome was also the same: a year later, the president "abruptly postponed" these reforms without explanation (NYT, Dec. 3, 1977; Feb. 5, 1978). The reason for their derailment was almost certainly opposition from Mexico's powerful private sector, which wielded massive, though veiled, political clout. Although he continued supportive of the private sector, Alan Riding condemned the "ultraconservative businessmen" who ignored "the problems of a real Mexico which exists outside their palaces," slowed the progress of the Mexican economy through "rapaciousness and greed," and were opposed to a "sorely needed fiscal reform to put an end to some of the mechanisms that lead to a concentration of riches" (NYT, Jan. 30, 1977; Nov. 29, 1978).

Despite such criticism of Mexico's private sector, the *Times*'s views on foreign investment in Mexico remained unaltered (figures 75–76). However, the paper did publish a few negative opinions, reflecting the spread of liberal ideas in the media. In 1978, for example, the *Times* ran an opinion piece by Philip Russell of NACLA, criticizing the negative impacts of foreign investment on countries like Mexico (Russell 1978). The paper also published a letter from the director of the American Friends Service Committee suggesting that "an international caste system" was creating "an unequal distribution of wealth" between Mexico and the United States (NYT, Nov. 15, 1979).

López Portillo, meanwhile, hoping to encourage competitiveness in Mexico's business community, ordered the country's protectionist trade barriers lowered (NYT, Jan. 30, Mar. 24, 1977). His government was also considering the possibility of joining the General Agreement on Tariffs and Trade (GATT). In fact, in February 1979 Clyde Farnsworth reported from Washington that Mexico had indeed agreed to enter the GATT, after "decades of protectionist commercial policies" and following "exhortations from Washington." But although López Portillo was close to deciding in favor of GATT membership, in the end he backed down, a move explained in the United States as reflecting an unusual alliance between "left-wing economists and right-wing businessmen" (NYT, Feb. 2, 1979). The *Times* reported on the disappointment of the U.S. business community, which viewed Mexico's entry into the GATT as a prerequisite for improved trade relations between the two nations and as a potential stimulant to the economic reforms so needed in Mexico (NYT, Mar. 24, 1980). Ultimately Mexico opted to rely instead on its newly discovered petroleum deposits to meet all these objectives (NYT, Oct. 19, 1978).

THE EARLY DAYS OF THE OIL BOOM

In October 1974, in the middle years of the Echeverría presidency, the *Washington Post* reported the discovery of vast oil fields in Mexico.[1] This announcement ushered in an era in which oil dominated U.S. perceptions of Mexico: Daniel Yergin (1978) wrote that "the most addictive drug coming out of Mexico is no longer marijuana: it is oil." U.S. enthusiasm was driven by the country's recollection of the 1973 oil embargo, when oil supplies dried up and prices skyrocketed—and the Arab oil-producing nations demonstrated their independence from the United States. This shakeup also boosted theories of interdependence and global visions of the international system (Keohane and Nye 1977; Wallerstein 1974). In light of this globalization, geographic proximity greatly enhanced the importance of Mexican crude for the United States' grand security strategy, a fact reflected in the rising number of articles published by the *Times* (figure 1).

Another indicator of the growing interest in Mexican affairs was Presidential Review Memorandum 41, prepared for Jimmy Carter in 1978. It identified Mexico as an "emerging energy power," with the potential to help reduce the United States' dependence on the Middle East (NSC 1978: 2).[2] Although PRM-41 was a classified document, once it was declassified it became apparent that the ideas it contained did not differ significantly from those that were circulating publicly at the time. For example, U.S. government officials had already confirmed that Mexico's vast oil reserves would allow them to drive OPEC's inflated prices from the market (NYT, Oct. 12, 1974; also Oct.

---

[1] The news had been leaked by a major U.S. oil company in hopes of eroding OPEC solidarity (NYT, Oct. 20, 1974).

[2] This idea was not new; it had been suggested by the secretary of the treasury in 1976 (ST 1976).

20, 1970; Mar. 21, 1977). There was also talk about ending dependence on Middle East–supplied oil. Richard Fagen (1978), Secretary of Energy James Schlesinger (NYT, Oct. 29, 1978), and the *Times* editors all agreed that Mexico had "enough oil to supply the United States by short and safe routes for 40 years" (NYT 1978). Had these estimates of Mexico's reserves been accurate, Mexican oil and gas would certainly have been the easiest and cheapest solution to the problem of supply in the United States.[3]

Private and public opinion in the United States was based on a central assumption: Mexico would not fail the United States because, under the tacit understanding that regulated the bilateral relationship, the two countries were pledged to provide mutual assistance in times of need. Americans were doubly disconcerted, therefore, when López Portillo failed to behave as expected, setting in motion a fascinating period in the bilateral relationship, one that brought to the surface many of its previously submerged tensions. Oil would illustrate the depths of anti-American sentiment in Mexico and the pragmatism that guided U.S. policy along lines that protected U.S. interests. Sadly, although the Mexican leadership was willing to exploit the new power that the oil discoveries conferred on the country, the administration lacked the know-how to take full advantage of the moment.

Echeverría had already hinted that an empowered Mexico could amend the rules of the bilateral understanding. Just prior to meeting with Gerald Ford in Nogales, Sonora, in 1974, Echeverría had declared that Mexico would exploit its oil "in a nationalist and profoundly anti-imperialist manner" and that he would request "observer" status in OPEC (NYT, Oct. 15–16, 1974). In his meeting with Ford, Echeverría acknowledged that "substantial amounts of oil have been discovered." He added, maliciously, that "they would be sold on the world market." He was willing, however, to make a concession to the United States: Mexico would abstain from joining OPEC if President Ford would support Echeverría's proposed new economic charter for resolving the world's problems (NYT, Oct. 21, 1974). Ford capitulated, despite Washington's avowed dislike for Echeverría's world diplomacy campaigns (NYT 1974). In any case, the Americans were not seriously worried; Echeverría continued to give U.S. officials private guarantees and reassurances. In a confidential letter the U.S. secretary of the treasury informed Ford that Echeverría had decided not to join OPEC although he would declare the opposite in public (ST 1976: 5).

The U.S. elite remained calm and did not demand oil concessions in exchange for the financial support extended to Mexico in 1976.

---

[3]PRM-41 suggested that Mexico could be in a position to "satisfy 30% of the United States' importation needs by the mid-eighties" (NYT, Feb. 13, 1979).

They were confident that, one way or another, Mexico would supply the needed oil and at a reasonable price. However, it was also clear that the time had come to pay closer attention to Mexico, and Washington included the bilateral relationship among "its highest priorities" (NYT 1978).

This desire for a closer relationship was widespread. During the presidential campaigns of 1979, four candidates (including Jimmy Carter and Ronald Reagan) supported the idea of a North American common market. Carter was very candid about his reasons: the establishment of a common market would allow the United States to end its "dependency on Middle Eastern oil" (Hill 1979).[4] Interestingly, this did not seem to displease the Mexican leadership. James Reston quoted López Portillo as saying that "it was possible to think of a common market" (Reston 1979a), and this is fully consistent with the tenor of the relationship as expressed in confidential documents.

Americans are a pragmatic people, able to admit their mistakes. Consequently, there soon followed expressions of regret for having treated Mexico as a "minor power" and having taken it for granted (NYT, Feb. 11, 1979). Reston suggested that Carter did not visit Mexico in February 1979 so much to "address the price of Mexican gas" as to "address the price of [past U.S.] indifference" (Reston 1979b).

The need to defend U.S. interests, the population's inherent pragmatism, and broadening consciousness all encouraged Americans to reinterpret contentious chapters in the two nations' shared history, such as Mexico's "expropriation" of its oil industry in 1938. Historian Karl Meyer agreed with U.S. Ambassador to Mexico Josephus Daniels that "Mexicans had a legitimate grievance, and they had a [legal justification] for the expropriation." Meyer acknowledged that Lázaro Cárdenas had offered generous compensation to foreign oil companies, and he concluded, with a certain sadness, that if the United States "had accepted, today Mexico would be [its] partner" (K. Meyer 1979). At this same time, negative references to Cárdenas vanished from the *Times*, and a few positive references appeared (figure 20).

THE ARROGANT YEARS

Despite the United States' efforts to improve the relationship, Mexico pursued a path of independence. Mexico's sudden oil wealth provided an opportunity to promote development and to fulfill at least some of the dreams of international independence and social justice inherited from the Mexican Revolution. López Portillo embarked, therefore, on what he haughtily termed an "administration of abun-

---

[4]One view opposing the common market was that of Aaron Segal (1979).

dance," whose consequences were as immediate as they were unexpected.

Tensions soon appeared in the bilateral relationship, and they would not ease for several years. In August 1977, Mexico signed an agreement to supply natural gas to six U.S. oil companies. Based on this agreement, the Mexican government immediately began construction of a U.S.$1.2 billion pipeline, without awaiting U.S. government approval of the contract. Robert Pastor, then Latin American staff director at the National Security Council, noted that the Mexicans were clearly warned that the contract might not be approved and that initiating construction of the pipeline was both premature and risky (author interview with Pastor, 1985). Nonetheless, the López Portillo government proceeded with construction, for reasons that are still unclear.

In December 1977, Secretary of Energy James Schlesinger proved the truth of the warnings: the United States would not approve the price set for the Mexican gas. Schlesinger somewhat arrogantly asserted that "sooner or later" Mexico would "sell its gas to the United States" and at prices set by the United States.[5] The pipeline was left unfinished, and PEMEX director Jorge Díaz Serrano claimed that Mexico was willing to wait "two or three years to sell natural gas" (NYT, Jan. 6, 1978). Yet just two years later Mexico capitulated and began to supply gas under conditions set by the United States (NYT, Dec. 30, 1979).

A disgusted López Portillo vented his anger at a meeting with President Carter in Mexico City in February 1979, in what was the most contentious presidential summit in history. Carter arrived with the hope of repairing "a growing rift between our two nations," and he reiterated that mending the relationship was a priority issue for the hemisphere (NYT, Feb. 11, 1979). López Portillo, somber to the point of rudeness, refused to cross the tarmac to greet the deplaning Carter at the official airport welcome. Instead, he waited for Carter to come to him where he stood waiting (Levy and Székely 1983: 183). López Portillo also refused to organize the usual welcoming parade. No multitudes greeted Carter, as they had Truman, de Gaulle, Tito, Johnson, Kennedy, and so many others. No flags, no mariachis, only a sullen López Portillo who, over a grim official dinner, stated that "our peoples need definitive accords, and not circumstantial concessions." He added that Mexico "resented [the United States'] mistrust, hostility and disdain" and that Mexico had become the center of the United States' attention only as a result of its new-found oil wealth (NYT, Feb. 15, 1979).

---

[5]On the evolution of this affair, see NYT, Aug. 5 and 16, Sept. 24, and Dec. 17, 24, 30, 1977.

Carter, not anticipating such open and public hostility, erred in keeping to his prepared script. His speech, presented in a tense atmosphere punctuated with nervous titters, began with some light humor about Carter's stomach upsets during his honeymoon in Mexico, hardly an auspicious opening, given the general mood.

It is highly revealing of U.S. culture that, rather than rebut López Portillo's statements, Americans accepted them as "harsh realities." For years, noted Alan Riding, "Mexico has been perhaps too well-mannered, and certainly too weak, to state them" (NYT 1979b). No previous encounter between the U.S. and Mexican heads of state had produced such extensive criticism of a U.S. president in the *Times*. A number of journalists interpreted López Portillo's words as a "public chastisement of the United States." Carter's weakness was never forgiven.[6]

The relationship between Carter and López Portillo, already severely strained, was further tested when the shah of Iran, who had been deposed a month before the Carter–López Portillo summit, was granted political asylum in Mexico. The shah, elderly and in poor health, left his luxurious residence in Cuernavaca in November 1979 to travel to New York for medical treatment, with Mexico promising to readmit him when the treatment ended. While the shah was in the United States, "students" seized the U.S. Embassy in Tehran, took hostages, and demanded that the shah be returned to Iran. Mexico then reneged on its promise to readmit the shah, stating simply that a return visa could not be provided. The United States was forced to allow the shah to remain on American soil and endure a prolonged and ugly hostage situation in the Middle East.

In response to Mexico's refusal to honor the rule of providing mutual support in times of need, Senator Lloyd Bentsen of Texas accused Mexico of "egoism and cowardice" (Levy and Székely 1983: 188–91). Secretary of State Cyrus Vance wrote later that the U.S. government never understood why "López Portillo reneged on his commitments" (Vance 1983: 382). In his memoirs, Carter recalled that he was "furious. . . . We were guaranteed that the Shah would be welcome. . . . López Portillo's word was not to be trusted" (1983: 468). This was the only time during the period under study that a Mexican president failed the United States. The incident also produced the most extended reference to a Mexican president to be found in any U.S. president's memoirs.

Carter's failure to deal decisively and successfully with the hostage crisis in Iran was largely responsible for his loss to Ronald Reagan in November 1980. Never before had Mexico exerted such influence on a U.S. presidential election. It was an exceptional moment,

---

[6]One Carter critic was Tom Wicker; see, for example, Wicker 1979.

and it also demonstrated the U.S. elite's broad tolerance for the Mexican leadership. This was not the result of any respect on the part of the United States for the principles of Mexican foreign policy since, as mentioned above, Washington has never taken Mexican nationalism very seriously. What underlies this tolerance are the issues of stability and proximity: events in Mexico can have immediate repercussions on U.S. territory. When Eisenhower wrote that "we have an over 2,000–mile, undefended border" (1965: 515), he was voicing one of the United States' chronic anxieties.

The U.S. elite tolerated López Portillo's discourtesies because it was in their interest to do so: they wanted access to Mexico's oil bonanza. In 1979, despite the ill-fated Carter–López Portillo summit, the U.S. media's references to the Mexican economy were typically optimistic (figures 67–68). Riding, for example, suggested that López Portillo was "betting heavily on industrial expansion," which would lead to "less inflation and more jobs." By the year 2000, Riding predicted, the Mexican economy would be completely transformed (NYT, Dec. 9, 1979).

A Temporarily Independent Diplomacy

López Portillo felt that the time was ripe for a foreign policy more suitable to a nation with rich oil resources. For the first and only time in the four decades examined in the content analysis, Mexico's independence went beyond rhetorical, ceremonial radicalism to address more concrete issues such as political events in Central America. Predictably, this new configuration provoked "conflict with the United States on a growing number of issues" (NYT, Apr. 24, 1980).

Conflicts did not surface immediately. In fact, during the Sandinista insurrection in Nicaragua (1977–1979), there was relative agreement between Carter and López Portillo. Carter had already denounced Anastasio Somoza for his human rights violations. López Portillo, eager to flex Mexico's new oil-based muscle in the international arena, was happy to back the Nicaraguan guerrillas, to the point of stating that Mexico would "defend the cause of Nicaragua as its own" (NYT, May 8, 1981).

López Portillo became one of the Sandinistas' staunchest supporters. According to Cheryl Eschbach (1991), Mexico funneled over U.S.$1 billion to the Sandinistas, due in large part to the fact that they appealed to something deep within López Portillo—in the oft-repeated pattern of a Mexican president with a revolutionary's soul.[7]

---

[7]Carlos Salinas, for example, professed deep admiration for Emiliano Zapata, although his government program would scarcely have pleased the late revolutionary.

In 1981 López Portillo, when asked whether he was a socialist, responded, "no, but I am a converted revolutionary. The Mexican Revolution of 1910 offers a third path between the two great currents that are now vying for world hegemony" (NYT, Aug. 29, 1981). The Sandinistas reaped the benefits of the president's empathy; a Sandinista leader recalled that, in meetings with López Portillo, the latter would "sometimes slap the table and say, 'Well, *muchachos*, what do you need?'" (NYT, May 8, 1981).

Mexico's new vigor in foreign policy found other outlets as well. One was Mexico's recognition, along with France, of the Farabundo Martí National Liberation Front as a "representative political force" in El Salvador (NYT, Aug. 29, 1981). Another was Mexico's support for Cuba; López Portillo identified Cuba as the Latin American nation "best loved" by Mexico and as an example for "our region, the continent, and the world" (NYT, Feb. 21, 1981).

Although Mexico's activism was made possible by oil revenues, it was also nourished by an increasingly acrimonious debate on Central America taking place in the United States. New ideas were opening unexplored areas and challenging the rules that governed relationships of domination in the hemisphere. There were widespread feelings of solidarity with Central America. Documents from the era reveal that Mexico's policies toward Central America enjoyed substantial support from liberal and progressive sectors in the United States. A *Times* editorial urged Washington to allow Mexico and France to assume "the risks of promoting a political accord" in El Salvador (NYT 1981). Richard Fagen (1981) suggested that Mexico's proposals, informed by a "historically conditioned understanding of the forces at work in Central America and the Caribbean" could be useful. In the spring of 1981, one hundred U.S. congressmen called upon the State Department to "consider the Franco-Mexican initiative, which supported the Frente Farabundo Martí de Liberación Nacional and the Frente Democrático Revolucionario as legitimate actors in El Salvador" (Hannon 1984: 5).

U.S. conservatives, of course, were highly critical of Mexico's position, calling it a mistake due either to naiveté or bad faith. The Republicans—who came to power with Ronald Reagan in January 1981—felt that Mexico was turning a blind eye to Cuban and Soviet involvement in Nicaragua and support for the Salvadoran guerrillas (see Menges 1988; Hannon 1984).

U.S. explanations for Mexico's new foreign policy direction were many and diverse. Some analysts saw López Portillo's stance in the international arena as intended, as in the past, "to appease Mexican leftists who frequently criticize his conservative domestic economic policies" (NYT, Apr. 25, 1980). Others suggested that Mexico's new diplomatic posture was an appropriate one for a midsized, emerging power that sought to establish "political leadership in Central America and the Caribbean to offset the traditional influence of both the United States and Cuba." Still others noted that Mexico could not afford to see the region become a focus of "East-West tensions" (NYT, Aug. 20, 1980). It is very revealing that not a single U.S. analyst even considered the possibility that López Portillo's foreign policies might be guided by the traditional principles of Mexican diplomacy—despite the fact that this message was repeated over and over again in official Mexican discourse.

The situation in Central America also hastened Mexico's opening to the outside. During this era, Mexican intellectuals like Carlos Fuentes and Jorge Castañeda began defending Mexico's foreign policy in the U.S. press (Fuentes 1980; Castañeda 1982a, 1982b). Their efforts were seen as one more step in the internationalization of Mexican diplomacy, which would eventually transform the bilateral relationship and generate feedback effects on Mexico's political system. Traditional Mexican definitions of sovereignty and nationalism gave way as key Mexican actors maneuvered for influence or alliances with U.S. sectors concerned with Mexico.

PROLOGUE TO CRISIS

Policy differences regarding Central America faded into the background and economic considerations assumed center stage as the López Portillo administration wore on. In order to open its oil fields for exploration—and thereby reinvigorate the nation's stalled economy—Mexico needed money. To get it, the government decided to borrow, increasing its external debt burden and consigning fiscal reform to the dustbin. Foreign bankers, eager to share in Mexico's oil boom, were happy to oblige. They competed among themselves to finance a $117 billion, six-year expansion program to develop Mexico's oil industry and economy (NYT, Jan. 10, 1979). For Mexico, this meant an enormous and sudden influx of financial resources—from oil sales, foreign investment, and foreign loans. Mexico's foreign debt skyrocketed from $20 billion in 1976 to $80 billion in 1982.

By 1980, Mexico's economy was showing serious signs of strain. In August of that year, Alan Riding noted that the "feeling is growing that President José López Portillo will pass along an economic crisis in 1982" (NYT, Aug. 22, 1980). Riding's comment mirrors the frustration with Mexico that was gaining ground in the United States and coming from a variety of sources, both obvious and obscure. One incident that clearly detracted from Mexico's reputation in the United States was the blowout of the Ixtoc I oil well in the Gulf of Mexico in summer 1979. Mexico refused to accept liability for the spill's damage to the U.S. coastline, despite numerous protests from Washington. This incident, in which U.S. interests were directly affected, provoked a stream of criticism of Mexico's oil policies as a whole. These included accusations of corruption, some directly targeted against PEMEX director Jorge Díaz Serrano (NYT, Aug. 22, 1979).

The disillusionment of U.S. participants in this debate also derived in part from guarded reappraisals of Mexico's real, rather than proclaimed, oil wealth (author interviews). During the early days of the oil boom, the Mexican government trumpeted the news of vast reserves. Even normally cautious U.S. government officials seem to have accepted Mexico's claims, and U.S. official documents, including PRM-41, report that Mexico had proven reserves totaling some 57 billion barrels of crude and an additional 220 billion barrels in probable future discoveries, a supply for which Washington was clearly willing to do almost anything (NSC 1978).

In 1980, David Ronfeldt, Richard Nehring, and Arturo Gándara of the Rand Corporation concluded that in fact Mexico had no more than 18.9 billion barrels in proven reserves and only 19 billion barrels in probable reserves (Ronfeldt, Nehring, and Gándara 1980: v, ix–x). The disappointing downward adjustment in estimates of Mexican oil had serious repercussions in Washington and prompted thoroughgoing revisions to U.S. oil strategies. U.S. interest in Mexican oil diminished, and the Mexican leadership's margins for maneuver narrowed. Washington's long-standing mistrust of Mexican government data appeared to have been validated.

Reports of endemic corruption in Mexico were soon widespread. They included details about the first family's expenditures and "persistent reports of numerous high officials with interests in private companies that win government contracts" (NYT, Sept. 6, 1981). References to Mexican corruption reached their highest point in forty-one years in 1982, the last year of the López Portillo administration (figure 93). Interestingly, although corruption received substantial, though intermittent, attention in the United States, there were no serious or systematic analyses of it. The first text dedicated to this topic did not appear until 1991 (Morris 1991). Nor were there any Mexican studies on corruption, which may explain some of the relative indifference regarding this topic in the United States.

What is undeniably clear is that in the latter years of his term, López Portillo's image suffered. Between 1976 and 1981, *Times* references to him were overwhelmingly favorable. This pattern reversed itself when the Mexican economy went into a tailspin, and López Portillo's image sustained further injury as a result of later media coverage of corruption in high places in Mexico (figures 22–23).

16

The 1982 Crisis and Its Consequences

FROM REFORMISM TO A CONSERVATIVE REVOLUTION

Although the devaluation of the peso in 1982 followed the pattern set by the preceding devaluation in 1976, it differed in the details. During the earlier period, the United States, in fact the entire global economy, was undergoing important transformations, which must be included in any analysis of this critical moment in Mexico's recent history. Attesting to the viability and adaptability of the American system, many of the changes incubating in the United States throughout the turbulent 1960s were being institutionalized: Congress imposed new limits on executive power, placed stricter controls on intelligence agencies, and strengthened protections for individual rights. The Freedom of Information Act (which permitted the release to the public of many of the documents quoted in this volume) dates from this period.

Meanwhile, the enormous power the United States had amassed since the end of World War II began to wane (though only in relative terms; it would rebound spectacularly a few years later). As U.S. power lessened, Washington had to make corresponding adjustments to the nation's foreign policy. The balance of world power was also affected by the dramatic economic recovery of Japan and the countries of Western Europe, intersecting with a downturn in U.S. productivity and a surge in the United States' rate of inflation, federal budget deficit, and trade deficit. This process was exacerbated by the crushing costs—human, political, and economic—of the Vietnam War (Brittan 1983; Garten 1985; Hormats 1986). Not surprisingly, a realignment of world power became a charged issue during the 1970s.

Congressional hearings convened by Representative Donald Fraser in 1973 reflected another important change. The hearings focused on how the United States could, through the implementation of foreign policy, encourage repressive regimes to improve their human rights record. One outcome of this new linkage was the International Security Assistance and Arms Export Control Act of 1976–77, which prohibits the granting of "security assistance to a government which has a consistent pattern of gross violations [of human rights]"(B. Smith 1982: 279).[1]

The implementation of these revamped U.S. foreign policy priorities fell to a new generation of congressional politicians. Following in the wake of the Watergate scandal, the 1974 midterm elections gave Democrats an overwhelming majority in the U.S. Congress.[2] The elections also opened congressional doors to a new school of politicians (including Fraser) who had been sensitized by personal experience in Latin America, Africa, and Asia, usually as academics or Peace Corps volunteers. These new politicians had witnessed first-hand the grimmest aspects of oppression and the direct impacts of U.S. foreign policies. They enjoyed the support—and felt the pressure—of a number of nongovernmental human rights organizations and religious groups with links to counterpart groups in Latin America.

Jimmy Carter's election in 1976 transformed U.S. discourse and policies toward Latin America. Inspired by recommendations put forth in the Linowitz Reports of 1975 and 1976, which called for increased respect for national sovereignty and human rights, Carter cut back, and sometimes suspended, military aid to Argentina, Chile, Brazil, El Salvador, Guatemala, Nicaragua, and Uruguay. Further, to demonstrate Washington's determination on the human rights front, Carter decided to make an example of Nicaraguan dictator Anastasio Somoza, incidentally facilitating the triumph of the country's left-wing Sandinista Front for National Liberation (FSLN). And yet U.S. attitudes toward human rights abuses in Mexico remained unchanged: indifference and silence continued to prevail.

Republicans retook the White House four years later, putting an end to Carter's activist policies. The upswell that carried Ronald Reagan to the presidency in 1980 reflected a realignment of social forces in the United States and the appearance of new political strategies. This movement—the New Right—evolved in California and other southwestern states and drew its strength from the growing community of religious fundamentalists. It arose in direct response to the country's socioeconomic problems and the general malaise stemming from the United States' diminished global status. And it fed on a

---

[1] For a general overview of the role of human rights in U.S. foreign policy, see P. Fagen 1980. A series of yearly State Department reports on the global human rights situation, commissioned by Congress in 1976, provides valuable insight into the nature and evolution of the United States' policies toward Mexico.

[2] There were 243 Democrats in the House, versus 188 Republicans (four seats were vacant at the beginning of the session). The tally in the Senate was 57 Democrats, 41 Republicans, and 2 Independents.

swelling undercurrent of anger and prejudice kindled by the activism of racial and sexual minorities and antiwar protesters (Wolfe 1981).

Another important factor in the Right's ascent was that its ideological pronouncements rested on a well-articulated theoretical foundation, developed in generously financed conservative research centers. This foundation included, among other elements, the theory of supply-side economics (Laffer and Seymour 1979; Wanniski 1978; Gilder 1981). The international-level counterpart of this intellectual and political revolution was "structural adjustment policies"—or neoliberalism. Throughout this period, liberal and progressive sectors failed to generate new ideas to counter those of the conservative camp, underscoring once again the fundamental role that ideas play in political action.

The conservatives, pledged to a thoroughgoing reorientation of U.S. foreign policy, aimed to reimplement containment measures and return to a period in which the will of the United States prevailed worldwide and "anti-Communism" was a magical incantation used to reduce and simplify realities that were in fact enormously complex. Not only had Carter been naive, conservative arguments ran; he had put the security of the United States at risk, and the clearest example of this was Central America. The Sandinistas in Nicaragua and the guerrillas in El Salvador had to be stopped. As Reagan put it, the stakes were no less than "the security of America as a whole." The conservatives were absolutely convinced that the Communists saw Mexico as their next target and the prize jewel in their hemispheric sphere of influence.

This view served only to aggravate—and probably prolong—the conflict in Central America. Conservative Washington proved unable to impose its will absolutely; it could eradicate neither the Sandinistas nor the Salvadoran guerrillas. It succeeded only in debilitating and destabilizing both forces, in the process contributing significantly to the devastation and human suffering in both countries. The conservatives' failure to prevail was due in large part to opposition within the United States. This is remarkable, especially when contrasted with the broad freedom that Eisenhower, also a Republican, enjoyed in his actions against Jacobo Arbenz in 1954.

The U.S. movement for solidarity with progressive forces in Central America was to become one of the most expansive in the history of the United States. It grew out of the social networks established in the 1960s and owed its existence, first, to a higher level of awareness regarding Central American affairs and, second, to the appearance of new actors (Europe, Cuba, and Mexico) with both the will and the margins for maneuver needed to oppose regional policies advocated by the United States. Developments in Central America attest to the profound transformations that had taken place, in both the United

States and the world: despite the rise of conservatism and the might of the United States, a Republican administration ultimately had been unable to impose its will on even the smallest of nations.

This outcome reflects the deeper forces that were at work within the international system. The globalization of economic and political activity introduced new actors onto the world stage who were undermining the great powers' entrenched hegemony. Large corporations were creating economic networks that were relatively autonomous from any nation-state. Meanwhile, independent social organizations proliferated and linked up in new global networks with counterpart organizations in other countries. Acting jointly on issues such as the defense of human rights or the environment, these groups have succeeded in severely hindering government action and have themselves become an important new force.

Over the course of the 1980s, the way in which relationships of domination operated underwent significant change. Although it followed traditional lines in its intervention in Central America, the United States was simultaneously working to reorient its economic policies and the manner in which it implemented these policies, both regionally and globally. One individual's evolution illustrates these changes. Robert McNamara, a hawkish secretary of defense under President Kennedy, became a converted liberal; as president of the World Bank (1968–1982), McNamara announced his intention to serve the basic human needs of the poorest populations by reorienting development policies toward addressing the root of the problem—inequality. What is remarkable about McNamara's metamorphosis is the fact that, in the new environment produced by the profound transformations in U.S. worldview, society was easily able to take it in stride; such personal evolution was, in effect, socially acceptable.

A World Bank report issued in 1981 suggests that, by that year, McNamara's era and its accompanying notion of development with equality had come to an end (World Bank 1981). The pattern had reverted, once again, to the North imposing its will on the South through the establishment of adjustment programs tailored to "liberalize trade regimes, privatize state enterprises, cut government expenditures, raise interest rates, and generally become 'market-friendly'" (Mkandawire 1995: 1). These were the beginnings of a neoliberal revolution that would redefine development and the arsenal of mechanisms with which to promote it, generally via international financial institutions.

In Mexico, the now exhausted economic model inherited from the revolution and the equally exhausted leadership entrenched around it—along with the rapid rise of a new group of "technocrats"[3] through

---

[3]Headed by Carlos Salinas de Gortari and José Córdoba Montoya.

the ranks of the de la Madrid administration—allowed this neoliberal revolution to gain a firm foothold in Mexico. The fortunes of the new technocrats rose at a rate on par with the rate of the peso's decline in 1982; following the devaluation this group appeared to be the only one with a seemingly viable plan for economic recovery and the know-how to conduct negotiations with the U.S. government and international institutions.

These extensive transformations forced a redefinition of concepts previously thought to be immutable, such as "border," "sovereignty," and "intervention," to name a few. This process of redefinition can even be seen as almost imperceptibly laying the foundations for a new universal culture, whose complexity stems in part from the fact that it brings together ideas and assumptions traditionally considered to be mutually exclusive. The ramifications of these new definitions have touched the United States, Mexico, the bilateral relationship, and the Mexican political system, but not in equal measure.

THE RITE OF DEVALUATION

The U.S. elite was acutely aware of the deterioration of the Mexican economy. The *Times* began publishing reports critical of the country's financial situation, inflation, unemployment, and declining living standards as early as 1981. Most analysts were convinced that the peso was overvalued vis-à-vis the dollar (figures 69–70) (NYT, Apr. 6, 1981). Repeating the pattern of events in 1976, the *Times*'s first reference was to a "possible devaluation in the future" (NYT, Jan. 8, 1981), with the author noting that "business executives and senior Government officials, reveling in the fruits of record company profits, exorbitant salaries, and endemic corruption," were becoming visibly nervous (NYT, Jan. 11, 1981). The *Times* also suggested that "more than half of the capital which enters as foreign investment exits the country as profits or royalties" (NYT, Mar. 24, 1979). Meanwhile, high-ranking members of the López Portillo administration continued to cater to the fantasies of this president who seemed to have lost touch with reality; they dismissed warnings of approaching economic crisis as the pessimistic prognostications of traitors, malcontents, or "enemies of the president."

López Portillo's unreal universe—the product of a political system in which there are no restraints on presidential power—was at the root of an incident reported widely in the U.S. media. In mid–1981, with the international oil market glutted with oversupply, PEMEX director Jorge Díaz Serrano cut the price of Mexican crude. An indignant López Portillo summarily fired Díaz Serrano and in June 1981 declared that Mexico would not be coerced by forces in the international market. He reimposed the higher price for Mexican crude and warned clients that if they refused to pay his price they could forget about Mexico as an energy source in the future (NYT, June 17, 1981). When France refused to pay the price, the Mexican government canceled several French purchase contracts. López Portillo's feud with the international oil market was short-lived; after only two months PEMEX lowered its price to the level Díaz Serrano had proposed (NYT, Aug. 5, 1981).

The media continued to allude to a possible devaluation of the peso, whose parity with the dollar depended on Mexico's oil revenues. López Portillo blustered along, even declaring that he would defend the peso "like a dog" (NYT, July 18, 1981). While the president rehearsed his memorable one-liners, the *Times* published the facts on Mexico's foreign debt, which would exceed $10 billion in 1981. And the situation would get worse in light of the fact that international banks were continuing to make loans to Mexico (NYT, July 6, 1981).

Despite Mexico's rapidly deteriorating economic situation, Washington remained supportive of López Portillo and his government. In August 1981, the United States signed a five-year purchase contract under which Mexico would supply oil for the U.S. strategic reserves at a price that slightly exceeded expectations (NYT, Aug. 21, 1981). The agreement was remarkable in many respects, not least of which was the way in which the Mexican government manipulated how it was presented to the public. By changing the way it categorized the types of exported oil, "Mexico's leadership was able to create the impression that a small price increase had been won" (NYT, Sept. 2, 1981), although the government's official releases stated simply that sales would be made "at current official prices" (*El Nacional*, Aug. 21, 1981).

In late 1981 and early 1982, the *Times* began alerting its readership to the massive amounts of capital fleeing Mexico and predicting that "a repetition of the large devaluation in August 1976" was imminent (NYT, Dec. 24, 1981). The first devaluation in 1982, on February 19, shattered López Portillo's image; henceforth he would be "a devalued President" (NYT, May 23, 1982). In May 1982, López Portillo appointed Jesús Silva Herzog as minister of finance, and Mexico's economy began to show some signs of improvement, though these were transitory. The temporary upswing was due largely to the U.S. government's raised expectations, which grew out of its respect and admiration for Silva Herzog. The new minister was praised for displaying "a frankness rare among those responsible for the Mexican economy" and described as a "scrupulously honest man," high distinction indeed at a moment when references to Mexico's endemic corruption were at an all-time high (NYT, Aug. 21, 1982).

However, respect for Silva Herzog alone could not prevent another devaluation, which occurred in August 1982 and required yet another U.S. rescue operation. Although internal government documents from this period have not yet been released, events seem to have followed lines very similar to those of 1976, and U.S. aid to Mexico was conditional on Mexico's agreement to significant concessions. For example, the *Times* quoted a confidential State Department memorandum to the effect that, because of the crisis, Mexico would sell "more oil and gas [to the United States] at better prices," might be forced to reduce restrictions on foreign investment, would cooperate in reducing illegal migration, and would negotiate a trade agreement with the United States (NYT, Aug. 14, 1982).

An enraged Mexican government stridently denied making any such concessions. These denials were almost simultaneous with López Portillo's discussions with IMF experts regarding the conditions for yet another loan (NYT, Aug. 17, 1982). No agreement was reached, and as the summer of 1982 wore on, Mexico's foreign currency reserves diminished to next to nothing. Silva Herzog had no option but to travel to Washington where, in one weekend, he was able to negotiate a multi-million-dollar loan. Eventually it came to light that in his negotiations Silva Herzog had been forced to accept many of the concessions predicted in the leaked State Department memorandum (NYT, Aug. 21, 1982). Once again, the avowed nationalism of government officials aside, it is clear that Mexico's sovereignty and independence are often infringed upon by foreign interests as long as these interests are willing to remain in the background.

The concessions were significant. Mexico would increase its oil and gas exports to the United States, and a price ceiling of $35 dollars/barrel was set for Mexican crude, to remain in effect even if it was overtaken by prices on the world market. A energy specialist writing for the *Times* noted that "the United States, so far as is known, never before has been able to obtain price protection." Furthermore, Mexico promised to increase the quality of its crude. It is revealing that the U.S. elite saw these extraordinary concessions as their due; the *Times* noted that Mexico could now be accepted as a friend and "ally" of the United States (NYT, Aug. 21, 1982).

Yet despite these significant concessions, Mexico was not yet out of the woods. As a condition for Silva Herzog's "jumbo" loan, the Mexican government would have to institute an IMF-approved economic program. To this end, the World Bank and the U.S. Federal Reserve set up a committee to "analyze Mexico's total debt picture and . . . establish a realistic fiscal and monetary program" (NYT, Aug. 21, 1982). Mexico's ambassador to Washington during this period, Bernardo Sepúlveda, conceded that these accords were "the bitter medicine we will have to swallow" (NYT, Aug. 31, 1982). Of course, what was really being negotiated in Washington was no more and no less than the economic model created by the Mexican Revolution. In 1982, unlike 1976, there was a conservative in the White House and the basic attitude of international financial institutions was completely changed. Coercion was no longer carried out by government agencies but by impersonal multilateral financial institutions.

THE NATIONALIZED BANKS AND THE IMF ACCORDS

Obstinately refusing to accept the conditions laid down by the IMF, an entrenched López Portillo hunkered down in Los Pinos to prepare his final State of the Nation Address, to contain the surprising announcement that he had nationalized the Mexican banking system.[4] Interestingly, U.S. banks reacted favorably to the address, at least initially, believing that nationalization was the only measure that could "save the private banks from insolvency." After this surprising first reaction, the U.S. elite switched position and united in vociferously condemning the nationalization, interpreted as a blow against private enterprise, the desperate act of a president seeking to "shift some of the blame for Mexico's severe economic problems away from his administration" (NYT, Sept. 2, 1982; also Apr. 4, 1982). Mexican politicians, on the other hand, applauded López Portillo. Alan Riding interviewed one anonymous "influential Government politician" who believed that the nationalization of the banking system was destined to become "a political symbol that no future President would dare touch" (NYT, Sept. 3, 1982).[5] But even this spectacular initiative did not derail negotiations between Mexico and the International Monetary Fund. Apparently hoping for a miracle, López Portillo continued to reject the IMF's conditions.[6] When no miracle was forthcoming and Miguel de la Madrid was only days away from being inaugurated as Mexico's next president, López Portillo finally agreed to the IMF's "austerity program" in November 1982 and signed a confidential memorandum of understanding that included "details of how Mexico's public sector deficit would be reduced," such as doubling domestic gasoline prices and the value-added tax, cutting food subsidies, and imposing a government hiring freeze (NYT, Nov. 19, 1982). Throughout this process, Washington continued to support Mexico's

---

[4] Only a week prior to the announcement, the international banks had warned Mexico that it "must affirm its support of the private banks or . . . be cut off from all credit" (NYT, Sept. 2, 1982).

[5] It is likely that this same politician was among the congressmen who later willingly reprivatized the banking system when ordered to do so by Carlos Salinas de Gortari.

[6] The *Times* noted that López Portillo wished to avoid creating the "impression that he had allowed the IMF to dictate Mexico's economic policies."

established order, repairing somewhat the damage to the nationalistic image of Mexico's government officials.

The full significance of the IMF accord was not immediately apparent. Clearly, the economic model inherited from the Mexican Revolution was failing—largely because of the mistakes of administrations that had been either unable or unwilling to make needed adjustments to it. But in jettisoning the economic model, Mexico was also abandoning its long-standing myths, its "collective dreams" of social justice and a development path independent of the United States. And here we must not forget that, in Mexico, democracy had been largely sacrificed in the pursuit of these objectives.

Further, the impacts of the IMF accord were not limited to the economic sphere. Mexico's insolvency had serious repercussions on its foreign policy. U.S. analysts noted that Mexico's activism in Central America waned as the crisis deepened. In September 1981, the *Times* noted that "Mexico's self-assurance has suddenly been shaken by the drop in world oil prices" (NYT, Sept. 13, 1981). The flood of tens of thousands of Guatemalan refugees into Chiapas in the early 1980s allowed Mexico to experience first-hand some of the consequences of the Central American conflict and provoked a response that clearly demonstrated the shallowness of the Mexican government's commitment to the cause. Invoking national security—and in direct contradiction to Mexico's traditional hospitality to asylum-seekers—the government strongly resisted admitting the refugees encamped just beyond Mexico's southern border (NYT, Nov. 23, 1980, Mar. 21, 1982). Tens of thousands were eventually admitted but only after the international community and scores of independent organizations brought pressure to bear.

Moving out of its role as activist for change in Central America, Mexico began to take up the relatively lighter mantle of mediator. In November 1981, the *Times* reported that Mexico had offered its services as an "intermediary" between Nicaragua and the United States (NYT, Nov. 27, 29, 1981). U.S. strategists were relieved to see Mexico return to its traditional—and more familiar and less irritating—diplomatic principles. In fact, Mexico had no choice. This was the only option open to a nation whose dreams of vast oil wealth had rapidly devolved into nightmares of crisis, debt, and devaluation.

Thus 1982 marked the end of the only period in recent history in which Mexico attained real independence in its foreign policy and could challenge the U.S. government on matters of substance in which Mexico had a direct interest. President Miguel de la Madrid Hurtado, inaugurated in late 1982, redirected Mexican diplomacy along a path of pragmatic moderation, although defending Mexican government interests remained an important consideration. De la Madrid also continued to uphold the traditional myth that Mexico's foreign policy is based on principles rather than self-interest.

SEARCHING FOR SCAPEGOATS

The U.S. elite certainly believed that it was responsible for saving Mexico from insolvency—and thereby keeping the PRI in power, although the media tended to remain silent on the issue out of courtesy. Nevertheless, a few journalists, including conservative columnist William Safire, did state publicly what many held privately. Safire noted that, until recently, "Mexican politicians delighted in denouncing the United States; . . . during the worst of the oil squeeze of the 70's [they] rejected our requests for oil and gas . . . thumbing their noses at the needs of the 'colossus of the north.'" But now that Mexico was bankrupt, he added, those very "oligarchs turned for help to the ally of last resort," the United States (Safire 1982). What Safire did not mention is that this "ally of last resort" supported the Mexican oligarchy only because it was in its best interest to do so.

The U.S. elite also began assigning culpability for the devaluation. The consensus was that responsibility lay with governing officials in Mexico. However, a few observers with a fuller knowledge of Mexico suggested that blame should probably be dispersed more broadly. For example, Susan Kaufman Purcell noted that although the devaluation was largely a "result of serious miscalculation and incautious economic conduct," it was due in part to "foreign banks' willingness to keep pouring money into the country" (Purcell 1982). Other analysts blamed U.S. companies for encouraging corruption by funneling bribes to officials in Mexico, such as the millions of dollars that went to PEMEX officials (NYT, May 5, 1982). At least some segment of the U.S. elite was willing to accept that the United States had contributed, in part, to the Mexican debacle.

Alan Riding explored an interesting vein when he placed a share of the responsibility on Mexico's "prosperous businessmen" and government officials.[7] According to Riding's calculations, private businessmen and politicians had spirited at least U.S.$14 billion out of Mexico and invested approximately $30 billion in U.S. real estate. He noted that "even close members of the President's family are reported to have acquired homes in Miami and Seville, Spain" (NYT, Sept. 4, 1982). Riding later quoted an anonymous government official, who suggested that the business community "was given such generous subsidies and tax incentives. It earned such incredible profits. And

---

[7]Mexico's business sector was criticized more frequently in 1982 than in any year since 1946 (figure 76).

now it won't make any sacrifices" (NYT, Apr. 12, 1982). Such criticism of the business sector was rare, however.

Also mentioned in discussions of what lay behind the peso devaluation was "the consumer frenzy of the upper classes" (NYT, Jan. 11, 1981). The *Times* reported the case of a rich Mexican who went to Houston to buy "silk sheets, at $1,400 a pair, for his 9-year-old girl" (NYT, Oct. 7, 1982). Examples along these same lines raised U.S. awareness regarding what such extravagance on the part of politicians and businessmen might mean for those on the lower rungs of Mexican society. Reporters also noted in passing that "one result of the boom was an even greater concentration of income in a country where 10% of the population has traditionally controlled 50% of the wealth" (NYT, Aug. 23, 1982).

THE EMBODIMENTS OF CONSCIOUSNESS

Perceptions of Mexico during the López Portillo administration tended to follow one of two lines. The traditional (and predominant) inclination was to view Mexico through the rose-colored glasses of self-interest, always accentuating the positive. The second and more critical tendency was to see Mexico's flaws as well as its strong points. Both viewpoints were based on an improved, though still imperfect, understanding of Mexico.

The most revealing window on the predominant and more optimistic tendency is what its proponents deliberately *did not say*. For example, the U.S. government was well aware of the excesses of Mexico's security police and security agencies, but it decided not to speak out. The U.S. government's appreciation of the true situation in Mexico is confirmed in Presidential Review Memorandum–41. This document, prepared in 1978, notes that "Mexico's domestic human rights record leaves room for significant improvement." However, it continued, "it would be ill-advised and counter-productive for us to take Mexico to task publicly for its violations of human rights." PRM–41 went on to conclude that the most advisable course of action was "to continue our multilateral cooperation, manage a quiet and reasonable dialogue, and encourage human rights improvement on both sides without undue cost to our other interests" (NSC 1978: 1, 3). The United States' decision to overlook the human rights abuses committed by the authoritarian Mexican regime also appears in the annual reports on the human rights situation worldwide that the U.S. State Department has prepared since 1976. A clear pattern emerges in these documents: they consistently minimize the seriousness of the problem and thus avoid criticizing the Mexican government.

This pattern has held true across administrations, some liberal, others conservative. Its durability can be attributed to the fact that the U.S. government, although fully apprised of the true nature of the PRI, also recognized that it needed the PRI in order to guarantee its own interests. Thus, on the one hand the media reported that even though the Mexican government made concessions in order to maintain its "democratic image," these concessions did not apply to "Indians and peasants, striking workers or squatter organizers" and, further, that "the heirs of the Zapatistas are still impoverished, many lacking lands or the means to maintain themselves." The Mexican regime was no longer portrayed as democratic; "authoritarian" and "a combination of authoritarianism and democracy" became the new descriptors (NYT, July 31, 1979; Feb. 17, 1980; Jan. 11, 1981). On the other hand, however, the media credited the PRI with preserving Mexico's cherished stability, even though it now did so through "a complex network of loyalties, favors, and influences."

Alan Riding sometimes criticized corruption in Mexico while at other times he praised the PRI as "one of the world's most efficient political machines," admired by "many governments that would like to perpetuate themselves in power" (NYT, Mar. 4, 1979). Peter Smith also expressed admiration for the system's capacity to overcome crises. Thus the U.S. elite remained (and remains) ambivalent toward Mexican authoritarianism. They do not respect it; but because they need it they are willing to support and solidify it.

Despite their ability to entertain this fundamental contradiction, the U.S. elite had overcome many entrenched misportrayals of Mexico and amplified their potential consciousness. Thus, although Mexico's Communist Party received no positive references during the 1980s, the *Times* published only 6 negative ones; the overwhelming majority (42) were informative (figure 33). The Left no longer received more attention than the PRI, as it had during the Cold War, though apparently it did still cause some uneasiness, as reflected in the fact that there were twice as many references to the Mexican Communist Party as to the center-right National Action Party (figures 31–33).

In 1977, for the first time since 1946, a leader of Mexico's Communist Party consented to an interview with the *Times*. Arnoldo Martínez Verdugo outlined to Alan Riding the transformations his party had undergone (NYT, Dec. 27, 1977). Other Riding articles reported on Heberto Castillo and the Mexican Workers' Party (PMT) (NYT, Nov. 23, 1979). Although the media's general disapproval of the Left persisted, it was now tempered by an increasingly realistic awareness of the Left's strengths and weaknesses. Riding provided very accurate portrayals of left-wing organizations which, he noted, were no more than a "domesticated left . . . incapable of exploiting the country's worst domestic crisis in 40 years" (NYT, Oct. 1, 1978). He also emphasized a "persistent problem that has long plagued the Mexican left: its leaders prefer control over small factions, and are unwilling to accept positions of lesser authority in larger organizations" (NYT, Nov. 9, 1981). Media attitudes had come a long way since 1944, when Ambassador George Messersmith chastised *Times* correspondent Camille Cianfarra for interviewing "people of the extreme left" (DOS 1944).

Another indicator of the media's search for a better understanding of Mexican affairs was a new interest in previously ignored issues and actors. The middle classes, intellectuals, students, and the Church were some of the new topics covered in the pages of the *Times* (figure 39). Fascinating new subjects included the artists of CLETA, an independent theater group in Monterrey (referred to as a "Maoist commune"); Mexico City's marginalized underclasses, described as "a vast though as-yet silent urban proletariat"; feminists and dissident intellectuals; the political *desaparecidos*; *pepenadores* (squatters in city dumps who scavenge items for resale), all within a strictly controlled, hierarchical organization.[8]

Such coverage was not limited to the front section. The *Times*'s travel section published an emotional article on the 1968 student movement, in which the reporter recalled "beatings in the night . . . firing squads and tanks and the rights of the people . . . union between the students, workers, and peasants . . . land and bread" (NYT, Oct. 13, 1974). The paper's opinion section also ran a story on the life of a Mexican exile in the United States (NYT, Apr. 1, 1979) and reviewed a novel by Carlos Fuentes about "a group of men enriched through corruption" who betrayed the Mexican Revolution (Shorris 1985).

At about this time, a group of Mexicanists began publishing interpretations of Mexican reality that broke with earlier, more optimistic viewpoints. Two books that appeared about midway through the López Portillo administration characterize this new perspective: Peter Smith's *Labyrinths of Power: Political Recruitment in Twentieth-Century Mexico*, published in 1979, was based on more than six thousand Mexican political biographies. This rigorous piece of work dissected the Mexican political scene and distilled from it twenty-two rules that a would-be politician in Mexico should follow in order to succeed. The absence of principles and prevalence of blatant opportunism that Smith describes are depressingly realistic. If this is how the U.S. elite perceives the Mexican leadership, it is not surprising that they should

---

[8]For a sampling of these topics, see NYT, Sept. 25, 1976; Oct. 23 and Dec. 28, 1977; May 3, Aug. 17, Dec. 2, and Dec. 31, 1979; Aug. 15, 1980; Mar. 19 and 21, Apr. 18, and Dec. 26, 1981; and June 22, 1982. This material also served as a basis for Riding's very successful *Distant Neighbors*.

have been skeptical about Mexican politicians' claims that they were motivated by principles.

Another superb piece of research was Judith Adler Hellman's *Mexico in Crisis*, published in 1978,[9] which includes an excellent description of the mechanisms of co-optation, opposition, and repression employed in Mexico.[10] In her preface, Hellman states that "much of what has been written by Americans regarding contemporary Mexico consists of praise centered on the political stability and economic growth assured by a one-party system" (pp. xii–xiii), while her objective is to present a critical, sophisticated analysis, an objective she fully achieves.

No Mexicanist has ever evaluated or even considered the impact that the United States has on developments in Mexico. When the U.S. government rescued Mexico after the peso devaluation in 1982, it was motivated by the need to defend its own interests. One has to wonder what would have been the outcome had the United States decided not to bail Mexico out of its financial crisis. Although there are no easy answers, Mexico's political crisis might well have deepened. In 1983 discontent had built to the point that the opposition National Action Party was able to score significant electoral victories. The resources that the United States provided gave the Mexican government—and Mexican authoritarianism—a powerful boost. Even so, the International Monetary Fund and the World Bank were able to impose extremely harsh economic guidelines on the government of Miguel de la Madrid, ushering in an era of economic adjustment and a changing of the guard in Mexico's governing elite.

---

[9]According to the *Social Sciences Citation Index*, Hellman's volume is among the most frequently cited analyses of the Mexican political system. Between 1985 and 1995, her book was quoted thirty-four times; Smith's, fourteen.

[10]These mechanisms are very similar to the concepts of hegemony and coercion as used in the present volume.

17

The Technocrats Arrive

For Mexico, the years 1982 to 1986 mark an extraordinary period. The ruling elite's capacity to govern continued to deteriorate, and the impact of external factors on events within the country intensified, to the point that Washington was able in 1986 to dictate a series of key changes to Mexico's economic model. But because these changes were implemented with the utmost sensitivity, the Mexican leadership was able to preserve its nationalistic rhetoric—and remain in power. Thus, by executing a delicate balancing act the two nations were able to sustain their long-term understanding. At the same time, new independent social forces and political actors were appearing and gaining strength in Mexico, although they were not yet able to influence the country's economic policies or liberalize its political system.

THE EARLY DAYS OF THE DE LA MADRID PRESIDENCY

Miguel de la Madrid's administration was characterized by its incorporation of technocrats into the upper echelons of government; 63 percent of his cabinet members had studied abroad (Peter Smith 1986: 103, 109). One of the first Americans to realize the full import of this transformation was Alan Riding. In 1981, while de la Madrid was still campaigning, Riding reported, "over the last four years, politicians have lost ground to the technocrats who now dominate the administration" (NYT, Jan. 11, 1981). Riding also noted that the governing elite itself had failed to perceive the trend: "long accustomed to savoring the past, improvising the present and ignoring the future, the Mexicans woke up one day to find that they were governed by economic planners" (NYT, Apr. 4, 1980).

After missing the mark so widely in his early assessments of Echeverría and López Portillo, Riding was very cautious in his statements

about de la Madrid. Although Riding had always stressed the positive aspects of Mexico's presidents, his coverage of de la Madrid
tended to be very reserved. He called him a "political moderate . . .
popular among the private sector" and someone inclined "to favor
good relations with the United States" (NYT, Sept. 26, 1981). Riding
later noted that "the only untested aspect [of the new president was]
the nature of his response to the extraordinary powers he is beginning
to acquire." An experienced observer of political habits and customs
in Mexico, Riding recalled that "Mexican Presidents invariably sur-
round themselves with sycophants and eventually lose touch with the
country" (NYT, Dec. 2, 1982).

Despite Riding's warnings, the U.S. media continued to perceive
the evolution of Mexico's political system as it had since 1946. The
Times proclaimed that Mexico was making progress on the road to
democracy, and the 1982 elections were described on several occasions as "an important step in Mexico's cautious move away from a
one-party state towards a more democratic society" (NYT, June 29,
1982). As evidence of the prevailing optimism regarding Mexico, of
the 12 references to democratization printed in the *Times* in 1982, 8
were informative and 4 were positive; there were no negative references (figures 35–38).

However, there were some new elements in the media coverage,
such as unprecedented realism. While praising Mexico's progress toward democracy, Riding also faithfully described the "vast propaganda apparatus set in motion" during the 1982 presidential campaign (estimated to have cost close to U.S.$300 million) and the
diversion of government funds into the coffers of the PRI. Riding observed, for example, that during his campaign de la Madrid traveled
in "aircraft from such state entities as the Bank of Mexico, the Federal
Electricity Commission and Petróleos Mexicanos" (NYT, May 25, July
4, 1982). Another novel element was the overall pattern in the media's
assessment of the new administration. During the Echeverría and
López Portillo presidencies, media coverage had followed a progres-
sion from praise early on in the administration to severe criticism by
its end. In contrast, during de la Madrid's term, the media combined
positive and negative references throughout the administration
(figures 22–27).

Respite, but with a Social Cost

When Miguel de la Madrid became president of Mexico on December
1, 1982, the country's economy was in crisis and the regime's room for
maneuver was severely constricted. It came as no surprise, therefore,
that in his inaugural address de la Madrid outlined a new austerity

program, inspired by neoliberal proposals and López Portillo's pledges to the International Monetary Fund (NYT, Jan. 1, 1983). The pay-off came on December 23, when the IMF granted final approval for a U.S.$3.9 billion loan, with a further $2 billion to be provided by ten industrialized nations (NYT, Dec. 24, 1982). Although it is not known exactly what Mexico promised in exchange for this loan, it seems highly probable that one outcome was the government's decision—announced a week later—to sell 34 percent of the shares in Mexico's nationalized banks. The dismantling of the old economic model proceeded apace, and in May 1983 Citibank's vice president, William Rhodes, was able to report that Mexico's economic behavior during the year's initial trimester was "in line with targets set in its agreement with the IMF" (NYT, May 18, 1983). This entailed a "realistic" devaluation of the peso, a reduction in the budget deficit, and the sale (already under way) of "non-essential" state-owned companies.

As part of this process, Mexico enhanced its support to foreign investment. For example, the Mexican government agreed to pay the total construction costs (U.S.$23 million) for a gas pipeline to supply a new Ford manufacturing plant in Hermosillo—prompting varied reactions from Mexican politicians. Although Minister of Trade Héctor Hernández emphasized that "the government was not loosening its regulations on foreign investment," some of his colleagues suggested that "the government would now allow certain foreign companies to acquire majority ownership." In an act charged with historical symbolism, the government allowed IBM to hold total ownership of a new plant in Mexico, even though under Mexican law the computer sector is reserved for domestic producers only (NYT, Sept. 26, 1983; Jan. 11, Feb. 17, May 22, 1984; July 24, 1985).

The Mexican government also remained committed to repaying the country's foreign debt, even as other Latin American nations were debating whether to declare a joint debt moratorium. Washington clearly applauded de la Madrid's decision not to ally with these nations in a united debtors' front, something the United States (faithful to old-style hegemonic domination) claimed would "do grave harm" to Mexico (NYT, Sept. 21, 1984). When in 1984 Mexico successfully renegotiated the terms of its debt with international banks, U.S. praise for the regime rose still further.

De la Madrid's actions in 1983 and 1984 earned him high marks from bankers and international financial institutions (NYT, July 17, 1983). According to World Bank Vice President Ernest Stern, it was "fair to say that the way the people and Government of Mexico have managed their crisis has filled the whole world with admiration" (NYT, Aug. 23, 1983). In "recognition of Mexico's progress in accepting and sticking to a rigid austerity program," the international banking system decided to extend new loans to Mexico toward the end of 1983 (NYT, Dec. 31, 1983). Peaks of improvement in the Mexican economy and the additional loan funds that these peaks elicited explain the positive references that appeared in the *Times* between 1982 and 1984 regarding the general situation of the country's economy and finances (figures 67–70). There was a similar pattern in media assessments of Mexican policies toward foreign investment (figures 77–78).

But austerity policies carried social costs, and there was a rising number of references to issues such as the unequal distribution of income, under- and unemployment, low wages, high prices, inflation, and low living standards in both urban and rural areas (figures 82–90). Barbara Crossette observed that budget cuts were "making health care in Mexico more precarious than ever" (NYT, June 17, 1983), and Richard Meislin noted the "dramatic plunge in the standard of living of workers" (NYT, June 29, 1983). These comments appeared despite Mexican government efforts to downplay the deleterious side effects of the new economic model. Some officials tried to persuade a *Times* correspondent that there were no more "vendors than usual despite the sharp economic downturn" (NYT, Apr. 16, 1984).

Although U.S. interest in the social costs of austerity was increasing, this was not yet a priority issue. For example, income distribution received only 100 mentions between 1946 and 1986 (79 of them negative). In another revealing comparison, over the same 41–year period, poverty was mentioned only 211 times, compared to 596 mentions for tourism and 649 for transportation.

On the Road to Moral Renewal

The cronyism and corruption that pervaded the administration of President López Portillo were so blatant that one of de la Madrid's first acts in office was to initiate a campaign of "moral renewal." This is the period when corruption in Mexico finally took center stage in the U.S. consciousness, and the idea spread that corruption was an integral aspect of Mexican reality. In just four years—1982 to 1986—there were 183 references to corruption, approximately 40 percent of the total of 451 such references in the 41–year period between 1946 and 1986 (figures 91, 93).

De la Madrid's proclamation of an era of moral renewal sparked an enthusiastic response in the United States. The arrest of former PEMEX director Jorge Díaz Serrano was viewed as an important step along this path; more such steps were expected, given that "many top politicians were believed to have enriched themselves illicitly" under López Portillo. However, this morality campaign had limits; the *Times* explained that "a decision had been reached at the highest level" not to prosecute López Portillo for corruption, despite the "widespread belief among Mexicans that he profited greatly" during his incumbency (NYT, June 30, July 6, 1983).

Another welcome announcement was de la Madrid's promise to end the government's unhealthy influence over media coverage, although it was soon reported that "some ministries are beginning to pay off journalists again" (NYT, Apr. 10, 1983). Corruption in the oil workers' union was another target of government attention, but it ultimately became clear that the regime had no intention of taking decisive action against the union. The *Times* resignedly concluded that "the corruption campaign has taken second place to the need to keep Mexican oil—and the foreign dollars it brings—flowing" (NYT, Jan. 18, 1984).

In 1983, disparities within the regime's morality campaign provoked an unprecedented and realistic note in the *Times*: despite the good intentions that each new Mexican administration expressed during its early stages, these tended to "wane in intensity" with each president's "exposure to the system" (NYT, July 27, 1983). This phrase also recalls the United States' usual practice of disassociating Mexican presidents from the negative aspects of the system that sustains and supports them.

Acknowledging the organic relationship between corruption and the political system created an additional problem: how to justify the extensive support given to the Mexican leadership. The solution that was settled on runs as follows: corruption was "essential to the operation and survival of the country's complex and peculiar form of government. The political system has never existed without it, and may well disintegrate if it tries to do so" (NYT, Dec. 16, 1984). That is, corruption—organically linked to the very essence of the regime— was seen as a useful mechanism for maintaining stability.

THE DISPUTE OVER CENTRAL AMERICA

Central America was the primary source of tension in the bilateral relationship between 1982 and 1984. Conservatives in Washington hoped that Mexico's economic crisis would compel de la Madrid to terminate his country's support for leftist forces in Central America. They were to be disappointed; Mexico merely reduced the level of its aid. The National Security Council concluded that Mexico "maintained its public and covert support for the extreme left" in Central America, adding that only "the tone, and not the substance," of its policy had changed (NYT, Apr. 17, 1982). Washington's strong criticism of the Mexican government's activism in Central America stemmed from Ronald Reagan's obsession with Communism. Reagan believed that the goal of the guerrilla movements was both simple and sinister: to destabilize all of Central America, from the Panama Canal to Mexico.[1] The idea of "losing" Mexico—which could affect the United States' status on a global level—was inconceivable.[2]

Convinced that the Mexican government was playing with fire, Washington blamed that country's Ministry of Foreign Affairs, envisioned as a nest of intransigent leftist nationalists (author interview with Elliott Abrams, 1991). Against this backdrop a theory developed regarding Mexico's border with Guatemala: this region of impoverished peasants and refugees was a weak point through which the virus of revolution could escape from Central America and spread northward. That is, the domino theory could be applied to this hemisphere (see Russo 1985; E. Williams 1986; Hannon 1984; Applegate 1985). Some authors were outright alarmists. For example, although he did make certain important points, including the observation that the U.S. government had a "vested interest in viewing the Mexican situation with rose-colored glasses," Sol Sanders nevertheless gave his book the less-than-subtle title *Mexico: Chaos on our Doorstep* (Sanders 1986: 193).

Meanwhile, the de la Madrid administration was transforming the activism developed by López Portillo into a policy of mediation through the Contadora Group. How could an economically conservative government such as de la Madrid's diverge so dramatically from prevailing world opinion and, in the process, put itself at odds with U.S. policy toward Central America? First, it was in Mexico's interest to support a negotiated settlement of the conflict. Hundreds of thousands of impoverished refugees were amassing along Mexico's southern border; there were frictions between the Mexican military and their Guatemalan counterparts; and the stability of southern Mexico was at risk of being upset by events in neighboring countries. Further, it was important to preserve the image of independence that had served for decades to pacify the domestic Left and co-opt foreign liberal and progressive sectors.

A second reason was outlined in the preceding chapter: Mexico was able to diverge from the U.S. policy line because U.S. society was deeply divided over their country's aggressive position on Central America. In 1983, an internal National Security Council document acknowledged that Reagan was having "serious difficulties with public opinion and Congress," and that this was undermining U.S. policies in Central America (NYT, Apr. 7, 1983). Mexico's policy of

---

[1]Constantine Menges, of the National Security Council, also believed that Mexico's destiny was in play in Central America (Menges 1988: 27–28).

[2]There are many references to the importance of Mexican stability for the United States and the costs that its absence would imply. See Schoultz 1987; Jordan and Taylor 1984; Hannon 1984, 1986, 1987; Linn 1984; Sanders 1987; Wilson 1989.

mediation drew support from, and was seconded by, U.S. sectors opposed to Reagan's conservative ideas.

In a June 1, 1983, memorandum, Representative Bill Alexander, a Democrat, called on his fellow members of Congress to support the Contadora Group. Sol Linowitz described Contadora as "the only promising path towards peace in the region" (NYT, Mar. 20, 1984). The *Washington Post* concurred, noting that Contadora was the only mechanism able to "reduce the war's escalation" (NYT, Mar. 2, 1984). Democrat Robert Kastenmeier, representative for Wisconsin, defended Mexico's policies from the attacks of Republican Senator Robert Kasten.[3] The *Times* also lined up behind the Contadora Group, which the paper called "the only plausible alternative to a brutal, illegal and unwinnable war" (NYT 1986b, 1986c).

Divisions within the U.S. elite mirrored those that had emerged during the Vietnam War, but now they were intensified by highly successful solidarity actions that Central American revolutionaries were carrying out in the United States.[4] These activities won the revolutionaries broad-based support, reinforced through the American and Latin American networks that had formed during the 1960s.

U.S. conservatives' criticisms of Mexico were balanced by the praise and support coming from liberal sectors in the United States. Mexico's independent stance in foreign policy making was always understood as an exercise in pragmatism (not an expression of principles), intended to enhance the government's prestige on the home front: "independence from the United States is a concept Mexicans hold dear" (NYT, Apr. 14, 1984). Holding to this perspective enabled the United States to tolerate de la Madrid's emphasis on the policy differences between Mexico City and Washington—as was the case, for example, when de la Madrid and Reagan met in May 1984 and the former publicly expressed his "disagreement over Central America" (NYT, May 16, 1984).

Paradoxically, among the elements underpinning the Mexican government's prestige was its record of maintaining a cordial relationship with the Latin American Left while simultaneously controlling its own domestic Left. That is, Mexico's progressive foreign policies attracted admiration in the United States because they had proven their worth as mechanisms for controlling leftist sectors, not because they encouraged greater social freedom. This was part of the old game of simulations: Mexico pretended to be independent, and the United States pretended to respect its independence.

---

[3]For both sides of the debate, see NYT, June 17, July 4, 1985.
[4]Well-informed sources noted that at one point during the 1980s Central American organizations affiliated with the Farabundo Martí National Liberation Front had some two hundred full-time activists promoting solidarity with their movement.

REDEFINING THE RELATIONSHIP

During the 1982–1984 period, the Mexican government undertook a fundamental modification in its policy toward the United States: it began searching for long-term, permanent mechanisms through which it could influence U.S. decision-making processes. Its first efforts were oblique and would certainly not classify as interventionist. In May 1983, for example, Minister of Foreign Affairs Bernardo Sepúlveda met with a delegation of Democrats opposed to Washington's conservative polices. And the Mexican government applauded writers who came out in the U.S. press in support of Mexico's policies, criticizing Reagan and praising de la Madrid (see, for example, Fuentes 1984, 1985). Not since Plutarco Elías Calles had a Mexican president penned an essay for *Foreign Affairs*, the establishment's magazine on U.S. foreign policy.[5] Yet in the Fall 1984 issue, de la Madrid contributed an article in which he insisted that ignoring "the Central American conflict would entail an abandonment of Mexico's historic responsibility," a renunciation of "the defense of our own national interest and security." Although this was not explicit lobbying, this kind of action laid the foundations for Mexican society to accept the legitimacy of actively promoting Mexico's interests and ideas in the United States.

It is possible that this gradual modification in the bilateral understanding arose as a reaction to the Republicans' decision to pressure Mexico more overtly and consistently, making dissent in Mexico increasingly expensive. In February 1984, Paul Gorman, chief of the United States' Southern Command, declared that Mexico could become "the No. 1 security problem for the United States" over the next ten years "unless it drastically transformed" its policies. He added that Mexico was a "center for subversion," a nation following "a policy of accommodation with its own left and international leftist interests." He concluded that Mexico was characterized by the "most corrupt Government and society in Central America," which—according to the NYT—was "in line with the views that have been expressed by some intelligence officials" (NYT, Feb. 26, 1984).

Such comments reveal that the margins of tolerance toward the Mexican regime were narrowing in some sectors. In its April 2, 1984, issue, *Newsweek* reported that, despite objections from the State Department and Ambassador John Gavin, President Reagan had signed National Security Directive 124, ordering the creation of a "master plan in communications and diplomacy" to persuade de la Madrid and his key advisers of "the virtues of the struggle . . . against Communism in Central America."

---

[5]Calles published an article in *Foreign Affairs* in October 1926.

In May 1984, de la Madrid traveled to Washington, just as the U.S. bureaucracy was discussing how to address the Mexican situation. The mood was contentious; that same month, the CIA's foremost analyst on Latin American affairs, John Horton, had resigned in protest when CIA director William Casey asked him to prepare a report exaggerating Mexico's economic and political problems. This was prior to the Mexican president's upcoming visit, and the CIA hoped to use the report to persuade the White House to authorize increasing the pressure on Mexico (NYT, Sept. 28, 1984).

Such pressure tactics appear to have worked; in 1983 the Mexican government had begun to reevaluate the merits and disadvantages of its policy on Central America and had made some changes. The *Times* reported that, after heated debate, the Ministries of Finance and Government—despite opposition from the Ministry of Foreign Affairs—had determined that oil shipments to Nicaragua would be suspended if that country remained unable to pay for the oil it received. The United States had been urging Mexico to take this step for some time; one U.S. diplomat frankly admitted, "we have pressured Mexico because we feel that Nicaragua is not the type of government which deserves this kind of financing" (NYT, Aug. 11, 1983). In 1984, according to the *Times*, "Salvadoran rebels living in Mexico" admitted that they were "feeling pressure from the Mexican Government of President Miguel De la Madrid to curtail their public activities" (NYT, July 19, 1984).[6] And in August 1983, Susan Kaufman Purcell noted that "Mexico finally seems willing to take the United States' security concerns more seriously" (Purcell 1983).

Outside pressures were perhaps not the only reason for the changes. The economic crisis and the conservatism of many Mexican government officials were probably also factors. Whatever the reason, by 1984 Mexico's foreign policy direction had changed; an analyst from the conservative Heritage Foundation was able to state that Mexico was moving toward "a less ideological position, and a more pragmatic foreign policy" (Hannon 1984). After 1984 Mexico's attention necessarily shifted from Central America to the country's own economic and political system, and to its relationship with the United States; and tensions between the two countries over Central America eased rapidly.

THE EMERGENCE OF NEW SOCIAL FORCES

The 1980s witnessed the appearance and consolidation of new social actors in Mexico who would acquire a great deal of importance in

---

[6] After this point, positive references to Mexico's foreign policy in the *Times* multiplied (figure 45).

subsequent years, and whose presence confirmed the continuing erosion of the government's control mechanisms. The National Action Party, founded in 1939, gained an increased following during this period. The center-right PAN, which has always viewed elections as the appropriate path for moving toward a democratic regime, was frequently praised in the *Times* between 1983 and 1986 (figures 28, 31–32), largely because of spreading U.S. discontent with the PRI government.

The PAN's growing popularity led it to electoral victories in twelve cities in northern Mexico in July 1983. The *Times* noted that this was "the worst reversal" in the PRI's 54–year history and was partly the result of a middle-class protest against the government's economic policies (July 12, 1983). The paper applauded the "decision by the Government of President Miguel De la Madrid, then new to office, to permit a fair count of the vote and see what would happen if non-fraudulent elections were held" (NYT, Mar. 11, 1984). This flowering of democracy proved short-lived. With Operation Dragon, conducted in Baja California in September 1983, and Operation Tango Papas, carried out in Mérida in November 1984, the de la Madrid administration demonstrated that it was still prepared to resort to electoral fraud to defeat an increasingly influential opposition.

Another important factor in this process was the emergence of an independent media, a prerequisite for the consolidation of social movements. Previous chapters have described the government's control of the press, and hence its control over the flow of ideas. In September 1984 a new daily, *La Jornada*, began publication in Mexico City. This newspaper, founded by center-left journalists and intellectuals, would give voice to sectors that had no other avenue of expression and would become an indispensable source of information for a range of social movements. Numerous other independent magazines and dailies appeared throughout the country during this period.

Another sector that benefited from the freer atmosphere was that of nongovernmental organizations, especially those dedicated to human rights. The Mexican Academy for Human Rights (AMDH) and the Fray Francisco de Vitoria Center for Human Rights (CDH), established in 1984, brought together Christian and other activists and scholars who had previously been working independently for the protection and promotion of human rights. Their rapid growth (by 1994 there were more than 250 human rights NGOs) also reflected Mexico's growing openness to the outside.

The anger spurred by continuing electoral fraud and the economic crisis led some sectors to suggest that armed struggle was inevitable. We now know that around 1983–1984 a group of survivors from the guerrilla movements of the 1970s arrived in Chiapas to lay the political groundwork that would culminate in the appearance of the Zapatista Army of National Liberation (EZLN) in 1994. Chiapas, meanwhile, was providing a gateway for Central Americans seeking refuge in Mexico, and the NGOs played an important role in protecting them and promoting their interests. The international community was also becoming increasingly concerned about the Central American refugees, especially those from Guatemala. This convergence enabled many social organizations to break out of isolation, further accelerating the ongoing process of internationalization in Mexican politics.

18

The Death of the Mexican Revolution

The economic model inherited from the Mexican Revolution, once presented as a viable alternative to socialism and capitalism, expired in 1985–1986. Its demise was not due to natural causes. Rather, the Mexican leadership had reached agreement with Washington to terminate its existence. In exchange, the PRI received U.S. support, infusing new strength into Mexico's authoritarian system, which was showing serious signs of wear.

UNLOCKING THE MEXICAN ENIGMA

Because of some exceptional circumstances, both the number and the prominence of *Times* articles on Mexican affairs rose sharply over 1985 and 1986.[1] Correspondents increased their annual production on Mexico by nearly 300 percent (figures 1, 6–7). John Bailey's analysis of coverage of Mexican affairs by the *New York Times*, the *Washington Post*, and three television networks (ABC, CBS, and NBC) between 1979 and 1988 confirms this pattern, showing a remarkable increase in 1985 and 1986 and a return to the status quo ante in 1987 (Bailey 1989). This heightened attention corresponds to events that were drastically reshaping the Mexican system and the intense debate under way regarding its prospects for the future. In 1986, Peter Smith voiced U.S. sentiments when he noted that "Mexico is in the midst of a profound transition. . . . [W]here is Mexico going?" (p. 101).

Proffered answers ranged across an extremely broad spectrum. Some forecasts were apocalyptic. In 1985, Rex Applegate warned that Mexico displayed "all the necessary elements and conditions for a Communist take-over" (p. 87). Even sophisticated analysts such as

---

[1] Nine percent of all front-page articles, as well as 10 percent of all editorials, printed during the period covered by the content analysis appeared in 1986.

Brian Latell, chief observer of Mexican affairs at the CIA, predicted that "Mexican stability will be threatened by a deepening crisis which is both economic and political" (1986: 3). Such extreme opinions were not generalized, however; most views of Mexico's future were more optimistic. In 1984, the CIA concluded that "the majority of Mexicans still accepts the legitimacy of a system dominated by the PRI" (Harper's 1987). In 1985, the State Department commissioned a number of studies that arrived at similar conclusions (Camp 1986). And a "national intelligence estimate"—the most complete form of intelligence analysis carried out by the U.S. government, leaked to the press in 1987—argued that under the most likely scenario the "Mexican political system will remain intact" (in Anderson and Atta 1987a, 1987b).

Despite this consensus, the attention of the U.S. elite focused once again on the need for economic and political reform in Mexico, and by 1985–1986 reform was an idea whose time had definitely arrived. Because any reform process would be administered by the PRI and the only viable opposition was the right-leaning PAN party, the United States was assured that Mexico would implement the kind of liberal economic policies that the elite explicitly, unanimously, and vociferously recommended (that is, demanded). The U.S. elite also believed that with the right kind of reform, Mexico would finally overcome all traces of its traditional anti-American nationalism and ultimately pursue economic integration with the United States. As it turned out, the United States had to exert significant pressure to bring about a transformation in Mexico's economic system, and the issue of reform of the political system was relegated indefinitely to the background.

THE REEMERGENCE OF DRUG TRAFFICKING

Turbulence gripped Mexico in 1985, driven by the unleashing of a series of accumulated though completely unforeseen forces. The first sign of the approaching storm was the escalating trade in illegal narcotics. After the 1960s, drug trafficking as a variable in the bilateral relationship displayed dramatic and unpredictable peaks and valleys. From a total of 408 *Times* references to drug trafficking between Mexico and the United States, 191 appeared in 1985–86, and of a total of 153 negative references on this topic, 123 appeared during this same two-year span (figures 58, 66).

Following Operation Intercept and the 1976 agreement to exchange prisoners, drug-related issues had faded from the bilateral agenda. They made only rare appearances during the López Portillo presidency, probably because Mexico's economic boom was fueling a surge of optimism in the United States that overshadowed any negative issues in the relationship. During this period, reports in the United States on Mexico's anti-drug programs usually applauded the Mexican authorities' efforts.[2] This overall approval continued into the first two years of de la Madrid's term in office; and in 1984 a U.S. House committee concluded that "Mexico was the only country where the Government recognized its obligation to detect and eradicate the illicit cultivation of narcotic crops," an observation that "greatly pleased the Mexican Government officials" (NYT, Sept. 13, 1984).

But praise abruptly gave way to condemnation. In November 1984, Mexican authorities—tipped off by U.S. agents—raided El Búfalo Ranch in Chihuahua State and confiscated over 10,000 tons of marijuana in the largest marijuana seizure in history. The drug dealers were quick to retaliate; in February 1985 they seized Drug Enforcement Agency (DEA) agent Enrique Camarena and his pilot, Alfonso Zavala, in Guadalajara.

When Camarena and Zavala failed to surface, the U.S. media speculated that the kidnappers "may be working under the protection of local Guadalajara officials" (NYT, Feb. 22, 1985). Mexico was criticized as never before.[3] The United States' response was not limited to oratory; both the U.S. Customs Service and the DEA increased the pressure on Mexico and closed the border to bring their point home. The collapse of relations on the border was dramatic (see figure 62).

In early March 1985, the tortured bodies of Camarena and Zavala were found in Michoacán. Secretary of State George Shultz declared that the United States' "level of tolerance has been exceeded" (NYT, Mar. 8, 1985). This—the strongest public statement in many decades—signaled a fundamental shift in the United States' attitude—and in the bilateral understanding. U.S. Ambassador to Mexico John Gavin publicly affirmed that at least two of Camarena's kidnappers were Mexican policemen (NYT, Mar. 16, 1985).

There were other indications of U.S. displeasure. Although Washington had referred publicly to the complicity between drug dealers and some government officials as early as 1969, the U.S. government never revealed the names of the twenty Mexicans against whom it claimed to have evidence. In 1985, on the other hand, it released the names of state governors, chiefs of police, ministers, and even relatives of the president alleged to be involved with criminal organizations. In April 1985, Ambassador Gavin stated that he could not have "full confidence in the honesty and integrity of De la Madrid's Cabinet," adding that "at least one Cabinet member and the

---

[2]See figures 65–66; NYT, Feb. 24, 1980; Aug. 15, 1983.
[3]The *Times* published its highest number of hostile declarations in 1985; see figure 66.

son of a Cabinet member may have links to drug traffickers" (NYT, Apr. 30, 1985).

Mexican officials were vehement in their country's defense. In 1985, the number of Mexican officials and scholars quoted in the *Times* rose sharply, as did the number of correspondents willing to interview them (figure 10). There was a corresponding increase in anti-American sentiment in Mexico (figure 94). Although these data reflect genuine Mexican anger, they also reflect the fact that the Mexican government played on this anger, using nationalism as a rallying cry against Yankee interventionism. Such calls for national unity could still produce results; a number of Mexican intellectuals rushed to their government's defense in the U.S. press (see, for example, Castañeda 1985).

As 1985 wore on, U.S. displeasure with Mexico began to ease, apparently because there were signs that the Mexican government was showing increased willingness to cooperate. In November 1985, U.S. government officials once again were expressing satisfaction with the Mexican government, which was "increasing its overall effort and cracking down on corruption" (NYT, Nov. 10, 1985).

OTHER DRUG-RELATED MATTERS

Camarena's assassination coincided with certain changes in the U.S. elite's perception of the drug issue. Nancy Reagan's "Just Say No" campaign tacitly acknowledged that demand was part of the problem. Mexico may have helped bring about this transformation; Ambassador Gavin acknowledged that "[the Mexicans] are right" regarding the importance of demand (NYT, May 14, 1986). A *Times* editorial also noted that "the problem truly begins with the demand for drugs in the United States" (NYT 1985b).

Camarena's assassination also reaffirmed U.S. perceptions that the entire Mexican system was riddled with corruption (figure 93). His murder revealed two divergent U.S. attitudes, which are still in place. On one side were those who called for intensifying the pressure on Mexico, arguing that official corruption was so widespread and damaging to the United States that only a very firm hand could compel the Mexican government to carry out in-depth reform. And on the other side were those who opposed harsh or explicit sanctions that would, they warned, aggravate the economic crisis, reduce the regime's legitimacy, tarnish the bilateral relationship, and curtail Washington's influence. The wisest course of action—according to this second camp, which ultimately prevailed—was to stick to the rules of the unwritten understanding, urging the Mexican regime into ever broader concessions.

A paradoxical consequence of the Camarena affair was that it accelerated the breakdown of the government's authoritarian controls over Mexican society. De la Madrid's 1985 decision to dissolve the Federal Security Directorate—the regime's most important political police force but also a key source of protection for drug dealers—came largely as a result of pressure from the United States. This proved to be a decisive step in the loosening of authoritarian control mechanisms. With the demise of the DFS, the Mexican government lost a central piece of its coercion machine, and this coincided with a reevaluation within the armed forces regarding the wisdom—or convenience—of using troops to repress independence or opposition movements. Coercion is an essential element in any authoritarian regime; when it ceases to be employed, the population becomes less afraid and dissident groups and ideas begin to emerge and coalesce. Thus it was that Washington, acting in line with its own interests, unwittingly contributed to the liberalization of the Mexican political system by attacking the corruption that pervaded its security forces.

ELECTIONS AND THE ECONOMY

Elections for the Mexican Congress and for the governorship of Sonora in 1985 were marred by irregularities masterminded by the central government. In follow-up coverage, the *Times* ran a series about the lack of democracy in Mexico. In fact, 50 percent of all negative opinions on electoral fraud registered for the entire period of the content analysis appeared in 1985–86 (figures 35, 38). Richard Meislin, *Times* correspondent from 1983 until mid–1985, may have contributed to this focus. More critical of Mexico than was Alan Riding, Meislin devoted an article in late 1984 to a PAN leader from Hermosillo who claimed to have compiled a list of more than 100 different techniques the PRI used to perpetrate electoral fraud (NYT, Dec. 2, 1984). The U.S. media's willingness to notice and report on the more negative aspects of Mexican politics became increasingly evident. For example, "Foreign journalists observing the elections on Sunday found several seeming abnormalities in voting procedures. In one case, acting on a tip, a group stopped a taxicab and found three ballot boxes full of uncounted votes on the back seat" (NYT, July 9, 1985).

The *Times* editorial line as a whole grew increasingly critical during 1985–86. Addressing the 1985 elections, for example, the paper asserted that "Mexico's democratic system . . . is an undemocratic anomaly. Citizens may vote for parties of their choice, but only one of them, the PRI, is allowed to win. This puts Mexico in the uncomfortable company of Chile, Haiti, Paraguay, Cuba and Nicaragua" (NYT 1985c).

The 1985 elections in Sonora and Nuevo León were obviously fraudulent. Sam Dillon, of the *Miami Herald*, noted that "not a single independent observer believes in the official results." The *Washington Post*'s Robert McCartney was equally direct: "many reporters observed even less regard for the law and democratic procedure in Sonora than in recent elections in El Salvador and Nicaragua" (in Bailey 1989: 5). Such unfettered criticism reflected priorities on international agendas, which—informed by Reagan-era ideologies—now viewed democracy as a fundamental legitimating factor for political systems.

Attitudes and priorities were changing on other fronts as well. In 1983 and 1984 the government of Miguel de la Madrid had been lauded for its strict enforcement of IMF austerity policies (figures 67–70). But in 1985 there were calls for another round of reforms of the economic model. In early 1985 a foreign investment analyst noted that the Mexican government's "flexibility" toward foreign investment "pleased the United States." However, he went on, this would no longer suffice: "the Government says, Yeah, we wrote the law, but it doesn't work, so don't worry about it. Well, we worry about it. American businessmen want things laid out 1 to 10 and A to Z" (NYT, Jan. 19, 1985). This quote is particularly indicative of a growing concern in the United States: as Mexico's economic instability intensified, the American business community began calling for reforms that would protect their investments, and that meant a more thorough-going reform of Mexico's economic and legislative systems.

U.S. impatience intensified as the Mexican economy continued to deteriorate (NYT, Feb. 11, 1985). By July 1985, inflation was skyrocketing, growth was lagging, the peso was losing ground vis-à-vis the dollar, and the price for exported crude oil was plummeting. In this worsening context, certain previously ignored links were suddenly explicitly clear. In August the *Times* noted that "while both sides have been careful not to link economic aid with the anti–drug-trafficking effort, the Mexicans knew that the price for substantial economic concessions would be promises of greater efforts to stem the flow of drugs" (NYT, Aug. 17, 1986). Far from being ignored, the linking of aid would be broadened to encompass a number of other issues.

By early September the economic situation had turned desperate. Mexico announced that it would request new negotiations with the international banks and offer further concessions. One analyst of Mexican affairs noted that "no previous Mexican President has gone so far to meet the needs and demands of the United States," and he wondered whether "he could go further" (NYT, Sept. 2, 1985). The Mexican government was indeed willing to go much, much further. In fact, it would accept any concession, no matter how harsh, as long as the ruling elite was allowed to remain in power.

THE 1985 EARTHQUAKES

Two brutally damaging earthquakes shook Mexico on September 19, 1985. The first was a geological event that devastated broad sections of Mexico City's historic downtown. Actually a series of earthquakes, this seismic activity could almost stand as a metaphor for the profound transformations under way in Mexican society at the time. The second earthquake was by nature international and financial. It was catalyzed by the United States' announcement that its tolerance of Mexico's economic policies had reached an end, and hence these policies would have to change.

The geological activity was ably covered by the *Times*, which published over sixty articles on the disaster, written with sensitivity and respect for the victims but without shying away from reporting on the endemic official corruption laid bare in the quakes' horrific aftermath. The media noted that many of the collapsed buildings had failed to comply with even the most rudimentary construction codes. The macabre discovery of mutilated and tortured bodies in the basement of a building owned by the Mexican judicial police was also reported.

One consequence of the earthquakes was to cast the Mexican government's indecisiveness and authoritarianism into sharp relief. An example was the government's response to offers of assistance from the United States. The day after the quakes, the de la Madrid administration curtly informed Washington that it would "decline its offers of financial assistance." Four days later, it accepted the proffered resources. A spokesperson for the Office of the President explained that the delay was due to an "incomplete understanding of the problem's full extent and gravity" (NYT, Sept. 21–22, Oct. 24, 1985). This explanation is highly unsatisfactory; the enormity of the damage was more than evident immediately after the event.

Why did the Mexican government initially reject U.S. assistance? Was it arrogance, resentment, pride? Was it de la Madrid's lack of leadership, or perhaps authoritarian inertia, that led him to seek to control every detail? It seems likely that all these factors played a part in that early decision. Whatever the reason, how the government responded in the earthquakes' aftermath made the deterioration of its mechanisms of control painfully apparent.

September 19, 1985, was also symbolic in that it marked the first anniversary of the independent Mexico City newspaper *La Jornada*, which had survived despite tremendous financial difficulties and government harassment. This paper, which would become the key forum for social groups that appeared during the emergency, also provided the most steady coverage of new actors such as the "coordinating committees" (*coordinadoras*) of urban, peasant, and teachers' movements (Haber 1994: 282).

To curtail the influence of the new social organizations operating in Mexico, the country's Ministry of Tourism insisted that all emergency assistance coming from abroad be channeled through Mexico's Embassy or consulates, rather than through other organizations (NYT, Sept. 22, 1985). The government directive went largely unheeded; many foundations put resources directly into the hands of the independent organizations, significantly enhancing their position in the process.

The second earthquake of September 19, 1985, was the financial one. By that date, Washington had concluded that Mexico was "no longer adhering to the austerity program accorded with the IMF." The implications were immediate and devastating: Mexico would lose "900 million dollars in assistance from the Fund," which would "greatly complicate its relationship with the international banking system" (NYT, Oct. 20, 1985). In other words, Mexico would soon be bankrupt. To demonstrate its sensitivity toward the geological tragedy that had just befallen Mexico, the IMF judiciously agreed to postpone imposing sentence for a few weeks; an IMF delegation didn't arrive until late October "to discuss Mexico's economic problems" (NYT, Oct. 31, 1985). Although the full story of these tense and drawn-out negotiations has never been made public, what was clearly being decided was the future configuration of Mexico's political and economic system.

Indications as to the nature of these confidential negotiations soon surfaced. In November 1985, the Mexican government announced that it would apply for entrance into the General Agreement on Tariffs and Trade, a move hailed by U.S. diplomats and analysts as one of Mexico's boldest moves in decades (NYT, Dec. 9, 1985). No one mentioned that by entering the GATT, Mexico was fulfilling an old desire of the United States.[4]

The Christmas of 1985 was a bitter one for official Mexico. Throughout that winter, oil prices plummeted, dragging the peso down with them. The government's options were so few that, despite the crisis, it decided in January 1986 not to join other oil-producing nations in a joint strategy to raise international crude oil prices. The *Times* reported that Mexico made this decision for two reasons: to minimize the impacts on the Mexican economy, and to avoid "offending the United States," the main beneficiary of the falling oil prices (NYT, Jan. 23, 1986). In February 1986 Mexico cut its price for a barrel of crude by $8.65, bringing the country "to the brink of eco-

---

[4]Julián Nava must have allowed himself a satisfied smile. Five years earlier, when the López Portillo government had decided not to enter into the GATT, Nava, then U.S. ambassador to Mexico, declared that "sooner or later" Mexico would be forced to reverse its decision. The Mexican ruling elite condemned Nava's statement as further evidence of "United States intimidation" (NYT, May 15, 1980).

nomic disaster" (NYT, Feb. 15, 1986). U.S. Secretary of State George Shultz declared that Mexico, the IMF, and the international banking system were making every effort to "prevent a Mexican financial collapse" (NYT, Feb. 10, 1986). With each passing week, it became increasingly evident that Mexico would have to reach some new accord with international financial institutions.

REINING IN THE ECONOMIC MODEL

In order to appreciate fully the degree of pressure being exerted by the United States on Mexico, we must look to the broader context. Mexico's policy toward Central America was probably the primary, but not the only, irritant to the Reagan administration; other contentious issues were drug trafficking, Mexico's failed economic model, electoral fraud, and de la Madrid's lack of leadership. Concern on these specific topics intermingled with general concern for Mexico's stability—and for what repercussions a loss of stability in Mexico might have on U.S. security just as conservatives were trying to influence the global balance of power.

It is very difficult to reconstruct those months with any detail. Nonetheless, there can be no doubt as to the anger that the U.S. elite felt toward Mexico. It was much in evidence throughout the congressional hearings convened by Senator Jesse Helms in May 1986, when high-ranking government officials issued a series of blistering accusations against the Mexican government, citing corruption, collaboration with drug cartels, electoral fraud, and administrative ineptitude.

William Von Raab, United States Customs Service commissioner, observed that the drug problem had become "a horror story, increasing logarithmically," and that Mexico was "doing nothing about it." The situation, he added, was "totally out of control" and was only aggravated further by "inept and corrupt" Mexican authorities. Von Raab also suggested that his view was shared by "the entire executive branch of Government" (NYT, May 12, 1986). Other prominent members of Reagan's cabinet, including Assistant Secretary of State Elliott Abrams, expressed similar opinions.

The White House soon received a strongly worded note of protest from an enraged Mexican government. An unidentified "senior Mexican official"—probably the minister of foreign affairs—was quoted in the *Times* to the effect that Washington's response to the note would "most likely determine the future course of [bilateral] relations" (NYT, May 15, 1986). Although there is no reason to doubt the sincerity or patriotism of the anonymous author of this prognostication, it was empty bluster, no more. The Mexican leadership, by then utterly dependent on the U.S. government for its survival, was forced to accept even the harshest American criticism with good grace.

Succeeding events followed a well-trodden path. Once again the Mexican leadership assumed a nationalistic pose for the benefit of its domestic audience, secure in the knowledge that it was in the United States' own interest to help maintain a facade of Mexican autonomy. The Mexican population was informed that Elliott Abrams had sent a conciliatory letter to the Mexican government and that the U.S. attorney general had held a fruitful telephone conversation with his Mexican counterpart (NYT, May 25, 1986). The Mexican press reported that the nation's sovereignty was intact, with the White House collaborating actively in this whitewash: Attorney General Edwin Meese publicly criticized the comments of Commissioner Von Raab. The *Times* observed that "the Mexicans were delighted; they had stood up to the giant, they concluded, and the giant had backed down" (NYT, June 1, 1986).

There were other, significantly different interpretations, however. Mexico's note of protest, on which the future of the relationship supposedly hinged, was interpreted by the *Times* as a maneuver designed to "pacify internal opposition" (Aug. 3, 1986). U.S. officials, who chose to remain anonymous, noted that if Washington had indeed given Mexico's official nationalism a boost, this was only because "Mexicans are exceptionally sensitive to criticisms from the United States" and because the contentious atmosphere might make it "difficult to carry through with some important initiatives" (NYT, May 25, 1986). This reasoning was developed further in a *Times* observation that Washington had eased up on Mexico because "Mexico's problems can have serious impact not only in Mexico but also in the United States," and "the more stable and confident the system is," the easier it would be to push through the reforms that the White House desired (NYT, Aug. 13, 1986).

This interpretation was, in fact, exactly on target. With its image untarnished, the Mexican government did everything in its power to allay U.S. concerns, although in as discreet a manner as possible. Mexico signed an accord in June 1986 that allowed "six United States airplanes with civilian pilots under contract to the State Department" to take part in a program designed "to eradicate opium fields," noting only that their participation was "unusual" (NYT, July 18, 1986). Washington, hoping to take full advantage of the Mexican government's cooperative stance, also sought permission for U.S. agents to "chase drug smugglers up to 100 miles into Mexican territory" (NYT, Aug. 14, 1986). This request, intended to authorize agents "in hot pursuit" to enter Mexico, was never approved and it is still a contentious point between the two countries.

However, by early summer of 1986 the U.S. elite had reason to hope for far more than concessions in the area of anti-drug measures. The statements of high-ranking U.S. officials testifying about Mexico in the Helms hearings revealed the existence of a new strategy to address definitively several features of this traditionally problematic country. These officials sought to impose a new economic model, curtail the country's independent diplomatic initiatives, and, if at all possible, create conditions conducive for extending democracy without threatening stability. Participants in the Helms debates have suggested that Washington, after carefully evaluating Mexico's presidential succession, had decided to support Carlos Salinas de Gortari.

While Helms and his allies were attacking the Mexican government, there was an intense debate under way within the de la Madrid cabinet about how to deal with the economic crisis and the pressure being applied by the United States. Although there are many gaps in the information pertaining to this crucial period, its broad outlines are clear. By June 1986, Mexico's negotiations with the United States had stalled, and Minister of Finance Jesús Silva Herzog was hinting that the only remaining alternative was a moratorium on debt payments, the option preferred by Mexico's most nationalistic sectors (NYT, June 8, 1986). Soon thereafter, Paul Volcker, chairman of the Federal Reserve, went to Mexico at Silva Herzog's invitation. Volcker met with a number of high-ranking Mexican officials, but it is not known to what purpose. A few days later, de la Madrid dismissed Silva Herzog, publicly describing him as "disloyal." De la Madrid named as his successor Gustavo Petricioli, "not a man with a strong political base of his own" (NYT, June 18, 1986).[5]

Alan Riding was in Mexico at the time, and it was he who filled in the details surrounding Silva Herzog's dismissal, noting that the minister had acted "without even consulting the President," becoming "a defender of the IMF without considering the internal repercussions." Ironically, Silva Herzog's chief critic in Mexico was Minister of Budget and Planning Carlos Salinas de Gortari; later, as president, Salinas would become a loyal implementer of the adjustment policies dictated by the IMF and the World Bank (NYT, June 18, 1986).

Following Silva Herzog's dismissal, Salinas took control of the debt negotiations and sent Pedro Aspe to join the negotiating team in Washington (NYT, July 14 , 1986). A broad accord was reached within weeks. Although its details have never been made public, this accord clearly entailed a readjustment of Mexico's economic policy. The level of pressure that the United States exerted on Mexico during these ne-

---

[5]For the accusations against Silva Herzog, see *El Nacional*, June 20, 1986. One particularly acute analysis of this transformation was Granados Chapa 1986.

gotiations was probably commensurate with the level of U.S. irritation with that country. In June 1986, the Mexican economy was a
shambles and democracy was stalled. The United States' disappointment was voiced frequently in the media; for example, *Times* correspondent Richard Meislin, who covered the elections of summer 1985,
wrote, "the problem for Mexico is that these elections were supposed
to be different. Foreign reporters seemed to take at face value President Miguel De la Madrid's pledges that the elections would be conducted cleanly and that the 'moral renewal' would extend to the
democratic process" (NYT, July 16, 1985). At that time, the media also
detected a link between the economic and political arenas: some
bankers, it was reported, believed that the crisis was largely a result
of the government's practice of "stimulating the economy in preparation for important state elections" (NYT, Sept. 21, 1985).

This was the backdrop for the fraudulent elections held in Chihuahua on June 6, 1986. In his coverage for the *Times*, William Stockton noted that "state electoral laws stack the deck against the opposition and clearly invite fraudulent voting and counting" (NYT, July 10,
1986). The *Times* published an important editorial that explored the
deterioration of Mexico's image in the United States. The editorial
recalled that when Jesse Helms and other critics of Mexico had attacked the PRI for its lack of "legitimacy," the *Times* had advised "the
critics to stop bashing Mexico and show some sympathy for its problems. Well, look who's bashing now. State elections in Mexico last
Sunday were rife with fraud. And the accusers, accused and victims
are all Mexicans" (NYT 1986d).

One particularly insightful editorial, published on June 11, 1986,
contained both an affirmation and a question: "Negotiations imply a
deal. Money for something. What should the Reagan Administration
be asking for?" (NYT 1986e). For the *Times*, the answer was clear:
Washington had to take advantage of the Mexican situation to press
for a reduction in the "state's role in the economy and the privileges
of the PRI–favored few. Mexico's leaders may find it hard to ditch
their props of power. But let them stare at the alternatives and feel
some friendly pressure from next door" (NYT, June 11, 1986). That
such sentiments were expressed in the *Times* was remarkable. Never
before had the paper so explicitly urged the U.S. government to use
"friendly pressure"—that is, coercion—on Mexico.

Negotiations ultimately produced a new accord with the IMF,
signed on July 22, 1986, under which Mexico pledged to carry out a
"series of economic reforms in return for $1.6 billion in emergency
assistance," to be provided over the following eighteen months (NYT,
July 23, 1986). Mexico would also have access to a further $6 billion
from commercial banks and $4.4 billion from other official U.S.
sources (NYT, July 25, 1986). "The key to this agreement is that the

Mexicans have agreed to make certain structural changes in their economy in order to reach these targets" (NYT, Oct. 1, 1986). The exact details of these "structural changes" were never made public, but Mexico was accepted into the GATT that same month.

This highly important period was capped, perhaps unwittingly, by a group of influential U.S. Mexicanists, some of whom were well known for their liberal views. Under the auspices of the Stanley Foundation, they prepared a document that made several unusually harsh observations regarding the Mexican regime, such as the following: "President De la Madrid, who has proved totally incapable of translating national interest into concrete programs, has protected his country's institutions by appealing to nationalist sentiments, much like the Presidents who preceded him." Mexico can no longer, it added, "continue to hide behind a pseudo-patriotic nationalism, waiting for the United States to solve its internal problems" (Stanley Foundation 1986: 8).

Two months later, in December 1986, the *Times* reported that over the coming year Mexico would carry out "further sales of state tourist, banking, and industrial enterprises," reduce "trade subsidies," and promote "more open investment policies and other market-oriented measures." This was not wishful thinking. It accurately reflected the commitments undertaken by Mexico in exchange for the "new loan programs accorded with the IMF" (NYT, Feb. 12, 1986).

Interestingly, despite their groundbreaking importance, these accords received relatively little attention. Drug-related issues continued to dominate public awareness in the United States that summer, overshadowing this extremely important item (Bailey 1989: 66, 74). Another factor contributing to the relative inattention given to the accords was the involvement of new actors. In earlier periods, coercion as a foreign policy tool had been wielded by U.S. officials through the CIA, the armed forces, the United States Information Agency, and so on. In this instance, it was banks and multilateral organizations who filled this role. While they acted in an apparently impersonal and objective fashion, they clearly answered to the industrial powers. It was a different mechanism of domination, less direct and more diffuse, and it was to become an essential aspect of domination in the age of globalization.

The Mexican government, which could engineer the information it released domestically, trumpeted the accords as a triumph. Given the nation's dire economic situation, perhaps they were. Nonetheless, the accords represented the final nail in the coffin of the economic model created by the Mexican Revolution and its substitution by another model more in line with the needs and interests of the United States. This, in turn, generated important changes in Mexico's foreign policy, which would also be increasingly attuned to U.S. interests.

Many aspects of the IMF accords remain hidden in an official twilight of confidential documents. Although the Mexican economy's subsequent progress reveals that the pressure from Washington yielded many of the results that the United States had hoped for, there are no documents or testimony to fill in the details of this process. Only by learning which institutions and individuals in the United States applied the greatest pressure, and which Mexican actors reacted and how, can we hope to gain a full understanding of the combined forces of hegemony and coercion that were to have such a decisive impact on Mexican history.

The United States, as usual, did everything in its power to let the Mexican government off the hook, at least on the domestic level, allowing it to maintain its traditional image of independent nationalism—largely because Washington had decided to maintain its support for the incumbent authoritarian regime. This reveals some curious paradoxes: the nation that has historically been the greatest threat to Mexican sovereignty in effect acted as the staunchest supporter of Mexico's official nationalism. And a superpower that claims to promote democracy around the world has in fact been the truest friend of the longest-lived authoritarian political system. There can be little doubt as to the fruitfulness of the accord reached between Morrow and Calles in 1927.

19

The Reign of Neoliberalism

The year 1986 signaled the end of an era for the bilateral relationship, and it might have made a natural endpoint for this book. However, a chapter covering the years from 1986 to 1997—the "reign of neo-liberalism"—was called for in light of this period's extraordinary relevance for Mexico's history and for the country's relationship with the United States.

In 1989, three prominent Mexicanists compiled an anthology that opened with a query: "Where is the Mexican political system head-ing? By 1988, Mexico had clearly begun to experience a major political transition; but a transition to *what?*" (Cornelius, Gentleman, and Smith 1989: 1). Although answers were slow to appear, Mexico's new shape came into sharp focus on July 6, 1997, when the ruling PRI party suffered a critical electoral defeat, the consequence of several key variables outlined in preceding chapters. The train of events from 1986 to 1997 can be explained in terms of (a) the gradual exhaustion of Mexican authoritarianism and its ability to control society, (b) the strengthening of already existing and/or the appearance of new so-cial forces, and (c) the increasing impact and importance of external factors, a variable that has been largely ignored. These trends, which are likely to endure, suggest that Mexico will continue to advance toward a more democratic system, whose most important features—such as its economic model and its relationship with the United States—will now be debated and decided differently.

DETERIORATION OF THE ECONOMY

In 1986, after months of wrangling, the Mexican government finally signed a letter of intent with the International Monetary Fund in which it agreed to modify its economic model. This was the beginning of an era of neoliberal governments which, over the following decade, would privatize state-owned holdings, slash subsidies and deficits, raze protectionist barriers, and implement tight fiscal controls. This called for major structural adjustments, which generated a series of spectacular macroeconomic successes during the presidency of Carlos Salinas: inflation fell from 159 percent in 1987 to 12 percent in 1992; the public-sector deficit, which stood at 17 percent of GNP in 1987, had been erased by 1991. And after a decade of economic downturn, Mexico's GNP showed an average annual growth rate of 3.9 percent in the first three years of the 1990s (Centeno 1994: 16).

Mexico's new economic policies—which were very much in line with the views of the U.S. elite—were greeted with favor in the United States. However, by 1990, 18 percent of Mexico's economically active population (EAP) was unemployed, and between 25 and 40 percent was underemployed. In 1991, the minimum wage had only two-thirds of its 1982 purchasing power; and in 1990, approximately 70 percent of Mexican families were unable to afford a minimum basket of basic foodstuffs. Nutrition levels suffered, especially among children in rural areas (where about half were believed to be undernourished), and supposedly eradicated diseases reappeared (Centeno 1994: 19). The extreme costs of the new economic policy, which fell heavily on the impoverished majorities, were viewed as necessary and inevitable.

This indifference toward the repercussions of economic policy also reflects the Left's inability to put forward an alternative and viable worldview or to translate discontent into effective protest. The technocrats remained in control of a population resigned to an absence of political options and compelled to make do with government promises of a brighter future. When Ernesto Zedillo won the presidency in August 1994, the U.S. elite interpreted his victory as the people's ratification of their country's economic orientation. However, the peso's devaluation in December 1994 thrust Mexico into an economic and financial debacle that shattered popular optimism and accentuated a shift in U.S. perceptions. The election results of July 1997 will force new discussions of some aspects of the country's economic policy.

DETERIORATION OF AUTHORITARIAN CONTROL MECHANISMS

Although the technocrats were not particularly interested in liberalizing the political system, they were unable to prevent a progressive deterioration in their capacity to control an increasingly organized society.[1] The proliferation of obstacles inhibiting the use of coercion

---

[1]Washington viewed this process with a degree of satisfaction, given that it preferred a peaceful and gradual transition.

was both cause and effect of this deterioration. As the armed forces became more professional, they also became less willing to repress peaceful demonstrations or opposition movements (Benítez 1994). Police units, meanwhile, were under intense scrutiny by human rights organizations and a growing body of independent media, both domestic and international. Further, the illegal drugs trade diminished the cohesion and the role of the police and the "rural guards," paramilitary forces which at one time numbered over 120,000 peasants under the command of army officers; they are no longer considered faithful allies of the regime.

As noted earlier, when the use of force is curtailed, populations lose their fear—an essential ingredient for any authoritarian regime—and they begin to play an increasingly active role in public affairs and in confrontations with the government. Paradoxically, political repression in Mexico was replaced by an equally worrying wave of criminal violence unleashed by the economic crisis and the corrupting power of drugs, and new fears simply replaced the old.

The fact that there are impediments to the use of coercion does not mean that the regime has completely lost its power to coerce. Mexico's security apparatus as a whole is now better trained and better armed than before, and the number of political assassinations remains high in many areas. Violence—either political or drug-related—introduces disturbing variables for the immediate future. The preservation of authoritarianism is a scenario that cannot be discounted, especially in certain regions.

DIVISIONS WITHIN THE RULING CLASS

In the mid–1980s the legendary discipline and unity of the PRI began to disintegrate, partly as a result of changes in the elite's profile and partly as a result of ideological differences and disputes over power.[2] By 1986 the technocrats were clearly in control of the bureaucracy. However, the economic reforms they implemented aroused a great deal of contention within the governing group, and in September 1986 the press reported that a "Democratic Current" had arisen within the PRI that aimed to democratize the party's selection of its presidential candidates. Then-president de la Madrid, in no mood for democratically minded experiments, had the current's leaders summarily expelled from the PRI in 1987. They coalesced in the National Democratic Front (FDN) and supported Cuauhtémoc Cárdenas's unsuccessful bid for the presidency in the turbulent elections of 1988,

---

[2]Some sectors in the United States responded by stepping up their support for the regime.

from which Carlos Salinas emerged the victor (but only after resorting to a range of illegal and immoral tactics).

Salinas was—and is—a master politician. Lacking both ethics and a democratic vocation, he did have a project for Mexico and a cohesive and sophisticated support group. His election, combined with the system's accelerating disintegration and the cleavages between groups with diverging styles and projects, gave rise to powerful tensions within the ruling elite, which would erupt into overt violence in 1994 with a series of politically motivated murders. Recent electoral defeats of PRI candidates have exacerbated disarray within this party that was once considered the paradigm of monolithic power.

STRENGTHENING NEW POLITICAL AND SOCIAL FORCES

After the mid–1980s, the relaxation of authoritarian controls, in combination with Mexico's economic reorientation and increasing openness, allowed a surprisingly wide range of independent political and social forces to appear and/or coalesce. This process has generated important benefits for Mexico's opposition parties. Although the most remarkable such case up until 1997 was the PAN, the Party of the Democratic Revolution's (PRD) impressive showing in the 1997 elections effectively transformed Mexico into a multiparty political system. The growth of the PRD (which had endured ferocious harassment throughout the Salinas administration) indicates the presence of a broad social base that is only now beginning to find outlets other than the PRI for a center-left party in Mexico.

The media play a strategically important role in political processes. They can be the bastions of democracy, or they can be the instruments by which authoritarian governments control what information reaches the population. The Mexican government—which has never underestimated the importance of this privileged mechanism of domination—has traditionally made every effort to control it, usually with success.[3] This began to change during the 1990s. Although the large private television networks are latecomers to this transition, relatively speaking, the press and several radio stations and/or programs have gained substantial independence.

Over recent years, nongovernmental organizations have established themselves as important new players on the national scene. Their influence has increased exponentially through national or international "networks" able to galvanize joint action.[4] The NGOs are a further expression of a "social capital" that has been accumulating for decades, and which is at the very heart of democratic culture (Fox

---

[3]For good analyses of the regime's favorite methods, see Camp 1985; Hellman 1983.
[4]An analysis of these organizations appears in Aguayo and Parra 1996.

1995). Groups such as Alianza Cívica have played a key role in the construction of a more democratic political culture—which is the central incentive in citizen mobilizations for free and transparent elections. Social movements have appeared simultaneously on every level of society. The Urban Popular Movement (MUP) remains active; the number of unions breaking free of corporate control is on the rise; and aggressive peasants' and debtors' organizations like El Barzón have appeared.

In the opening years of the decade, most observers of Mexico were convinced that the country had definitively crushed all guerrilla movements in the 1960s and 1970s. They were wrong; an armed struggle was gestating in southern Mexico. In January 1994, the Zapatista Army of National Liberation (EZLN) erupted on the scene in the mountainous regions of Chiapas, signaling the beginning of a dramatic reversal in the fortunes of the Salinas administration. This peasant rebellion was still unresolved in June 1995, when the Peoples' Revolutionary Army (EPR) appeared in Guerrero, Oaxaca, and other states, adding a further degree of complexity regarding Mexico's future.

Any list of new actors appearing in Mexico during the 1990s must include the increasingly powerful groups associated with the production, trafficking, and distribution of illegal narcotics. As Peter Andreas has pointed out, economic liberalization, together with the United States' successful effort to close off Caribbean drug routes, has strengthened Mexico's position in the international drugs market. The result has been to "narcotize the state and economy in Mexico" (Andreas 1996: 23). Beginning in 1987, each Mexican successive president has asserted that drug cartels pose a grave threat to Mexico's national security, although each has proved unable to halt their spread (Aguayo 1990; Chabat 1994).

And no effort at a comprehensive analysis can ignore the impact of the international community, and especially the United States, whose influence continues to grow while also becoming increasingly differentiated.

THE EXTERNAL FACTOR

The importance of external actors is intimately linked to Mexico's opening to the world, and this, in turn, has gone hand in hand with economic, political, and social globalization. From 1986 to 1997, society and government in Mexico developed their respective international agendas, establishing ties with groups around the world and creating processes of extraordinary complexity. The ideas and politics of external actors now influencing events in Mexico can be roughly

divided into those who support the PRI and those who support opposition or democratic groups (this second category will be examined
later).

The influence of the U.S. government and intellectual and political
elite upon Mexico grew during these years, confirming the notion that
the understanding between the elites of these two nations had
reached a point of perfect and unprecedented harmony. Although
certain traditionally nationalist and leftist sectors within the Mexican
leadership resisted this new intimacy, they had no clear alternative
project or antidote with which to confront the peculiarities of relationships of domination in a neoliberal age. The new and diffuse form of
government interventionism—in which economic policies were imposed by international financial organisms, albeit organisms controlled by Washington—placed traditional schools of nationalism,
such as the Mexican one, in a serious dilemma.

Another element was the United States' increasing preference for
hegemonic forms of domination, under which the Mexican leadership
would voluntarily adopt American policies and priorities. To encourage such a result, the United States has traditionally sought out allies
who hold compatible viewpoints. An earlier chapter documented the
case of Ambassador Antonio Carrillo Flores in the 1960s. His 1990s
counterpart was a Harvard-educated economist, a leader adept in the
secret codes of the Mexican political system, who was able to navigate
this country's corridors of power with ease. This is, of course, Carlos
Salinas de Gortari, who was to benefit enormously from the U.S.
elite's absolute and unconditional support.

The 1988 Elections

During the 1988 campaign, leading newspapers, the U.S. government,
and many scholars threw their combined weight behind candidate
Carlos Salinas de Gortari. This support, which was to endure
throughout Salinas's administration, reflects the limitations and bi-
ases of U.S. consciousness. The elections, marred by inequities and
fraud, failed to meet even the minimum international standards for
believability. Nonetheless, the United States did everything in its
power to legitimate them, using tactics fine-tuned over decades. For
example, government spokespersons frequently pointed out that, despite some problems, Mexico was advancing toward democracy,
thanks to Carlos Salinas, who was explicitly disassociated from a series of negative signals such as severe criticism of the opposition and
a whitewash in official documents.

Three days after the election, and with no prior announcement
from electoral authorities, Salinas declared himself the victor in the

presidential race, also noting that the opposition had made important advances and that "the days of the one-party system are finished" (*Washington Post*, July 8, 1988). *Times* corespondent Larry Rother praised Salinas's "remarkable speech" (NYT, July 10, 1988). Simply by acknowledging that the PRI had suffered some defeats, Salinas validated his democratic and reformist credentials. It is worth recalling that a view of Salinas as reformer was already established before the elections; a *Times* editorial appearing just prior to the election proposed that "Mr. Salinas represents the most radical break with the past" and urged the PRI to "heed his pleas to respect the integrity of the electoral process" (NYT 1988a).

The *Times* was not alone in its belief that Salinas would bring a wave of democratic change to Mexico. On July 18, 1988, William Branigin, correspondent for the *Washington Post*, noted that "Carlos Salinas de Gortari already appears to be succeeding in his stated aim of fundamentally changing the country's outmoded political system." Salinas had proved his commitment to a "Mexican-style *glasnost* [by] admitting unprecedented losses in state-level presidential voting and congressional races" (*Washington Post*, July 12, 1988). In an editorial published on July 15, the *Wall Street Journal* offered a daring assertion: "many of the maneuvers around the vote-counting look like attempts to undermine Mr. Salinas, who pushed for clean elections" (*Wall Street Journal* 1988).

To justify their early assessment, the media resorted to the old argument that there was "an internal struggle within the PRI." The *Washington Post* stated that this was a struggle between "Salinas supporters who want to recognize party losses [and the] old guard stalwarts who do not" (July 8, 1988), a view that continued to serve Salinas well. A *Times* editorial that explicitly disassociated Salinas from "the most retrograde elements in his own party" also praised him as a "convinced and capable free-market exponent" (NYT 1988b).

Even experienced correspondents like Alan Riding joined in the legitimating chorus: "Salinas, a 40-year-old Harvard-trained economist, has repeatedly pledged to 'perfect' Mexico's democracy." Riding portrayed Salinas as a direct opposite of the "old-time political bosses in the governing party who believe that no concessions should be made to the opposition" (NYT, July 8, 1988). The U.S. elite believed in Salinas—as they had in Echeverría and López Portillo—because they wanted to. Throughout his career and even during his presidential campaign, Salinas had never displayed even a hint of pro-democratic yearnings. However, he did display intelligence and an unquenchable thirst for power, which lay at the heart of his uncanny ability to navigate Mexico's labyrinthine corridors of power. Moreover, he had an economic project for Mexico that coincided with theoretical paradigms then in vogue in Washington and around the world.

It was this vitally important coincidence that explains an unprecedented editorial that appeared in the *Washington Post* on July 18, 1988. Never before had such statements been published in this newspaper known for its liberal principles. The article justified electoral fraud in Mexico, arguing that the country was "in the midst of an extraordinary series of reforms led from within the dominant party. Ballot fraud always deserves attention, but it's the reform that is the great and historic change."

John Bailey, who has studied coverage of Mexican affairs in the U.S. media, also recorded efforts to minimize the fraud: "when the results were announced, reporters conveyed the opposition's protests less emphatically than in 1985. The press concentrated nearly as much on the struggle within the PRI as on the significance of the elections, and editorial comments were generally more positive about the elections, noting that Mexico had begun the transition to genuine democracy" (1989: 85). The notion of a country that has not achieved, but is advancing toward, a brilliant future is one of the oldest and most persistent of U.S. perceptions. It has surfaced many times since 1946, and especially during irregular or contested elections.

At the same time, there were ongoing efforts to shoot down the opposition, especially the Left. The *Wall Street Journal* presented Cuauhtémoc Cárdenas as the son of Lázaro Cárdenas, "the founder of the modern PRI and the inventor of much of its vote-stealing machinery."[5] The *Wall Street Journal* added that the party proposing Cuauhtémoc Cárdenas as its presidential candidate was no more than "the Echeverría wing of the PRI" and that much of its electoral muscle came from "'La Quina', Joaquín Hernández Galicia, head of the PEMEX union, long a PRI stalwart but in constant combat with the De la Madrid government in its efforts to control corruption" (*Wall Street Journal* 1988).

Although most of the U.S. media backed Salinas, they also urged his government to acknowledge opposition victories. A *Times* editorial advised Salinas to "honor his pledge to recognize what he calls Mexico's 'new political reality' [and allow both the Left and the Right to] translate their gains into institutional political forms" (NYT 1988c). The media also reported on the manipulation of information in Mexico, criticizing the government-leaning news program anchored by

---

[5]Although the elder Cárdenas's authoritarianism is unquestioned, we must also remember that it was in the 1929 elections that the Revolutionary National Party (PNR), the PRI's direct predecessor, tested techniques for stealing elections in the first great electoral fraud of the postrevolutionary era, with the willing cooperation of U.S. Ambassador Dwight Morrow.

Jacobo Zabludovsky and praising the objectivity and professionalism of Monterrey's *El Norte* (NYT, July 16, 1988).

As had been the case since the days of Miguel Alemán, the media's support for Salinas consisted of both what was said and what was not said. No major U.S. newspaper ever considered publishing a serious piece on the fraud perpetrated in Mexico's 1988 presidential election or its impact on the outcome. Information on electoral irregularities was easily available: in thirty-five rural districts, Salinas's vote total fell between 105 and 125 percent of the total adult population as reported in the 1980 census.[6]

The U.S. government made every effort to shore up Salinas's controversial victory. One of the *Times's* most prestigious journalists, R.W. Apple, Jr., suggested that "although they will not say so for publication, American officials are pulling for Mr. Salinas in what they consider an honest attempt to make a new start. They appear unconcerned about voting irregularities." Apple also noted that these same officials were "giving considerable weight to reports from Mexico City suggesting that Mr. Salinas has allied himself with a reform group within the PRI" (NYT, July 11, 1988).

Washington's actions were more eloquent than any declaration. On October 17, 1988, Washington agreed to loan Mexico $3.5 billion which, according to the *Times*, was intended to "underwrite existing policies at a time of great political ferment." In this same article, author Larry Rother quoted an anonymous U.S. banker in a prophetic assertion: "Don't think for a minute that this is the last chapter. Mexico will be back at the well again, and the United States will once again have to help, if for no other reason than that it cannot afford to turn its back" (NYT, Oct. 20, 1988).

As of 1976, the U.S. State Department began producing annual congressional reports on the human rights situation in Mexico and around the world. These reports are useful—and often ignored—barometers of the bilateral relationship. Despite the cautious language of the reports, it is clear that both Democratic and Republican administrations overtly supported the PRI, using techniques such as those described in preceding chapters. For example, although the reports sometimes included references to human rights abuses, these were generally followed by praise for the government's efforts to eradicate them.

The congressional report from 1980, for example, described instances of torture, but it followed up by noting that "the government has prosecuted some police officers who obtained evidence or confessions through torture." The 1991 report asserted that the Mexican

---

[6]In Ocosingo, Chiapas, Salinas's vote was 105 percent of the total electoral roll, and in Comitán it was 124 percent. Chiapas, with 3 percent of the total national population, contributed 6 percent of Salinas's votes nationwide (López 1988: 31–33; Fox 1996).

government had not ceased in its "efforts begun in 1990 to reduce the incidence of torture and similar abuse by officials" (DOS 1981: 479–80, 1992: 667). Other assumptions made in these reports were that the existence of a legal framework necessarily meant that the framework was being adhered to, and that official statements could be accepted at face value without independent confirmation.

The kinds of guidelines followed in the reports colored most perceptions of the Mexican electoral process. They can be best appreciated by comparing coverage of the 1986 and 1988 elections. The State Department's report for 1986 states that the July elections in Chihuahua were plagued by irregularities, and it scrupulously noted that charges of electoral fraud were "leveled by both Mexican *and foreign* investigative journalists as well as by opposition party activists." It added that "following the Chihuahua State elections, prominent leftist intellectuals in Mexico as well as *members of the Catholic Church hierarchy* publicly denounced what they believed to be blatant electoral frauds in those elections" (DOS 1987: 565, emphasis added). This text unequivocally reveals that there was a full awareness of the extent of Mexico's electoral irregularities; the inclusion of foreign journalists and members of the Catholic hierarchy in the list of critics was an indirect manner of validating these charges.

The report for 1988 differed considerably. Despite the importance of the 1988 elections, the State Department report for that year merely noted that "opposition parties and other observers have charged the PRI with electoral fraud." The report offered an absurdly baroque justification: "given the PRI's greatly reduced margin of victory compared to previous years, many observers believe that the extent of electoral fraud in 1988 was considerably reduced." This was followed by a list of the government's glowing advances for 1988: an increased number of opposition seats in the Senate and the Chamber of Deputies, and the entry of a woman (a state governor) into the administration's upper echelons (DOS 1989: 631, 637). Such distortions allowed the United States to persevere in its defense of an authoritarian regime without violating its own self-view as an exceptional and objective nation.

Salinas de Gortari and NAFTA

Although the *Times* coverage of the Salinas administration has not been subjected to content analysis, the overriding impression left by important articles published during this period is that Salinas was the international community's favorite Mexican president, even surpassing Miguel Alemán in popularity. A statement appearing in the *Economist*—extreme even at the time of its publication in 1993—

reflects this: "despite his controversial entrance [the 1988 elections], four years into his administration, Mr. Salinas has earned the right to be acclaimed as one of the great men of the 20th Century" (*Economist* 1993).

Such enthusiasm has been explained in a number of ways. Some observers have emphasized Salinas's propaganda and public relations apparatus, which was adept at creating images the United States was predisposed to accept. Its central message—that Mexico's new technocrats were a modernizing elite without whom the country would inevitably slide into instability—played on some of the United States' most deep-seated anxieties while portraying Salinas not just as the best but as the only viable option.

Of course, not everything was propaganda. Salinas carried out a fundamental reorientation of the Mexican national project, and many of the changes he wrought were necessary. He was able to reduce the state's role in the economy, regularize the Church's legal status, and establish a less tortured relationship with the United States.[7] One of his most important reforms was the decision to negotiate a free trade agreement that would consolidate the trends outlined above. The process through which Mexico arrived at this hugely important decision reflects the extensive powers vested in the presidency. In a conversation with Robert Pastor, Salinas explained that one of his reasons for seeking a North American trade agreement was that "changes in Europe and East Asia and an apparent reliance on blocs *convinced me* that we should also be part of an economic trading bloc with the United States and Canada" (Pastor 1990: 32, emphasis added).

The traditional political class obediently implemented a presidential order that entailed a historic turnabout in Mexico's perceptions of, and manner of establishing relations with, the United States. All opposition was easily brushed aside by Salinas's public relations mechanisms, which cemented the belief that this was the road to a more prosperous society.

Debate on NAFTA in the United States revolved around its potential benefits for the U.S. economy and for Mexico's general well-being. Grinspun and Cameron's analysis of the literature on Mexico's economic links with the rest of the world reveals that most analysts in the United States believed not only that NAFTA was inevitable, but also that it was in Mexico's best interests. NAFTA, it was frequently argued, would result in "stable growth of the Mexican economy and sustained capital inflows to fund that growth; slow but sure improvement in the standard of living of poor Mexicans as wages and

---

[7]Unfortunately, many changes were implemented in such a hurried and disorderly manner that catastrophic errors were unavoidable. For example, corruption soared to unprecedented levels, although—as happened during the oil boom—this was downplayed by the U.S. media.

working conditions improve; improvement in social indicators as the benefits of growth 'trickled down'; and lagged, but steady liberalization of the political system" (Grinspun and Cameron 1996). That is, economic liberalization would eventually lead to greater democracy. This dovetailed neatly with a chronology developed by Salinas: "when you are carrying out a strong economic reform, you must make sure that you build the political consensus around it. If you are at the same time introducing additional drastic political reform, you may end up with no reform at all. And we want to have reform, not a disintegrated country" (*New Perspectives Quarterly* 1991: 8). Although important advances have been made toward liberalizing the political system, these have had to overcome continued resistance from the ruling elite.

The United States was so enthralled with Salinas's reform program that it glossed over the most negative aspects of his administration. One serious consequence was that the drug cartels were able to acquire a great deal of power without calling attention to themselves. In December 1995, the *Economist* acknowledged that "during Mr. Salinas' tenure, drug bosses consolidated their fiefs. . . . American anti-drug agents knew of the spreading rot, often refusing to work with counterparts they knew to be crooked. But other American officials, keen to cement Mr. Salinas' economic reforms with the NAFTA, turned a blind eye, often issuing statements praising his anti-drug efforts, despite evidence to the contrary" (Andreas 1996: 24).

The U.S. elite's commitment to Salinas and NAFTA must be evaluated in terms of the story so far. Washington's rationale appears in an April 1991 confidential memorandum from U.S. Ambassador to Mexico John Negroponte, which states that reforms in Mexico's foreign policy and economy began in the mid–1980s, a process that was "dramatically accelerated by Salinas after he came to office in 1988. The proposal for an FTA is in a way the capstone of these new policy approaches." In foreign policy terms, an "FTA would institutionalize acceptance of a North American orientation to Mexico's foreign relations," and in economic terms, the FTA would be an "instrument to promote, consolidate and guarantee continued policies of economic reform beyond the Salinas administration" (DOS 1991: 1).[8]

From a broader perspective, although the understanding between the two countries had functioned for almost a century, there were still unsatisfactory aspects from Washington's point of view. Salinas presented the United States with an opportunity to quell the occasional irritations that resulted when this potentially unstable neighbor held an independent attitude. Through Salinas, Mexico would finally adopt the United States' model for political and economic organiza-

---

[8]Orme (1993: 17) reached similar conclusions.

tion. NAFTA would also help assuage any residual guilt left from a long history of U.S. aggression. As a U.S. government official stated in private conversation, Salinas was like a priest who could absolve the United States from all historical sins (author interview, March 1996).

THE INTERNATIONALIZATION OF POLITICS

The interests of the new actors involved in the bilateral relationship became increasingly apparent as part of a broader phenomenon after the mid–1980s. A number of historical trajectories merged in an internationalization of Mexican politics that had two distinct expressions. A growing number of Mexican actors incorporated the external factor into their tactical and strategic thinking, and foreign groups became more interested in Mexican affairs. In the case of the United States, the dialogue between the two societies intensified and the myth of official Mexican independence and nationalism was gradually laid to rest.

During the Central American conflicts, Mexico's geographical situation made it a natural point of confluence for international organizations with an interest in the region. Foundations and organizations concerned with the safety of refugees and displaced populations established close ties with independent Mexican organizations such as the San Cristóbal and Tapachula dioceses and NGOs from around the country. Such ties raised awareness and extended the vision of Mexican NGOs—traditionally semi-clandestine, inward-facing, and insular groups, very much in the shadow of an authoritarian government—regarding the importance of international networks. This, in turn, laid the foundation for a relationship that would facilitate the flow of support and financial resources at critical moments, such as electoral observation in 1994 and the peace process in Chiapas. Today, complex networks of Mexican, U.S., and Canadian organizations have become an important influence on inter-governmental relations in North America.

Simultaneously, the long-standing taboo against Mexicans discussing Mexican problems in foreign arenas gave way, and the United States became a forum for a number of highly critical Mexican commentators (see Castañeda 1986).[9] In August 1986, members of the PAN leveled serious charges of electoral fraud and corruption against the Mexican government in an informal hearing convened by Senator Jesse Helms (NYT, Aug. 15, 1986), prompting an outcry in Mexico

---

[9]Castañeda began to criticize the Mexican government as early as summer 1985.

and accusations that the PAN members were inviting a U.S. intervention.[10]

After 1986, the flame of official patriotism dimmed rapidly, and its
occasional flare-ups were not particularly bright or effective. Salinas's
economic policies, along with the increasing closeness between the
two governments, laid bare the incongruence of the official pose of
independence and facilitated greater dialogue between the two societies. Slowly, fueled by the pioneering labors of many scholars, a wide
range of groups in the United States began to take a greater interest in
Mexico. In 1986, the *Times* published a letter from the United States
section of Amnesty International expressing concern for "over 400
instances of disappearances, torture, ill-treatment and the detention of
those we consider to be prisoners of conscience," adding that Mexico
was "second only to Chile" in the list of hemispheric human rights
violators (Acker and King 1986).

In 1988, the Minnesota International Human Rights Committee[11]
established the first program dedicated exclusively to Mexico. In
1989, Americas Watch began an investigation on Mexico with the goal
(as described by executive director Juan Méndez) of "responding to a
growing interest from non-official sectors—churches, unions, and social organizations—in what is going on in Mexico" (author interview,
July 1990). The U.S. section of Amnesty International was simultaneously conducting further investigations thanks to increasing financial
and human resources freed up by the democratization of Latin
America (author interview with Beth Kempler, July 1990).[12] These organizations soon discovered Mexican NGOs able to provide them
with accurate information (and not intimidated by fears of being labeled unpatriotic).

The Mexican government was an involuntary contributor to this
internationalization. Coincidentally, an Americas Watch report
(*Human Rights in Mexico: A Policy of Impunity*) was presented in Los
Angeles in June 1990, only days before the presidents of Mexico and
the United States announced their decision to begin negotiations for a
free trade agreement in North America. Realizing that human rights
issues could pose obstacles to a trade accord, Salinas immediately
ordered the creation of the National Commission on Human Rights

---

[10]Paradoxically, that same month the Mexican government quietly embarked on a deliberate attempt to influence the United States. In August 1986, the Mexican government hired a number of U.S. lobbyists to promote its official image in Washington. For some unknown reason these enthusiastic lobbyists dumped fourteen
informational dossiers on Mexico—each weighing over five kilos—at the *Times*'s
doorstep (NYT, Aug. 29, 1986).

[11]Today the Minnesota Advocates for Human Rights.

[12]This report did not appear until 1991. See Amnesty International 1991.

(CNDH), and his team oversaw its formal establishment a mere seventy-two hours later.[13]

Despite its hasty origins and the fact that it was set up with no jurisdiction over labor or electoral matters, by concentrating on the defense of basic individual rights the CNDH constructed new barriers to the use of coercion, and this, in turn, allowed independent social movements to appear and evolve. Another unexpected consequence was that the CNDH fueled the internationalization of Mexican politics. In order to bolster the image of the regime, CNDH officials embarked on a campaign of intense international activity, which ultimately legitimated the concept of international activism as a whole, including that being carried out by independent organizations.[14]

Mexico's human rights NGOs benefited from yet another positive consequence of the CNDH's creation. For many years such groups had focused on defending individual rights. With the creation of the CNDH, the NGOs were able to expand their agendas to include broader rights and freedoms. After 1991, political rights, civil rights, and freedom of information would become pivotal issues for the vigorous civic movement that would reach a high point in 1997. Such are the paradoxes of history: an authoritarian action nourished the very forces that would eventually rise up against authoritarian forms of government.

1994–1997

In December 1993, Mexico's ruling elite seemed likely to remain in power, postponing hopes for political liberalization. Then on January 1, 1994, the EZLN burst onto the national scene; in August came the all-important presidential election; and in December 1994 Mexico devalued the peso. These events and others can all be interpreted—though in differing ways—in light of the variables described above.

Salinas's triumphant dream showed its first signs of turning into a nightmare on January 1, 1994, when an Indian uprising in Chiapas laid bare the limitations and defects of the economic model, exposed the weaknesses of the political classes, and accelerated processes of democratization. The government's initial inclination was to respond with force. When this elicited a strong negative reaction from large sectors of Mexican society and the international community, the government entered into negotiations with the rebels, and a truce, albeit an uneasy one, was eventually established in Chiapas.

---

[13]General Directorates for Human Rights were established in the early days of the Salinas administration, both in the Ministry of Government and in the Ministry of Foreign Affairs.

[14]For an analysis of Mexico's new style of foreign policy, see Eisenstadt 1992.

Just as the situation seemed to be coming under control, PRI presidential candidate Luis Donaldo Colosio was assassinated in March 1994. His death was followed by a second major political assassination, that of PRI president José Francisco Ruiz Massieu in September 1994. Meanwhile, Manuel Camacho Solís, passed over in the PRI's choice of its candidate for the presidency, begun to distance himself from the official party.

This mood of political violence, together with the situation in Chiapas, heightened the importance of the August 1994 presidential election, in which two strong opposition candidates were challenging the man deputed to candidacy after Colosio's death—Ernesto Zedillo Ponce de León. The elections were carefully monitored by organizations such as Alianza Cívica, a coalition of hundreds of NGOs and thousands of Mexican citizens. Alianza Cívica not only provided a clear picture of a host of electoral irregularities, but it also exposed the poverty of Mexico's civic culture: it was clear that much of the electronic media were anything but impartial and that there were absolutely no effective limits on campaign expenditures.[15]

Reactions in the United States—and among the international community—dramatically reflected the extent to which opinion was divided. The U.S. government responded to the Chiapas situation by giving strong support to the Mexican authorities. And in August 1994, Washington clearly placed peaceful elections ahead of democratic elections, in an attitude reminiscent of U.S. support for the Mexican regime during the contested elections of 1929, 1940, 1946, 1952, and 1988.

Such government responses were in stark contrast to the newfound breadth of social reaction and the attitude of the U.S. media. Members of an American human rights organization, invited by their Mexican counterparts, arrived in Chiapas only four days after the rebels first appeared on the scene. Then in July, the presidential elections were closely monitored by a wide range of organizations; Global Exchange and the Washington Office on Latin America were but two of the many groups that contributed observers to back their Mexican counterparts. And foundations, such as the John D. and Catherine T. MacArthur Foundation, underwrote activities to promote democracy.

Some of the most dramatic expressions of these shifting perceptions came from *Newsweek* correspondent Tim Padgett, whose reflections on his Mexican experiences summarize a radical change in attitudes. He acknowledged that Salinas was in many ways an extraordinary Mexican president. However, he went on to sum up a very generalized feeling: "he fooled us into thinking he had modern-

---

[15]For the first time in history, in 1994 a number of organizations were able to provide a clear x-ray of Mexico's electoral processes. See Aguayo 1995; Alianza Cívica 1994a, 1994b.

ized Mexico." Salinas changed "the image but not the substance of Mexico." His "economic reforms failed to modernize Mexico because he failed to modernize the corrupt, repressive and inefficient apparatus that *controls* Mexico's economy in the first place." Salinas "charmed us into forgetting that most Mexican politics is a byzantine, mafioso affair. I would have been better off during his Presidency if I'd remembered the rule of thumb I was taught as a young reporter in Chicago: 'If your mother says she loves you—check it out!'"— something far too few journalists or scholars bothered to do.

"Why was Salinas able to fool the United States?" Padgett wondered. The reason was that he was *just like an American*: "he wore Armani business suits and talked like a Wall Street broker . . . and while most Mexican Presidents take pride in a certain Latin lover's mystique, gossip columnists complained that Salinas was a sexual bore. He was just like an American (or at least a Brit)." This

> public relations maestro . . . promised that the money we'd pour into Mexico as a result of his economic reforms would transform his country into a modern democracy with a healthy and happy middle class. Here's the problem: in reality, Salinas was firmly allied with Mexico's oligarchy, which meant he wasn't interested in fostering either democracy or a middle class.

Padgett described some of Salinas's preferred strategies:

> One of his favorite gimmicks was to take the billions of dollars his government was earning from the auction of state-run companies and fly around the country giving roads, water or electricity to the poor, as if it were all a gift from him instead of their right as Mexican citizens. And he always took U.S. journalists along to show everyone he was a world player.

Tim Padgett—like many other observers, both Mexican and foreign—had a profound change of heart regarding Salinas's Mexico following the Zapatista rebellion. After government troops slaughtered rebels at Ocosingo during the conflict's early days, Padgett realized that "there was something very wrong beneath the surface of the 'Mexican Miracle'" (T. Padgett 1996).

This premonition was confirmed by the December 1994 devaluation, which even economists favorable to the regime acknowledged was "caused, most of all, by the fiscal and monetary policies implemented throughout 1994" by the Salinas administration, policies that were "wholly inconsistent with the rate of exchange." Another catalyst, for which the regime was also to blame, was the conversion of "the entire short-term government debt [*tesobonos*] which had been originally set in pesos, into dollars, which exacerbated the risk of insolvency" (Lustig 1995). Once again, presidential authoritarianism and the absence of controls over Mexico's presidents were to stand the country in poor stead.

The devaluation called for yet another financial bailout of the Mexican economy. As in 1976, 1982, 1985, 1986, and 1988, the Mexican government was again dependent on the goodwill of Washington and the international community. Their reaction was unprecedented. By authorizing an enormous relief package, the White House confirmed that the bilateral understanding remained very much in place. In late January 1995—in record time—the United States announced that it had put together a package of up to $U.S.50 billion, including $20 billion from the U.S. government, $17.8 billion from the International Monetary Fund, $10 billion from the Bank for International Settlements, $1 billion from Canada, and $1 billion from other Latin American countries.

The proposed financial bailout package evoked a furor in Washington. The Clinton administration was charged with having obscured, or even concealed, the truth about Mexico's economic situation in 1994 (D'Amato 1995: 7–13), and these accusations were not without some basis. Later, when the time came for the State Department to certify Mexico's fight against drugs, as it does annually, certain U.S. sectors expressed outright disgust. Senator Robert Bennet noted,

> the certification is clearly a joke, if the purpose is to determine what is going on in Mexico. At the same time, I understand why it was done. It was done because the President felt that we could not undercut President Zedillo to the point where the problem could get worse, so we lied. We can't de-certify Mexico. We have to lie about what is going on because our relationship with Mexico is so important that we can't let it go down the tubes (Andreas 1996: 26).

Other critics, such as Representative David Bonior, argued that the United States should not send "money to Mexico just to prop up a nation with the fastest growing number of billionaires in the world." The Clinton administration defended its decision with arguments relating to the economy, national security, and prestige.[16] Secretary of State Warren Christopher testified before the House Banking and Financial Services Committee on January 25, 1995, that the United

---

[16]Curiously, a former U.S. administration once defended its involvement in Vietnam in very similar terms.

States had an immense economic and political stake in Mexico's stability and, further, that the financial bailout would not only have "far-reaching implications for the prosperity and stability of Latin America and of emerging market economies around the world," but that it would also serve as "a test of American leadership" (Roett 1996: 37–38). In order to divert criticism (and to protect its interests), the U.S. government attached an unprecedented series of strings to this loan, forcing the Mexican government to accelerate the process of economic restructuring even further.

As the decade progressed, it became apparent that the United States' impact on Mexico was becoming increasingly multidimensional. Although Washington continues to support the incumbent regime, a wide range of groups promoting peace or democracy have consolidated their positions, creating new spaces for dialogue and facilitating social transformations. Although these forces are still a minority, their capacity to hinder the implementation of authoritarian government policies has been in evidence during the search for peace in Chiapas and the ongoing struggle for free and fair elections which, since the 1997 elections, has made remarkable progress.

To summarize, between 1986 and 1997 it was clear that the old bilateral understanding, though somewhat modified, continued in force. And it became clear that analyses of Mexico's contemporary history could no longer ignore the role of the United States. There is ample evidence that external support for the PRI was instrumental in allowing the party to extend its stay in power and to set an agonizingly slow rate of transition. In this context, President Clinton's decision to meet with the heads of Mexico's opposition parties during his May 1997 visit to Mexico was a clear signal that Washington has accepted the inevitability of a more democratic Mexico. Although Clinton's actions did not influence the electoral results, they did indicate an extremely important policy shift.

For Mexico, the dramatic results of the July 1997 elections provide a golden opportunity to debate and define the profile of a new political system. In this process—which is far from concluded—an important point for discussion will be the kind of relationship that Mexico must establish with the United States, a nation now challenged to achieve a better understanding of the problems and aspirations of the Mexican people.

CONCLUSION

Washington has staked everything on a slow transition in Mexico. The Mexican government is determined to remain in power. And a dizzyingly varied and growing range of forces is exerting unrelenting pressure for change. It is extremely hard to predict what the outcome will be. The situation continues to be unstable. Schisms and divisions within the PRI continue to appear; during the party's 17th National Assembly, for example, the traditional political classes rebelled against the new technocrats, who found the road to the presidency suddenly blocked.

The year 1997 was one of struggle for the entrenched authoritarian regime. Despite being seriously weakened, it still refused to relinquish its grip on power and privilege, while the forces arrayed against it gained in strength. In this ongoing process Mexico appears to oscillate between reaching some kind of consensus and succumbing to the threat of ungovernability and the proliferation of regional pockets of violence.

Will Washington continue to constitute an obstacle to democracy in Mexico? Will groups in the United States attain the coherence they need to thwart their government's antidemocratic efforts? No clear answer can emerge until this major transformation is complete. But as the finishing touches are put to this book in late 1997, there is reason for optimism.

20

The United States and Mexican Nationalism

This volume has sketched in broad strokes the U.S. elite's perceptions of Mexico, and it has presented an extensive base of information for a reinterpretation of certain aspects of recent Mexican history. This exploration of the past fifty years of Mexico's evolution and its relationship with the United States demonstrates that many myths should be revised. These include the assumptions that Mexico is hard to understand, that the U.S. elite is exceptional, and that Mexicans are passive and unwilling to open up to foreigners (that is, that they are insular and nationalistic).

The material contained in the 6,903 articles on Mexico published in the *New York Times* was used in two ways. The first was to digest and utilize the vast amount of information contained in these articles. The second was to interpret trends in perception and the evolution of ideas. In both cases, the results were complemented with sources from academia and government.

Time and again, the evidence reveals that there is a prevailing worldview in the United States that has colored that country's perceptions of many aspects of life in Mexico. With some exceptions,[1] this worldview is characterized by a perennial optimism toward Mexico's ruling party and governments and a total rejection of any current that leans even slightly toward the Left. The confluence in perceptions was not the product of a plot hatched by a CIA mastermind of ideologies; it was the result of the convergences of widely shared beliefs, such as belief in the exceptional character of the United States and in the inherently benign nature of capitalism and liberalism.

---

[1]The importance of these exceptions has increased steadily since the 1980s.

While most of the individuals quoted in this volume are likely convinced of the originality of their respective contributions, all were nevertheless "collective speakers," their words socially determined by ideas that evolved in tandem with the evolution of U.S. society—in the process modifying the parameters within which the United States viewed Mexico.

To argue that there was a collective consciousness is not to suggest that there was no room for individual contributions; it is simply to emphasize the importance of their overarching context. The works of Galdwin Hill, Oscar Lewis, Henry Giniger, Susan Kaufman Purcell, Kevin Middlebrook, Bruce Bagley, Roderic Camp, Roger Hansen, John Womack, Evelyn Stevens, Alan Riding, John Bailey, Friedrich Katz, David Brooks, Susan Eckstein, Wayne Cornelius, Judith Hellman, David Ronfeldt, Peter Smith, Jonathan Fox, John Coatsworth, Ellen Lutz, George Grayson, and many others, were all individual contributions to knowledge that helped expand and enrich the collective consciousness. Each of these authors absorbed and processed ideas and information that circulated in the United States, in Mexico, and around the world; and after being subjected to their individual imaginations and explored with the tools of scientific rigor, these ideas then bred new ideas in a dialectical process that is as interminable and ancient as history.

However, the incorporation of a fact or idea into an individual or collective consciousness is not dependent solely on its validity; the idea must also be compatible with the interests of the person who develops it, or of the community or country that is its context. When there is no such compatibility, mechanisms of evasion, denial, or rationalization come into play.

PERCEPTIONS OF MEXICO

How accurate is the U.S. elite's perception of Mexico? Although this question may seem inevitable, it is also fundamentally misconceived. The United States has all the information it needs to attain a full understanding of Mexico. The question, better put, would be how much the United States really wishes, or is able, to know about Mexico. And here enter the individual and collective limits of consciousness, as well as the mechanisms that are frequently employed to disguise them. Neither are exclusive to the United States; on the contrary, they are a common denominator across all of human culture.

A particularly persistent myth among foreigners is that Mexicans are difficult, if not impossible, to understand, due to their inherent tendencies toward isolation. In 1985, Cathryn Thorup noted that few Americans "seem to understand Mexico, despite our long and close relationship" (Thorup 1985; see also NYT 1985a). This was not for lack of accurate information, especially after the 1960s, when the margins of U.S. consciousness began to broaden, methodologies improved, and the number and quality of Mexicanists soared. Many Mexicans were willing to speak with foreigners and foreigners were willing to listen, catalyzing a fruitful dialogue between U.S. and Mexican scholars.

Yet not all members of the elite chose to incorporate this growing wealth of information into their understanding of Mexico and Mexicans. The new data transcended their maximum limits of consciousness. This is not unusual; most people tailor the information they are willing or able to accept. Thus lacunae can appear in consciousness, whether as the result of incomplete information or of the need to defend established interests. Following paragraphs outline some of the most glaring lacunae, although one must remember that these are generalizations; there are many exceptions to the rule.

The U.S. elite has never conducted a rigorous probe of Mexico's private sector, even though, during the period under study, this sector frequently showed itself to be as corrupt and inefficient as many of the government institutions that came in for constant (and often accurate) criticism.[2] Little was said, for example, about the poor business practices that characterized Mexico's banking sector prior to its nationalization in 1982, even though drawing attention to such problems would not have implied any opposition to free-market economies or the business sector. To the contrary, it might well have promoted a more efficient administration. And for purposes of comparison, the business community in the United States is under the constant and highly critical scrutiny of the media and a range of industry watchdogs.

Another gap is the meager attention paid to the coercive structure and perverse workings of the Mexican government. Some scholars might argue that this was a result of incomplete or nonexistent information, but the U.S. government can make no such claim. It has deliberately ignored this subject—even in the face of the very accurate and comprehensive information it has received on Mexico's corrupt law enforcement organizations and the tactics they employ. A broad range of documents makes reference to the "innumerable police forces that have become symbols of corruption, abuse of power, and in some instances, blatant criminality" (NYT, Feb. 13, 1983). There is also clear evidence that, as early as 1951, the CIA was well aware of

---

[2]There are a few critical analyses of the Mexican business sector, but this subject has received little attention in the literature.

the close relationship between Mexico's Federal Security Directorate and some of Mexico's most powerful drug lords (CIA 1951: 58).[3]

The government's turning a blind eye has been justified on a number of grounds—for example, that the United States did not wish to intervene in Mexico's internal affairs. The Mexican government welcomed such a justification, which tied in neatly with its nationalistic rhetoric. But for the United States' disregard of such issues to be credible required the quiescence of the Mexican population. As Mexican society becomes increasingly articulate and organized, it is attracting the attention of various sectors within the United States.

THE MYTH OF THE PASSIVE MEXICAN

U.S. consciousness is shot through with a thinly veiled contempt toward Mexico which is reflected in a certain fatalism regarding the Mexican population's ability to free itself from authoritarianism and secure a democratic form of government. This point of view was articulated frequently and publicly in the past. Not long after the United States gained independence, John Adams commented that there could never be democracy "amongst the birds, the beasts or the fish, or amongst the peoples of Hispanic America" (in Vázquez 1974). In the early twentieth century, Ambassador James Sheffield insisted that Mexicans could "recognize no argument but force" (L. Meyer 1985: 23). And only a few years ago Alan Riding closed his influential *Distant Neighbors* with this observation: "in spirit, Mexico is not—and perhaps never will be—a Western nation" (1985: 439). Such ideas are nourished—and intensified—by the United States' poor opinion of the Mexican population's will to struggle.

Both Mexicans and non-Mexicans frequently lament the passivity of the Mexican population in the face of government abuse. On June 29, 1983, the *Times* suggested that "what is most surprising for foreigners is the calm with which the Mexican system seems to absorb [the damage wrought by the economic crisis]." On July 7, 1984, the paper observed that despite the crisis, Mexican society appeared to display "no rage, nor even any resentment towards the government," and added that instead, there was "a placid resignation." In private, many in the United States were even more explicit.

---

[3]This knowledge came via the U.S. government's long association with these police organizations. In 1982 the U.S. justice system sought an indictment against Miguel Nassar Haro of the DFS for allegedly heading up a group of professional thieves specializing in California luxury cars for resale in Mexico. The CIA halted the indictment, arguing that Nassar Haro was one of their most useful Mexican collaborators (NYT, Mar. 28, 1982).

The author's research on state coercion and social resistance provided an opportunity to test the veracity of this interpretation and to postulate certain hypotheses. Files and archives, collective and individual memories, all attest to the fact that the regime has quashed a great number of protests and protesters, whose importance has been systematically downplayed or distorted in the Mexican and U.S. media. When these protests and the movements they represented were denied any kind of overt recognition, they suffocated, reinforcing the myth of the passive Mexican.

Not everyone was unaware of the situation in Mexico, however. An active academic current within the United States, which emerged during the 1960s, has helped assemble a more faithful representation of the Mexican government's transgressions. Evelyn Stevens, Susan Eckstein, Kenneth Johnson, Judith Adler Hellman, and Ellen Lutz, among others, have documented the price paid by those who dared oppose Mexican government authoritarianism. Overall, however, *Times* coverage, as well as the State Department's annual reports on human rights in Mexico, reveals that such analyses have failed to penetrate the consciousness of the majority in the United States, which remains comfortable with the myth of the passive Mexican and a reformist president courageously dealing with the reactionary dinosaurs in his government.

These lacunae allow the United States to justify its continued support for the authoritarian Mexican regime and to defend its own interests. They also reflect the extreme U.S. concern over the potential ungovernability of its neighbor, as well as the desire for extraordinarily broad margins of security. The United States has always protested even the slightest threat of ungovernability in Mexico, whether it came from the Left or the Right. In 1986 the *Times* quoted a U.S. diplomat who urged the PAN to forget "about hunger-strikes and protesters," and instead "become more organized, gather funds, and work hard at providing the people with a real alternative to the PRI" (NYT, July 13, 1986). Would his advice be the same today, following the July 1997 elections? All must now be reevaluated in the context of a general transformation of U.S. perceptions of Mexico.

SILENCE ON THE ROLE OF THE UNITED STATES

The most remarkable and important gap in understanding was the generalized disinterest of scholars, journalists, and government officials regarding the United States' impact on Mexican affairs. While many Mexicans have blamed the United States for everything imaginable, many Americans have done the opposite: with the exception of a few leftist analysts, they have never even considered the possibility that U.S. policies could produce negative repercussions in Mexico.[4]

For example, the U.S. government and media often criticized Mexico for allowing the Soviets and Cubans to operate intelligence units on Mexican soil, but they rarely mentioned (and certainly never denounced) the fact that the United States' own intelligence services were also operating there.[5] This was not the result of ignorance; a broad range of official documents bore witness to the many operations of U.S. intelligence services in Mexico. Even the *Times* was well aware, for example, that "the CIA has an extensive representation" in Mexico (NYT, June 23, 1985).

U.S. specialists on Mexico's national security also failed to acknowledge their country's role. One such was Lieutenant Colonel Alden M. Cunningham, who admitted (though only in a footnote) that "space limitations only permit acknowledging that other important national security factors also exist. These would be the United States–Mexican relationships, moral renovation, demographic initiatives" (Cunningham 1984).

This phenomenon was similar to that which colored the U.S. media's coverage of Mexico's private sector. That is, in the United States, the activities and operations of the security and intelligence services are closely monitored, but in Mexico these same services are given free rein. This silence was born of an extraordinarily important assumption: the U.S. elite simply cannot imagine that any of their actions could negatively impact their southern neighbor. This assumption—founded on the premise that the United States is an exceptional nation and that its interests and Mexico's are common and shared—has always been accepted, and never examined, much less proven.[6]

Such basic and deeply rooted assumptions produced important consequences. If the United States is, by definition, no threat to Mexico's security, then Mexican nationalism can be nothing more than an irrational (and irritating) refusal to cooperate fully with a powerful potential ally. But although the two nations do have a number of shared interests—the war on drugs is one example—there are many other areas where there is no concordance. It is also clear that many U.S. policies have had far-reaching repercussions on Mexico. Refusing to acknowledge this fact can only perpetuate a series of baseless myths and fantasies—and generate a detrimental feedback effect on reality.

---

[4]Examples include Cunningham 1984; Ronfeldt 1984; Moorer and Fauriol 1984; Applegate 1985. An exception is Dziedziec (1996), who acknowledges this influence but does not develop it.

[5]For a discussion of the United States' impact on Mexico's security, see Aguayo 1990.

[6]For examples of this, see DAF 1955; DOS 1956, 1959; Fauriol 1988; Ganster and Sweedler 1987; Wilson 1989.

PRESERVING MYTHS

When analyzing an extensive body of writings by journalists, scholars, government officials, and others who have sought to tread lightly around difficult questions and thorny subjects (a mind-set that crosscuts national boundaries), we begin to find traces of the techniques they used and to see how these strategies may play a role in the construction and preservation of myths. One of the most effective means for detecting a particular author's (or newspaper's) leanings is to note the author's (or paper's) sources. For the *Times*, this was the members of Mexico's political and economic elite—clearly the sector to which the *Times* could best relate.

To look at how this coverage might have differed, we need only compare it with the *Times* coverage of a government that the United States had no interest in protecting: Fidel Castro's Cuba. Content analysis of a sample of *Times* articles on revolutionary Cuba published in the early 1960s reveals that the paper frequently quoted the opposition and maintained a systematically critical and skeptical attitude toward the statements of the Cuban government. The opening sentence of a 1960 article is representative: "Cuba begins its second year under Castro's regime with fear and uncertainty, despite the rosy panorama painted by the government" (NYT, Jan. 13, 1960).[7] Official reports were clearly being rejected out of hand; opposition statements dominated throughout the remainder of the article.

Another useful strategy used in "shading" U.S. analyses of Mexico involves references to time and place. This technique was apparent in a 1986 article by James Reston: "there are those in the United States who would rather focus on political corruption and the one-party system, rather than recall that, unlike the rest of Latin America, the Mexican government has been able to maintain the peace and avoid a military dictatorship for over half a century" (Reston 1986). Clearly the Mexican system, warts and all, still compared favorably with those of other countries, and therefore it should be supported and maintained. It is worth mentioning that this mechanism has recently fallen into disuse; a global wave of democracy and the collapse of socialism have made it increasingly difficult to make favorable comparisons between Mexico and other countries.

Another technique involves the use of fragmentary analyses that hinder the development of a global vision. This ploy has proved particularly effective for relieving Mexico's presidents of blame by disassociating them from the political system's most negative aspects. From Miguel Alemán to Ernesto Zedillo, topics such as repression,

---

[7]The sample includes every first article on Cuba published annually by the *Times* between 1958 and 1964. See NYT, Jan. 8, 1958; Jan. 14, 1959; Jan. 13, 1960; Jan. 11, 1961; Jan. 10, 1962; Apr. 8, 1963; Jan. 17, 1964.

local political bossism, corruption, or electoral fraud have all been described as being totally separated from the president in office, who is usually portrayed as an embattled reformer struggling to overcome retrograde opponents. It is rarely noted that individuals who reach the apex of political power in Mexico must necessarily be highly skilled at manipulating even the most sinister aspects of the system in their favor. This tactic is complemented by a total disinclination to examine the biographies of Mexico's presidents once out of office, which belie the myth—restated every six years like a revelation from heaven—of their vocation of democracy.

Understanding how such mechanisms work is particularly important because researchers in the United States have earned a reputation for objectivity. Deliberate lies or the kind of governmental control long tolerated by the Mexican media have rarely featured in the U.S. press. What has been present, however, is a subtle process of interpretation that "massaged" thinking along a certain course. Whether this process was deliberate or unconscious varies case by case, but its pervasiveness confirms a pattern of selective denial of certain realities.

These considerations lead naturally to a discussion of the United States' belief in its own exceptional character. While living and studying in the United States for extended periods, the author developed a profound respect for the openness of this society and the deeply rooted consciousness of its citizens, which allows them to defend their rights and keep a tight rein on the activities of their government and business sectors. And, of course, one must acknowledge the United States' vast, indeed overwhelming, economic and military might. However, its continued support for an authoritarian and corrupt Mexican regime belies its self-image. How can the exceptional citizens of an exceptional country have persisted so long in their support for actions and policies that directly contradict their ideals of democracy and good government? The most obvious answer is that, for a long time, this support was believed to be in the best interests of the United States. (The idea that U.S. interests might include a more democratic Mexico has gained currency only very recently.) In effect, in foreign policy terms the United States behaves much like any other power.

The evidence collected in this volume reveals that, although in some cases the United States' vaunted rigor and objectivity is a reality, in other cases it is only a myth. Information and ideas became a privileged instrument for the maintenance of relationships of domination between the two countries, and for the preservation of the established order. For the majority of the Mexican population, this was to have disastrous consequences.

HEGEMONY AND COERCION

This brings us back to the very first questions posed in this book. What is the true extent and nature of the United States' impact on Mexico's history? What have been the costs and benefits to Mexico of being this superpower's neighbor? What role has the United States played, or can it play, in shaping a fairer and more democratic Mexico? Let us risk a few answers in what is still a very hazy area.

We cannot take the easy way out—blaming the United States for every Mexican crisis and misfortune. Mexico's government and society must shoulder a large share of responsibility for the prolonged and multidimensional crisis that has gripped the country since the 1970s. However, we cannot ignore the enormous impact of the United States on Mexican history. To shed some light on this hitherto cryptic topic—and perhaps assign at least some measure of responsibility—we must begin to unravel the true nature of this impact.

Any appraisal of the relationship between the two countries must recognize its most salient feature: since the earliest days of their independent existence, there has been a huge disparity in terms of power, and the United States has dominated Mexico continuously through varying combinations of hegemony and coercion. During the nineteenth and early twentieth centuries, the principal instrument was brute force, justified with moral arguments based on myths of racial and cultural superiority. For example, the Mexican War of 1846, in which Mexico lost half its territory, was "a war of valued conquest, covered in a coloring cloak of holy justification called 'Manifest Destiny'" (Virden 1957).[8] And Woodrow Wilson's intervention in Veracruz in 1914 was purportedly intended to help Mexico attain a greater level of democracy.

The era of brute force ended in 1927, when Ambassador Morrow and President Calles reached an understanding whose intricacies were to have a fundamental effect upon Mexican history in the twentieth century. Washington has since tended to emphasize hegemony as its policy tool of choice, and coercion has become rare. This emphasis on hegemony results in part from the nature of the two government systems and the countries' close geographic proximity (any miscalculation on the part of the U.S. government can have immediate repercussions upon U.S. territory) but also because the Mexican government has proved itself able to maintain stability and willing to respect the interests of the United States.

For these reasons, and because Mexico's leadership has always adhered to certain implicit restrictions, the U.S. elite tolerated policies and outbursts from Mexican officials that under other circumstances

---

[8]This war was justified, in one way or another, by most of the U.S. analysts who have written about it. See, for example, Bauer 1956; Rees 1960; Logfren 1967; Swan 1983.

would have been unacceptable. A high-ranking official from the Bush administration explained this attitude quite clearly:

> It is true that we allowed the Mexicans to behave in ways that would be unacceptable in other governments. We did so because we knew that in their attitude there is a great deal of rhetoric; their actions never go beyond certain implicit limits. If, during negotiations, we became stalled on a point they did not like, they immediately resorted to hypernationalism. We would sit back and listen, because we knew that this was something transitory, which would pose no real obstacles for the solution of concrete problems (author interview).

Despite any and all "implicit limits," it is clear that Mexican governments have enjoyed broad margins for action, especially when compared to other Latin American countries. An important question, then, is: How well has Mexico exploited these broad margins for maneuver? The governments that arose from the Mexican Revolution were able to carry out a novel economic experiment, develop an independent diplomacy, and reject at least some U.S. demands. In exchange for the freedom to take these steps toward Mexican self-determination, they gave way on other points to ally more closely with U.S. interests.

The Mexican government was usually persuaded to make concessions through rational arguments but coercion was used when needed. The Republicans, rather than the Democrats, were probably more prone to use coercion. However, whenever the U.S. government decided to use pressure against Mexico, it was implemented unilaterally and without warning—and it always produced results, which leads to the following points.

THE UNITED STATES AND MEXICAN NATIONALISM

These final pages reflect on the relationship between the United States and Mexican nationalism and on the challenges that Mexico faces in the closing years of the twentieth century. One of the most frustrating characteristics of Mexico's political transition has been its glacial pace—that is, the regime's capacity to resist change. This has been explained in various ways. Kevin Middlebrook has suggested that labor movements and their activities have been key to the regime's extraordinary longevity (Middlebrook 1995: 288). Other analysts have emphasized the sophistication of Mexico's political classes, the regime's inclusive character, the passivity of the Mexican population (sometimes attributed to the present-day population's indigenous roots), the opposition's inability to reach even limited accords, and/or the use of coercion.

Although such explanations may be valid, the PRI's survival has been greatly enhanced by the support of the international community, and in particular the United States. The United States' financial aid to Mexico and its colossal disinterest in Mexico's pro-democracy movements have no precedent in recent history. Impoverished and marginalized activists for democracy, challenging an affluent and entrenched regime, must figure prominently in any analysis of recent developments in Mexico.

The United States—theoretically a bastion of democracy—has repeatedly had to justify its continuing support for an authoritarian regime. To do so, it most frequently simply overlooked the most problematic aspects of Mexican reality. These were excised from the American consciousness and banished into the black hole of forgotten knowledge. On other occasions, Washington justified its policies on the grounds that they laid a foundation for a brilliant, though still unachieved, future and were, therefore, in Mexico's best interests. One of the most paradoxical justifications appears in a State Department document from the Reagan era:

> [E]very dictatorship—both of the left and of the right— perpetrates grave violations of human rights. Every human rights violation, furthermore, should be condemned. However, inasmuch as non-communist dictatorships are able, in varying degrees, to evolve in a democratic direction, communist dictatorships are especially resistant to democratization (DOS 1984: 10).

Thirteen years after these lines were written, the majority of the world's Communist dictatorships are fading into history, but the authoritarian Mexican regime is still in place (although the PRI's electoral defeats in 1997 appear to signal the beginning of the end).

Not every sector within the U.S. elite agreed with this Reagan-era perspective. Over the last three decades an important number of academics, journalists, politicians, and members of social organizations have become increasingly critical of the Mexican regime's rampant corruption and inefficiency, its violation of human rights, and the absence of democracy. While such views will ultimately entail some revision in U.S. policies toward Mexico, and their supposedly beneficial and benign nature, until recently these ideas have been confined to limited sectors of U.S. society.

Why did the United States decide to support the PRI so firmly and unquestioningly? The usual response is that this party gave the United States what it was looking for: stability in Mexico. But this argument is flawed; the system's potential for instability has always been high. During the last thirty years Mexico has suffered cyclical economic crises, the country's foreign debt has soared from U.S.$3 billion in 1970 to over $100 billion in 1996, political upheavals (both peaceful and violent) have become commonplace, the population's living standard has been brutally undercut, and drug trafficking and crime have skyrocketed.

Then perhaps the United States' support was due to the fact that there was no actor dedicated to a continuing and systematic broadening of its margins of collective consciousness. Unlike the Irish, Israelis, Central Americans, and others, Mexicans who opposed their government were, for a long time, unable to promote their cause—a more democratic Mexico—in the United States. Their ability to lobby in the United States was hindered by obstacles to consciousness among both Mexicans and Americans; and perhaps one of the greatest of these obstacles has been Mexican nationalism.

After its defeat and loss of territory in 1848 (and after a whole series of other European and U.S. intrusions), Mexico turned inward behind a barrier of mistrust. Foreigners were viewed as hostile, and Mexicans were urged to unite against them. For example, President Luis Echeverría noted in his fourth State of the Nation Address that "in 1848 we lost half of the territory inherited from our Indian and Spanish forefathers, as a result of an unfair war with the United States of America" (Echeverría 1974: 22). Echeverría's words sum up some of the central theses of a nationalism that arose from a revolution against the excesses of Porfirio Díaz's dictatorship and/or the constant interventions by Western powers. During the early decades of the twentieth century, such ideas served as a healing balm, helping make some sense of the death and destruction that accompanied the Revolution. Nationalism also played an important role in the construction of new institutions, helping the elite win and hold the support of the masses. It was a key referent for national identity and guided government actions and policies in a hostile, seemingly incomprehensible world.

The revolutionaries' fiery nationalism was eventually tempered by pragmatism, and by 1927 they had established an understanding with the United States, an implied understanding cloaked in ambiguity from its inception. In time, the Revolution became bureaucratized, and nationalism and the United States became important symbols in the Mexican elite's rhetorical efforts to hold on to power and privilege. And at some point nationalism and its associated revolutionary myths ceased to be a collective dream, to be converted into a mechanism of control with little relation to day-to-day existence in Mexico—in the process undermining the credibility of the institutions that had been erected on the foundation of nationalism and its myths (see Basáñez 1991).

By presenting the United States as a potential threat, the Mexican government had also been able to restrain Mexicans who sought to bring global attention to the country's problems, as well as to legitimate its call for national unity around a regime that portrayed itself as the real champion of national integrity and sovereignty. Although there have been moments in Mexican history when a united front against threats from the United States or elsewhere has been critically important, over the last fifty years the United States has been anything but an enemy of the regime, and any threat is far more imagined than real. In fact, Washington has been one of the regime's closest allies; even when it resorted to coercion, it did so as an adversary, not an enemy.

The United States elite cooperated fully with the regime's posturings. It not only ignored or glossed over certain events in Mexico, it also maintained a discreet silence in response to the nationalistic expostulations of the regime, having received private assurances from the government that Washington should not take its public pronouncements to heart. The United States also had a fairly clear view of public opinion in Mexico. From 1946 to 1980 the only opinion polls on Mexican attitudes toward the United States were those carried out by the U.S. government. These revealed that Mexico was not unlike other countries in Latin America: a portion of the population distrusted the United States, another group expressed pro-American views, and the remainder wavered between the two positions (Favela and Morales 1991). Polls carried out after Mexico's economic opening reveal that anti-American sentiment has declined (Poll 1992). This explains the Mexican population's weak opposition to NAFTA and the government's claim that proximity to the United States is, after all, a blessing, not a curse.

The United States' indifference toward Mexican nationalism was often in evidence. In 1958 a *Times* editorial noted that "traditional anti-Yankee feeling is a political artifice, and not a reality" among Mexicans (NYT 1958b). In 1980, Alan Riding commented that "despite the nationalistic rhetoric espoused by a number of governments, the Mexicans are not anti-American" (NYT, Nov. 9, 1980). And Ronfeldt, Nehring, and Gándara (1980: 47) observed that Mexico's "nationalist symbolism has served to embellish internal rhetoric, parochial demagoguery, and bureaucratic maneuvering." In 1984, U.S. Ambassador to Mexico John Gavin informed correspondent Richard Meislin that "a number of Mexican government officials," with whom he had an extremely "cordial relationship" and who would often privately "praise the help provided by the United States," would on other occasions "publicly criticize him and the United States" (NYT, Nov. 11, 1984).

The United States even found Mexico's official posturing to be useful because it cajoled many of the world's revolutionaries and neutralized and isolated Mexico's more genuinely nationalistic and far more disquieting Left. For the U.S. elite, Mexico's official nationalism became a paper tiger: sleek and threatening, but with little real substance.

The understanding between Mexico and the United States has produced different consequences for each. Mexico has always been only a marginal concern for the United States. But for Mexico, its neighbor to the north has long been, in equal parts, an enigma and an obsession, despite the fact that the population has, until recently, affected an attitude of indifference. This feigned indifference, the result of a traumatic nineteenth-century conflict, was an unwise strategy. Mexico forgot that knowledge and intelligence are critical tools that a weak nation can use to guide its deployment of scarce resources for maximum effect. As border areas have become increasingly integrated, ignorance has allowed the Mexican population to imagine a host of conspiracies originating in Washington, while they have failed to realize that the real threat for Mexico comes from a rigid, corrupt, and inefficient political system.

When the history of these two societies is written, it will note that this situation began to change in the 1970s, when a vast intellectual effort finally provided better and more critical evaluations of Mexico's political system and its ruling class, as well as an increasingly thorough understanding of the United States which eschewed both excessive praise and unthinking criticism. This book forms part of a revisionist school (which has yet to identify itself as such) that has been nurtured by a decades-long dialogue among scholars. Over these three decades, many Mexicans have learned to understand the United States as a vehicle for serving their own national interests. As perceptions have become less simplistic, tolerance has grown and relationships have improved. If Mexicans of divergent viewpoints had not intensified their relationship with the United States, we might not have access today to writings that challenge the rosy panorama sketched out by the two governments.

The final years of the twentieth century have proved to be a difficult period, one of uncertainty and crumbling myths. Mexico's July 1997 elections, which seem to mark a watershed for Mexican authoritarianism, raise complex new challenges. Mexico urgently needs a development model that will allow it to achieve democracy, social justice, and sovereignty. Will it reach these goals? If so, how and when? As Mexico debates its choices, the United States must make some decisions as well, based on national priorities and a reevaluation of Mexican reality.

Neither a simplistic rejection of neoliberalism nor a nostalgia for the populism of days gone by will suffice. What is needed are new intellectual and political proposals that will allow us to reconceptualize the past. One important future task will be to reevaluate the Mexican Revolution. Were the foundational principles and aspirations of the Mexican Revolution in error? Are the men who were charged with bringing these principles and goals to fruition to blame? Or does the fault lie with an anemic society that tolerated the abuses? And regardless of who is to blame, what was the role of the U.S. elite?

This is not merely an intellectual exercise. It has political relevance, for as we consider what really happened and develop proposals about what should be done in the future, we must continue to dismantle the structures of authoritarianism and create democratic institutions that allow us to achieve the kind of consensus needed to overcome an obsolete presidentialism. The task will be arduous. Mexican democracy faces complex obstacles, set in place by a cunning and still deeply entrenched authoritarian regime and culture, and by a superpower long convinced that its national security is linked to the perpetuation of a single party in Mexico.

Despite all obstacles, change continues. The Mexican government has lost control over much of society, and its monopoly over the nation's channels of communication with the outside is crumbling rapidly. Mexico City, the Chamber of Deputies, and several state governments are now in the hands of the opposition. The population is poised to take on authoritarianism and to call upon world opinion in its struggle. Slowly but surely, U.S. consciousness regarding Mexico has broadened, nourishing a new critical attitude among scholars and journalists. Will these new ideas influence Washington's traditional and absolute support for the Mexican leadership? Will an important change in attitude—foreshadowed in President Clinton's 1997 meeting with opposition leaders—take root? If so, what will be the results, and when will they become apparent?

In all likelihood a growing chorus of Mexican voices will be heard in the United States, creating awareness and broadening consciousness in a polyphonic concerto in which one melody is carried by those who support the incumbent regime and the other by those who hope for change, all singing together but absent a conductor. In 1997, the second melody, the voice of change, was strongest. If it prevails, we shall have to revise another assumption: that the U.S. elite is always and in every circumstance an obstacle to democracy and change.

The future calls for a mature and democratic nationalism, in tune with a pantheon of myths where past, present, and future merge; a pantheon that is permanently revised and updated through scientific reason and patriotic passion. Ideally, this new pantheon of myths will contain a more exact view of the United States, and will allow Mexico to achieve its maximum potential for independence as neighbor to a superpower. To attain this view by accumulating knowledge and intelligence, to maintain it and continue to build on it, these will be the threads guiding Mexico's evolution in the twenty-first century.

Appendix A

Figures

The following figures present a small portion of the information yielded by the processing of 6,903 articles on Mexico and Mexican affairs published by the *New York Times* between January 1, 1946, and December 31, 1986. The information is organized into broad categories that coincide in general terms with the code manual (appendix B): visible characteristics, sources of information, political system, foreign policy, economy, and national character. The following brief commentaries introduce the figures by highlighting some of their most relevant aspects. Although many variables were excluded because of space considerations, a careful selection was made to include those illuminating at least some of the most important findings. This is why some statistics mentioned in the text as forming part of the database do not figure in this appendix.

VISIBLE CHARACTERISTICS

Visible Characteristics refers to an article's most immediately apparent aspects: date, page, column, and section within the paper; author; filing location; placement on the page; allotted space (in columns and centimeters); style of headline; and so on.

- Figure 1
The number of published articles reflects the United States' cyclic spurts of interest in Mexico, which were aroused by a spectrum of specific topics. In 1946–1947, for example, attention was drawn to oil-related matters, as it was in 1951 and 1954, when this topic overlapped interest in the Korean War and the overthrow of Jacobo Arbenz in Guatemala. In the 1960s, it was the Cuban Revolution that awakened U.S. interest, and in the late 1960s it was the student movement of 1968. Between 1976 and 1979 the salient issues were, first, Mexico's oil boom and, second, the country's financial crisis. Finally, in 1985–1986, attention focused solely on the economic crisis.

Miguel Acosta was instrumental in the preparation of this appendix; I alone am responsible for the interpretation.

- Figure 2

This figure reveals two remarkable aspects: the failure of persons writing about Mexican affairs from within the country to travel beyond Mexico City, and the tendency of correspondents writing about Mexico from within the United States to file their articles from locations other than Washington, D.C. This reflects Mexican centralization, as well as the disperse nature of power in the United States.

- Figure 3

This figure indicates the little importance given to information about Mexico. Only 30 percent of all articles can be considered relevant by virtue of their location on one of the principal pages of the newspaper's several sections: on pages 1–5 in Section A; on the editorial page; or on the first page of the financial section.

- Figure 4

This figure illustrates the distribution that the most important articles enjoyed; in general, it coincides with the continuing cycles of interest in Mexico. A similar pattern holds for editorials, op-ed pieces, and first-page articles in the financial section.

- Figure 5

This figure confirms that about a third of the analyzed articles are of real importance. For this calculation, I have taken into account pieces authored by correspondents or special envoys, editorials, and opinion pieces.

- Figure 6

The *Times* had eleven correspondents in Mexico—all men—between 1946 and 1986. Paul Kennedy and Alan Riding, whose sojourns there were the most extended, were also the most prolific. A comparison of the topics that attracted these two writers reveal the many evolutionary stages through which the United States' vision of Mexico has passed. The *Times* correspondents in Mexico were not unaffected by their own work. Camile Cianfarra, for example, was harassed because of her coverage of Mexican radicals, while Richard Severo and Alan Riding developed a mutual animosity because of the divergent perspectives from which they wrote. How the *Times* correspondents perceived, and were transformed by, Mexican culture is a fascinating subject for future research.

- Figure 7

The *Times* ran few opinion pieces on Mexican affairs. Their concentration after 1977 is noteworthy.

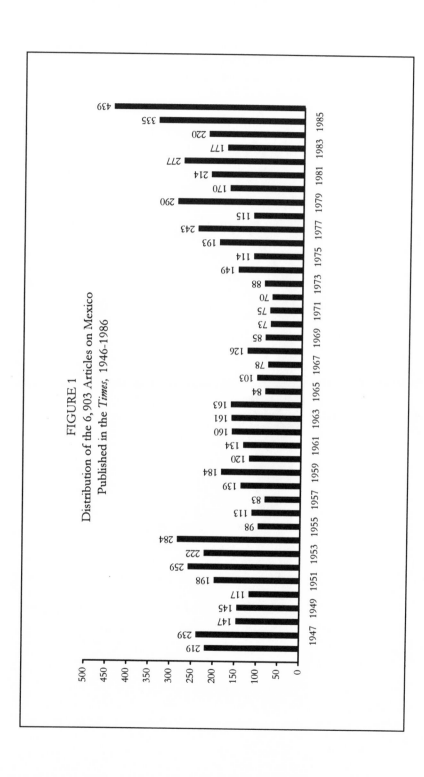

FIGURE 1

Distribution of the 6,903 Articles on Mexico
Published in the *Times*, 1946-1986

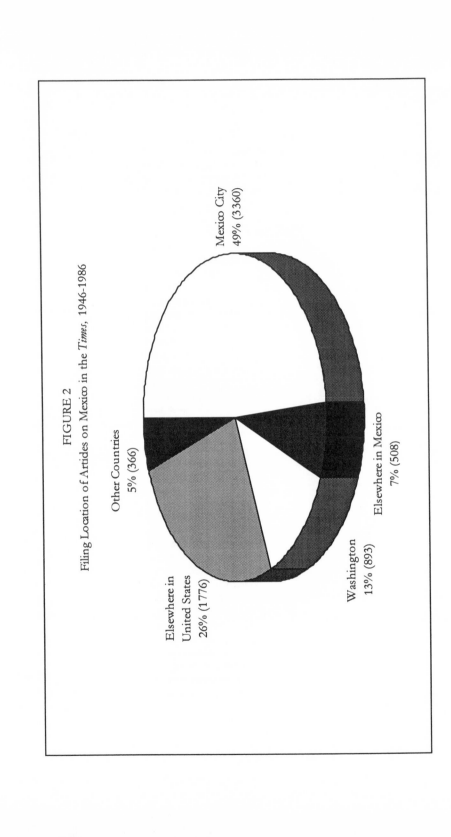

FIGURE 2

Filing Location of Articles on Mexico in the *Times*, 1946–1986

Other Countries
5% (366)

Elsewhere in
United States
26% (1776)

Washington
13% (893)

Elsewhere in Mexico
7% (508)

Mexico City
49% (3360)

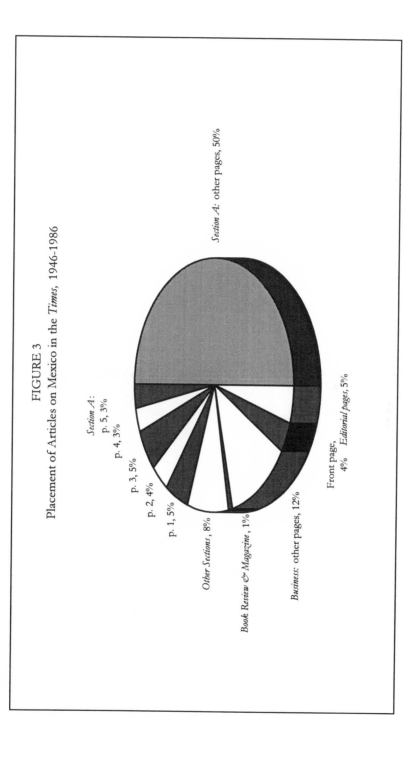

FIGURE 3

Placement of Articles on Mexico in the *Times*, 1946-1986

Section A:
p. 5, 3%

p. 4, 3%

p. 3, 5%

p. 2, 4%

p. 1, 5%

Other Sections, 8%

Book Review & Magazine, 1%

Business: other pages, 12%

Front page,
4%   *Editorial pages,* 5%

Section A: other pages, 50%

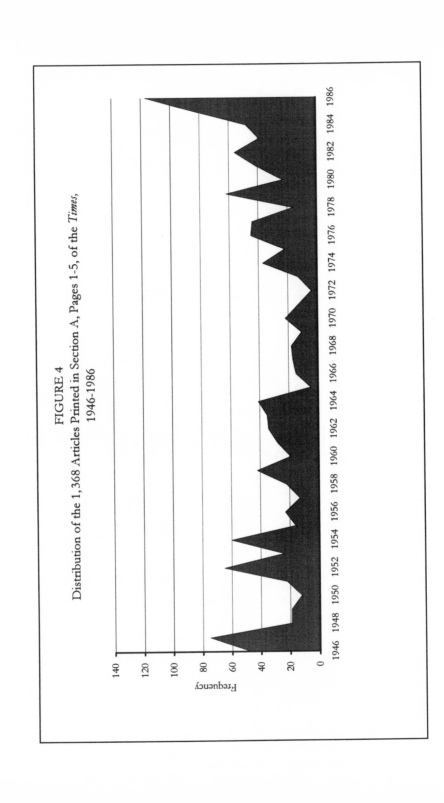

FIGURE 4

Distribution of the 1,368 Articles Printed in Section A, Pages 1-5, of the *Times*,
1946-1986

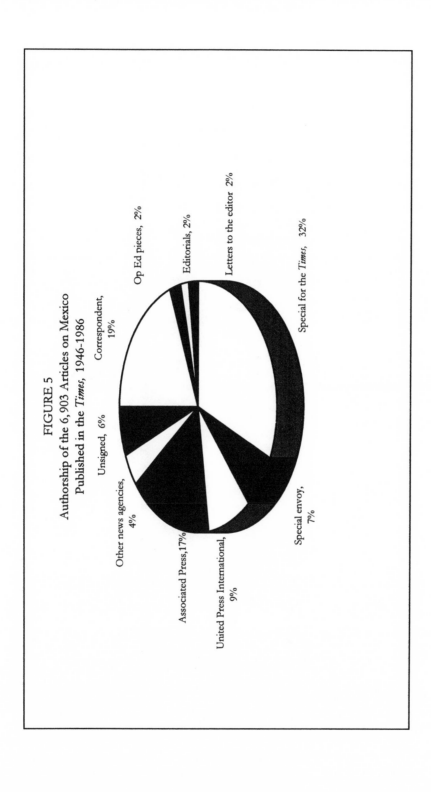

FIGURE 5

Authorship of the 6,903 Articles on Mexico
Published in the *Times*, 1946-1986

Op Ed pieces, 2%

Editorials, 2%

Letters to the editor 2%

Correspondent, 19%

Special for the *Times*, 32%

Unsigned, 6%

Other news agencies, 4%

Special envoy, 7%

Associated Press, 17%

United Press International, 9%

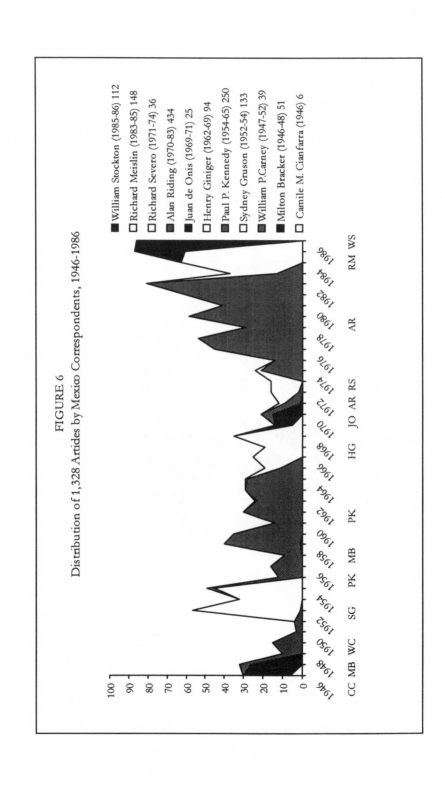

FIGURE 6

Distribution of 1,328 Articles by Mexico Correspondents, 1946-1986

■ William Stockton (1985-86) 112
□ Richard Meislin (1983-85) 148
■ Richard Severo (1971-74) 36
▨ Alan Riding (1970-83) 434
■ Juan de Onis (1969-71) 25
□ Henry Giniger (1962-69) 94
▨ Paul P. Kennedy (1954-65) 250
□ Sydney Gruson (1952-54) 133
▨ William P.Carney (1947-52) 39
■ Milton Bracker (1946-48) 51
□ Camile M. Cianfarra (1946) 6

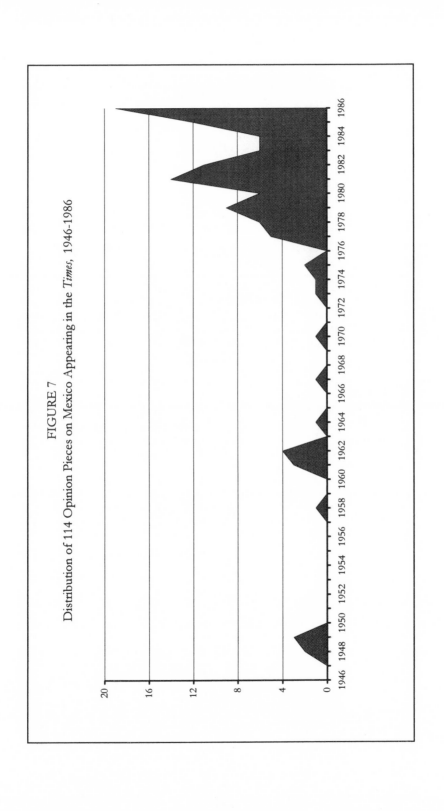

FIGURE 7

Distribution of 114 Opinion Pieces on Mexico Appearing in the *Times*, 1946-1986

Sources of Information

These variables are fundamental in content analysis. By identifying who has been granted a "voice," we can obtain a concrete indicator of the degree of objectivity displayed by a specific correspondent or in a specific piece. Balanced opinion is usually reflected in a range of sources that represent the variety of attitudes and players engaged in an issue.

- Figure 8

Certain images speak volumes. This figure clearly reveals which sectors were given greatest voice. The largest number of quotes corresponds to Mexican or U.S. government officials; the opposition was usually ignored. The *Times* was a forum for elite opinions.

- Figure 9

Other ways to organize quotes is by nationality or by whether their authors were identified or anonymous. Fifty-five percent of the individuals quoted in *Times* articles about Mexico were Mexicans, and of these, the greatest majority were members of the ruling elite.

- Figures 10–11

These figures indicate that both Mexican and U.S. government officials became increasingly willing to speak, albeit anonymously, to the U.S. press.

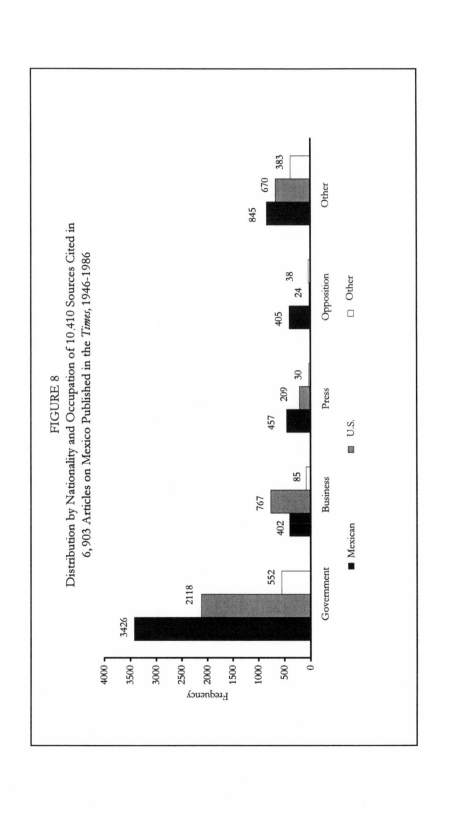

FIGURE 8

Distribution by Nationality and Occupation of 10,410 Sources Cited in 6,903 Articles on Mexico Published in the *Times*, 1946-1986

FIGURE 9

Nationality of Quoted Sources, 1946-1986

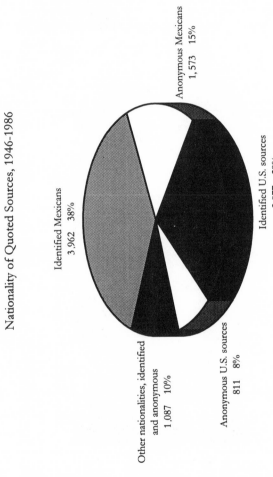

Identified Mexicans
3,962   38%

Anonymous Mexicans
1,573   15%

Identified U.S. sources
2,977   29%

Other nationalities, identified
and anonymous
1,087   10%

Anonymous U.S. sources
811   8%

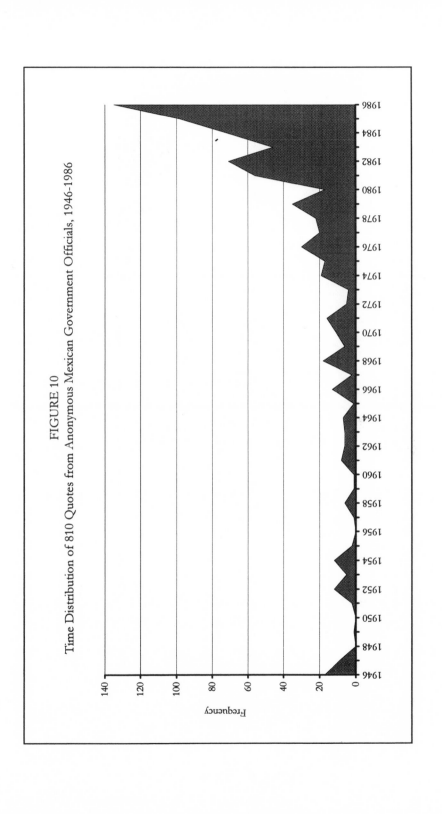

FIGURE 10

Time Distribution of 810 Quotes from Anonymous Mexican Government Officials, 1946-1986

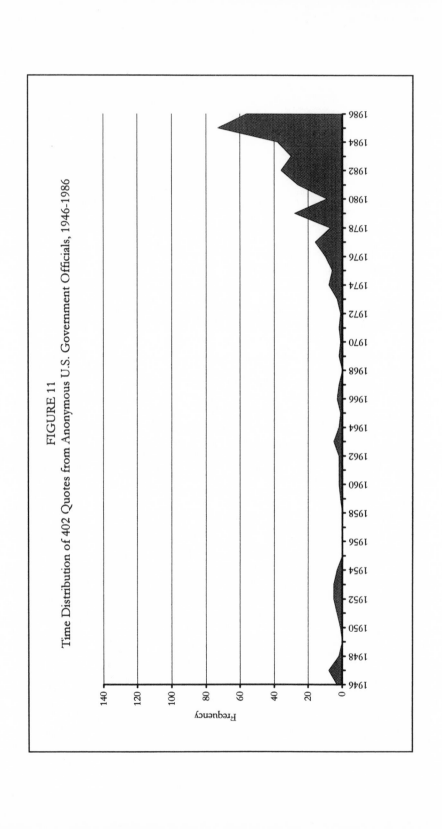

FIGURE 11

Time Distribution of 402 Quotes from Anonymous U.S. Government Officials, 1946-1986

THREE MEXICAN WATERSHEDS IN THE *TIMES*

The history of every nation is marked by events or moments that symbolize transitions from one era to another. These watersheds are usually subjected to a range of differing interpretations, which are inevitably transformed as society gains increased awareness and/or increased information. In the United States, the Civil War, World War II, and the Vietnam War are all events whose interpretations have changed dramatically in response to changes in society. Three of Mexico's fundamental twentieth-century watersheds, and the manner in which they were perceived by the *Times*, are the subject of the following figures.

• Figure 12

Three of the most decisive events in twentieth-century Mexican history were the Mexican Revolution, the nationalization of the petroleum industry, and the student movement of 1968. Figure 12 presents how the *Times* reported on these events between 1946 and 1986. The following three figures present the evolution that these variables underwent as social consciousness broadened over the years.

• Figure 13

Perhaps the most remarkable aspect of this figure is the United States' reevaluation of the Mexican Revolution between 1958 and 1968. Given the apparent threat posed by the success of the Cuban Revolution, the United States needed to offer an alternative, and the Mexican Revolution was now portrayed as an "acceptable" and nonthreatening revolutionary model.

• Figure 14

The *Times*'s view of nationalization was consistently negative, although the stridency of its opposition waned over the years. The relative concentration of criticism during the 1940s and 1950s reflects the fact that Washington was then hoping to pressure Mexico into opening its petroleum sector to foreign investment.

• Figure 15

This figure reveals the extent to which U.S. consciousness had broadened by 1968. Despite its scant treatment of previous social mobilizations in Mexico, the *Times*'s tendency was now to report on and condemn the regime's harsh suppression of the student movement.

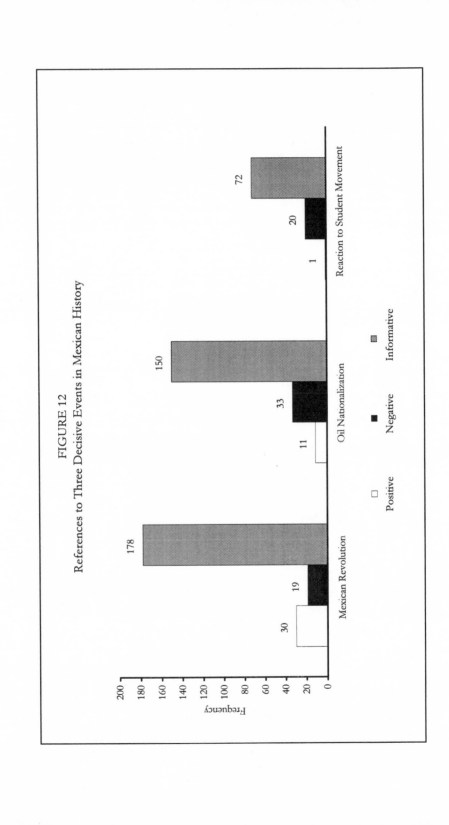

FIGURE 12

References to Three Decisive Events in Mexican History

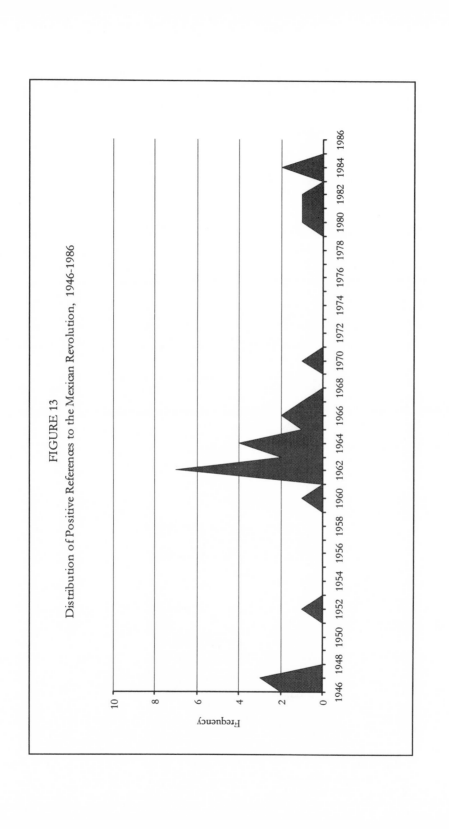

FIGURE 13

Distribution of Positive References to the Mexican Revolution, 1946-1986

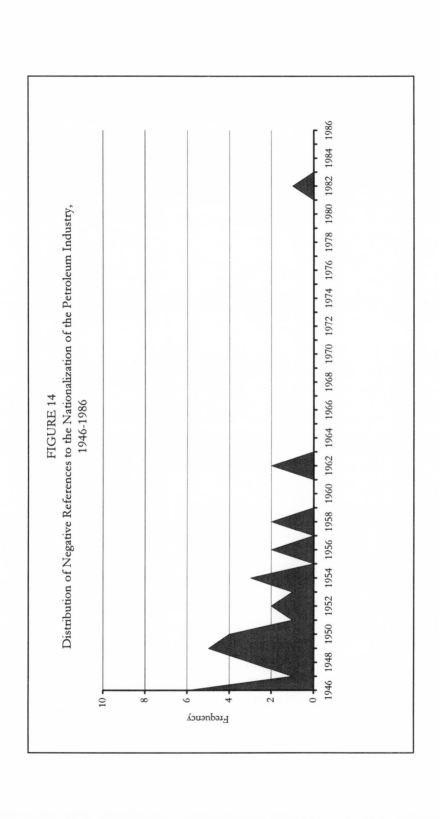

FIGURE 14

Distribution of Negative References to the Nationalization of the Petroleum Industry,
1946-1986

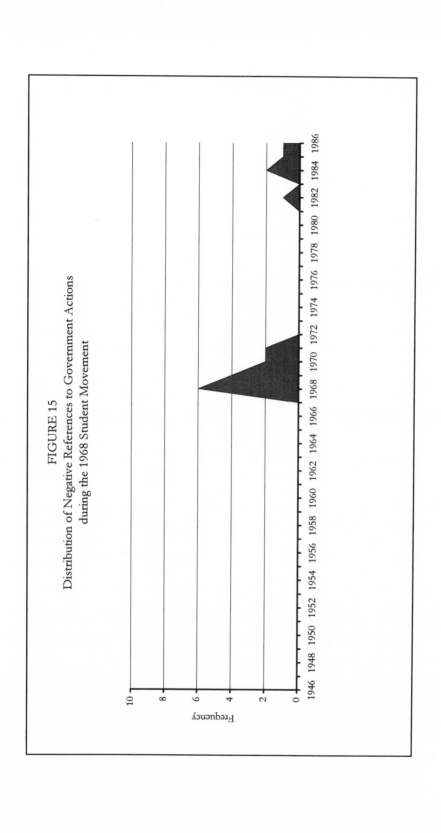

FIGURE 15

Distribution of Negative References to Government Actions
during the 1968 Student Movement

Mexican Policy as Perceived by the United States

A fascinating aspect of the results of the content analyses was the extent to which they revealed the differences between the two societies in terms of phobias and preferences. The figures in this section reflect the U.S. view on political evolution, Mexico's presidents, political parties, and Mexico's lukewarm commitment to democracy.

- Figures 16–17

These figures summarize the view of the Mexican political system held by the U.S. elite. Figure 16 displays the positive references, and its most noteworthy aspect is the consistency of U.S. approbation. The rare negative references (figure 17) remained low until 1976; their rise paralleled the convulsions within the Mexican political system.

- Figure 18

Figure 18 reveals two important elements. The first is the overwhelming weight of the Mexican presidency in *Times* coverage. The second is the fact that there were more positive than negative references to the executive branch. This reveals both that the *Times* was fully aware of who really held power in Mexico and that it was not excessively perturbed by the excesses of presidentialism.

- Figures 19–27

This series of figures is one of the most revealing in the study. It clearly indicates which Mexican presidents the U.S. elite favored and which they despised. The favorite, by far, was Miguel Alemán, followed by Miguel de la Madrid and José López Portillo. The most criticized were Luis Echeverría, Lázaro Cárdenas, and José López Portillo. These data reveal a great deal about prevailing moods in the United States, which evidently resonated differently to the distinct policies and styles of different Mexican presidents.

- Figures 28–33

These six figures reflect the *Times*'s view of Mexico's political parties, the orientation of the United States' worldview, and the extent of Washington's continued support for Mexico's established regime. Leftist parties attracted the most criticism, far more than the ruling party. Clearly the coverage of the PRI was more informative than opinion-based. Although there is an affinity between the United States and the PAN, this party usually aroused little media interest.

• Figure 34

Figure 34 sums up U.S. views on the many opposition movements that emerged in Mexico; it complements the previous series of figures and confirms an idea that emerges throughout this book: the U.S. elite has no sympathy for leftist groups, and even less for armed insurgencies. Although liberal opposition movements and parties are preferred, they are clearly not a priority: the total number of positive references—31—amounts to less than one a year.

• Figures 35–38

From a different perspective, this series confirms the United States' optimism regarding Mexican authoritarianism. Figure 35 reveals that opinion on the progress of democracy in Mexico was consistently positive (though if we observe the distribution of the 122 positive references, we can detect a very gradual decrease in enthusiasm (figure 36) and an equally slow rise in critical references (figure 37).

Although electoral fraud has been a permanent feature of political life in twentieth-century Mexico, it only drew U.S. attention on four occasions. Criticism of electoral fraud only gained importance in 1985 and 1986 (figure 38), a period that witnessed a crisis in U.S. tolerance toward the Mexican leadership.

• Figure 39

This figure charts the U.S. elite's perception of Mexican political actors. Evidently the greatest interest was aroused by the armed forces, the private sector, and students. The manner in which these groups were treated over time (which is not included here due to space constraints) reflects some of the battles ongoing in Mexico. For example, a period of criticism of the Mexican private sector coincides almost exactly with private-sector efforts to oppose the reformist policies of Presidents Echeverría and López Portillo.

• Figures 40–44

The *Times* condemned the Mexican government's use of force, but it also viewed with mistrust any threat to the established order. The data on seven problems related to Mexican government authoritarianism reveal the U.S. elite's deep disapproval of independent labor movements, peasant movements, demonstrations, or any form of public disorder. However, government repression or patronage politics were also considered unacceptable.

Some figures chart the evolution of certain variables over time. Although the independent labor movements (figure 41) were subjected to a fair amount of attention and criticism during the early decades (particularly during the railroad and oil workers' strikes), this interest waned, despite the fact that such mobilizations did not disappear.

Any sizable number of references to government repression (figure 43) is not in evidence until 1968. This reveals that the *Times* simply ignored much of the protest and repression that took place outside Mexico City. Patronage political relations (figure 44) were also mentioned only sporadically.

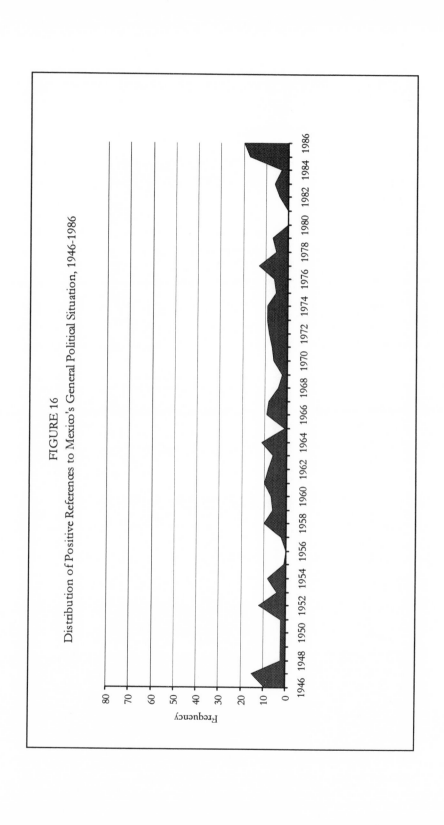

FIGURE 16

Distribution of Positive References to Mexico's General Political Situation, 1946-1986

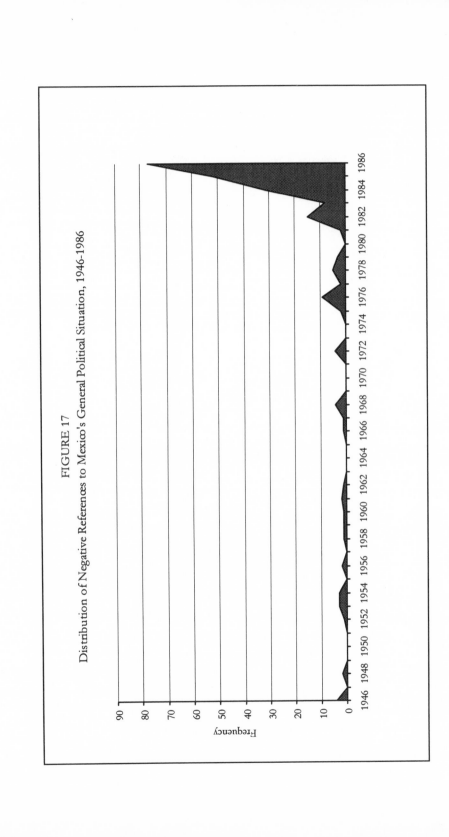

FIGURE 17

Distribution of Negative References to Mexico's General Political Situation, 1946-1986

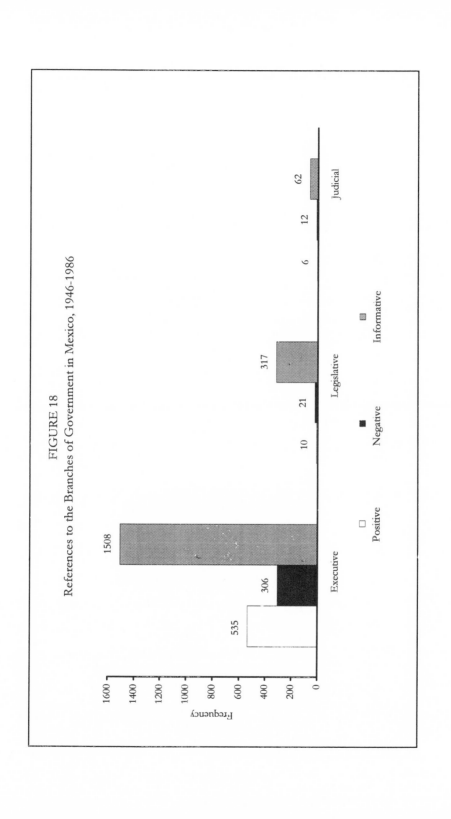

FIGURE 18

References to the Branches of Government in Mexico, 1946-1986

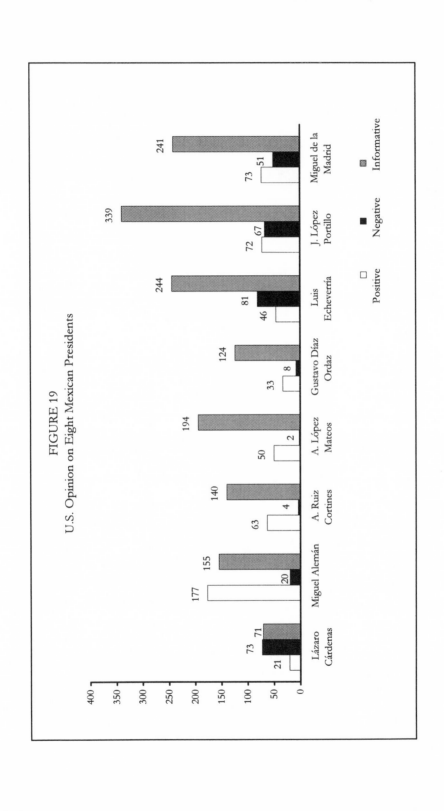

FIGURE 19

U.S. Opinion on Eight Mexican Presidents

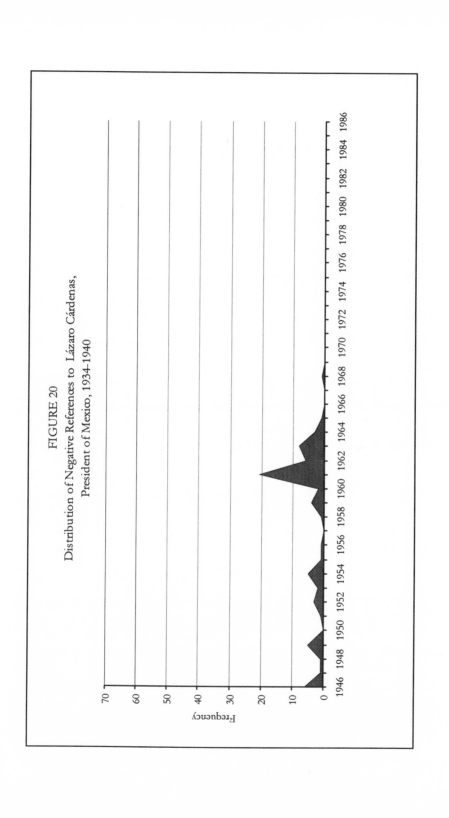

FIGURE 20

Distribution of Negative References to Lázaro Cárdenas,
President of Mexico, 1934-1940

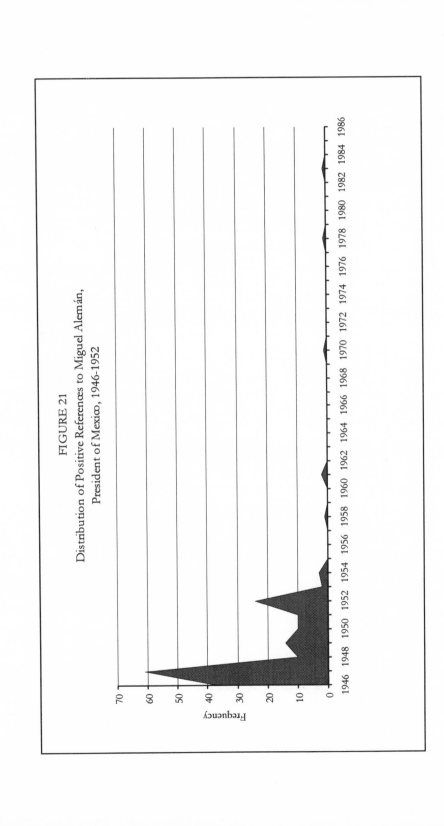

FIGURE 21

Distribution of Positive References to Miguel Alemán,
President of Mexico, 1946-1952

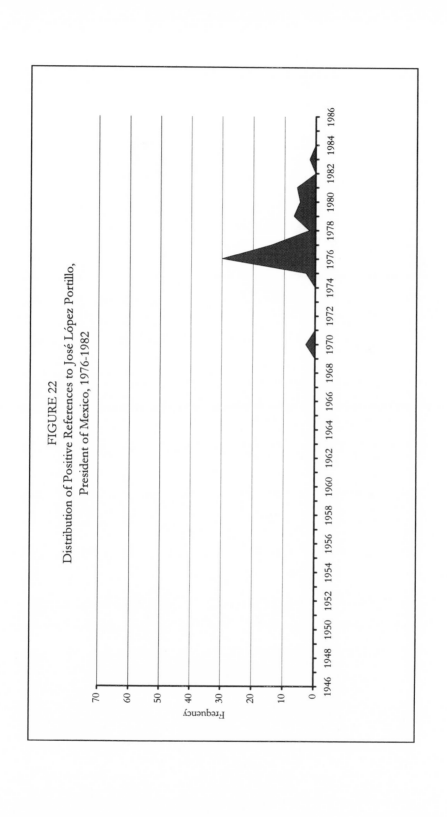

FIGURE 22
Distribution of Positive References to José López Portillo,
President of Mexico, 1976-1982

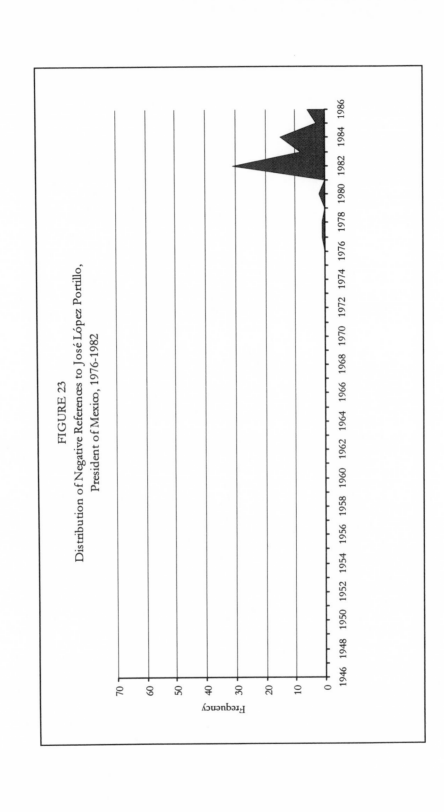

FIGURE 23

Distribution of Negative References to José López Portillo,
President of Mexico, 1976-1982

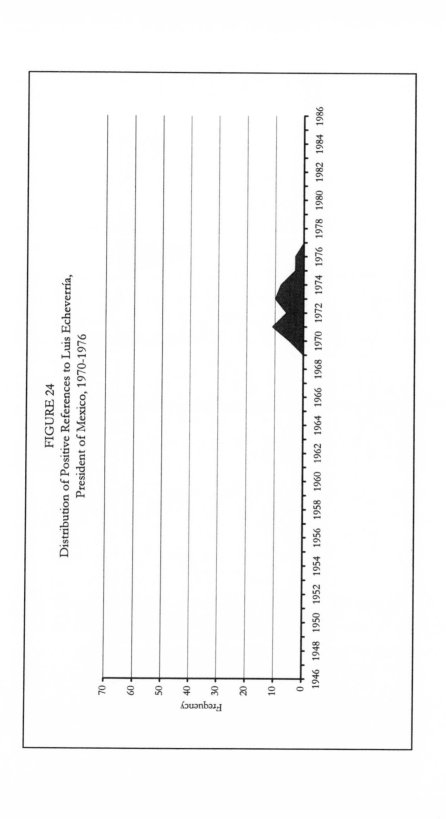

FIGURE 24

Distribution of Positive References to Luis Echeverría,
President of Mexico, 1970-1976

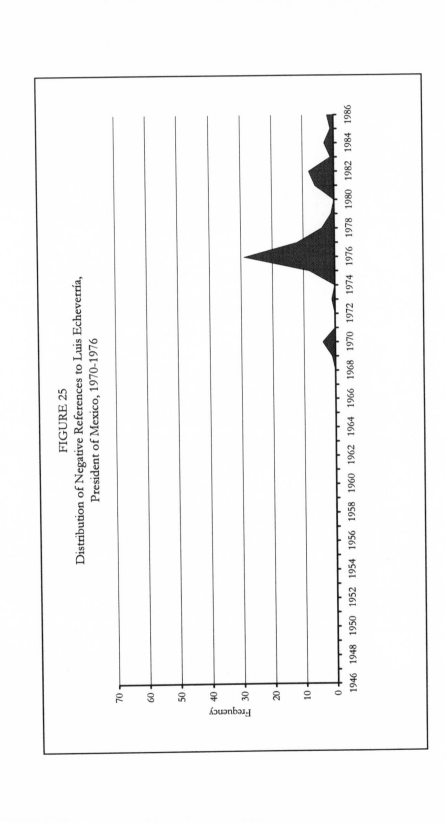

FIGURE 25

Distribution of Negative References to Luis Echeverría,
President of Mexico, 1970-1976

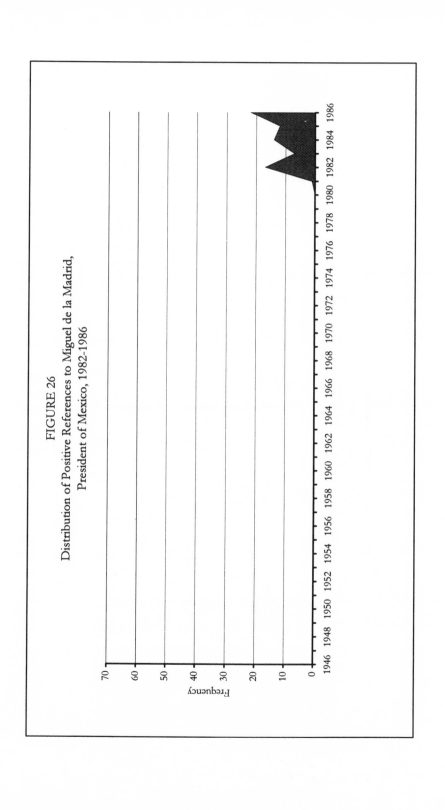

FIGURE 26

Distribution of Positive References to Miguel de la Madrid,
President of Mexico, 1982-1986

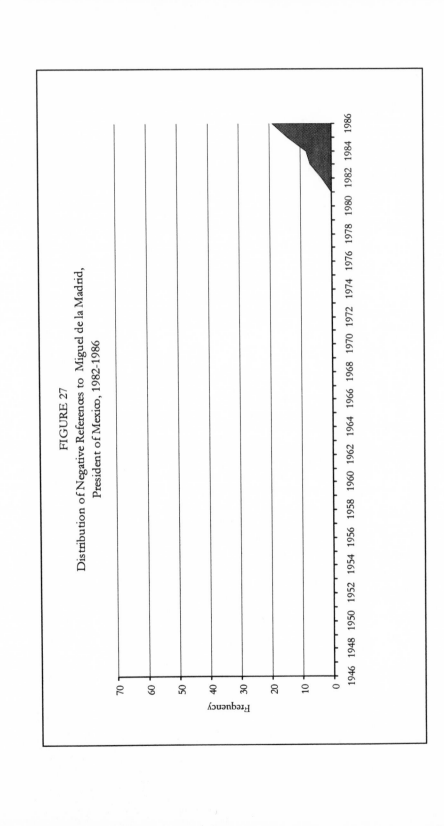

FIGURE 27

Distribution of Negative References to Miguel de la Madrid,
President of Mexico, 1982-1986

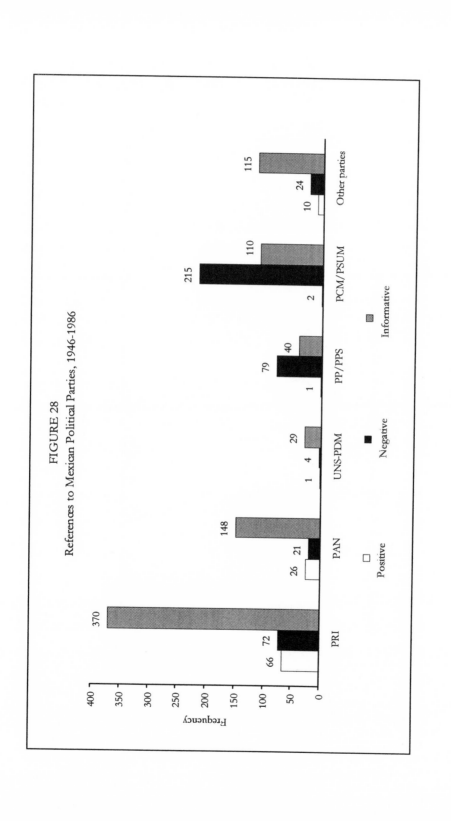

FIGURE 28

References to Mexican Political Parties, 1946-1986

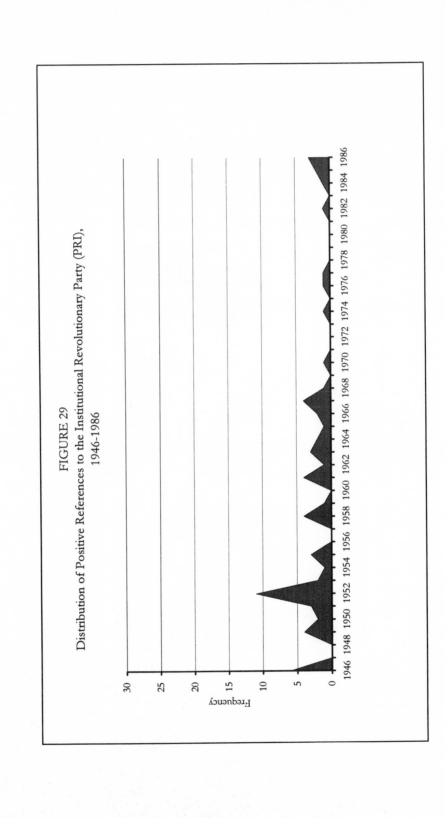

FIGURE 29

Distribution of Positive References to the Institutional Revolutionary Party (PRI), 1946-1986

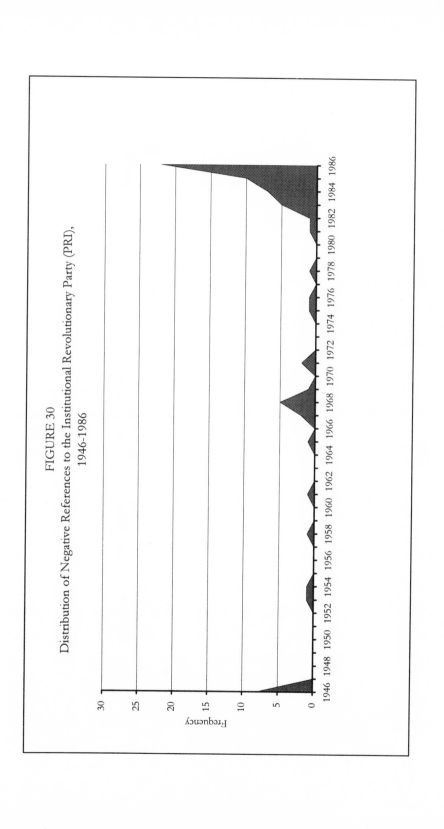

FIGURE 30

Distribution of Negative References to the Institutional Revolutionary Party (PRI), 1946-1986

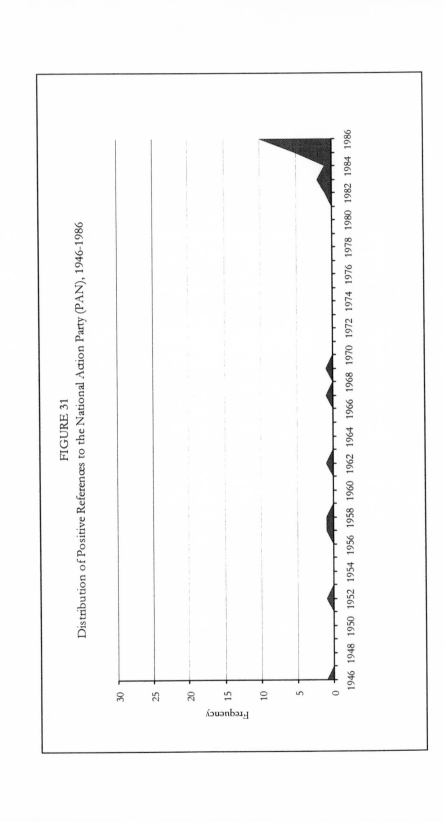

FIGURE 31

Distribution of Positive References to the National Action Party (PAN), 1946-1986

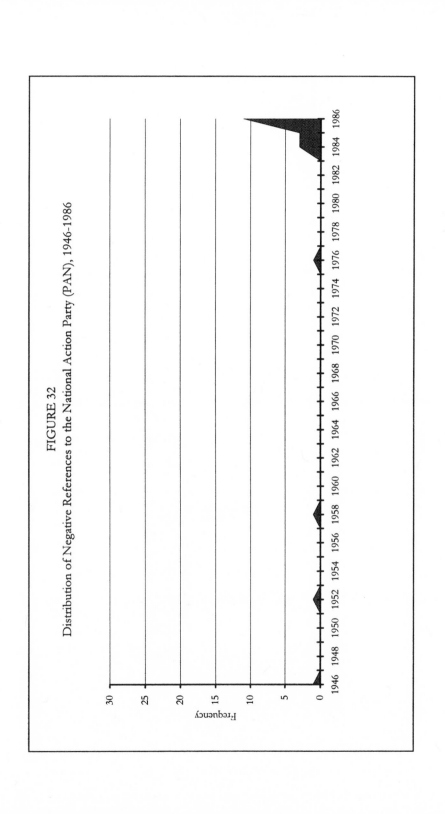

FIGURE 32

Distribution of Negative References to the National Action Party (PAN), 1946-1986

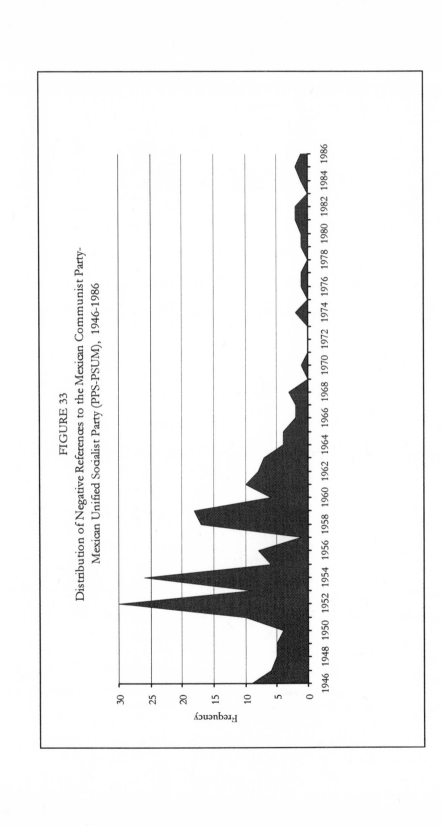

FIGURE 33

Distribution of Negative References to the Mexican Communist Party-
Mexican Unified Socialist Party (PPS-PSUM), 1946-1986

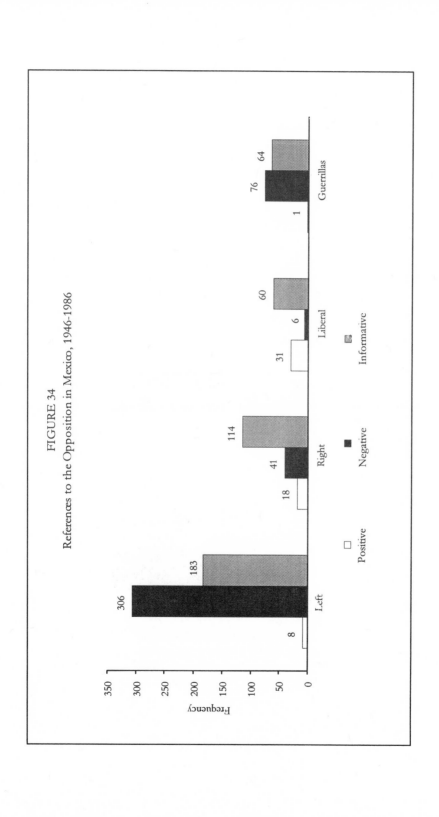

FIGURE 34

References to the Opposition in Mexico, 1946-1986

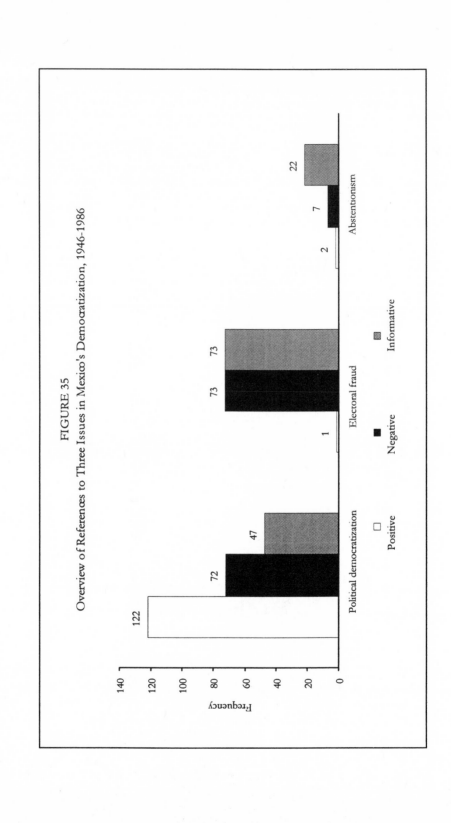

FIGURE 35

Overview of References to Three Issues in Mexico's Democratization, 1946-1986

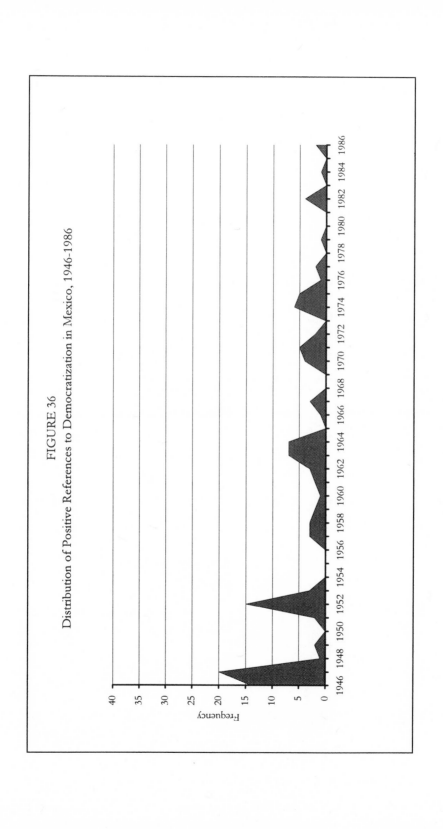

FIGURE 36

Distribution of Positive References to Democratization in Mexico, 1946-1986

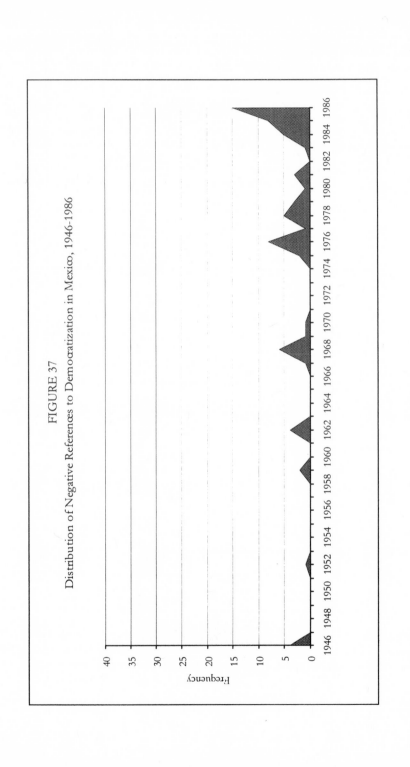

FIGURE 37

Distribution of Negative References to Democratization in Mexico, 1946-1986

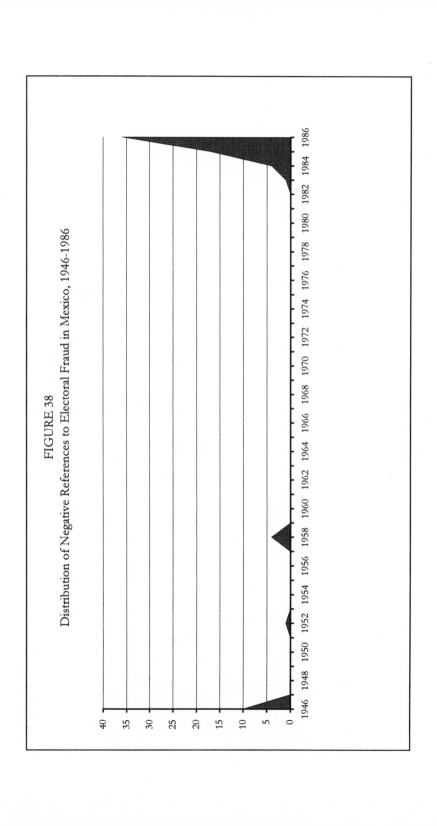

FIGURE 38

Distribution of Negative References to Electoral Fraud in Mexico, 1946-1986

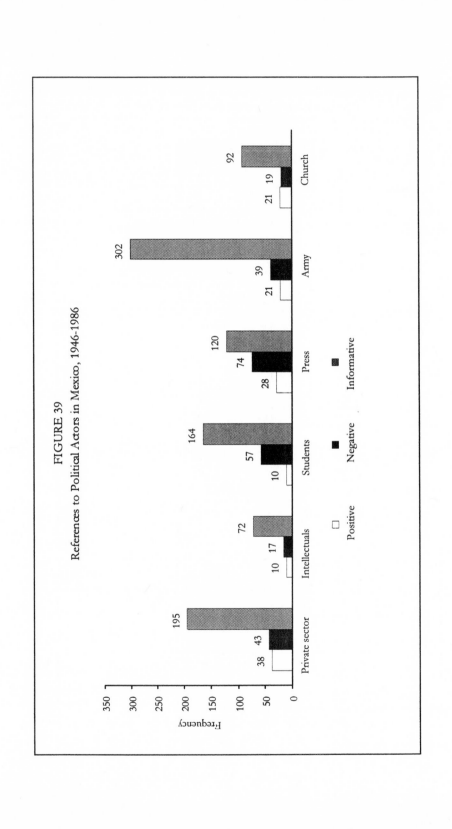

FIGURE 39

References to Political Actors in Mexico, 1946-1986

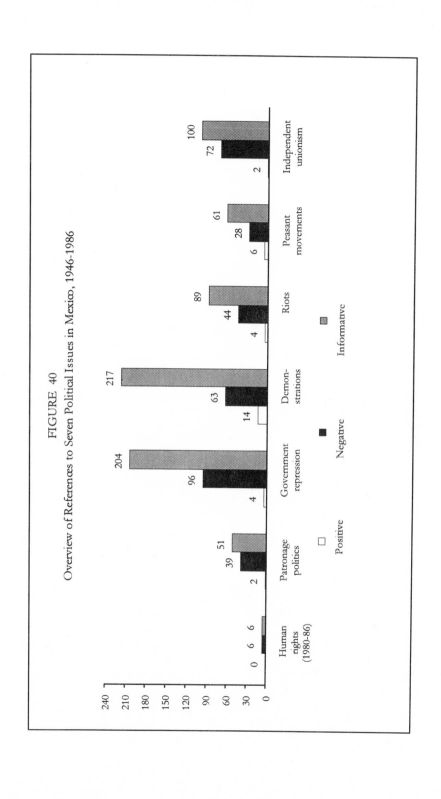

FIGURE 40

Overview of References to Seven Political Issues in Mexico, 1946-1986

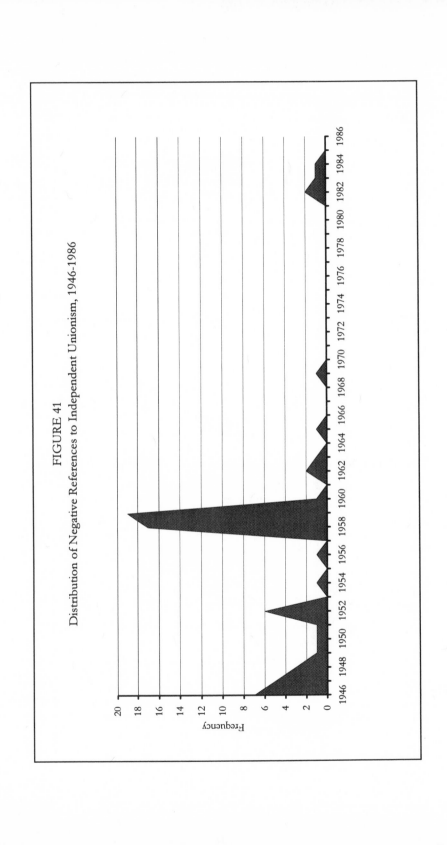

FIGURE 41

Distribution of Negative References to Independent Unionism, 1946-1986

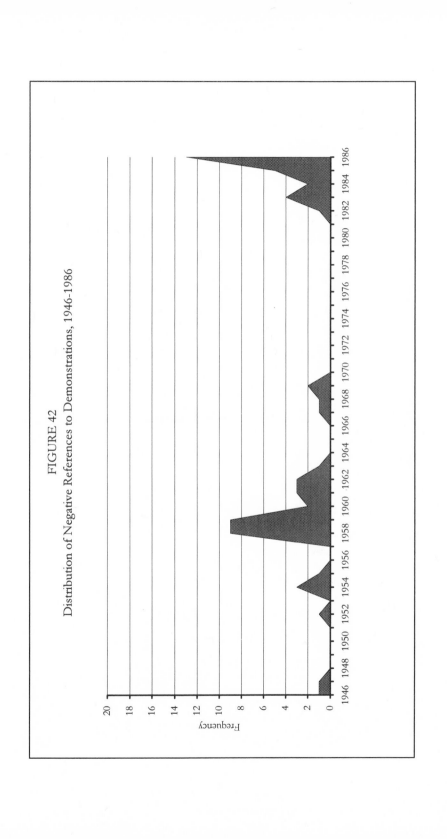

FIGURE 42

Distribution of Negative References to Demonstrations, 1946-1986

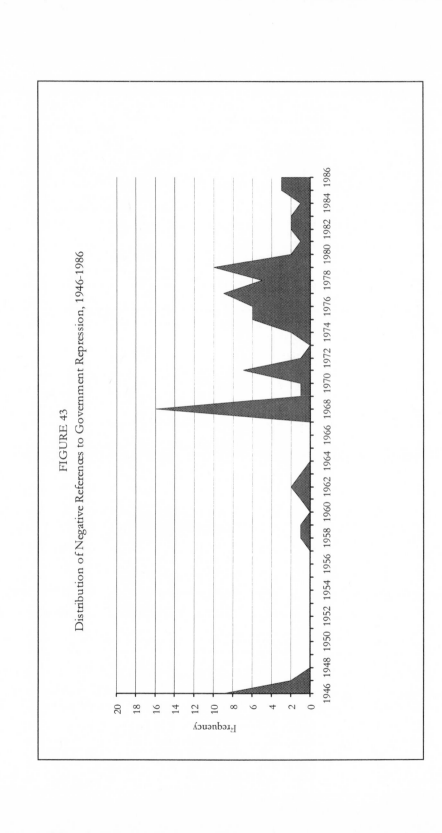

FIGURE 43

Distribution of Negative References to Government Repression, 1946-1986

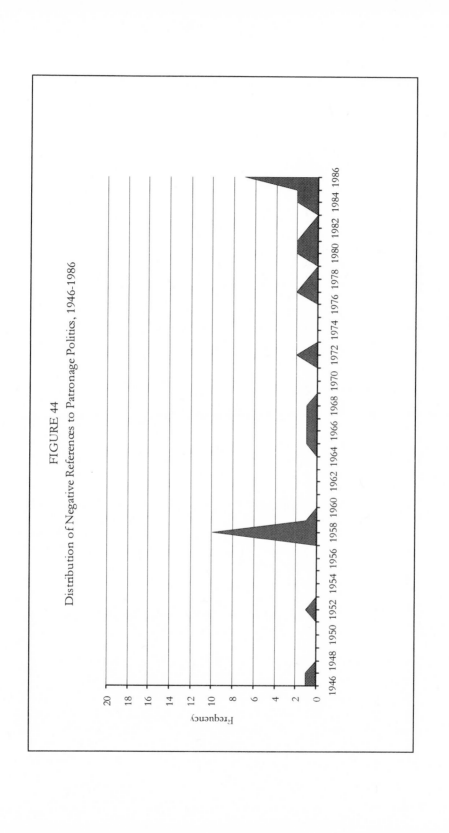

FIGURE 44

Distribution of Negative References to Patronage Politics, 1946-1986

MEXICO'S RELATIONSHIP TO THE WORLD

These 22 figures are a partial reflection of the manner in which Mexico's relationship to the rest of the world was perceived in the pages of the *Times*. Space constraints have forced the exclusion of a large number of variables concerning Mexico's relationship with Latin America, Europe, and Asia, in order to concentrate on Mexico–U.S. relations which, as might be expected, drew the greatest attention and are the most relevant for the present analysis.

- Figures 45–46

The United States evidently felt that Mexico's finest foreign policy hour came during the administration of Miguel Alemán. Other presidents were subjected to varying levels of criticism: Ruiz Cortines (as a result of his involvement in Guatemala), López Mateos (over Cuba and international activism, which included de Gaulle's visit to Mexico), Echeverría (due to the messianic activism he espoused in the latter years of his administration), and Miguel de la Madrid (over Central America).

- Figures 47–53

Numbers do not lie. Figure 47 is a numerical confirmation of the warm relationship between Mexico and the United States. The three variables—general relations, political relations, and economic relations—garnered a paltry 525 negative references over the 41–year period covered by the content analysis. In comparison, there were 960 positive and 998 informative references.

The distribution of these variables over time is fairly homogeneous. However, the favorite administration was that of Miguel Alemán (we should recall that Salinas de Gortari's administration was not part of this content analysis), followed by López Mateos and de la Madrid. The most criticized regimes were those of de la Madrid, López Portillo, Ruiz Cortines, and Echeverría, in that order. Of note here is the United States' ambivalence toward Miguel de la Madrid, a president who was simultaneously applauded and condemned.

- Figures 54–57

The first meeting between a U.S. and a Mexican president brought together Porifirio Díaz and Howard Taft in 1909. The next did not occur until World War II. However, presidential summits became routine after Truman's visit to Alemán and the latter's visit to the United States, the most spectacular and successful in the history of the relationship. This is clearly reflected in figure 55, as are the *Times*'s criticisms of López Portillo and Carter, and of de la Madrid and Reagan.

- Figures 58–66

Among the issues that have aroused the greatest U.S. interest and concern in this most complex of international relationships, migration occupies an undisputed first place; distant seconds are border relations, drug trafficking, and energy. However, these are aggregate figures that do not reflect temporal variations in interest.

Oil, which was an important issue between 1947 and 1952, also became a source of conflict between the two countries after 1976. The border became a contentious matter in the relationship only toward the end of the period analyzed. Migration has two great peaks of interest (at the beginning and at the end of the analyzed decades), although the United States has consistently perceived this as a domestic issue. Drug trafficking received sporadic references until the 1980s, at which point it became the thorniest problem in the relationship.

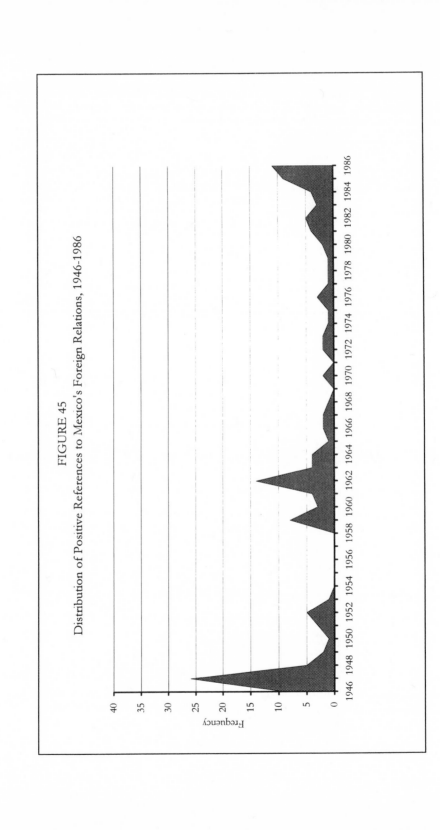

FIGURE 45

Distribution of Positive References to Mexico's Foreign Relations, 1946-1986

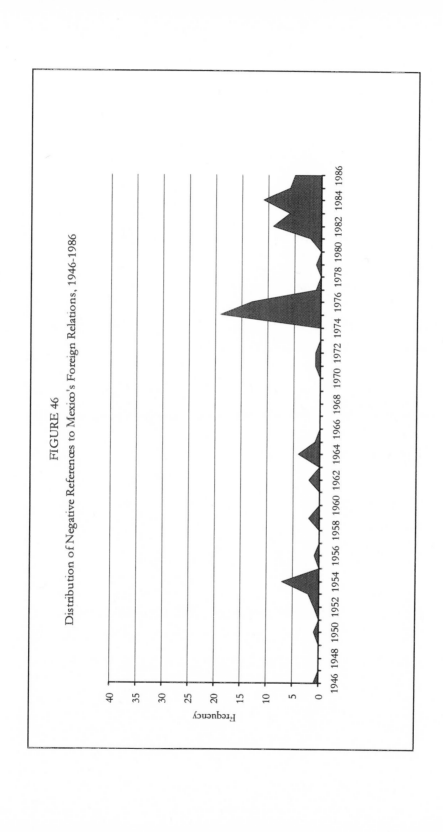

FIGURE 46

Distribution of Negative References to Mexico's Foreign Relations, 1946-1986

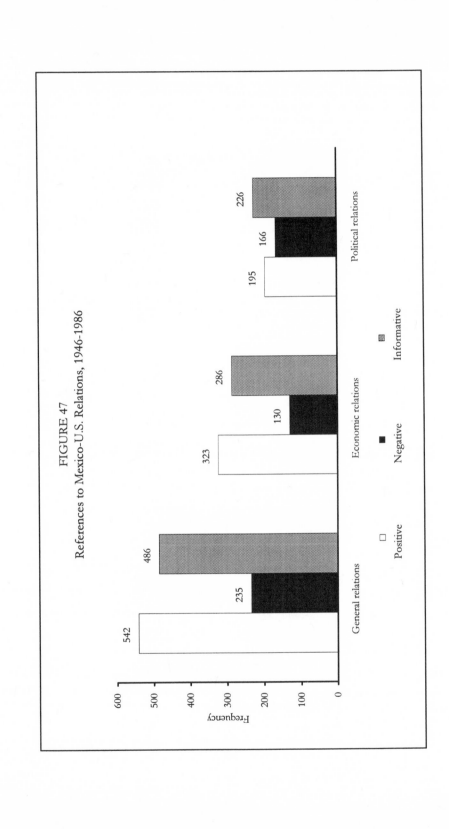

FIGURE 47

References to Mexico-U.S. Relations, 1946-1986

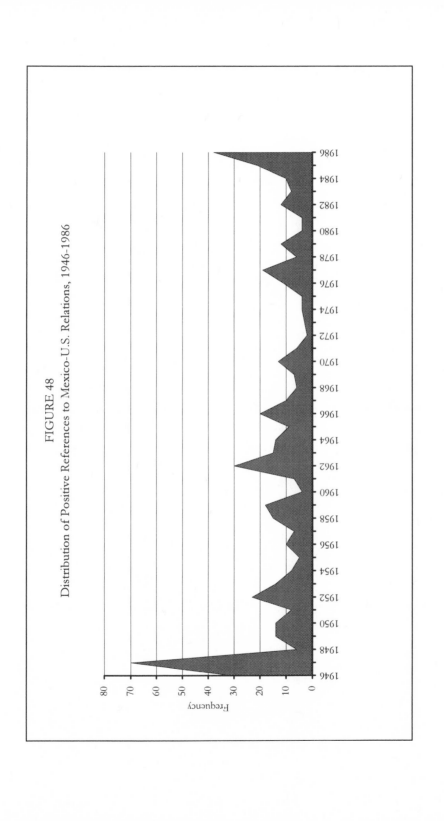

FIGURE 48

Distribution of Positive References to Mexico-U.S. Relations, 1946-1986

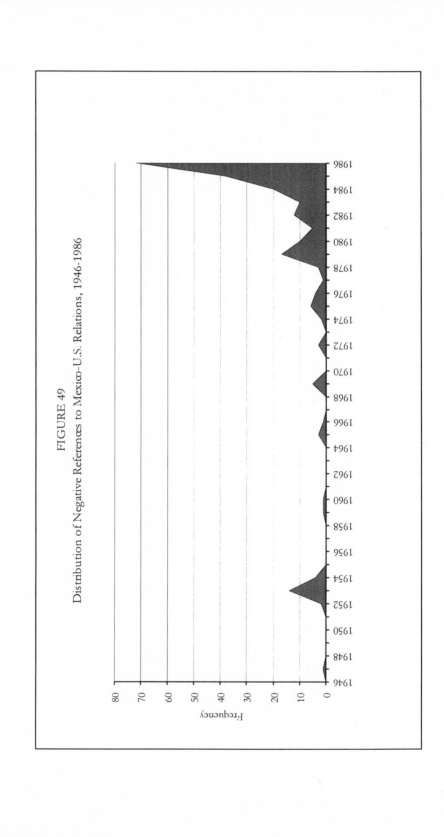

FIGURE 49

Distribution of Negative References to Mexico-U.S. Relations, 1946-1986

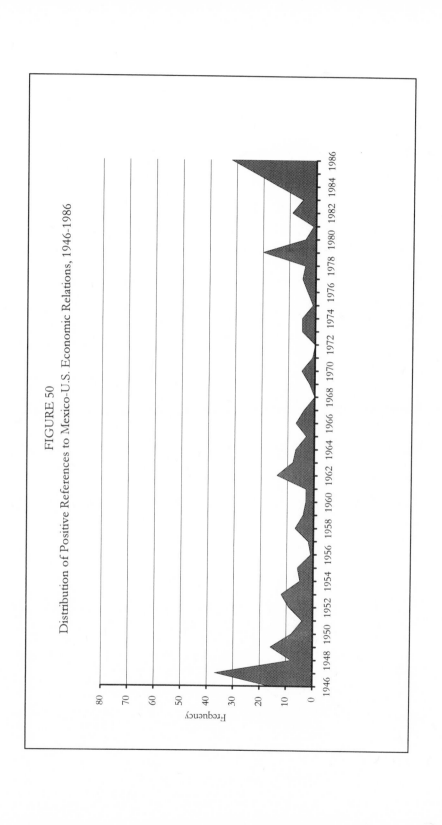

FIGURE 50

Distribution of Positive References to Mexico-U.S. Economic Relations, 1946-1986

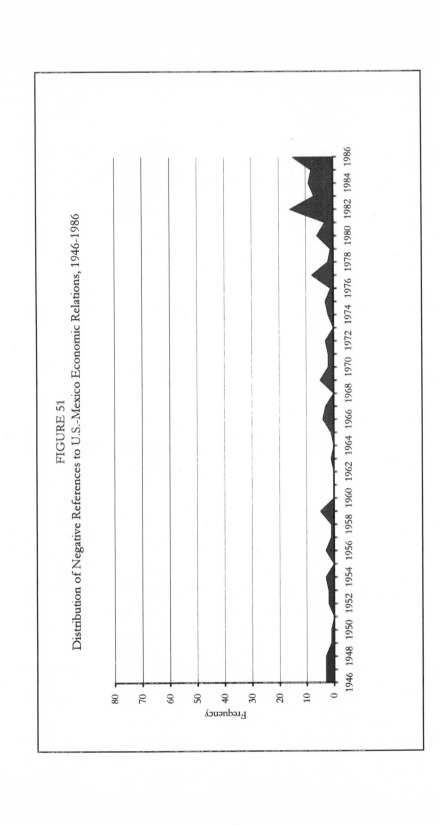

FIGURE 51

Distribution of Negative References to U.S.-Mexico Economic Relations, 1946-1986

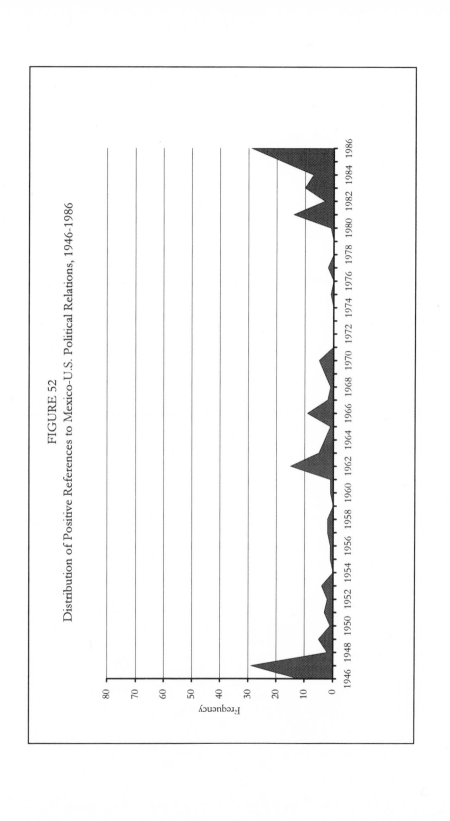

FIGURE 52

Distribution of Positive References to Mexico-U.S. Political Relations, 1946-1986

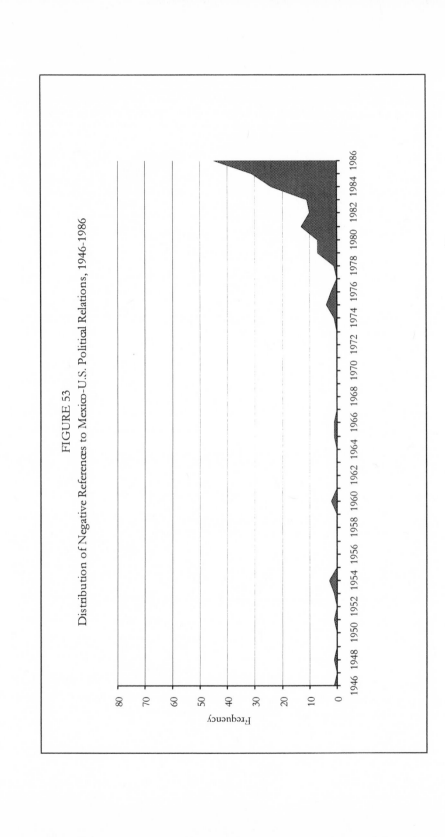

FIGURE 53

Distribution of Negative References to Mexico-U.S. Political Relations, 1946-1986

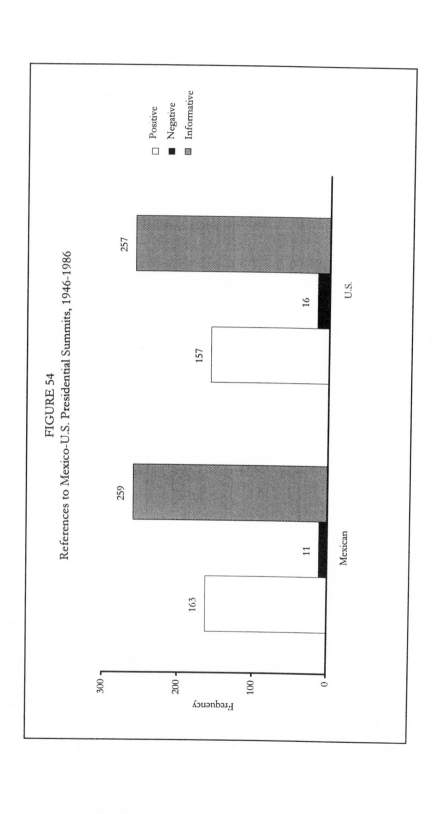

FIGURE 54

References to Mexico-U.S. Presidential Summits, 1946-1986

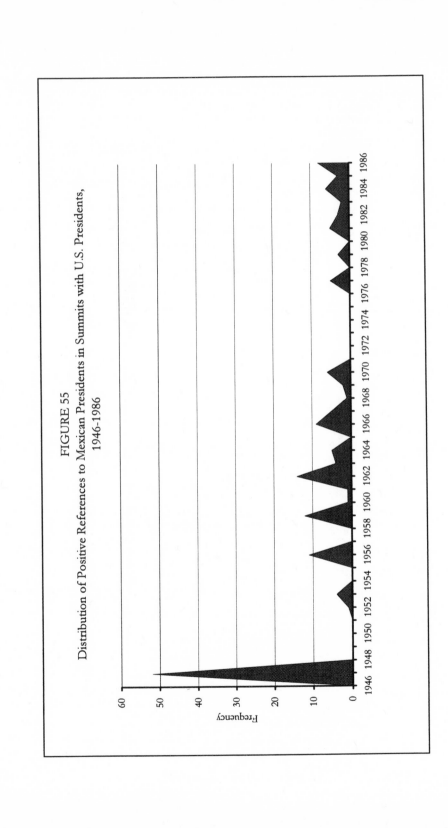

FIGURE 55

Distribution of Positive References to Mexican Presidents in Summits with U.S. Presidents, 1946-1986

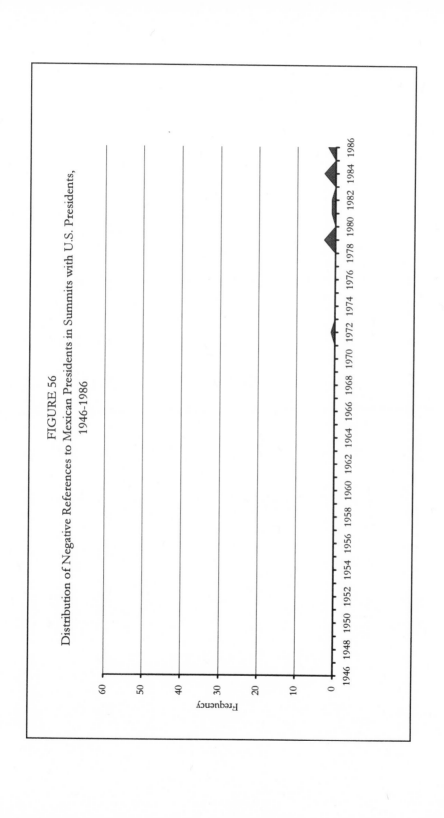

FIGURE 56

Distribution of Negative References to Mexican Presidents in Summits with U.S. Presidents, 1946-1986

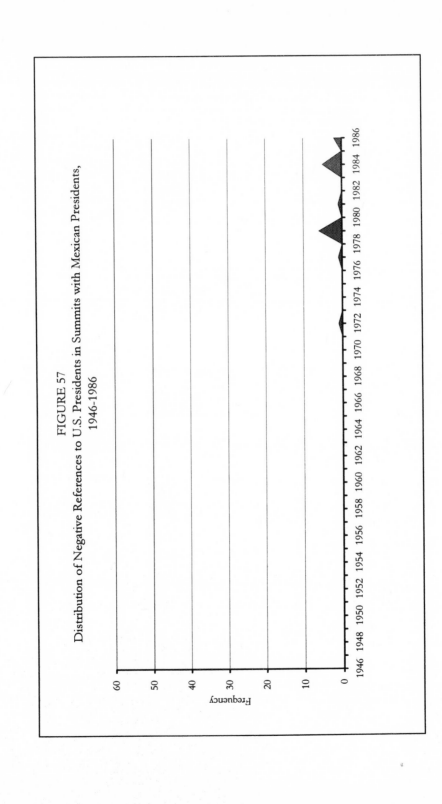

FIGURE 57

Distribution of Negative References to U.S. Presidents in Summits with Mexican Presidents, 1946-1986

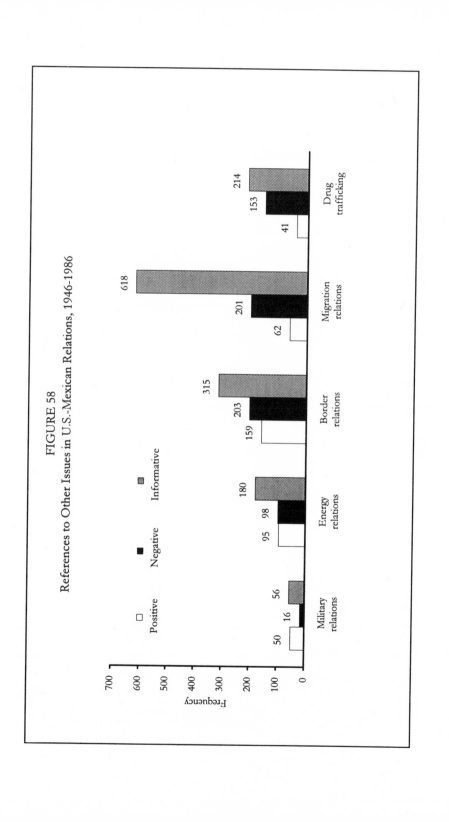

FIGURE 58

References to Other Issues in U.S.-Mexican Relations, 1946-1986

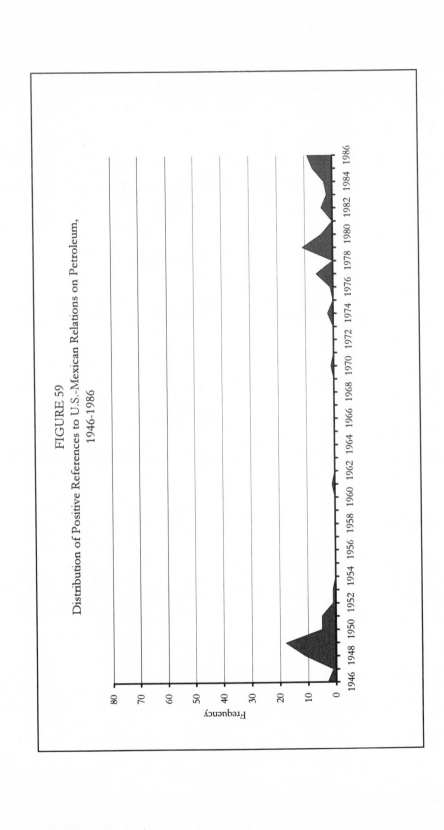

FIGURE 59

Distribution of Positive References to U.S.-Mexican Relations on Petroleum, 1946-1986

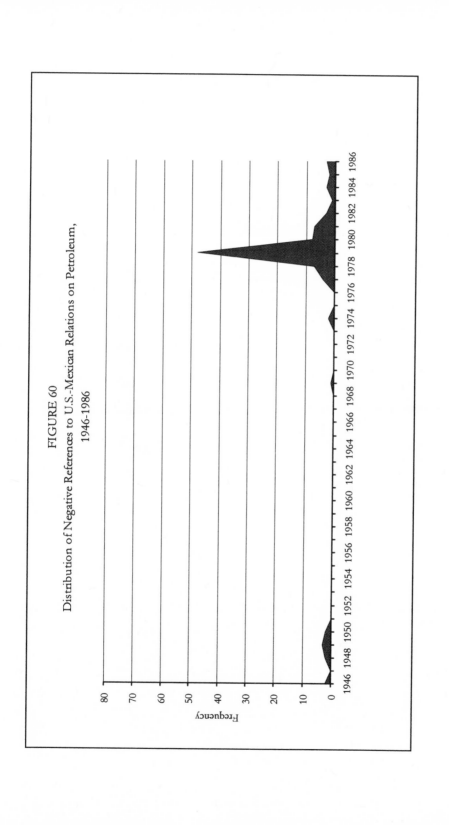

FIGURE 60

Distribution of Negative References to U.S.-Mexican Relations on Petroleum,
1946-1986

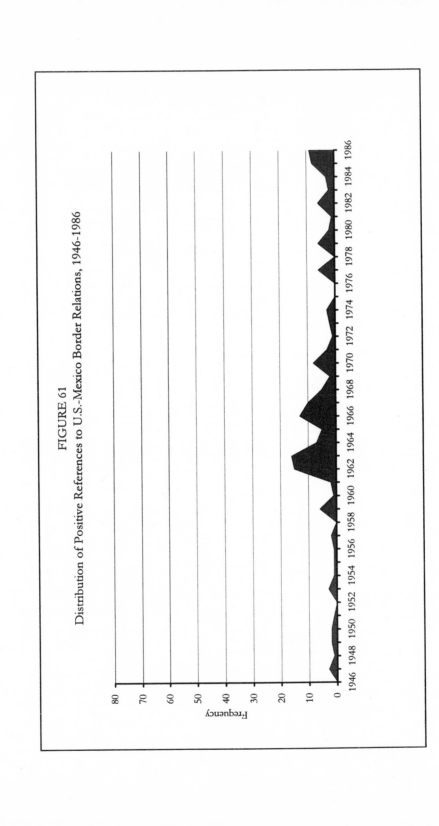

FIGURE 61

Distribution of Positive References to U.S.-Mexico Border Relations, 1946-1986

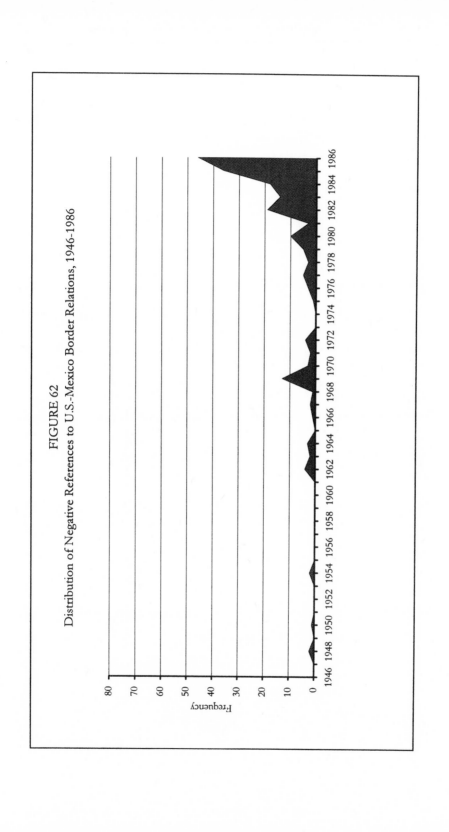

FIGURE 62

Distribution of Negative References to U.S.-Mexico Border Relations, 1946-1986

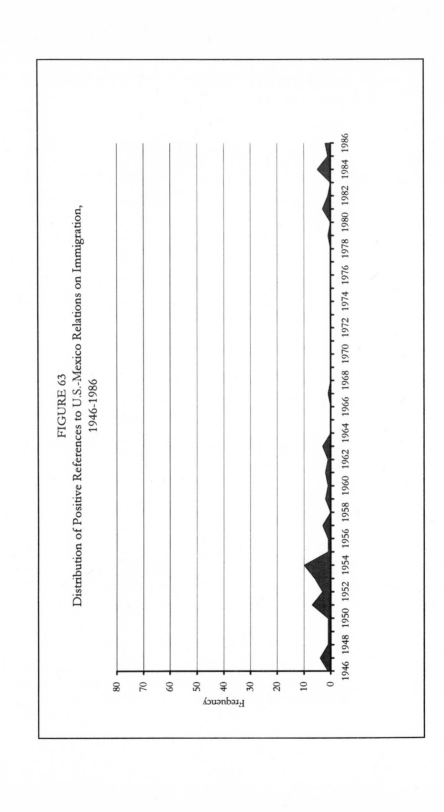

FIGURE 63

Distribution of Positive References to U.S.-Mexico Relations on Immigration,
1946-1986

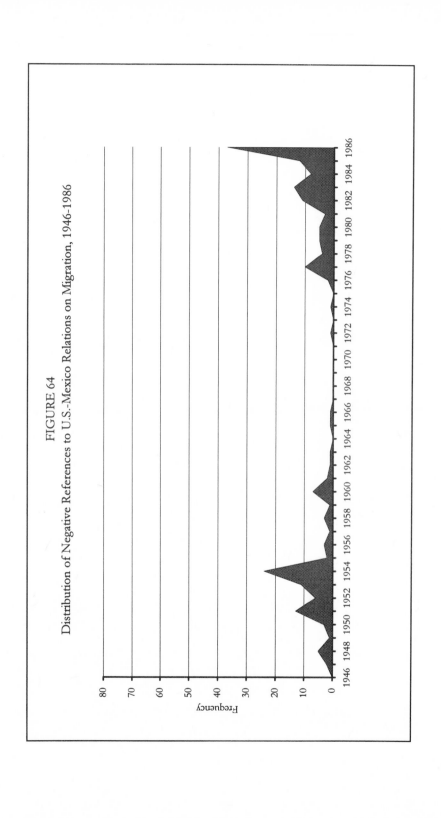

FIGURE 64

Distribution of Negative References to U.S.-Mexico Relations on Migration, 1946-1986

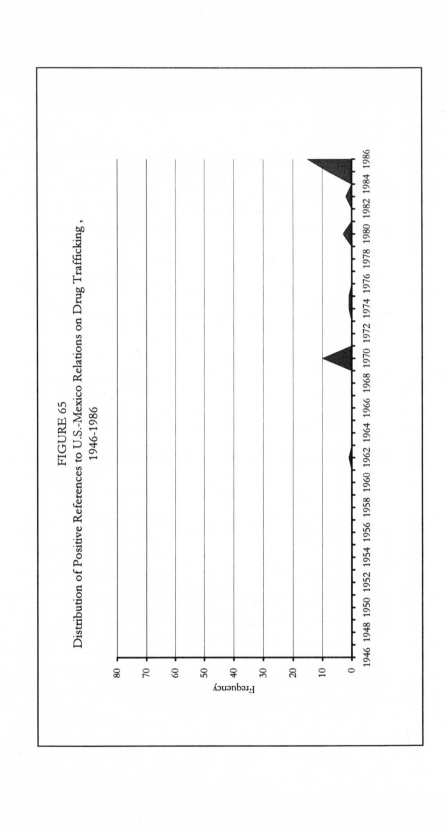

FIGURE 65

Distribution of Positive References to U.S.-Mexico Relations on Drug Trafficking, 1946-1986

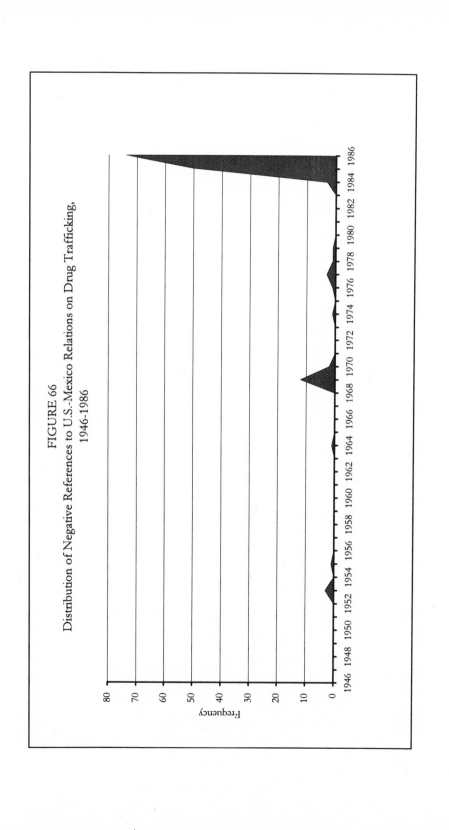

FIGURE 66

Distribution of Negative References to U.S.-Mexico Relations on Drug Trafficking,
1946-1986

THE MEXICAN ECONOMY

The figures on the economy are very important and very complex. They are subdivided according to the multiple topics that reflect the United States' worldview, rigidly anchored in a preference for capitalism.

A remarkable aspect that these figures reveal is the pragmatic balance the United States was able to strike between defending its principles and interests and tolerating the peculiarities of the Mexican model, especially Mexico's mixed economy. These figures also reflect the shift from tolerance to impatience that occurred during the 1980s.

- Figures 67–70

This series includes the broad categories the *Times* used to evaluate the Mexican economy. Figures 67 and 68 show the homogeneous way in which positive opinions on the general economic situation were distributed over time. The absence of negative references is remarkable until 1975, at which point the economic model's growing difficulties were suddenly and clearly identified. The jump in the curve in 1985–1986 is similarly eloquent.

Figures 69 and 70, which display references to the current account, display a similar pattern, as do a number of other unpublished variables.

- Figure 71

Mexico was upheld as a model for development on 54 occasions in the pages of the *New York Times*, 33 in positive terms. The moments of greatest praise came between 1961 and 1967, a period during which Washington was anxious to identify models that could contrast favorably with the Cuban Revolution. Criticism multiplied during the 1980s, when there was gathering impatience with the faltering Mexican economy.

- Figures 72–76

Mixed economies generally arouse mixed feelings as to the role of the state and private investment (both international and domestic). These figures depict the evolution of U.S. phobias and preferences.

Figure 72 indicates the number of references for each variable. The category that enjoyed the greatest number of positive references was the international private sector, followed by the Mexican private sector. State participation in the economy ranked last in the list of U.S. interests and preferences.

Figures 73 to 76 contrast the annual distribution of positive and negative references to the Mexican and international private sectors.

Praise for the international sector, which was strongest, was also the most evenly distributed over time. Negative references to international investors were few, but they tended to concentrate in a single period.

- Figures 77–79

The United States has always attached a great deal of importance to other nations' foreign investment climates. These figures depict the positive light within which Mexico was judged.

- Figure 80

There is a marked contrast between the United States' contempt for traditional agricultural techniques and its support for modern ones. The evolution of this variable over time, which has not been included due to space considerations, displays a remarkably high incidence of references during the 1960s. The Mexican countryside became the focus of unprecedented *Times* attention during this period.

- Figure 81

This figure reflects the United States' negative views of Mexican population growth and out-migration. References to international migration dwarf references to internal migration in numerical terms; this is because international migration out of Mexico, which has a direct impact on the United States, is viewed within the United States as a domestic, rather than a bilateral, issue.

There were a number of interesting aspects in the temporal evolution of these variables (which is not included here). There was an upsurge of interest in population growth during the late 1960s, as the topic gained increasing prominence on the international agenda. Interest in international migration surged and faded in cycles that reflected U.S. factors exclusively.

- Figures 82–85

The references to economic problems reveal that the *Times* was fully aware of the nature and gravity of Mexico's social problems, although they were given only limited priority, especially when compared to the number of references to variables such as tourism or communications (omitted due to lack of space).

By observing the evolving treatment of these topics, we can clearly trace the United States' broadening awareness; as time passed, there was an increasing interest and focus upon social problems.

- Figures 86–90

These figures include variables that allow us to measure the United States' sensitivity toward some of Mexico's most pressing national problems. Figure 86 reveals that the United States had a clear awareness of many of the depressing realities of day-to-day existence in Mexico. Their treatment over time reveals that consciousness broadened significantly only after the 1960s, when attention finally turned to Mexico's very real social problems. Nonetheless, it is still surprising how little attention such issues received in comparison with other matters.

- Figures 91–94

Certain variables are included in this content analysis with the aim of detecting the United States' perception of a range of more cultural issues (see Appendix B: Code Manual). Those that displayed the greatest consistency over the forty-one years covered in the content analysis were violence, corruption, and anti-American sentiment (usually associated to nationalism).

Although violence was mentioned frequently, it was generally associated with strikes, contested elections, and social movements. Corruption was most often mentioned toward the beginning or the end of successive administrations, especially those of Miguel Alemán, Luis Echeverría, José López Portillo, and Miguel de la Madrid. Finally, the highest levels of anti-American sentiment were detected during the administrations of Ruiz Cortines, López Mateos, López Portillo, and Miguel de la Madrid.

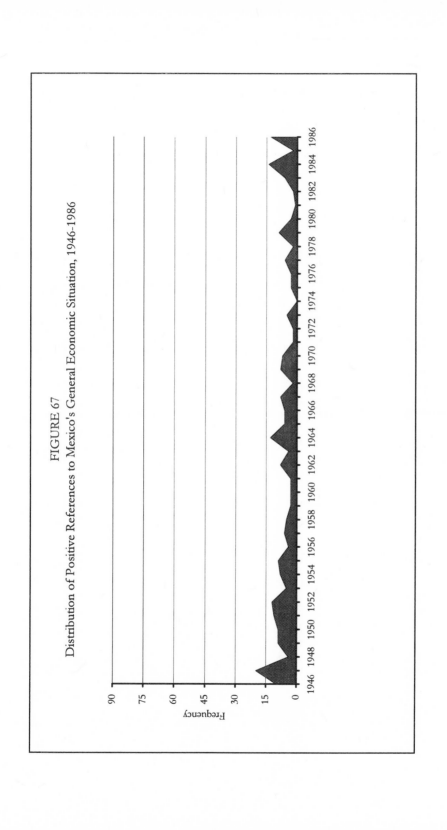

FIGURE 67

Distribution of Positive References to Mexico's General Economic Situation, 1946-1986

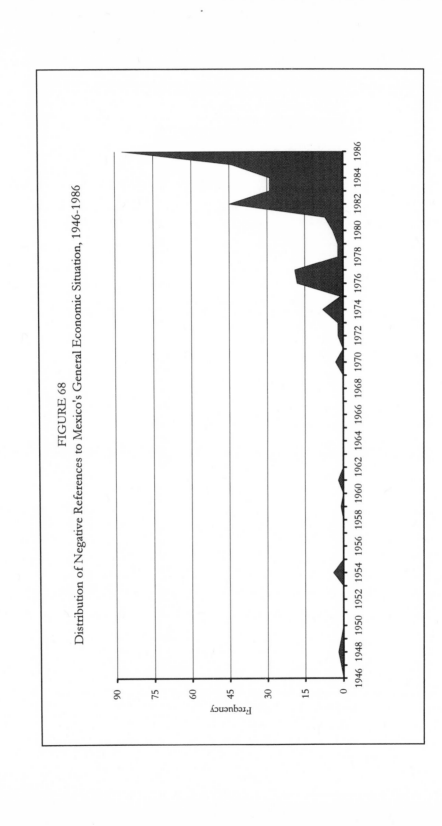

FIGURE 68

Distribution of Negative References to Mexico's General Economic Situation, 1946-1986

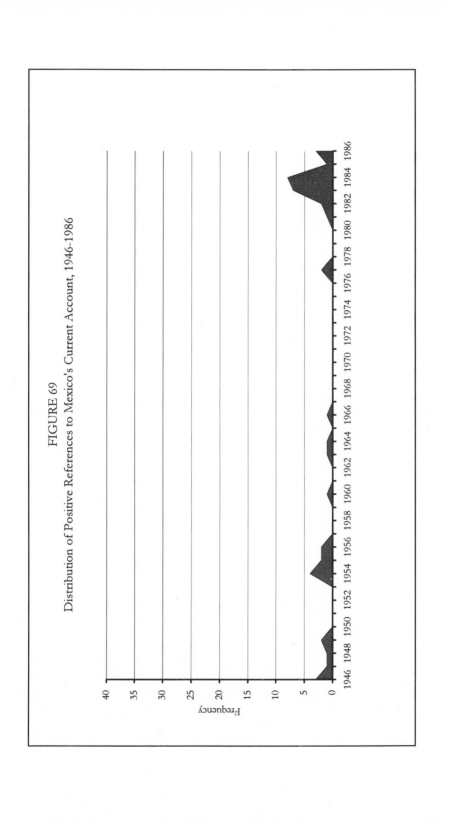

FIGURE 69

Distribution of Positive References to Mexico's Current Account, 1946-1986

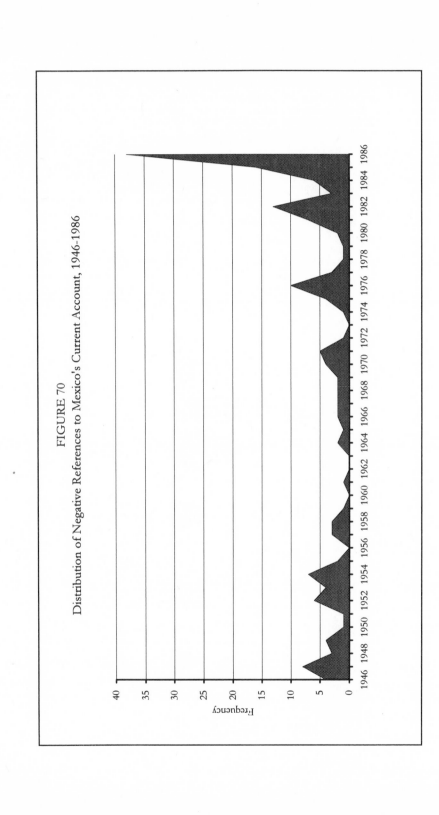

FIGURE 70

Distribution of Negative References to Mexico's Current Account, 1946-1986

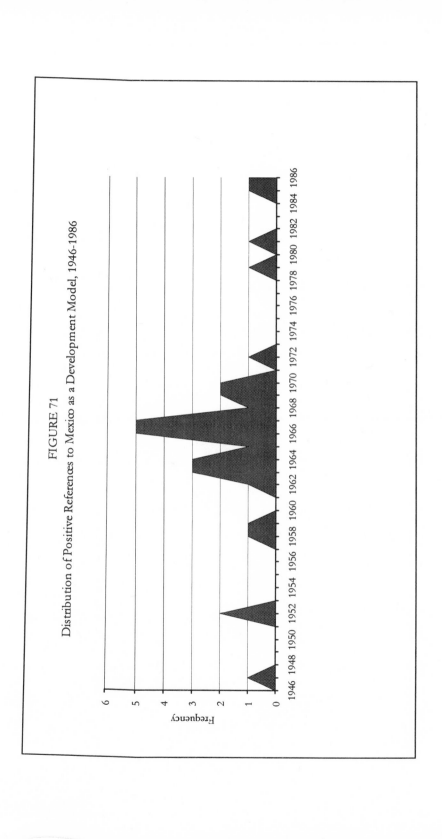

FIGURE 71

Distribution of Positive References to Mexico as a Development Model, 1946-1986

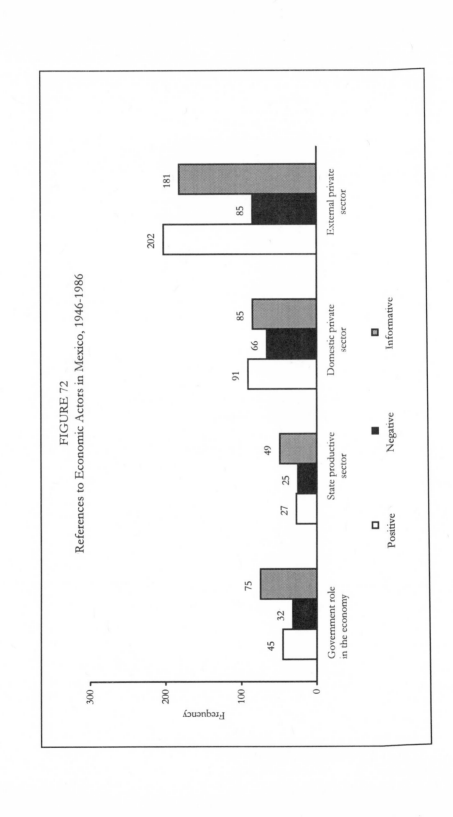

FIGURE 72

References to Economic Actors in Mexico, 1946-1986

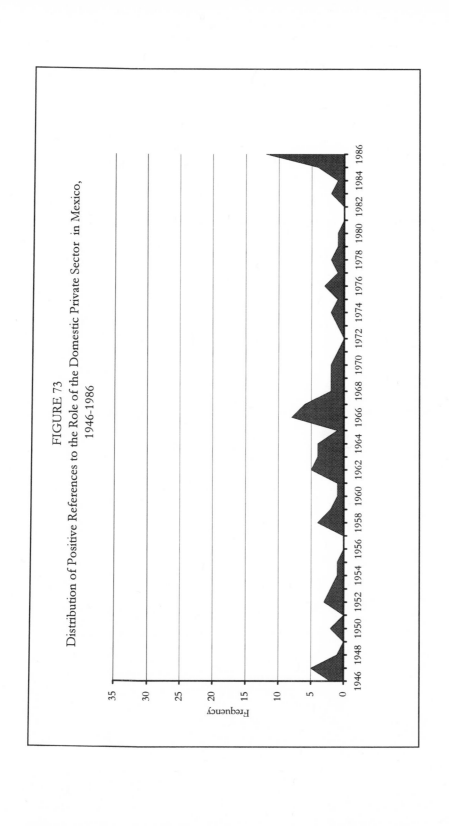

FIGURE 73

Distribution of Positive References to the Role of the Domestic Private Sector in Mexico,
1946-1986

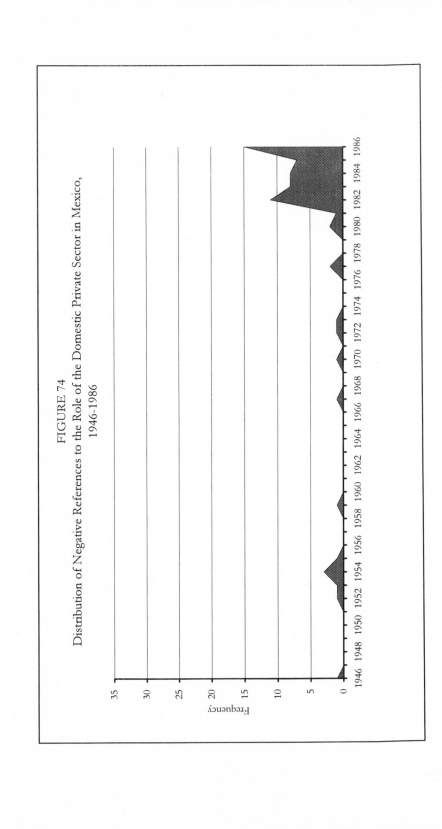

FIGURE 74

Distribution of Negative References to the Role of the Domestic Private Sector in Mexico, 1946-1986

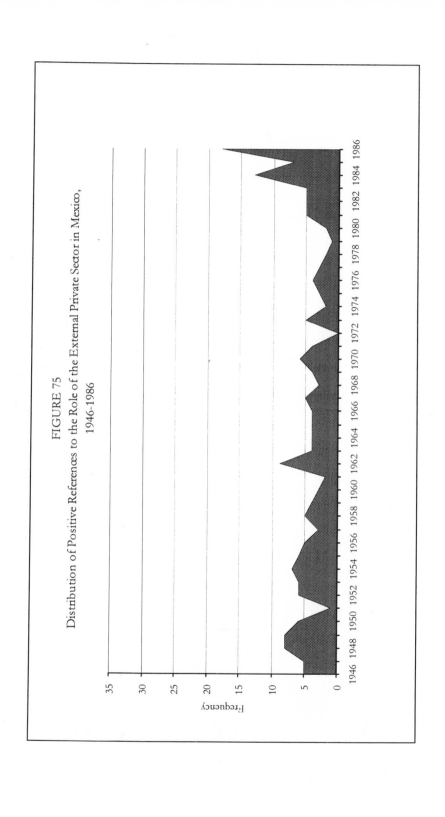

FIGURE 75

Distribution of Positive References to the Role of the External Private Sector in Mexico, 1946-1986

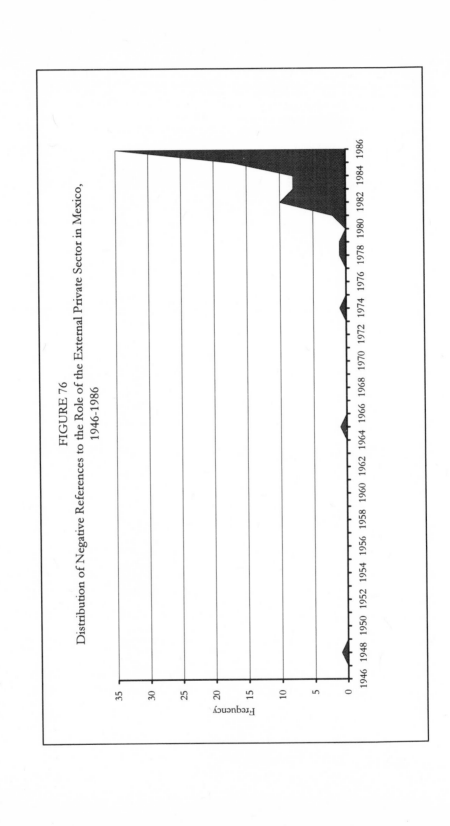

FIGURE 76

Distribution of Negative References to the Role of the External Private Sector in Mexico, 1946-1986

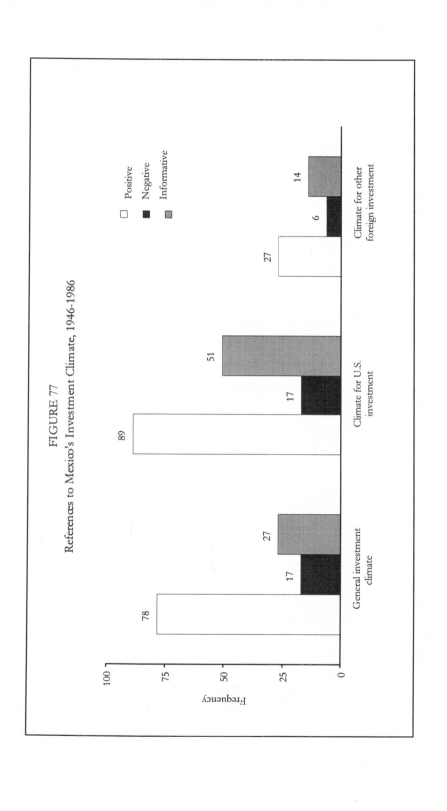

FIGURE 77

References to Mexico's Investment Climate, 1946-1986

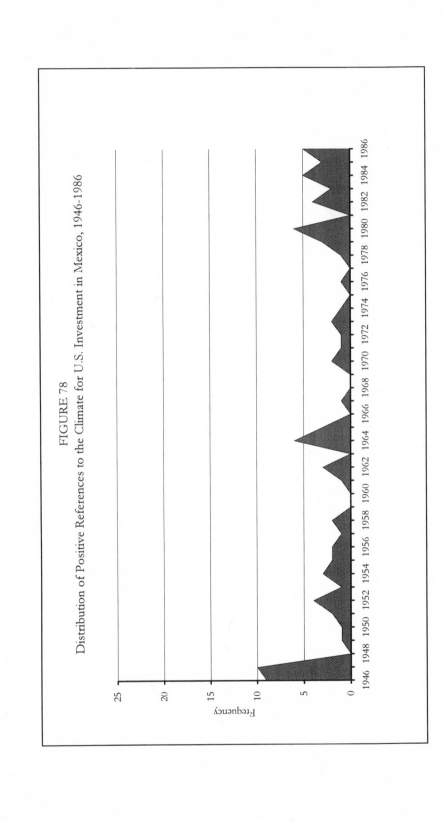

FIGURE 78

Distribution of Positive References to the Climate for U.S. Investment in Mexico, 1946-1986

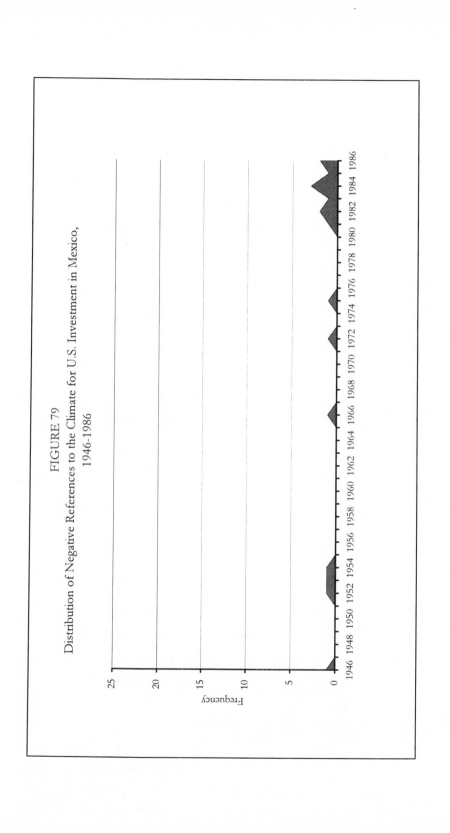

FIGURE 79

Distribution of Negative References to the Climate for U.S. Investment in Mexico, 1946-1986

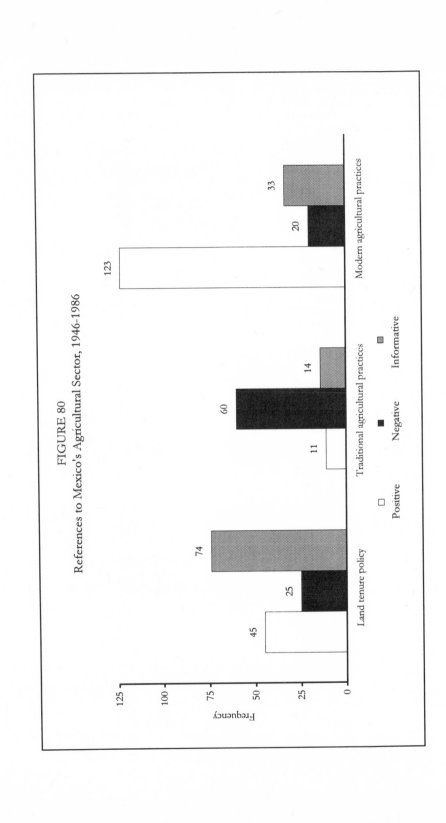

FIGURE 80

References to Mexico's Agricultural Sector, 1946-1986

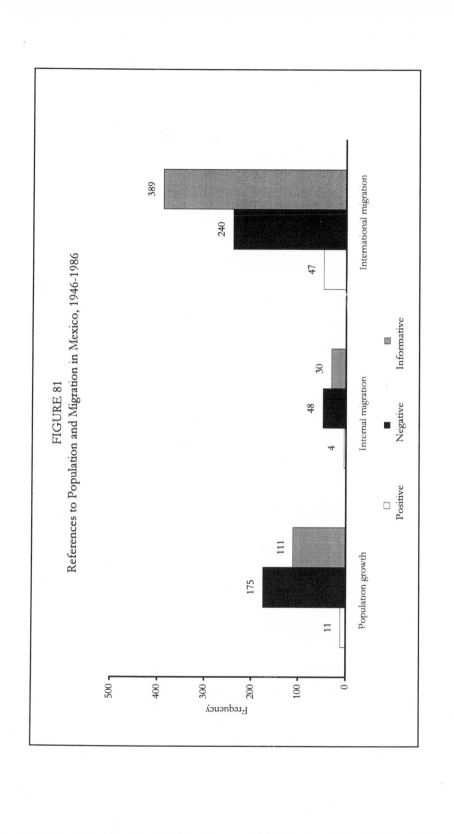

FIGURE 81

References to Population and Migration in Mexico, 1946-1986

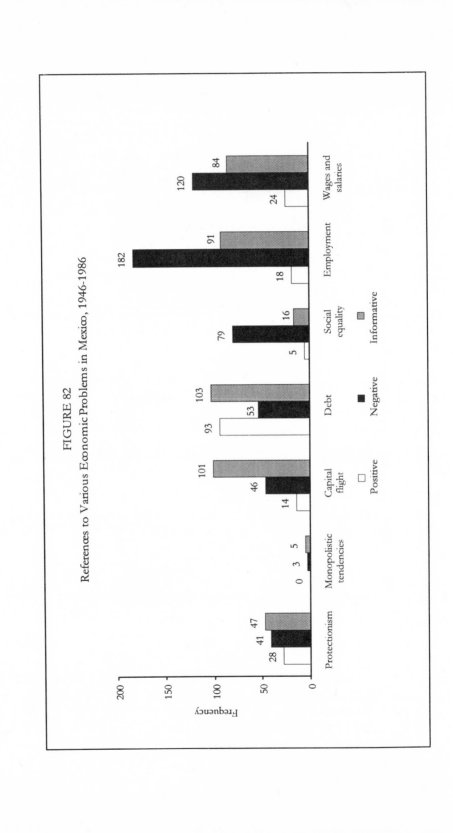

FIGURE 82

References to Various Economic Problems in Mexico, 1946-1986

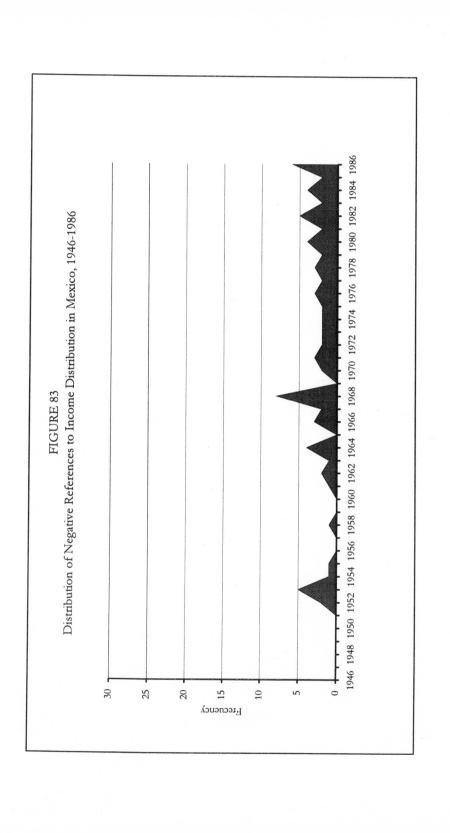

FIGURE 83

Distribution of Negative References to Income Distribution in Mexico, 1946-1986

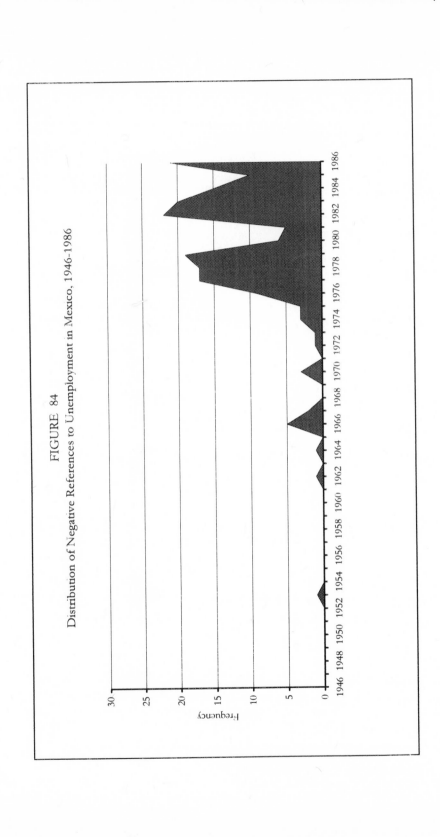

FIGURE 84

Distribution of Negative References to Unemployment in Mexico, 1946-1986

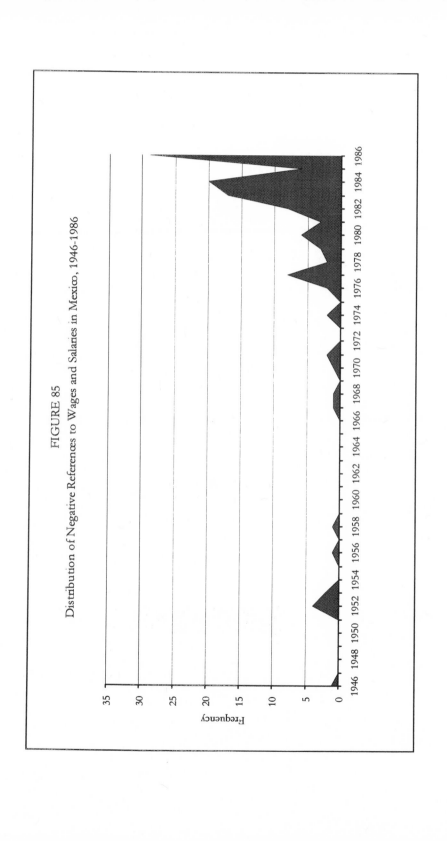

FIGURE 85

Distribution of Negative References to Wages and Salaries in Mexico, 1946-1986

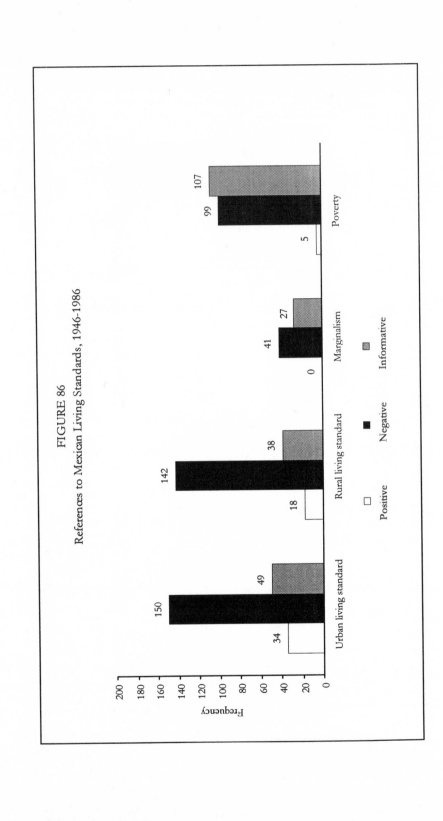

FIGURE 86

References to Mexican Living Standards, 1946-1986

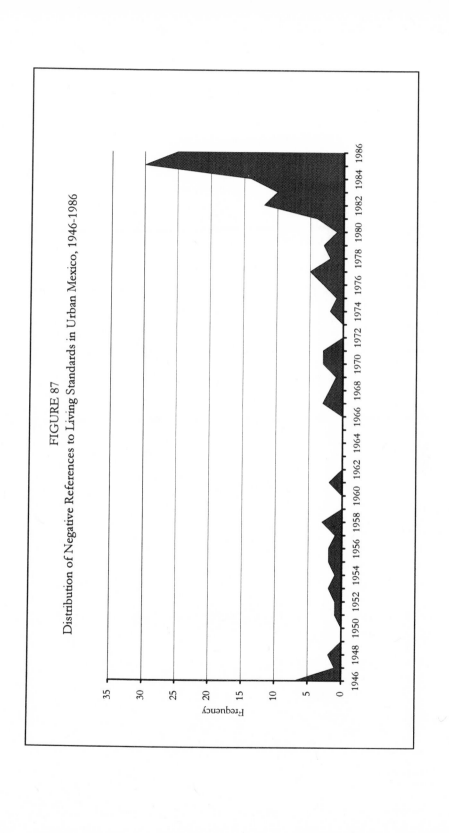

FIGURE 87

Distribution of Negative References to Living Standards in Urban Mexico, 1946-1986

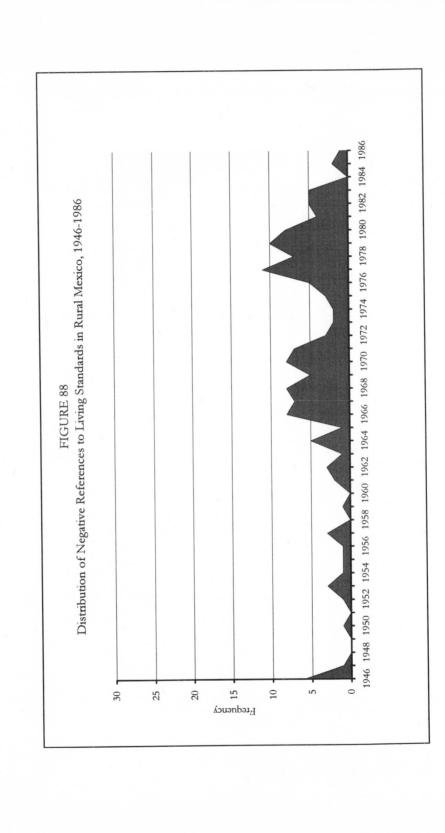

FIGURE 88

Distribution of Negative References to Living Standards in Rural Mexico, 1946-1986

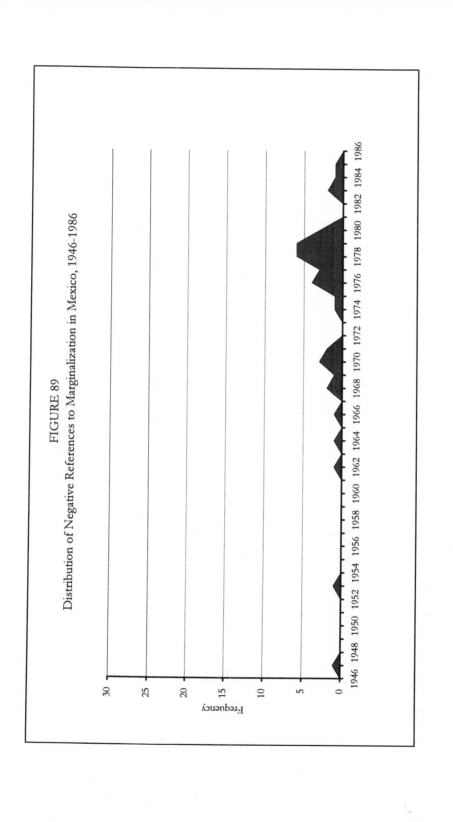

FIGURE 89

Distribution of Negative References to Marginalization in Mexico, 1946-1986

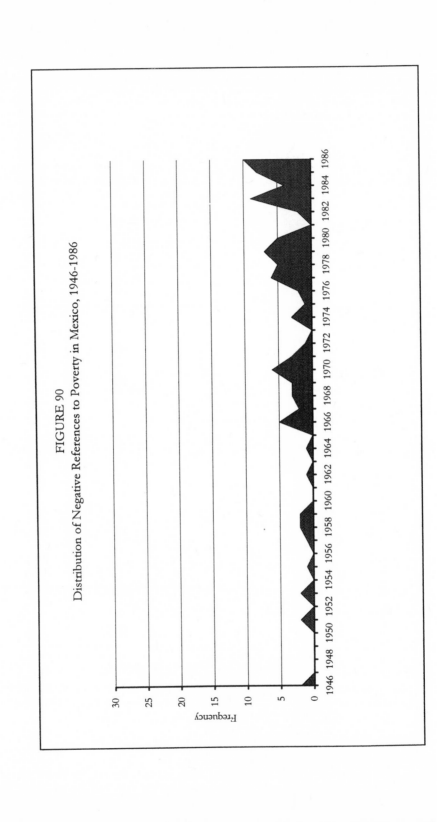

FIGURE 90

Distribution of Negative References to Poverty in Mexico, 1946-1986

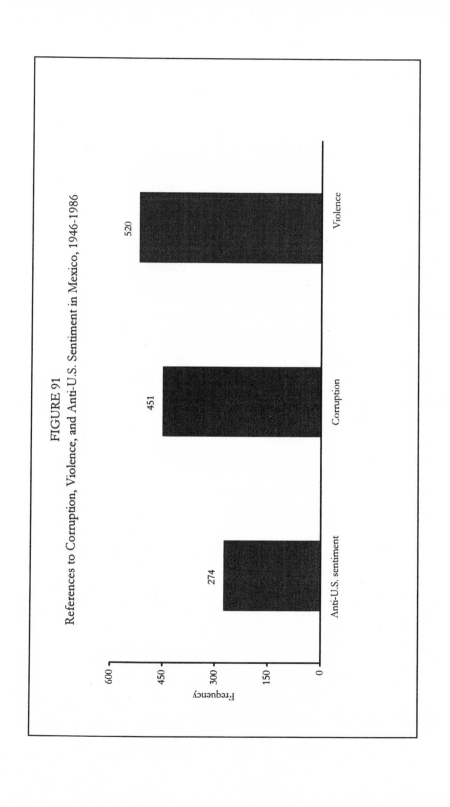

FIGURE 91

References to Corruption, Violence, and Anti-U.S. Sentiment in Mexico, 1946-1986

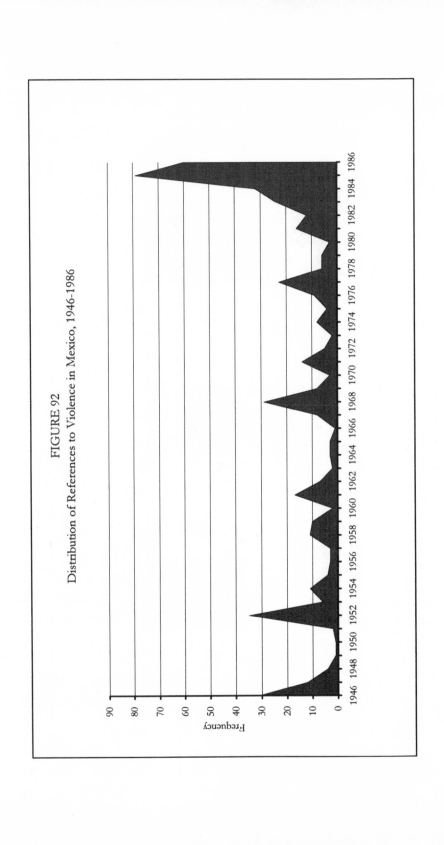

FIGURE 92

Distribution of References to Violence in Mexico, 1946-1986

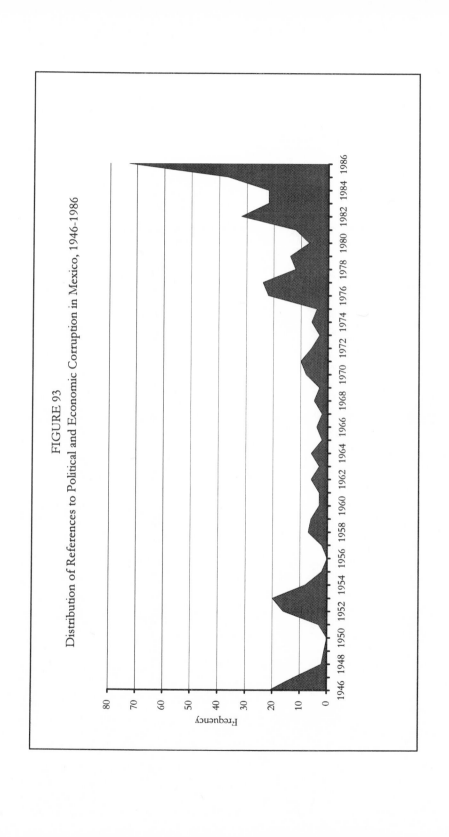

FIGURE 93

Distribution of References to Political and Economic Corruption in Mexico, 1946-1986

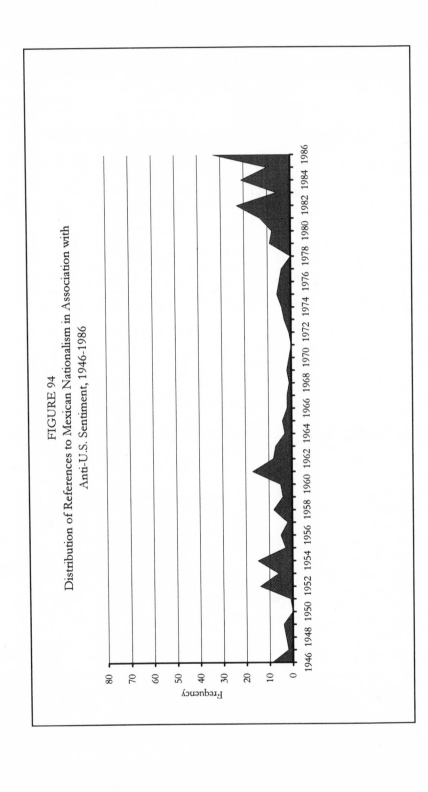

FIGURE 94

Distribution of References to Mexican Nationalism in Association with
Anti-U.S. Sentiment, 1946-1986

Appendix B

Methodology and Code Manual

The Code Manual, which lists the variables used to analyze the 6,903 pieces on Mexico published in the *New York Times*, developed over a number of stages. I first drew up a list of aspects that must necessarily be considered in content analysis. This list was derived from specialized texts on the subject;[1] consultations with a number of specialists on the economy, politics, and foreign affairs; and 236 randomly selected articles from the *Times*.

This yielded in a list of 127 variables organized into six categories. Although a number of modifications were carried out in later stages, these categories remained constant; they are: Visible Characteristics, Sources of Information, The Economy, The Political System, Foreign Policy; and Mexican National Character.

Visible Characteristics category refers to an article's most immediately apparent aspects: date, page, column, and section within the paper; author, and the geographic location from which the piece was posted; location on the page ("quadrant"); allotted space, in columns and centimeters; the nature of its headline; and so on.

The Sources of Information category identifies who is quoted within an article (government officials, businessmen, journalists, members of the opposition, and so on), their nationalities, and whether their declarations were public or anonymous. This indicator is useful for determining, among other things, which sectors have been granted an opportunity to speak and, hence, for establishing the preferences of the respective author or correspondent. The culture of journalism that has evolved in the United States has always prided itself on presenting a wide range of viewpoints.

Information for the Economy, Politics, and Foreign Affairs categories was gathered through a list of variables that I present below. Each variable also recorded whether a given reference was positive, negative, or neutral.

---

[1]See, for example, Battailer 1963; Berelson 1952; Covo 1973; Danielson n.d.; Duverger 1972; Gomis 1974; Jiménez de Ottalengo 1974; Kayser 1966; Stone 1966.

Finally, I grouped several variables under Mexican National Character, to gather together and analyze the wide range of comments on Mexican culture that must inevitably arise from the extreme diversity between the two societies. To formulate these variables, I revised a number of existing analyses of the manner in which Mexico and Mexican society have been portrayed in different cultural contexts in the United States, such as the cinema, western pulp fiction, textbooks, and so on (W. Anderson 1977; Paredes 1973; Zelman 1969).

The first iteration of the Code Manual, with its 127 variables and codification tables, was tested using 64 randomly selected articles: the first article in successive six-month periods between 1946 and 1977 that exceed 61 centimeters in length. To test for objectivity in the coding process, two readers analyzed these articles independently.

This pilot test led to a number of changes in the manual; 3 variables were dropped, 16 were modified, and 85 were added, for a total of 209. Certain errors in the design of formats for data collection were also corrected. The objectivity test (separate analysis carried out by two coders) produced agreement in 831 of the 852 coded variables; this margin of difference (2.5 percent) was deemed acceptable.

The revised, 209–variable Code Manual was then applied to 5,057 articles published between 1946 and 1979 (research for the author's doctoral thesis). An Ms-Editor program was used to translate the information-gathering formats, which were processed using the Statistical Package for the Social Sciences (SPSS). Later, for the preparation of this book, I included all articles published between 1980 and 1986. This entailed adding another 1,846 entries. This stage also required the addition of 6 new variables and produced the final version of the Code Manual, with a total of 215 variables. Because this research was carried out in two stages, there are certain gaps in the presentation of the variables. Miguel de la Madrid, for example, appears at the end of the list, and not with the other presidents.

After encoding, errors were eliminated and the information was processed Two caveats are in order: the following list is presented as it was handled by the statistical program; it does not correspond to the tables presented in Appendix B; and, to save space, I have removed the card number (each had three, with 80 columns), the code numbers used to identify the cards, and the four symbols (+, -, o, =) used to classify opinions.

CODE MANUAL

A. VISIBLE CHARACTERISTICS

Variable 1	Article identification number
V2	Date of article (day)
V3	Date of article (month)
V4	Date of article (year)
V5	Width of heading

        1 column
        2 columns
        3 columns
        4 columns
        5 or more

V6   Space allotted to article

        Up to 10 cm.
        11–30 cm.
        31–60 cm.
        61–121 cm.
        Half-page or more

V7   Location of article

        First section (including page number, 1 to 30)
        Other pages
        Editorial page
        Financial section
            First page
            Other pages
        Book Section
            First page
            Other pages
        Magazine
            First page
            Other pages
        Other Sections
            First page
            Other pages

V8   Page location, divided into four sections

        Top right
        Bottom right
        Top left
        Bottom left

V9   Filed from Mexico
                                      Mexico City
                                      Acapulco
                                      Elsewhere
                            Filed from the United States
                                      Washington, D.C.
                                      Elsewhere
                            Filed from another country
V10   Headline subject
                                      Economy
                                      Politics
                                      Foreign affairs
                                      National character
V11   Authorship
                                      Correspondent
                                      Editor
                                      Opinion piece
                                      Letter to the editor
                                      Special envoy
                                      Times special
                                      News agency
                                      UPI, AP, etc.
                                      No byline

B. INFORMATION SOURCES INCLUDED IN THE TEXTS

IDENTIFIED MEXICAN SOURCES
V12   Government official
V13   Businessperson
V14   Press
V15   Member of the opposition
V16   Other (clergy, citizens, intellectuals, etc.)

IDENTIFIED U.S. SOURCES
V17   Government official
V18   Businessperson
V19   Press
V20   Member of the opposition
V21   Other (clergy, citizens, intellectuals, etc.)

IDENTIFIED SOURCES OF OTHER NATIONALITIES
V22	Government official
V23	Businessperson
V24	Press
V25	Member of the opposition
V26	Other (clergy, citizens, intellectuals, etc.)

ANONYMOUS MEXICAN SOURCES
V27	Government official
V28	Businessperson
V29	Press
V30	Member of the opposition
V31	Other (clergy, citizens, intellectuals, etc.)

ANONYMOUS U.S. SOURCES
V32	Government official
V33	Businessperson
V34	Press
V35	Member of the opposition
V36	Other (clergy, citizens, intellectuals, etc.)

ANONYMOUS SOURCES OF OTHER NATIONALITIES
V37	Government official
V38	Businessperson
V39	Press
V40	Member of the opposition
V41	Other (clergy, citizens, intellectuals, etc.)

C. THE MEXICAN ECONOMY

V42	General overview of the economy
V43	Financial situation (minus balance of payments, part of another variable)
V44	Mexico as a model for development

FARMING AND AGRICULTURE
V45	Land ownership system
V46	Traditional agricultural techniques
V47	Modern agricultural techniques
V48	Cattle ranching

INDUSTRY
V49	General overview of industry
V50	Petrochemicals
V51	Electricity generation
V52	Manufacturing
V53	Mining
V54	Iron and steel
V55	Capital goods

SERVICE SECTOR
V56	Tourism
V57	Transportation
V58	Communications
V59	Other

TRADE
V60	Traditional marketing systems
V61	Modern marketing systems
V62	Subsidized commerce
V67	Speculative

BALANCE OF PAYMENTS
V64	Current account
V65	Capital account

MEXICAN POLICIES AND ECONOMIC GROWTH
V66	Protectionism
V67	Monopolizing tendencies
V68	Federal budget
V69	Education
V70	Health
V71	Nationalization of foreign companies
V72	Fiscal reform
V73	Capital flight
V74	Internal and external debt
V75	Income distribution
V76	Unemployment
V77	Salary
V78	Prices
V79	Inflation
V80	Foreign investors' use of Mexican "name-lenders"

THE MEXICAN POPULATION

V81	Growth
V82	Internal migration
V83	International migration
V84	Urban lifestyle
V85	Rural lifestyle
V86	Marginalization
V87	Poverty
V88	Livelihood
V89	Subsidized livelihood

PRINCIPAL ECONOMIC SECTORS

V90	State role in the national economy
V91	Public companies
V92	Role of the domestic private sector
V93	Role of the foreign private sector
V94	Federal policy toward the domestic private sector
V95	Federal policy toward the foreign private sector
V96	Relationship between domestic and foreign private sectors
V97	Other economic sectors

D. THE MEXICAN POLITICAL SYSTEM

V98	General overview of politics
V99	Government's general orientation
V100	Democratization

POLITICAL WATERSHEDS

V101	Mexican Revolution
V102	Nationalization of the oil industry
V103	Student movement of 1968

MEXICAN PRESIDENTS

V104	Lázaro Cárdenas
V105	Miguel Alemán
V106	Adolfo Ruiz Cortines
V107	Adolfo López Mateos
V108	Gustavo Díaz Ordaz
V109	Luis Echeverría Álvarez
V110	José López Portillo

Note: Miguel de la Madrid and Carlos Salinas de Gortari appear as variables 211 and 212.

OTHER FORMAL POWERS
| V111 | Legislative |
| V112 | Judicial |

OFFICIAL INSTITUTIONS
V113	Ministry of Government
V114	Ministry of the Presidency (later Ministry of Budget and Planning)
V115	Ministry of Defense
V116	Ministry of Education
V117	Ministry of Agrarian Reform
V118	Ministry of Labor
V119	Ministry of Treasury
V120	Ministry of Trade and Industry
V121	General Attorney's Office
V122	PEMEX (Mexican Petroleum Company)
V123	Bank of Mexico
V124	Nacional Financiera
V125	Federal Electricity Commission
V126	Other

POLITICAL PARTIES
V127	PRI (Institutional Revolutionary Party)
V128	PAN (National Action Party)
V129	UNS–PDM (National Sinarchist Union– Mexican Democratic Party)
V130	PP–PPS (Popular Socialist Party)
V131	PSUM (Mexican Unified Socialist Party)
V132	Other

POLITICAL OPPOSITION
V133	Left
V134	Right
V135	Liberal
V136	Armed

POLITICAL PROBLEMS
V137	Electoral fraud
V138	Abstentionism
V139	Independent labor movements
V140	Peasant movements
V141	Demonstrations
V142	Government repression
V143	Patronage politics
V144	Disturbances
V145	Other

POLITICAL ACTORS
V146	Private sector
V147	Labor
V148	Peasants
V149	Middle classes
V150	Intellectuals
V151	Students
V152	Press
V153	Armed forces
V154	Church
V155	Other

E. MEXICO'S RELATIONS WITH THE WORLD

V156	General overview of foreign relations

MEXICO–U.S. RELATIONS
V157	General appraisal of the relationship
V158	Economic relations
V159	Political relations
V160	Cultural relations
V161	Military relations
V162	Mexican attitude toward Alliance for Progress
V163	Oil-related relations
V164	Border relations
V165	Mexican migration
V166	Drug trafficking
V167	Contraband between Mexico and United States

PRESIDENTIAL SUMMITS
V168   Mexican president
V169   U.S. president

MEXICO'S FOREIGN INVESTMENT CLIMATE
V170   General
V171   Toward U.S. investment
V172   Toward investments from other countries

MEXICO'S FOREIGN DEBT
V173   General
V174   Contracted with private or public U.S. institutions,
            including multilaterals such as World Bank, IMF,
            Eximbank, etc.
V175   Contracted with other nations

MEXICO AND THE WESTERN HEMISPHERE
V176   Mexico–Central America
V177   Mexico–South America
V178   Mexico–Cuba
V179   Mexico–Chile

MEXICO AND THE REST OF THE WORLD
V180   Mexico–Europe
V181   Mexico–Asia
V182   Mexico–Japan
V183   Mexico–China
V184   Mexico–Soviet Union
V185   Mexico–other nations

MEXICO AND INTERNATIONAL ORGANIZATIONS
V186   Mexico–United Nations
V187   Mexico–Organization of American States
V188   Mexico–Latin American Free Trade Association
V189   Mexico–Central American Common Market
V190   Mexico–non-aligned countries
V191   Mexico–OPEC
V192   Mexico–General Agreement on Tariffs and Trades
V193   Mexico–specialized organisms

F. MEXICAN NATIONAL CHARACTER

V194	Pastoral image of Mexico
V195	Racial differences
V196	Violence
V197	Catholicism
V198	Economic and political corruption
V200	The "Mañana Syndrome"
V201	Machismo
V202	Traditionalism
V203	Family unity
V204	Canceled
V205	Creativity
V206	Folklore
V207	Folk crafts
V208	Other

G. OTHER VARIABLES (some added after study extended)

CORRESPONDENTS
V209	Camille M. Cianfarra
	Milton Braker
	William P. Carney
	Sidney Gruson
	Paul B. Kennedy
	Henry Giniger
	Juan de Onís
	Alan Riding
	Richard Severo

MORE CORRESPONDENTS
V210	Richard J. Meislin
	William Stockton
V211	Miguel de la Madrid
V212	Carlos Salinas de Gortari
V213	Human Rights
V214	Civil Society
V215	Earthquake of 1985

Appendix C

Author Interviews

Much of the information contained in this volume was gathered through formal interviews and through informal exchanges with individuals in the United States—in the latter case, often over a period of years. The following is a partial list of these individuals. When the exchange was a formal interview, the date, and sometimes the place, of the interview is included. The absence of an interview date indicates an ongoing exchange over several conversations at minimum.

Elliott Abrams, Under Secretary of State for Latin American Affairs under President Ronald Reagan, Washington, D.C., April 1991
Ruth Adams, MacArthur Foundation, Chicago
Cindy Arnson, The Wilson Center, Washington, D.C.
David Assman, *Wall Street Journal*, New York
Delal Baer, Georgetown University
Bruce Bagley, University of Miami
John Bailey, Georgetown University
Oscar Bolioli, Director of the Commission on the Caribbean and Central America, National Council of Churches, New York
David Brooks, U.S.–Mexico Diálogos, New York
Roderic Ai Camp, Tulane University, 1991
Richard Celeste, October 1991
Douglas Chalmers, Columbia University
John Coatsworth, University of Chicago, 1988
William Colby, former director of the Central Intelligence Agency, Washington, D.C., 1989
Mike Conroy, University of Texas at Austin
Pamela Constable, *Boston Globe*
Wayne A. Cornelius, Center for U.S.–Mexican Studies, University of California, San Diego, 1988
Margaret Crahan, Occidental College
Fred Cunny, Intertec, Dallas
Jorge I. Domínguez, Harvard University
William M. Dyal, Jr., American Friends Service Committee, New York
Michael Dziedziec, National Defense University
John Eagleson, Orbis Books, Maryknoll, New York

Richard Erkstad, American Friends Service Committee, Philadelphia
Patricia Weiss Fagen, United Nations High Commission for Refugees, Geneva
Richard Feinberg, Inter-American Dialogue, Washington, D.C.
John M. Fife, Tucson, Arizona
Murray Fromson, University of Southern California
Dennis Gallagher, Refugee Policy Group, Washington, D.C.
Manuel García y Griego, University of California, Irvine
Carl Gershman, National Endowment for Democracy, Washington, D.C.
Henry Giniger, former *New York Times* Mexico correspondent, New York
Piero Gleijeses, Johns Hopkins University
Tim Golden, former *New York Times* correspondent, Mexico
George Grayson, William and Mary College, 1988
Sidney Gruson, former *New York Times* correspondent, New York
Peter Hakim, Inter-American Dialogue, Washington, D.C.
Roger Hansen, Johns Hopkins University
Milton Jamail, University of Texas at Austin
Charles Keely, Georgetown University
Jared Kotler, Washington Office on Latin America
William Leogrande, Catholic University
Abraham Lowenthal, University of Southern California
Tommie Sue Montgomery, University of Miami
Richard Moss, Princeton University
Richard Nuccio, Inter-American Dialogue, Washington, D.C., 1988
Robert Pastor, Emory University, Mexico City, 1985
Alejandro Portes, Johns Hopkins University
Susan Kaufman Purcell, Council of the Americas, Washington, D.C., 1988
Clark Reynolds, Stanford University, Palo Alto, California
Alan Riding, former *New York Times* correspondent, 1981 and 1983
Riordan Roett, Johns Hopkins University
David Ronfeldt, Rand Corporation
Arthur Schmitt, Temple University
Lars Schoultz, University of North Carolina, Chapel Hill
Richard Severo, former *New York Times* correspondent, New York, 1983
Gene Sharp, Albert Einstein Institute, Cambridge, Massachusetts
Sally Shelton-Colby, Georgetown University
Michael Shifter, Inter-American Dialogue, Washington, D.C.
Diane Silver, Inter-Religious Task Force on El Salvador and Central America, New York
Clint Smith, Hewlett Foundation, Menlo Park, California
Peter H. Smith, University of California, San Diego
Kimberly Stanton, MacArthur Foundation, Chicago

Arturo Valenzuela, Georgetown University
George Vickers, Washington Office on Latin America
Stephen J. Wager, United States Military Academy, West Point
Christopher Welna, Ford Foundation, Mexico Office
Kenneth Wollack, National Democratic Institute for International
    Affairs, Washington, D.C.
Martin Zimmerman, United Methodist Church, New York, 1984
Aristide Zolberg, New School for Social Research

Acronyms

AMDH	Academia Mexicana para Derechos Humanos/ Mexican Academy for Human Rights
CCI	Central Campesina Independiente/Independent Peasant Central
CDH	Centro de Derechos Humanos Fray Francisco de Vitoria/Fray Francisco de Vitoria Center for Human Rights
CIA	Central Intelligence Agency
CIDE	Centro de Investigación y Docencia Económicas
CIDOC	Centro Intercultural de Documentación/Intercultural Center for Documentation
CNDH	Comisión Nacional de Derechos Humanos/National Commission on Human Rights
CONACYT	Consejo Nacional de Ciencia y Tecnología/National Council for Science and Technology
CONCANACO	Confederación de Cámaras Nacionales de Comercio/ Federation of National Chambers of Commerce
CTM	Confederación de Trabajadores de México/ Confederation of Mexican Workers
DEA	Drug Enforcement Agency
DFS	Dirección Federal de Seguridad/Federal Security Directorate
EAP	Economically active population
EPR	Ejército Popular Revolucionario/Peoples' Revolutionary Army
EZLN	Ejército Zapatista de Liberación Nacional/Zapatista Army of National Liberation
FBI	Federal Bureau of Investigation
FDN	Frente Democrático Nacional/National Democratic Front
FSLN	Frente Sandinista de Liberación Nacional/Sandinista Front for National Liberation
GATT	General Agreement on Tariffs and Trade
GNP	Gross national product

IMF	International Monetary Fund
INS	Immigration and Naturalization Service
ISI	Import-substitution industrialization
JMUSDC	Joint Mexican–U.S. Defense Commission
MUP	Movimiento Urbano Popular/Urban Popular Movement
NACLA	North American Congress on Latin America
NAFTA	North American Free Trade Agreement
NGO	Nongovernmental organization
NSC	National Security Council
OAS	Organization of American States
OPEC	Organization of Petroleum-Exporting Countries
PAN	Partido Acción Nacional/National Action Party
PCM	Partido Comunista Mexicano/Mexican Communist Party
PDM	Partido Demócrata Mexicano/Mexican Democratic Party
PEMEX	Petróleos Mexicanos
PMT	Partido Mexicano de los Trabajadores/Mexican Workers' Party
PNR	Partido Nacional Revolucionario/Revolutionary National Party
PP	Partido Popular/Popular Party
PPS	Partido Popular Socialista/Socialist Popular Party
PRD	Partido de la Revolución Democrática/Party of the Democratic Revolution
PRI	Partido Revolucionario Institucional/Institutional Revolutionary Party
PRM	Partido de la Revolución Mexicana/Party of the Mexican Revolution
PSUM	Partido Socialista Unificado de México/Mexican Unified Socialist Party
SELA	Sistema Económico Latinoamericano/Latin American Economic System
UNAM	Universidad Nacional Autónoma de México
UNS	Unión Nacional Sinarquista/National Sinarchist Union

Bibliography

Abrams, Floyd. 1981. "The Pentagon Papers a Decade Later," *New York Times Magazine*, June 14.

Acker, Jack, and Kathy King Wouk. 1986. "Mexico Must Do Better on Human Rights," *New York Times*, June 15.

Aguayo Quezada, Sergio. 1990. "Los usos, abusos y retos de la seguridad nacional mexicana." In *En busca de la seguridad perdida*, edited by Sergio Aguayo and Bruce M. Bagley. Mexico City: Siglo Veintiuno.

———. 1991. "Mexico in United States Military Literature, 1949–1988," *International Journal of Political Economy* 21:2 (Summer).

———. 1993a. "The Evolution and Implications of Mexican Nongovernmental Organizations Working on Behalf of Displaced Central Americans." Report DRU-257-FF. Santa Monica, Calif.: Rand Corporation, March.

———. 1993b. "The Inevitability of Democracy in Mexico." In *Political and Economic Liberalization in Mexico: At a Critical Juncture?* edited by Riordan Roett. Boulder, Colo.: Lynne Rienner.

Aguayo Quezada, Sergio, and Luz Paula Parra Rosales. 1996. "Los organismos no gubernamentales de derechos humanos en México: entre la democracia participativa y la electoral." Documento de Trabajo. Mexico City: Academia Mexicana de Derechos Humanos.

Albini, Joseph L. 1971. *The American Mafia: Genesis of a Legend*. New York: Appleton-Century-Crofts.

Alemán Valdés, Miguel. 1987. *Remembranzas y testimonios*. Mexico City: Grijalbo.

Alianza Cívica. 1994a. "Las elecciones presidenciales de agosto de 1994: entre el escepticismo y la esperanza. Un informe sobre las condiciones previas." Mexico City: Alianza Cívica, August 19.

———. 1994b. "La calidad de la jornada electoral del 21 de agosto de 1994." Mexico City: Alianza Cívica, September 19.

Almond, Gabriel A., and Sidney Verba. 1963. *The Civic Culture: Political Attitudes and Democracy in Five Nations*. Princeton, N.J.: Princeton University Press.

Amnesty International. 1986. *Mexico Human Rights in Rural Areas. Exchange of Documents with the Mexican Government on Human Rights Violations in Oaxaca and Chiapas*. London: Amnesty International.

———. 1991. *México. Tortura e impunidad*. Madrid: Editorial Amnistía Internacional.

Anderson, Jack, and Dale Van Atta. 1987a. "The Mexican Time Bomb," *Penthouse*, May.

———. 1987b. "CIA: Disorder Could Overwhelm Mexico," *Washington Post*, June 5.

Anderson, William W. 1977. "The Nature of the Mexican Revolution as Viewed from the United States, 1910–1971." Ph.D. dissertation, University of Texas at Austin.

Anderson-Barker, Cynthia. 1994. "A Case Study of Elections in the State of Michoacan on July 12, 1992," *International and Comparative Law Journal* 16:2 (February).

Andreas, Peter. 1996. "Narcotizing the State and Economy in Mexico: Side-effects of Free Market Reform and Drug Market Prohibition." Paper prepared for the "Transnational Organized Crime" panel at the International Law and Society Conference, Glasgow, July 10–13.

Applegate, Rex. 1985. "The Evil Empire Eyes the Big Enchilada," *Soldier of Fortune*, August.

Armstrong, Robert. 1983. "By What Right? U.S. Foreign Policy, 1945–1983," *NACLA Report on the Americas* 17:6 (November–December).

Aron, Raymond. 1966. *Trois Essais sur l'Age Industriel*. Paris: Plon.

Baer, Delal. 1987. "Mexico: Ambivalent Ally," *Washington Quarterly*, Summer.

———. 1988. "Between Evolution and Devolution: Mexican Democracy," *Washington Quarterly*, Summer.

Bailey, John. 1988. *Governing Mexico: The Statecraft of Crisis Management*. New York: St. Martin's.

———. 1989. "Mexico in the U.S. Media, 1979–1988: Implications for the Bilateral Relation." In *Images of Mexico in the United States*, edited by John H. Coatsworth and Carlos Rico. La Jolla: Center for U.S.–Mexican Studies, University of California, San Diego, for the Bilateral Commission on the Future of United States–Mexican Relations.

Bailey, John, and Sergio Aguayo Quezada. 1996. *Strategy and Security in U.S.–Mexican Relations beyond the Cold War*. La Jolla: Center for U.S.–Mexican Studies, University of California, San Diego.

Baird, Peter, and Ed McCaughan. 1974. "Golden Ghetto. The American Colony in Mexico," *NACLA's Latin America and Empire Report* 8:1 (January).

———. 1975. "Hit and Run. U.S. Runaway Shops on the Mexican Border," *NACLA's Latin America and Empire Report* 9:5 (July–August).

Baker, James A., III. 1995. *The Politics of Diplomacy: Revolution, War and Peace, 1989–1992*. New York: Putnam.

Bartra, Roger. 1978. *El poder despótico burgués*. Mexico City: Era.

———. 1993. *El oficio mexicano*. Mexico City: Grijalbo.

Basáñez, Miguel. 1991. "Encuesta electoral, 1991," *Este País* 5 (August).

Battailler, Francine, Alain Schitres, and Claude Tannery. 1963. *Analyses de Presse*. Paris: Presses Universitaires de France.

Bauer, K.J. 1956. "The Veracruz Expedition of 1847," *Military Affairs* 20 (Fall).

Benítez Manaut, Raúl. 1994. "Las fuerzas armadas mexicanas a fin de siglo: su relación con el Estado, el sistema político y la sociedad," *Sociología* 25, year 9 (May–August).

Bennett, Douglas C., and Kenneth E. Sharpe. 1985. *Transnational Corporations versus the State: The Political Economy of the Mexican Auto Industry*. Princeton, N.J.: Princeton University Press.

Berelson, Bernard. 1952. *Content Analysis in Communication Research*. New York: Stratford.

Birnbaum, Norman. 1960. "The Sociological Study of Ideology (1940–1960): A Trend Report and Bibliography," *Current Sociology* 2.

Bourne, Kenneth, and D. Cameron Watt, eds. 1989. *Latin America, South America and Mexico, 1924–1927.* Part II, Series D, Vol. 4 of *British Documents on Foreign Affairs,* edited by George Philip. Bethesda, Md.: University Publications of America.

Brandenburg, Frank. 1964. *The Making of Modern Mexico.* Englewood Cliffs, N.J.: Prentice-Hall.

Bray, Howard. 1980. *The Pillars of the Post. The Making of a News Empire in Washington.* New York: Norton.

Brenner, Anita. 1946. "Newsboy to President, Mexican Style," *New York Times,* July 21.

———. 1948. "Mexico's New Deal Two Years After," *New York Times Magazine,* November 28.

Brittan, Samuel. 1983. "A Very Painful World Adjustment," *Foreign Affairs* 61:3.

Brown, Betty H. 1969. "Make Mine Guadalajara (for retirement)," *Air Force Times,* August 13.

Camp, Roderic A. 1980a. "Mexican Military Leadership in Statistical Perspective since the 1930s." In *Statistical Abstract of Latin America,* vol. 20, edited by James Wilkie and Peter Reich. Los Angeles: University of California, Los Angeles.

———. 1980b. *Mexico's Leaders: Their Education and Recruitment.* Tucson: University of Arizona Press.

———. 1982. *Mexican Political Biographies, 1935–1981.* 2d ed. Tucson: University of Arizona Press.

———. 1984. *The Making of a Government: Political Leaders in Modern Mexico.* Tucson: University of Arizona Press.

———. 1985. *Intellectuals and the State in Twentieth-Century Mexico.* Austin: University of Texas Press.

———. 1989. *Entrepreneurs and Politics in Twentieth-Century Mexico.* New York: Oxford University Press.

———. 1990a. "Mexico." In *Handbook of Political Science Research on Latin America,* edited by David W. Dent. New York: Greenwood.

———. 1990b. "*Camarillas* in Mexican Politics: The Case of the Salinas Cabinet," *Mexican Studies* 6:1 (Winter).

Camp, Roderic A., ed. 1986. *Mexico's Political Stability: The Next Five Years.* Boulder, Colo.: Westview.

Cannon, Lou. 1991. *President Reagan: The Role of a Lifetime.* New York: Simon and Schuster.

Cano Andaluz, Aurora. 1993. *1968. Antología periodística.* Mexico City: Universidad Nacional Autónoma de México.

Cardoso, Fernando H. 1973. "Associated-Dependent Development: Theoretical and Practical Implications." In *Authoritarian Brazil: Origins, Policies, and Future,* edited by Alfred Stepan. New Haven, Conn.: Yale University Press.

Cardoso, Miriam L. 1975. *La ideología dominante.* Mexico City: Siglo Veintiuno.

Carey, James W. 1974. "Journalism and Criticism: The Case of an Underdeveloped Profession," *Review of Politics,* April.

Carr, Edward Hallet. 1963. *What Is History?* New York: Knopf.

Carter, Jimmy. 1980. "Speech Before the Caribbean/Central American Action," *In Action*, July.

———. 1983. *Keeping Faith. Memoirs of a President*. New York: Bantam.

Casaroli, Agostino. 1961. "Appeal of the Pontifical Commission to North American Superiors." Presentation to the Second Religious Congress of the United States, University of Notre Dame, August 17. Reprinted in *Mission to Latin America: The Successes and Failures of a Twentieth-Century Crusade*, by Gerald M. Costello (Maryknoll, N.Y.: Orbis, 1979).

Castañeda, Jorge. 1982a. "Caribbean Basin Security," *New York Times*, March 10.

———. 1982b. "Mexico's Peace Promoter," *New York Times*, March 20.

———. 1985. "Leaning Too Hard on the Mexicans," *New York Times*, March 29.

———. 1986. "Indebted Mexico Staggers On," *New York Times*, January 8.

Centeno, Miguel Angel. 1994. *Democracy within Reason: Technocratic Revolution in Mexico*. University Park: Pennsylvania State University Press.

Chabat, Jorge. 1994. "Seguridad nacional y narcotráfico: vínculos reales e imaginarios," *Política y Gobierno* 1:1.

Chalmers, Douglas, Judy Gearhart, et al. 1995. "Mexican NGO Networks and Popular Participation." Papers on Latin America, no. 39. New York: Institute of Latin American and Iberian Studies, Columbia University, January.

CIA (Central Intelligence Agency, U.S.). 1951. "Mexico." SR-18. January 24.

———. 1964. "Survey of Latin America." April 1.

———. 1965a. "Some Political and Economic Problems Arising from State Enterprise in Latin America." January 15.

———. 1965b. "The Role of Public Opinion in Latin American Political Stability." May 13.

———. 1966a. "Security Conditions in Mexico." Special National Intelligence Estimate Number 81-66. April 7.

———. 1966b. "Security Conditions in Mexico and Elsewhere in Latin America." May 6.

———. 1967a. "Mexico: The Problems of Progress." October 20.

———. 1967b. "Developments Relative to President Johnson's Trip to Mexico." October 25.

———. 1973. "Mexico's Toughening Policy toward Foreign Investment." Memorandum. Washington, D.C., November.

———. 1976a. "Mexican Economic Situation." October.

———. 1976b. "Policy Guidelines for the Incoming Administration of President-elect José López Portillo." Intelligence Information Cable, Directorate of Operations, October 27.

———. 1977. "The Forces for Change in Mexican Foreign Policy." June.

CIG (Central Intelligence Group, U.S.). 1947. "Soviet Objectives in Latin America." April 10.

Cline, Howard F. 1966. "Mexico: A Matured Latin American Revolution, 1910–1960." In *Is the Mexican Revolution Dead?* edited by Stanley R. Ross. New York: Knopf.

Coatsworth, John H. 1987. "Student, Academic and Cultural Exchanges between Mexico and the United States: A Report with Recommendations." Presentation at the "Cultural Relations" workshop of the Bilateral Commission on the Future of United States–Mexican Relations, Chicago, October 26.

Cockcroft, James D. 1983. *Mexico: Class Formation, Capital Accumulation, and the State.* New York: Monthly Review Press.

Cohen, Bernard C. 1963. *The Press and Foreign Policy.* Princeton, N.J.: Princeton University Press.

Comercio Exterior. 1971. "Las reformas fiscales para 1971," March.

Cook, Maria Lorena, Kevin J. Middlebrook, and Juan Molinar Horcasitas, eds. 1994. *The Politics of Economic Restructuring: State-Society Relations and Regime Change in Mexico.* La Jolla: Center for U.S.–Mexican Studies, University of California, San Diego.

Córdoba, Arnaldo. 1989. *La nación y la constitución. La lucha por la democracia en México.* Mexico City: Claves Latinoamericanas.

Cornelius, Wayne A. 1975. *Politics of the Migrant Poor in Mexico City.* Stanford, Calif.: Stanford University Press.

———. 1991. "The Center for U.S.–Mexican Studies at the University of California, San Diego: An Overview." La Jolla, Calif., May 14. Mimeo.

Cornelius, Wayne A., and Ann L. Craig. 1991. *The Mexican Political System in Transition.* La Jolla: Center for U.S.–Mexican Studies, University of California, San Diego.

Cornelius, Wayne A., Judith Gentleman, and Peter H. Smith, eds. 1989. *Mexico's Alternative Political Futures.* La Jolla: Center for U.S.–Mexican Studies, University of California, San Diego.

Corradi, Juan E., Patricia Weiss Fagen, and Manuel Antonio Garretón. 1992. *Fear at the Edge: State Terror and Resistance in Latin America.* Berkeley: University of California Press.

Cosío Villegas, Daniel. 1956. *Estados Unidos contra Porfirio Díaz.* Mexico City: Hermes.

———. 1968. "De la necesidad de estudiar a Estados Unidos," *Anglia* 1.

Costa, Dalmau. 1979. "Transfer of Technology and the Fuel Cycle," *AEI Foreign Policy and Defense Review* 1.

Costello, Gerald M. 1979. *Mission to Latin America: The Successes and Failures of a Twentieth-Century Crusade.* Maryknoll, N.Y.: Orbis.

Covo, Milena E. 1973. *Conceptos comunes en la metodología de la investigación sociológica.* Mexico City: Instituto de Investigaciones Sociales, Universidad Nacional Autónoma de México.

Crahan, Margaret E. 1982. *Human Rights and Basic Needs in the Americas.* Washington, D.C.: Georgetown University Press.

Crow, John A. 1957. *Mexico Today.* New York: Harper.

Cunningham, Alden M. 1984. "Mexico's National Security in the 1980s–1990s." In *The Modern Mexican Military: A Reassessment,* edited by David Ronfeldt. La Jolla: Center for U.S.–Mexican Studies, University of California, San Diego.

DA (Department of the Army, U.S.). 1949. "Defense Plan for the Continental United States." DA-DPI-49. Washington, D.C.: Plans and Operations Divisions, General Staff, April 4.

DAF (Department of the Air Force, U.S.). 1955. "Memorandum for Col. R.P. Grenshaw, Jr., Outline Plan of Operations for Mexico." From Colonel T.E. Holland. Washington, D.C., September 9.

Dalessandro, James. 1977–78. "Where Are the Next Revolutions?" *Military Electronics/Countermeasures* 2:3 (December 1977–January 1978).

D'Amato, Alfonse. 1995. "Report on the Mexican Economic Crisis." Washington, D.C., June 29.

Danielson, Wayne A. n.d. "El análisis de contenido y la investigación sobre la comunicación." Mexico. Mimeo.

D'Antonio, William V., and William H. Form. 1965. *Influentials in Two Border Cities: A Study in Community Decision-Making*. Notre Dame, Ind.: University of Notre Dame Press.

Davis, Charles L., and Kenneth M. Coleman. 1975. "Political Symbols, Political Decay and Diffuse Support for the Mexican Political System," *Journal of Political and Military Sociology* 3 (Spring).

De la Madrid, Miguel. 1984. "Mexico: The New Challenge," *Foreign Affairs* 66:1 (Fall).

De Sola Pool, Ithiel. 1952. *The "Prestige Papers."* Stanford, Calif.: Hoover Institute, Stanford University.

Deagle, Edwin A., Jr. 1981. "México y la política de seguridad nacional de los Estados Unidos." In *Las relaciones México–Estados Unidos*, edited by Carlos Tello and Clark Reynolds. Mexico City: Fondo de Cultura Económica. Published in English as *U.S.–Mexican Relations: Economic and Social Aspects*, edited by Clark W. Reynolds and Carlos Tello (Stanford, Calif.: Stanford University Press, 1983).

Del Villar, Samuel I. 1988. "The Illicit U.S.–Mexico Drug Market: Failure of Policy and an Alternative." In *Mexico and the United States: Managing the Relationship*, edited by Riordan Roett. Boulder, Colo.: Westview.

Derossi, Flavia. 1971. *The Mexican Entrepreneur*. Paris: Development Centre of the Organisation for Economic Co-operation and Development.

DOD (Department of Defense, U.S.). 1950. "Interests of Department of Defense in Development of Mexican Oil." Memorandum from Spiegel to Moline, August 2.

———. 1965. "US Policies toward Latin America Military Forces." February 25.

Donneley, Jack. 1986. "International Human Rights: A Regime Analysis," *International Organization* 40:3 (Summer).

DOS (Department of State, U.S.). 1925. Scoville to F.R. Martin, March 15. Record Group 59.

———. 1944. Letter from Ambassador [of the United States in Mexico] George Messersmith to E.L. James of the *New York Times*, August 5. NAW, RG59.

———. 1948. "A Report to the National Security Council on US Policy Regarding Anti-Communist Measures which Could Be Planned and Carried Out within the Inter-American System." June 28.

———. 1950. "A Mexican Oil Loan." Memorandum from Dean Acheson to the President, January 30.

———. 1951. "Policy Statement. Mexico." Washington, D.C., October 1.

———. 1952. "Latin America and US Policy." Washington, D.C., December 11.

———. 1955. Ambassador Francis White's "Letter to the President." Mexico City, August 29.

———. 1956. "Outline Plan of Operations for Mexico." Washington, D.C., January 13.

———. 1959. "Memorandum for the President. Visit to Acapulco, Mexico. February 19–20." Washington, D.C., February 14.

———. 1961a. "Fifth Regional Operations Conference. San Jose, Costa Rica, October 16–18, 1961." October 16.

———. 1961b. "Fourth Regional Operations Conference, Lima, Peru." October 10.

———. 1961c. "Brookings' Paper on Political Development." May 2.

———. 1961d. "Basic and Continuing Specific Themes for Latin America and the World at Large." Johnson Library, Vice Presidential Security File, NSC.

———. 1962a. Letter from Ambassador Thomas Mann to Robert M. Sayre, Officer in Charge, Mexican Affairs, January 8.

———. 1962b. "Current Situation in Mexico." Memorandum from Woodward to the Ministry, January 16.

———. 1963a. "Sino-Soviet Rivalry in Latin America." Memorandum, American Embassy, Mexico City, February 12.

———. 1963b. "A Strategy for Mexico." Memorandum from Walt W. Rostow, September 2.

———. 1963c. Memorandum from Walt W. Rostow to the President of the U.S., September 18.

———. 1964a. "Memorándum de conversación entre Presidente Lindon [sic] B. Johnson, Presidente electo Gustavo Díaz Ordaz, Embajador Antonio Carrillo Flores y Thomas C. Mann, Parte II de II." Number 12. This text was published in its entirety in Carlos Puig, "Díaz Ordaz proponía a Johnson aceptar divergencias menores," *Proceso*, June 24, 1996.

———. 1964b. "Mexican Policy Toward the Chinese Communists, Background Paper for the Meeting of President Johnson and Lopez Mateos in California, February 20–22, 1964." February 14.

———. 1964c. "Visit by General Charles de Gaulle to Mexico, March 16–19, 1964." March 26.

———. 1964d. "Memorandum for Mr. Bundy." February 18.

———. 1965a. "Latin American Relations with Communist Governments." January 18.

———. 1965b. "The Popular Socialist Party (PPS) and Vicente Lombardo Toledano." May 8.

———. 1966a. "Reaction to the President's Visit to Mexico." May 13.

———. 1966b. "Conversation between Presidents Johnson and Diaz Ordaz, Los Pinos, Mexico City." April 14–15.

———. 1969a. "Student Violence and Attitudes in Latin America." INR Working Draft, September 3.

———. 1969b. "Report of the Student Unrest Study Group." Memorandum from Ambassador-at-Large to the Secretary, January 17.

———. 1975. *Department of State Bulletin*, May 5.

————. 1976. "Economic Trend Report-Mexico. CERP-0004." American Embassy, Mexico to Department of State, July 13.

————. 1977a. "Government of Mexico External Borrowing." Cable from Ambassador to Mexico Patrick Lucey to Secretary of State, September.

————. 1977b. "Human Rights Practices in Countries Receiving U.S. Security Assistance." Report Submitted to the Committee on International Relations, House of Representatives. Washington, D.C.: U.S. Government Printing Office.

————. 1978. "Country Reports on Human Rights Practices." Report Submitted to the Committee on International Relations, House of Representatives, and Committee on Foreign Relations, U.S. Senate. Washington, D.C.: U.S. Government Printing Office.

————. 1979. "Reports on Human Rights Practices in Countries Receiving U.S. Aid." Report Submitted to the Committee on Foreign Relations, U.S. Senate, and Committee on International Relations, U.S. House of Representatives. Washington, D.C.: U.S. Government Printing Office.

————. 1980. "Country Reports on Human Rights Practices for 1979." Report Submitted to the Committee on Foreign Affairs, U.S. House of Representatives, and Committee on Foreign Relations, U.S. Senate. Washington, D.C.: U.S. Government Printing Office.

————. 1981a. "Country Reports on Human Rights Practices." Report Submitted to the Committee on Foreign Affairs, U.S. Senate, and Committee on Foreign Relations, House of Representatives. Washington, D.C.: U.S. Government Printing Office.

————. 1981b. *The Planetary Production in 1980.* Washington, D.C.: Bureau of Public Affairs.

————. 1982. "Country Reports on Human Rights Practices for 1981." Report Submitted to the Committee on Foreign Affairs, U.S. House of Representatives, and Committee on Foreign Relations, U.S. Senate. Washington, D.C.: U.S. Government Printing Office.

————. 1983. "Country Reports on Human Rights Practices for 1982." Report Submitted to the Committee on Foreign Affairs, U.S. Senate, and Committee on Foreign Relations, House of Representatives. Washington, D.C.: U.S. Government Printing Office.

————. 1984. "Country Reports on Human Rights Practices for 1983." Report Submitted to the Committee on Foreign Affairs, House of Representatives, and Committee on Foreign Relations, U.S. Senate. Washington, D.C.: U.S. Government Printing Office.

————. 1985. "Country Reports on Human Rights Practices for 1984." Report Submitted to the Committee on Foreign Affairs, U.S. Senate, and Committee on Foreign Relations, House of Representatives. Washington, D.C.: U.S. Government Printing Office.

————. 1986. "Country Reports on Human Rights Practices for 1985." Report Submitted to the Committee on Foreign Affairs, House of Representatives, and Committee on Foreign Relations, U.S. Senate. Washington, D.C.: U.S. Government Printing Office.

————. 1987. "Country Reports on Human Rights Practices for 1986." Report Submitted to the Committee on Foreign Affairs, U.S. Senate, and Committee on Foreign Relations, U.S. House of Representatives. Washington, D.C.: U.S. Government Printing Office.

———. 1988. "Country Reports on Human Rights Practices for 1987." Report Submitted to the Committee on Foreign Affairs, House of Representatives, and Committee on Foreign Relations, U.S. Senate. Washington, D.C.: U.S. Government Printing Office.

———. 1989. "Country Reports on Human Rights Practices for 1988." Report Submitted to the Committee on Foreign Affairs, U.S. Senate, and Committee on Foreign Relations, U.S. House of Representatives. Washington, D.C.: U.S. Government Printing Office.

———. 1990. "Country Reports on Human Rights Practices for 1989." Report Submitted to the Committee on Foreign Affairs, House of Representatives, and Committee on Foreign Relations, U.S. Senate. Washington, D.C.: U.S. Government Printing Office.

———. 1991. "Cable from John Negroponte to Assistant Secretary Bernard Aronson," April.

Douglas, H. Eugene. 1985. "The United States and Mexico: Conflict and Comity," *Strategic Review*, Spring.

Douglas, Joyce. 1960. "Mexican Journey Family Plan," *U.S. Lady*, October.

Dunn, Delmer D. 1969. *Public Officials and the Press*. Reading, Mass.: Addison-Wesley.

Duverger, Maurice. 1972. *Métodos de las ciencias sociales*. Buenos Aires: Ariel.

Dziedziec, Michael J. 1989. *The Mexican Challenge: Managing Change and Preserving a Strategic Relationship*. London: Adelphi.

———. 1996. "Mexico and U.S. Grand Strategy: The Geo-strategic Linchpin to Security and Prosperity." In *Strategy and Security in U.S.–Mexican Relations beyond the Cold War*, edited by John Bailey and Sergio Aguayo Quezada. La Jolla: Center for U.S.–Mexican Studies, University of California, San Diego.

Echeverría, Luis. 1974. *IV Informe de Gobierno*. Mexico City: Presidencia de la República.

Eckstein, Susan. 1977. *The Poverty of Revolution: The State and the Urban Poor in Mexico*. Princeton, N.J.: Princeton University Press.

Economist, The. 1993. "A Survey of Mexico," February 13–19.

Eisenhower, Dwight D. 1963. *Mandate for Change, 1953–1956. The White House Years*. Garden City, N.Y.: Doubleday.

———. 1965. *Waging Peace, 1956–1961. The White House Years*. Garden City, N.Y.; Doubleday.

Eisenstadt, Todd. 1992. "Nueva diplomacia. Cabildeo y relaciones públicas en Estados Unidos," *Este País* 15 (June).

El Nacional. 1954. "Los braceros que vuelven a México," January 25.

El Universal. 1961. "Los desorientados," September 10.

EMW (Embajada Mexicana en Washington). 1963. "Carrillo Flores, Antonio, al presidente de México Adolfo López Mateos, carta y memorándum, 4 de septiembre."

Engels, Frederick. 1955. "Letter to J. Bloch, 21–22 September 1890." In *Karl Marx and Frederick Engels, Selected Correspondence*. Moscow: Progress.

Eschbach, Cheryl. 1991. "Mexico's Relations with Central America: Changing Priorities, Persisting Interest." In *Mexico's External Relations in the 1990's*, edited by Riordan Roett. Boulder, Colo.: Lynne Rienner.

Este País. 1991a. "Integración económica y nacionalismo: Canadá, Estados Unidos y México." Vol. 1 (April).

————. 1991b. "Convergencias y divergencias en América del Norte." Vol. 2 (May).

————. 1992. "Opinión sobre Estados Unidos y México." Vol. 14 (May).

Fagen, Patricia Weiss. 1980. "The United States and International Human Rights, 1946–1977," *Universal Human Rights* 2:3 (July–September).

Fagen, Richard R. 1978. "El petróleo mexicano y la seguridad nacional de Estados Unidos," *Foro Internacional*, October–December.

————. 1981. "The U.S. and Mexico," *New York Times*, January 4.

Fagen, Richard R., and William S. Tuohy. 1972. *Politics and Privilege in a Mexican City*. Stanford, Calif.: Stanford University Press.

Fauriol, Georges. 1986. "Mexico: In a Superpower's Shadow." In *Emerging Powers: Defense and Security in the Third World*, edited by Rodney W. Jones and Steven A. Hildreth. New York: Praeger.

————. 1988. *The Third Century: U.S. Latin American Policy Choices for the 1990s*. Washington, D.C.: Center for Strategic and International Studies, Johns Hopkins University.

Favela, Margarita, and Pilar Morales. 1991. "México ante los ojos de Estados Unidos," *Este País*, July.

Fedler, Fred. 1978. *An Introduction to the Mass Media*. New York: Harcourt Brace Jovanovich.

Foucault, Michel. 1976. *Vigilar y castigar. Nacimiento de la prisión*. Mexico City: Siglo Veintiuno.

Foweraker, Joe. 1989. "Popular Movements and the Transformation of the System." In *Mexico's Alternative Political Futures*, edited by Wayne A. Cornelius, Judith Gentleman, and Peter H. Smith. La Jolla: Center for U.S.–Mexican Studies, University of California, San Diego.

Fox, Jonathan. 1995. "How Does Civil Society Thicken? The Political Construction of Social Capital in Rural Mexico." Paper presented at the conference "Government Action, Social Capital and Third World Development," American Academy of Arts and Sciences, Cambridge, Massachusetts, May 5–6.

————. 1996. "National Electoral Choices in Rural Mexico." In *Reforming Mexico's Agrarian Reform*, edited by Laura Randall. Armonk, N.Y.: M.E. Sharpe.

Fox, Jonathan, and Luis Hernández. 1992. "Mexico's Difficult Democracy: Grassroots Movements, NGOs and Local Government," *Alternatives* 17.

FR (Federal Reserve, U.S.). 1975. "Possible Increase in Swap Line with Bank of Mexico." From Arthur L. Broida to Federal Open Market Committee, August 13.

————. 1976a. "Executive Session, November 16, 1976. Tape 6." Transcript. Gerald Ford Library.

————. 1976b. "Comments on the Mexican Program in the Light of Recent Developments." Prepared by Yves Maroni, Division of International Finance, October 8.

————. 1976c. "$800 million loan to Mexico." From R.H. Mills, Jr., to Mr. Gemmill, October 19.

Frederick, Howard H. 1993. "North American NGO Computer Networking on Trade and Immigration: Computer Communications in Cross-Border Coalition Building." Report DRU-234-FF. Santa Monica, Calif.: Rand Corporation, March.

Freeland, Richard. 1975. *The Truman Doctrine and the Origins of McCarthyism.* New York: Knopf.

Fuentes, Carlos. 1980. "Dominoes—Again?" *New York Times,* August 19.

————. 1984. "Don't Push Mexico," *New York Times,* April 24.

————. 1985. "The Real Latin Threat," *New York Times,* November 5.

Gabel, Joseph. 1974. *Ideologies.* Paris: Anthropos.

Galloway, Clark H. 1953. "When Communists Take Over," *U.S. News and World Report,* February 20.

Gandhi, Mohandas K. 1993. *An Autobiography; The Story of My Experiments with Truth.* Boston, Mass.: Beacon.

Ganster, Paul, and Alan Sweedler. 1987. "The U.S.–Mexican Border Region: Implications for U.S. Security." San Diego, Calif., April. Manuscript.

Garten, Jeffrey E. 1985. "Gunboat Economics," *Foreign Affairs* 63:3.

————. 1989. "Trading Blocs and the Evolving World Economy," *Current History* 88:534 (January).

Gellner, Ernest. 1988. *Naciones y nacionalismo.* Mexico City: Alianza.

Gentleman, Judith, ed. 1987. *Mexican Politics in Transition.* Boulder, Colo.: Westview.

Gilder, George. 1981. *Wealth and Poverty.* New York: Basic Books.

Gill, Stephen R., and David Law. 1989. "Global Hegemony and the Structural Power of Capital," *International Studies Quarterly* 33:4 (December).

Glade, William P., and Charles W. Anderson. 1963. *The Political Economy of Mexico.* Madison: University of Wisconsin Press.

Gleijeses, Piero. 1991. *Shattered Hope: The Guatemalan Revolution and the United States.* Princeton, N.J.: Princeton University Press.

Goldmann, Lucien. 1969. *The Human Sciences and Philosophy.* London: Jonathan Cape.

————. 1976a. "The Importance of the Concept of Potential Consciousness for Communication." In *Cultural Creation in Modern Society,* by L. Goldmann. St. Louis, Mo.: Telos.

————. 1976b. "The Revolt of Arts in Advanced Civilizations." In *Cultural Creation in Modern Society,* by L. Goldmann. St. Louis, Mo.: Telos.

————. 1977. *The Hidden God.* London: Routledge.

Gomis, Lorenzo. 1974. *El medio media: la función política de la prensa.* Madrid: Seminarios y Ediciones.

González Casanova, Pablo. 1970. *Democracy in Mexico.* New York: Oxford University Press.

Gottlieb, Robert, and Irene Wolf. 1977. *Thinking Big: The Story of the Los Angeles Times, Its Publishers, and Their Influence on Southern California.* New York: Putnam.

Graham, Lawrence S. 1968. *Politics in a Mexican Community.* Gainesville: University of Florida Press.

Gramsci, Antonio. 1975. *Note sul Machiavelli.* Rome: Riuniti.

Granados Chapa, Miguel Angel. 1986. "Plaza Pública," *La Jornada*, June 22.

Grayson, George W. 1980. *The Politics of Mexican Oil*. Pittsburgh, Penn.: University of Pittsburgh Press.

Grayson, George W., ed. 1990. *Prospects for Democracy in Mexico*. New Brunswick, N.J.: Transaction.

Greenberg, Martin H. 1970. *Bureaucracy and Development: A Mexican Case Study*. Lexington, Mass.: Heath.

Grindle, Merilee S. 1977a. *Bureaucrats, Politicians, and Peasants in Mexico: A Case Study in Public Policy*. Berkeley: University of California Press.

———. 1977b. "Power, Expertise and the 'Tecnico': Suggestions from a Mexican Case Study," *Journal of Politics* 36 (May).

Grinspun, Ricardo, and Maxwell A. Cameron. 1996. "NAFTA and the Political Economy of Mexico's External Relations," *Latin American Research Review*, Fall.

Haber, Paul Lawrence. 1994. "The Art and Implications of Political Restructuring in Mexico: The Case of Urban Popular Movements." In *The Politics of Economic Restructuring: State-Society Relations and Regime Change in Mexico*, edited by Maria Lorena Cook, Kevin J. Middlebrook, and Juan Molinar Horcasitas. La Jolla: Center for U.S.–Mexican Studies, University of California, San Diego.

Haig, Alexander M., Jr. 1984. *Caveat. Realism, Reagan, and Foreign Policy*. New York: Macmillan.

Halberstam, David. 1980. *The Powers That Be*. New York: Basic Books.

Handleman, William S. 1973. "How Wars End," *Armed Forces* 110 (January).

Hannon, Esther Wilson. 1984. "Why Mexico's Foreign Policy Still Irritates the U.S.," *Backgrounder* (Heritage Foundation), September 26.

———. 1986. "What the U.S. Should Do as Mexico Heads for Crisis," *Backgrounder*, July 17.

———. 1987. "Keys to Understanding Mexico: Challenges for the Ruling PRI," *Backgrounder*, April 7.

Hansen, Roger. 1971. *The Politics of Mexican Development*. Baltimore, Md.: Johns Hopkins University Press.

Harper's Magazine. 1987. "The CIA Sizes Up the Mexican Domino," May.

Harrison, John M. 1974. "Media, Men and Morality," *Review of Politics*, April.

Hartz, Louis. 1955. *The Liberal Tradition in America*. New York: Harcourt Brace.

Harvey, Neil. 1994. *Rebellion in Chiapas: Rural Reforms, Campesino Radicalism, and the Limits to Salinismo*. La Jolla: Center for U.S.–Mexican Studies, University of California, San Diego.

Heath, Edward Allen. 1981. "Mexican Opium Eradication Campaign." Master's thesis, California State University.

Hegel, G.W.F. 1817. *Encyklopadie der philosophischen Wissenschaften im Grundrisse*. Heidelberg: A. Oswald.

———. 1942. *Philosophy of Right*. Oxford: Oxford University Press.

Hellman, Judith Adler. 1978. *Mexico in Crisis*. New York: Holmes and Meier.

Hill, Kenneth E. 1979. "Three Nations Together on Energy," *New York Times*, March 23.

Hirales, Gustavo. 1982. "La guerra secreta, 1970–1978," *Nexos*, June.

Hodges, Donald C. 1995. *Mexican Anarchism after the Revolution*. Austin: University of Texas Press.

Hoffmann, Stanley. 1968. *Gulliver's Troubles; or, The Setting of American Foreign Policy*. New York: McGraw Hill, for the Council on Foreign Relations.

Hormats, Robert. 1986. "The World Economy under Stress," *Foreign Affairs* 64:3.

Horowitz, Irving Louis, ed. 1967. *The Rise and Fall of Project Camelot: Studies in the Relationship between Social Science and Practical Politics*. Cambridge, Mass.: MIT Press.

Hulteng, John. 1973. *The Opinion Function*. New York: Harper and Row.

Humphrey, Nicholas. 1993. *A History of the Mind*. New York: Harper Perennial.

Huntington, Samuel P. 1971. "The Change to Change: Modernization, Development, and Politics," *Comparative Politics*, April.

———. 1991. *The Third Wave: Democratization in the Late Twentieth Century*. Norman: University of Oklahoma Press.

Ianni, Francis A.J. 1972. *A Family Business; Kinship and Social Control in Organized Crime*. New York: Russell Sage Foundation.

International Review Group of Social Science Research on Population and Development. 1979. *Social Science Research for Population Policy, Directions for the 1980s*. Mexico City: El Colegio de México.

Islam, Shafiqui. 1990. "Capitalism in Conflict," *Foreign Affairs* 68:1.

Jacobson, Harold, William Reisinger, and Todd Mathers. 1986. "National Entanglements in International Governmental Organizations," *American Political Science Review* 80:1 (March).

James, Daniel. 1954. "Showdown in Guatemala," *New York Leader*, February 15.

———. 1958. "Next Door Neighbor's Next President," *New York Times Magazine*, June 8.

———. 1962. "Kennedy Visits a 'New' Mexico," *New York Times Magazine*, June 24.

———. 1963. *Mexico and the Americans*. New York: Praeger.

JCS (Joint Chiefs of Staff, U.S.). 1954. "To Determine What the U.S. Should Do to Better Its World Position vis-à-vis the Soviet Bloc." (Confidential) memorandum, September 15.

———. 1959. "Memorandum for the Secretary of Defense. JCSM-52-59. Subject: U.S. Policy Toward Latin America (NSC-5902)," from N.F. Twining, Chairman. Washington, D.C.

Jellinek, James. 1969. "Zapata and the Mexican Revolution," *New York Times Book Review*, February 2.

Jensen, Jay. 1962, "Freedom of the Press: A Concept in Search of a Philosophy." In *Social Responsibility of the Newspress*. Milwaukee, Wis.: Marquette University School of Journalism.

JIC (Joint Intelligence Committee, U.S.). 1946. "Joint Basic War Plan-Mexico." JIS 248/M. Washington, D.C., April 29.

Jimenes de Ottalengo, Regina. 1974. *Las fuentes de información en México (la prensa como ilustración)*. Mexico City: Instituto de Investigaciones Sociales, Universidad Nacional Autónoma de México.

JIS (Joint Intelligence Service, U.S.). 1946. "Report by the Joint Intelligence Committee, Basic War Plan, Mexico." JIS 248/M. Washington, D.C., April 29.

Johnson, Kenneth F. 1971. *Mexican Democracy: A Critical View.* Boston, Mass.: Allyn and Bacon.

Johnson, Loch K. 1989. *America's Secret Power: The CIA in a Democratic Society.* New York: Oxford University Press.

Johnson, Lyndon Baines. 1971. *The Vantage Point; Perspectives of the Presidency, 1963–1969.* New York: Holt, Rinehart and Winston.

Jordan, Amos A., and William J. Taylor, Jr. 1984. *American National Security: Policy and Process.* Baltimore, Md.: Johns Hopkins University Press.

JSPC (Joint Strategic Plans Committee, U.S.). 1947. "Estimates of Probable Developments in the World Political Situation up to 1957." December 11.

Kayser, Jacques. 1966. *El periódico. Estudios de morfología, metodología y prensa comparada.* Quito: CIESPAL.

Kennan, George. 1947. "The Sources of Soviet Conduct," *Foreign Affairs*, July.

Kennedy, Paul. 1963. "Revolution and Evolution South of the Border," *New York Times Book Review*, September 22.

Keohane, Robert O., and Joseph S. Nye, Jr. 1974. "Transgovernmental Relations and International Organizations," *World Politics* 27:1 (October).

———. 1977. *Power and Interdependence. World Politics in Transition.* Boston, Mass.: Little, Brown.

Kristol, Irving. 1967. "The Underdeveloped Profession," *Public Interest*, Winter.

Krock, Arthur. 1948. "The Vital Question of Mexican Oil," *New York Times*, December 30.

———. 1949. "The Subterranean 'Crop' of Mexico," *New York Times*, March 31.

LaFeber, Walter. 1976. *America, Russia and the Cold War, 1945–1975.* New York: Wiley.

LaFeber, Walter, and Richard Polenberg. 1975. *The American Century.* 3d ed. New York: Wiley.

Laffer, Arthur, and Seymour, Jan P. 1979. *The Economics of the Tax Revolt.* New York: Harcourt Brace Jovanovich.

Lagos, Ricardo. 1977. "The Old Model and Its Abandonment." In *The Development of Development Thinking.* Paris: Development Centre of the Organisation for Economic Co-operation and Development.

Latell, Brian. 1986. *Mexico at the Crossroads: The Many Crises of the Political System.* Stanford, Calif.: Hoover Institution, Stanford University.

Lerner, Daniel. 1958. *The Passing of Traditional Society: Modernizing the Middle East.* Glencoe, Ill.: Free Press.

Levin, Harry. 1960. "Some Meanings of Myth." In *Myth and Mythmaking*, edited by Henry A. Murray. Boston, Mass.: Beacon.

Levy, Daniel C. 1980. *University and Government in Mexico: Autonomy in an Authoritarian System.* New York: Praeger.

———. 1986. "The Political Consequences of Changing Socialization Patterns." In *Mexican Political Stability: The Next Five Years*, edited by Roderic A. Camp. Boulder, Colo.: Westview.

Levy, Daniel C., and Gabriel Székely. 1983. *Mexico: Paradoxes of Stability and Change.* Boulder, Colo.: Westview.

Lewis, Flora. 1953. "Industrial Drive Changing Mexico," *New York Times,* January 7.

Lewis, Oscar. 1963. *The Children of Sanchez.* New York: Vintage Books.

Lieuwen, Edwin. 1968. *Mexican Militarism.* Albuquerque: University of New Mexico Press.

Linn, Tom. 1984. "Mexico and the United States: Recognition at Last," *Defense and Foreign Affairs,* December.

Linz, Juan. 1964. "An Authoritarian Regime: Spain." In *Cleavages, Ideologies and Party Systems: Contributions to Comparative Political Sociology,* edited by Erik Allardt and Yrjo Littunen. Turku, Finland: A. Tidnings.

Lippmann, Walter. 1957. *Public Opinion.* New York: Macmillan.

Lipset, Seymour Martin. 1963. *Political Man; The Social Bases of Politics.* Garden City, N.Y.: Anchor Books.

Logfren, Charles A. 1967. "Force and Diplomacy, 1846–1848: The View from Washington," *Military Affairs* 31 (Summer).

Lonergan, Bernard. 1970. *Insight: A Study of Human Understanding.* 3d ed. New York: Philosophical Library.

Loory, Stuart. 1974. "The CIA's Use of the Press: A 'Mighty Wurlitzer,'" *Columbia Journalism Review,* September–October.

López, Arturo, et al. 1988. *Geografía de las elecciones presidenciales en México. 1988.* Mexico City: Fundación Arturo Rosenblueth.

López Portillo, José. 1982. *Sexto Informe de Gobierno.* Mexico City: Presidencia de la República.

Lowenthal, Abraham. 1991. *Exporting Democracy.* Baltimore, Md.: Johns Hopkins University Press.

Lustig, Nora. 1995. "The Mexican Peso Crisis: The Foreseeable and the Surprise." Brookings Discussion Papers in International Economics. Washington, D.C.: Brookings Institution, June.

Lutz, Ellen L. 1990. *Human Rights in Mexico. A Policy of Impunity.* New York: Human Rights Watch.

Mabry, Donald J. 1973. *Mexico's Acción Nacional: A Catholic Alternative to Revolution.* Syracuse, N.Y.: Syracuse University Press.

———. 1982. *The Mexican University and the State; Student Conflicts, 1910–1971.* College Station: Texas A&M University Press.

Macluhan, Marshall. 1960. "Myth and Mass Media." In *Myth and Mythmaking,* edited by Henry A. Murray. Boston, Mass.: Beacon.

Mannheim, Karl. 1945. *Ideology and Utopia.* New York: Harcourt Brace.

Marcellesi, Jean Baptiste, and Bernard Gardin. 1974. *Introduction a la sociolinguistique, la linguistique social.* Paris: Larousse.

Marcus, John T. 1960. "The World Impact of the West: The Mystique and the Sense of Participation in History." In *Myth and Mythmaking,* edited by Henry A. Murray. Boston, Mass.: Beacon.

Marcuse, Herbert. 1968. *One Dimensional Man; Studies in the Ideology of Advanced Industrial Society.* Boston, Mass.: Beacon.

Margiotta, Franklin D. 1976. "Civilian Control and the Mexican Military: Changing Patterns of Political Influence." In *Civilian Control of the Mili-*

tary: Theory and Cases from Developing Countries, edited by Claude E. Welch, Jr. Albany: State University of New York Press.

Marx, Karl. 1906. Capital, a Critique of Political Economy. New York: Modern Library.

Marx, Karl, and Frederick Engels. 1975. The Holy Family, or Critique of Critical Criticism, against Bruno Bauer and Company. Moscow: Progress.

Masset, Pierre. 1970. Les 50 Mots-clés du Marxisme. Toulouse: Privat.

Maxfield, Sylvia, and Ricardo Anzaldúa Montoya, eds. 1987. Government and Private Sector in Contemporary Mexico. La Jolla: Center for U.S.–Mexican Studies, University of California, San Diego.

McCaughan, Ed, and Peter Baird. 1976. "Harvest of Anger. Agro-imperialism in Mexico's Northwest," NACLA's Latin America and Empire Report 10:6 (July–August).

Medina, Luis. 1979. Civilismo y modernización del autoritarismo. Mexico City: El Colegio de México.

Melzer, Richard. 1987. "The Ambassador Simpático: Dwight Morrow in Mexico 1927–1930." In Ambassadors in Foreign Policy, edited by C. Neale Ronning and Albert P. Vannucci. New York: Praeger.

Menges, Constantine. 1988. Inside the National Security Council. New York: Simon and Schuster.

Merrill, John C., and Harold A. Fisher. 1980. The World's Great Dailies: Profiles of Fifty Elite Newspapers. New York: Hastings House.

Meyer, Karl E. 1979. "What Mexico Remembers," New York Times, October 4.

Meyer, Lorenzo. 1972. México y los Estados Unidos en el conflicto petrolero (1917–1942). 2d ed. Mexico City: El Colegio de México.

———. 1973. México y los Estados Unidos en el conflicto petrolero (1917–1942). 3d ed. Mexico City: El Colegio de México.

———. 1978. "El auge petrolero y las experiencias mexicanas disponibles. Los problemas del pasado y la revisión del futuro," Foro Internacional 18:4 (April–June).

———. 1985. The Mexican Revolution and the Anglo-American Powers: The End of Confrontation and the Beginning of Negotiation. La Jolla: Center for U.S.–Mexican Studies, University of California, San Diego.

———. 1991. Su Majestad Británica contra la Revolución Mexicana, 1900–1950: el fin de un imperio informal. Mexico City: El Colegio de México.

Middlebrook, Kevin J. 1988. "Dilemmas of Change in Mexican Politics," World Politics 41 (October).

———. 1995. The Paradox of Revolution: Labor, the State, and Authoritarianism in Mexico. Baltimore, Md.: Johns Hopkins University Press.

Milliband, Ralph. 1978. El estado en la sociedad capitalista. Mexico City: Siglo Veintiuno.

Mills, C. Wright. 1956. The Power Elite. London: Oxford University Press.

Minnesota Advocates for Human Rights. 1992. Conquest Continued: Disregard for Human and Indigenous Rights in the Mexican State of Chiapas. Minneapolis: Minnesota Advocates for Human Rights.

———. 1993. Civilians at Risk: Military and Police Abuses in the Mexican Countryside. New York: World Policy Institute, New School for Social Research.

Mitchelmore, Garry E. 1975. "The Other Side of the Border," *Airman* 19 (January).

Mkandawire, Thandika. 1995. "The Adjustment Debacle and Democratic Consolidation in Africa." Paper presented at the conference "Winners and Losers in Neo-Liberal Experiments: Toward More Equitable Development," Princeton University, December 8–9.

Montalvo, Enrique. 1985. *El nacionalismo contra la nación.* Mexico City: Grijalbo.

Monteforte Toledo, Mario. 1976. *Literatura, ideología y lenguaje.* Mexico City: Grijalbo.

Montemayor, Carlos. 1991. *Guerra en el paraíso.* Mexico City: Diana.

Moorer, Thomas H., and Georges A. Fauriol. 1984. *Caribbean Basin Security.* New York: Praeger.

Morris, Stephen D. 1991. *Corruption and Politics in Contemporary Mexico.* Tuscaloosa: University of Alabama Press.

Mosk, Sanford A. 1954. *Industrial Revolution in Mexico.* Berkeley: University of California Press.

Moynihan, Daniel P. 1971. "The Presidency and the Press," *Commentary,* March.

Murray, Henry A. 1960. "The Possible Nature of a 'Mythology' to Come," In *Myth and Mythmaking,* edited by H. Murray. Boston, Mass.: Beacon.

NACLA (North American Congress on Latin America). 1972. "A New Stage in the Mexican Struggle: Interview with a Political Exile," *NACLA's Latin America and Empire Report* 6:3 (March).

Needleman, Carolyn, and Martin Needleman. 1969. "Who Rules Mexico? A Critique of Some Current Views of the Mexican Political Process," *Journal of Politics* 31 (November).

Needler, Martin. 1961. "The Political Development of Mexico," *American Political Science Review* 55 (June).

Neuchterlein, Donald E. 1985. *America Overcommitted; U.S. National Interests in the 1980's.* Knoxville: Kentucky University Press.

New Perspectives Quarterly. 1991. "North American Free Trade: Mexico's Route to Upward Mobility" (interview with Carlos Salinas de Gortari), 8:1 (Winter).

Nixon, Richard. 1978. *The Memoirs of Richard Nixon.* New York: Grosset and Dunlap.

Novedades. 1968. "Anoche en Tlatelolco," October 3

NSC (National Security Council, U.S.). 1948a. "A Report to the National Security Council on U.S. Policy Regarding Anti-Communist Measures which Could be Planned and Carried Out within the Inter-American System." NSC-16. June 28.

———. 1948b. "A Report to the National Security Council on Security of Strategically Important Industrial Operations in Foreign Countries," Department of the Army. NSC-29. August 26.

———. 1949. "Report to the National Security Council on US Policy Concerning Military Collaboration Under the Inter-American Treaty of Reciprocal Assistance," Secretary of Defense. NSC-56. August 31.

———. 1953a. "United States Objectives and Courses of Action with Respect to Latin America." NSC-144. March 4. Typescript.

———. 1953b. "Note by the Executive Secretary to the National Security Council on United States Objectives and Courses of Action with Respect to Latin America." NSC-144. March 4.

———. 1953c. "A Report to the National Security Council. United States Objectives and Courses of Action with Respect to Latin America." NSC-144/1. Washington, D.C., March 18.

———. 1954. "A Report to the National Security Council by the Executive Secretary on United States Objectives and Programs for National Security." NSC-68. Reprinted in *Naval War College Review*, May–June 1975.

———. 1976. "The Mexican Float: Many Unanswered Questions." Memorandum for Brent Scowcroft from Robert Hormats, September 14.

———. 1978. "Presidential Review Memorandum NSC-41: Review of U.S. Policies Toward Mexico." Washington, D.C., November 21.

———. 1984. Document published by the *New York Times*, April 7.

NYT (*New York Times*). 1947. "President Aleman's Visit," April 29.

———. 1951a. "Iran and Mexico," June 22.

———. 1951b. "Migrants from Mexico," March 27.

———. 1951c. "Drying Up the 'Wetbacks,'" November 4.

———. 1951d. "Migrant Labor," April 18.

———. 1951e. "Mexican Hat in the Ring," August 4.

———. 1952a. "Mexico at the Polls," July 6.

———. 1952b. "Mexican Elections," July 9.

———. 1952c. "Mexican Inaugural," December 1.

———. 1953. "Meeting of Presidents," October 19.

———. 1956a. "Hospital Diplomacy," March 29.

———. 1956b. "PanAmerica at Panama," July 18.

———. 1957a. "Mexico Sets an Example," April 1.

———. 1957b. "How the Mexicans Do It," November 24.

———. 1958a. "Mexico City via Augusta," December 1.

———. 1958b. "Mexico's Next President," July 6.

———. 1959a. "American 'Exploitation,'" December 20.

———. 1959b. "A Visit to Mexico," February 19.

———. 1960a. "Protection for Farm Labor," April 11.

———. 1960b. "Imported Mexican Labor," June 15.

———. 1960c. "The Forgotten People," August 31.

———. 1960d. "Mexico's Anniversaries," September 16.

———. 1961a. "The Farm Labor Bill," August 14.

———. 1961b. "Egyptian Socialism," August 16.

———. 1961c. "The Kennedy Plan," February 15.

———. 1961d. "The United States and Mexico," February 8.

———. 1961e. "The Mexican Conference," March 11.

———. 1962a. "Vivan Los Dos Presidentes," July 1.

———. 1962b. "The Kennedy Plan," March 15.

———. 1963a. "Ban on Braceros," June 3.

———. 1963b. "Defeat for the Migrants," November 3.

———. 1963c. "A Gesture for Mexico," December 23.

———. 1963d. "Mexico in 1963," September 3.

———. 1963e. "Mexico's Prospective President," November 6.

———. 1964a. "New Door for Braceros?" December 9.

———. 1964b. "Two Neighbors Meet," February 21.

———. 1964c. "De Gaulle in Mexico," March 16.

———. 1965. "The 'New Diplomacy,'" April 4.

———. 1966a. "Pledge on the Alliance," April 18.

———. 1966b. "Rural Mexico," June 18.

———. 1968. "Ferment in Mexico," October 12.

———. 1969a. "An Operation to Intercept," October 10.

———. 1969b. "Operation Intercepted," October 11.

———. 1970a. "Useful Mission to Mexico," August 25.

———. 1970b. "Mexico's President-Elect," July 7.

———. 1972. "Mexico's Example," June 24.

———. 1974. "Dialogue with Mexico," October 23.

———. 1975a. "Protests on Spain," October 3.

———. 1975b. "Shame of the United Nations," November 13.

———. 1976a. "Mexico's New President," July 13.

———. 1976b. "Mexico's New President . . . Loses a Free Press," July 13.

———. 1976c. "Legacy for Mr. Lopez," December 1.

———. 1978. "Mexican Oil and the United States," December 25.

———. 1979a. "Jeopardizing American Prisoners Abroad," August 8.

———. 1979b. "Carter Encounters Mexican Anger," February 18.

———. 1981. "The Tainted Ballot in El Salvador," September 8.

———. 1985a. "Stop Bullying Mexico," September 29.

———. 1985b. "Where Is Mexico's Pride," March 22.

———. 1985c. "Still One-Party Mexico," July 13.

———. 1986a. "Conflict-of-Interest Policy," July.

———. 1986b. "The Ninth Life of Contadora," February 15.

———. 1986c. "It Takes Two to Contadora," May 22.

———. 1986d. "Mexico Bashes Itself," July 11.

———. 1986e. "Another Moment of Truth for Mexico," June 11.

———. 1988a. "Mexico's Radical Insider," July 3.

———. 1988b. "Mexico Shatters a Monolith," July 9.

———. 1988c. "How Three Can Win in Mexico," July 14.

———. 1995. "Mexico's Political Crisis," October 11.

Oakes, John B. 1977. "Mexico's New Regime-I," *New York Times*, February 10.

O'Donnell, Guillermo. 1978. "Apuntes para una teoría del Estado," *Revista Mexicana de Sociología* 4 (October–December).

Orme, William A., Jr. 1993. *Continental Shift: Free Trade and the New North America*. Washington, D.C.: Washington Post Co.

Ottinger, John C., and Patrick D. Mainess. 1972. "Is It True What They Say about the New York Times?" *National Review* 15 (September).

Packenham, Robert A. 1973. *Liberal America and the Third World*. Princeton, N.J.: Princeton University Press.

———. 1978. "The New Utopianism: Political Development Ideas in the Dependency Literature." Washington, D.C.: Wilson Center, September.

Padgett, L. Vincent. 1966. *The Mexican Political System*. Boston, Mass.: Houghton Mifflin.

Padgett, Tim. 1996. "Confessions of a Gringo Correspondent: 'Salinas Fooled Me Too.'" Paper presented at Wabash College, February 15.

Page, Joseph A. 1972. *The Revolution That Never Was; Northeast Brazil, 1955–1964*. New York: Grossman.

Paredes, Raymond. 1973. "The Image of the Mexican in American Literature." Ph.D. dissertation, University of Texas at Austin.

Pastor, Robert A. 1990. "Salinas Takes a Gamble," *New Republic*, September 10, 17.

Pastor, Robert A., and Jorge G. Castañeda. 1988. *Limits to Friendship: The United States and Mexico*. New York: Knopf.

Pellicer, Olga. 1972. *México y la Revolución Cubana*. Mexico City: El Colegio de México.

Pellicer, Olga, and Esteban L. Mancilla. 1978. *El entendimiento con los Estados Unidos y la gestación del desarrollo estabilizador*. Mexico City: El Colegio de México.

Petrusenko, Vitalii. 1976. *The Monopoly Press*. Prague: International Organization of Journalists.

Piccone, Paul. 1978. "Introduction." In *The Essential Frankfurt School Reader*, edited by Andrew Arato and Eike Gebhardt. New York: Urizen.

Piñeyro, José Luis. 1987. *El ejército mexicano: pasado y presente*. Mexico: Universidad Autónoma Metropolitana–Azcapotzalco/Universidad Autónoma de Puebla.

Plamenatz, John. 1970. *Ideology*. New York: Praeger.

Portes, Alejandro. 1977. "Legislatures under Authoritarian Regimes: The Case of Mexico," *Journal of Political and Military Sociology* 5 (Fall).

Poulantzas, Nicos. 1975. *Political Power and Social Classes*. London: New Left Books.

Pratt, Raymond B. 1973. "The Underdeveloped Political Science of Development," *Studies in Comparative International Development* 8.

Purcell, Susan Kaufman. 1973. "Decision-Making in an Authoritarian Regime: Theoretical Implications from a Mexican Case Study," *World Politics*, October.

———. 1975. *The Mexican Profit-Sharing Decision: Politics in an Authoritarian Regime*. Berkeley: University of California Press.

———. 1982. "Banking on Mexico Badly," *New York Times*, August 24.

———. 1983. "Why Mexico Is Coming Around," *Washington Post*, August 1.

———. 1986. "The Prospects for Political Change in Mexico." Paper presented at the conference "U.S. Interests in Mexico: A Program for the Next Decade," Washington, D.C., August 21–22.

Reagan, Ronald. 1983. *Discussions on Central America in the Joint Session of Congress*. U.S. Cultural and Information Service, April 27.

Reed, Fred. 1979. "Fading Away in Mexico," *Air Force Times*, September 17.

Rees, David. 1960. "Texas, Buena Vista, and the Mexican War," *Royal United Service Institution Journal* 105 (November).

Reston, James. 1962. "View of the Cold War from below the Rio Grande," *New York Times*, December 12.

———. 1964. "How to Win in Mexico and Lose in Europe," *New York Times*, March 18.

———. 1975a. "The Coming Class War?" *New York Times*, August 27.

———. 1975b. "The Forgotten Americans," *New York Times*, July 17.

———. 1975c. "Mexico's Advice to Mr. Ford," *New York Times*, October 8.

————. 1979a. "Mexico Wants Full Review of Ties in Carter Talks," *New York Times*, February 8.

————. 1979b. "New Focus on Mexico," *New York Times*, February 7.

————. 1986. "The Mexican Time Bomb," *New York Times*, June 22.

Reuter, Peter, and David Ronfeldt. 1992. *Quest for Integrity: The Mexican–U.S. Drug Issue in the 1980s*. Santa Monica, Calif.: Rand Corporation.

Reyes Heroles, Federico. 1994. *50 preguntas a los candidatos. Elecciones mexicanas del 21 de agosto de 1994*. Mexico City: Fondo de Cultura Económica.

Reyna, José Luis, and Richard Weinert. 1977. *Authoritarianism in Mexico*. Philadelphia, Penn.: Institute for the Study of Human Issues.

Riding, Alan. 1985. *Distant Neighbors: A Portrait of the Mexicans*. New York: Knopf.

Rippy, J. Fred. 1931. *The United States and Mexico*. New York: Crofts.

Rodinson, M. 1968. "Sociologie Marxiste et Ideologies Marxistes," *Diogene* 64 (October–December).

Rodman, Selden. 1958. *Mexican Journal: The Conquerors Conquered*. New York: Devin-Adair.

Roett, Riordan. 1996. "The Mexican Devaluation and the U.S. Response: Potomac Politics, 1995-Style." In *The Mexican Peso Crisis: International Perspectives*, edited by R. Roett. Boulder, Colo.: Lynne Rienner.

Ronfeldt, David. 1973. *Atencingo: The Politics of Agrarian Struggle in a Mexican Ejido*. Stanford Calif.: Stanford University Press.

————. 1976. "The Mexican Army and Political Order since 1940." In *Armies and Politics in Latin America*, edited by Abraham F. Lowenthal. New York: Holmes and Meier.

————. 1983. *Geopolitics, Security, and U.S. Strategy in the Caribbean Basin*. Santa Monica, Calif.: Rand Corporation.

————. 1993. "Institutions, Markets, and Networks: A Framework about the Evolution of Societies." DRU-590-FF. Santa Monica, Calif.: Rand Corporation, December.

Ronfeldt, David, ed. 1984. *The Modern Mexican Military*. La Jolla, Calif.: Center for U.S.–Mexican Studies, University of California, San Diego.

Ronfeldt, David, Richard Nehring, and Arturo Gándara. 1980. *Mexico's Petroleum and U.S. Policy: Implications for the 1980s. Prepared for the U.S. Department of Energy*. Santa Monica, Calif.: Rand Corporation, June.

Roosevelt, Kermit. 1979. *Countercoup. The Struggle for the Control of Iran*. New York: McGraw-Hill.

Ross, Stanley R. 1966. "Introduction." In *Is the Mexican Revolution Dead?* edited by S. Ross. New York: Knopf.

————. 1972. *¿Ha muerto la revolución mexicana?* Mexico City: Secretaría de Educación Pública.

Roxborough, Ian. 1986. *Unions and Politics in Mexico: The Case of the Automobile Industry*. Cambridge: Cambridge University Press.

Russell, Phillip. 1978. "On Mexico," *New York Times*, July 20.

Russo, Daniel. 1985. *Conflict on Mexico's Other Border. A Challenge for United States Political and Military Relations*. Miami, Fl.

Sachs, Ignacy. 1972. "The Logic of Development," *International Social Science Journal* 24:1.

Safire, William. 1982. "Yankee Stick Around," *New York Times*, August 23.

Salisbury, Harrison E. 1980. *Without Fear or Favor. The New York Times and Its Times*. New York: Times Books.

Sandbrook, Richard. 1976. "The 'Crisis' in Political Development Theory," *Journal of Development Studies* 12:2 (January).

Sanders, Sol W. 1986. *Mexico; Chaos On Our Doorstep*. Lanham, Md.: Madison.

———. 1987. "Crisis Looms Down Mexico Way," *Pacific Defense Reporter*, April.

Sanderson, Steven E. 1981. *Agrarian Populism and the Mexican State*. Berkeley: University of California Press.

Sanderson, Susan Walsh. 1984. *Land Reform in Mexico: 1910–1980*. Orlando, Fl.: Academic Press.

Sauer, Franz A. von. 1974. *The Alienated "Loyal" Opposition. Mexico's Partido Accion Nacional*. Albuquerque: University of New Mexico Press.

Schlesinger, Arthur M., Jr. 1965. *A Thousand Days; John F. Kennedy in the White House*. Boston, Mass.: Houghton Mifflin.

Schmitt, Karl. 1965. *Communism in Mexico Today*. Austin: University of Texas Press.

Schoultz, Lars. 1982. "The Carter Administration and Human Rights." In *Human Rights and Basic Needs in the Americas*, edited by Margaret E. Crahan. Washington, D.C.: Georgetown University Press.

———. 1987. *National Security and United States Policy toward Latin America*. Princeton, N.J.: Princeton University Press.

Scott, Robert E. 1959. *Mexican Government in Transition*. Urbana: University of Illinois Press.

———. 1971. *Mexican Government in Transition*. 3d ed. Urbana: University of Illinois Press.

———. 1980. "Politics in Mexico." In *Comparative Politics Today: A World View*, edited by Gabriel Almond and G. Bingham Powell. Boston, Mass.: Little Brown.

SDN (Secretaría de la Defensa Nacional). 1945. "Informe final de los delegados que sostienen las pláticas conjuntas de Estados Mayores de México y Estados Unidos" (Secreto), March 27.

Seers, Dudley. 1973. "What Are We Trying to Measure?" *Development Digest* 11:1.

Segal, Aaron. 1979. "North American Energy," *New York Times*, September 29.

Segovia, Rafael. 1996. *Lapidaria política*. Mexico City: Fondo de Cultura Económica.

Selltiz, Claire, Lawrence S. Wrightsman, and Stuart W. Cook. 1976. *Research Methods in Social Relations*. New York: Holt, Rinehart and Winston.

Shafer, Robert J. 1973. *Mexican Business Organizations*. Syracuse, N.Y.: Syracuse University Press.

Shaff, Adam. 1969. *Sociología e ideología*. Barcelona: Anthropos.

Shapiro, Helen. 1981. "NACLA Reminiscences. An Oral History," *NACLA Report on the Americas*, September–October.

Shils, Edward. 1968. "Ideology." In *International Encyclopedia of the Social Sciences*, edited by David Sills, vol. 7. New York: Macmillan.

Shorris, Earl. 1985. "To Write, to Fight, to Die. The Old Gringo," *New York Times*, October 27.

Siebert, Fred S., Theodore Peterson, and Wilbur Schramm. 1963. *Four Theories of the Press.* Urbana: University of Illinois Press.

Sigal, Leon V. 1973. *Reporters and Officials.* Lexington, Mass.: Heath.

Skocpol, Theda. 1979. *States and Social Revolutions: A Comparative Analysis of France, Russia and China.* Cambridge: Cambridge University Press.

Smith, Brian H. 1982. "U.S.–Latin American Military Relations since World War II: Implications for Human Rights." In *Human Rights and Basic Needs in the Americas,* edited by Margaret E. Crahan. Washington, D.C.: Georgetown University Press.

Smith, David G. 1968. "Liberalism." In *International Encyclopedia of the Social Sciences,* edited by David Sills, vol. 9. New York: Macmillan.

Smith, Dwight C., Jr. 1975. *The Mafia Mystique.* New York: Basic Books.

Smith, Peter H. 1979. *Labyrinths of Power: Political Recruitment in Twentieth-Century Mexico.* Princeton, N.J.: Princeton University Press.

———. 1986. "Leadership and Change: Intellectuals and Technocrats in Mexico." In *Mexico's Political Stability: The Next Five Years,* edited by Roderic A. Camp. Boulder, Colo.: Westview.

Smith, Phillip R. 1971. "Amigos-Americans All," *Soldiers* 26 (September).

Solís, Leopoldo. 1969. "La política económica y el nacionalismo mexicano," *Foro Internacional* 9 (January–March).

Sorel, Georges. 1961. *Reflections on Violence.* New York: Collier.

Spengler, Joseph H. 1965. "Bureaucracy and Economic Development." In *Bureaucracy and Political Development,* edited by Joseph La Palombara. Princeton, N.J.: Princeton University Press.

Spero, Joan. 1988. "Guiding Global Finance," *Foreign Policy* 73 (Winter).

SRE (Secretaría de Relaciones Exteriores). 1958. *México en la Décima Conferencia Internacional Americana.* Mexico City: SRE.

ST (Secretary of the Treasury, U.S.). 1976a. "Trip to Chile, Brazil and Mexico." Memorandum for the President from the Secretary of the Treasury William E. Simon, May 24.

———. 1976b. "Financial Arrangements with Mexico." Memorandum for the President from the Secretary of the Treasury William E. Simon, September 20.

Stanley Foundation. 1986. "U.S. Policy Toward Mexico." Report Excerpt from the U.S. Foreign Policy Conference. Muscatine, Ia.: The Foundation, October.

Steinberg, Albert. 1950. "Human Villains," *New York Times,* September 8.

Stevens, Evelyn P. 1974. *Protest and Response in Mexico.* Cambridge, Mass.: MIT Press.

Stone, Philip J. 1966. *The General Inquirer. A Computer Approach to Content Analysis.* Cambridge, Mass.: MIT Press.

Story, Dale. 1986. *Industry, the State, and Public Policy in Mexico.* Austin: University of Texas Press.

Sulzberger, C.L. 1961. "B.C. and A.D. Attitudes in Mexico," *New York Times,* November 11.

———. 1962. "JFK and Another Kind of Democracy," *New York Times,* June 30.

———. 1973. "Too Much and Too Soon," *New York Times,* March 2.

Summers, Harry G., Jr. 1982. *On Strategy: A Critical Analysis of the Vietnam War*. Novato, Calif.: Presidio.

Sunkel, Osvaldo. 1977. *The Development of Development Thinking*. Paris: Development Centre of the Organisation for Economic Co-operation and Development.

Swaan, Mony de, Sergio Aguayo, and Jared Kotler. 1994. *The 1994 Mexican Election: A Question of Credibility*. Washington, D.C.: Washington Office on Latin America/Mexican Academy of Human Rights.

Swan, Guy C., III, et al. 1983. "Scott's Engineers," *Military Review* 63 (March).

Talese, Gay. 1969. *The Kingdom and the Power*. New York: New American Library.

———. 1971. *Honor Thy Father*. New York: World Publishing/Times Mirror.

Tannenbaum, Frank. 1966. "Some Reflections on the Mexican Revolution." In *Is the Mexican Revolution Dead?* edited by Stanley R. Ross. New York: Knopf.

Taylor, John M. 1982. "Lt. Grant and the Missing Money," *Army* 32:67–68 (February).

Teichman, Judith A. 1988. *Policymaking in Mexico: From Boom to Crisis*. Boston: Allen and Unwin.

Tello Díaz, Carlos. 1995. *La rebelión de las Cañadas*. Mexico City: Cal y Arena.

Thorup, Cathryn L. 1985. "Play It Smart with Mexico," *New York Times*, September 30.

———. 1993. "Redefining Governance in North America: The Impact of Cross-Border Networks and Coalitions on Mexican Immigration into the United States." DRU-257-FF. Santa Monica, Calif.: Rand Corporation, March.

Thorup, Cathryn L., and Robert L. Ayres. 1982. "Central America: The Challenge to United States and Mexican Foreign Policy." U.S.–Mexico Project Series, no. 8. Washington, D.C.: Overseas Development Council, July.

Treverton, Gregory V. 1988. "Narcotics in U.S.–Mexican Relations." In *Mexico and the United States: Managing the Relationship*, edited by Riordan Roett. Boulder, Colo.: Westview.

Truman, Harry S. 1955. *Memoirs*. Vol. 1, *Year of Decision*. Garden City, N.Y.: Doubleday.

———. 1956. *Memoirs*. Vol. 2, *Years of Trial and Hope*. Garden City, N.Y.: Doubleday.

Tucker, William P. 1957. *The Mexican Government Today*. Minneapolis: University of Minnesota Press.

Tuohy, William S., and Barry Ames. 1970. *Mexican University Students in Politics: Rebels without Allies?* Monograph Series in World Affairs. Denver, Colo.: University of Denver.

U.S. Army. 1963. "The Mexican-American War," *Army Information Digest*, September.

USC (US Congress). 1959a. Senate Committee on Foreign Relations. *United States–Latin American Relations*. Washington, D.C.: U.S. Government Printing Office.

———. 1959b. Senate Committee on Foreign Relations. *United States–Latin American Relations. Post World War II Developments in Latin America*. Washington, D.C.: U.S. Government Printing Office.

————. 1971. Senate Subcommittee on Western Hemisphere Affairs, Committee on Foreign Relations. *United States Policies and Programs in Brazil*, 92d Congress, 1st session, May.

————. 1975. Senate Select Committee to Study Governmental Operations. *Alleged Assassination Plots Involving Foreign Leaders*. Washington, D.C.: U.S. Government Printing Office.

USIA (United States Information Agency). 1956. "Mexican and Brazilian Public Opinion on International Issues." July 18.

————. 1964a. "Some Latin American Attitudes on Current Issues." July 11.

————. 1964b. "De Gaulle Visits Mexico." March 13.

Vance, Cyrus. 1983. *Hard Choices: Critical Years in America's Foreign Policy*. New York: Simon and Schuster.

Vázquez, Josefina Zoraida. 1984. "Cultural Linkages: A Mexican View," *Mexican Forum* (University of Texas at Austin) 4:1 (January).

————. 1985. "Teaching and Research in Mexico on United States History." In *Guide to the Study of United States History outside the U.S., 1945–1980*, edited by Lewis Hanke. Vol. 3. White Plains, N.Y.: Kraus.

Vázquez, Josefina Zoraida, and Lorenzo Meyer. 1982. *México frente a Estados Unidos. Un ensayo histórico, 1776–1980*. Mexico City: El Colegio de México.

Veraza, Sergio. 1968. "Dos monólogos no hacen diálogo," *El Día*, August 20.

Vernon, Raymond. 1963. *The Dilemma of Mexico's Development: The Roles of the Private and Public Sectors*. Cambridge, Mass.: Harvard University Press.

Virden, John M. 1957. "Destiny and Glory," *Army, Navy, Air Force Register* 78 (January 19).

Wager, Stephen J. 1992. "The Mexican Army, 1940–1982: The Country Comes First." Ph.D. dissertation, Stanford University.

Wager, Stephen, and Donald E. Schulz. 1994. *The Awakening: The Zapatista Revolt and Its Implications for Civil-Military Relations and the Future of Mexico*. Carlisle Barracks, Penn.: Strategic Studies Institute, U.S. Army War College.

Wall Street Journal. 1988. "Reading Mexico," July 15.

Wallerstein, Immanuel. 1974. *Capitalist Agriculture and the Origins of the European World-Economy in the Sixteenth Century*. Vol. 1, *The Modern World-System*. New York: Academic Press.

Walton, Richard J. 1973. *Cold War and Counterrevolution*. Baltimore, Md.: Penguin.

Wanniski, Jude. 1978. *The Way the World Works*. New York: Basic Books.

WD (War Department, U.S.). 1942. General Staff. "War Department's Objectives Respect to Mexico." Memorandum. Washington, D.C., February 5.

Weber, Max. 1946. *From Max Weber: Essays in Sociology*, edited by H.H. Gerth and C. Wright Mills. London: Oxford University Press.

Wendt, Lloyd. 1979. *Chicago Tribune: The Rise of a Great American Newspaper*. Chicago: Rand McNally.

WH (White House). 1956. "Memorandum of Conversation. Participants: Dwight D. Eisenhower, President Ruiz Cortines, Lt. Col. Vernon A. Walters." March 27.

————. 1960. "Memorandum of Conversation with the President. October 15, 1960," Gen. Brigadier A.J. Goodpaster. Washington, D.C., October 15.

———. 1961. "Report to the President on Latin American Mission, February 12–March 3, 1961," Arthur Schlesinger, Jr., March 10.

———. 1969. "Report to the President on US–Mexican Border Trade Problems," Harry R. Turkel, March 15.

Whines, David K. 1974. "The Measurement of Comparative Development: A Survey and Critique," *Journal of Modern African Studies* 12:1.

Whitehead, Laurence. 1980. "Mexico from Bust to Boom: A Political Evaluation of the 1976–1979 Stabilization Program," *World Development* 8.

———. 1991. "México y la hegemonía de Estados Unidos: pasado, presente y futuro." In *Las relaciones de México con el mundo,* edited by Riordan Roett. Mexico City: Siglo Veintiuno.

Wicker, Tom. 1979. "Time for a Leader," *New York Times,* February 18.

Williams, Edward J. 1986. "The Evolution of the Mexican Military and Its Implications for Civil-Military Relations." In *Mexico's Political Stability: The Next Five Years,* edited by Roderic A. Camp. Boulder, Colo.: Westview.

Williams, William A. 1959. *The Tragedy of American Diplomacy.* Cleveland: World.

———. 1964. *The Great Evasion.* Chicago: Quadrangle.

Wilson, Michael G. 1989. "The Security Component of U.S.–Mexico Relations," *Backgrounder* (Heritage Foundation), January 26.

Wionczek, Miguel S. 1967. *El nacionalismo mexicano y la inversión extranjera.* Mexico City: Siglo Veintiuno.

Wolfe, Alan. 1981. "Sociology, Liberalism, and the Radical Right," *New Left Review* 128 (July–August).

Womack, John. 1969. *Zapata and the Mexican Revolution.* New York: Knopf.

World Bank. 1981. *Accelerated Economic Development: An Agenda for Action.* Washington, D.C.: World Bank.

Wyden, Peter. 1979. *Bay of Pigs. The Untold Story.* New York: Simon and Schuster.

Yergin, Daniel. 1978. "The Mexican Oil 'High,'" *New York Times,* December 20.

Zamba, Michael. 1988. "Mexican Political Machine," *Journal of Defense and Diplomacy* 6 (June).

Zelman, Donald L. 1969. "American Intellectual Attitudes Toward Mexico, 1908–1940." Ph.D. dissertation, Ohio State University.

Zolberg, Aristide R., Astri Suhrke, and Sergio Aguayo. 1989. *Escape from Violence.* New York: Oxford University Press.

Index

About the Author

Sergio Aguayo Quezada has been a member of the research faculty of the Center for International Studies at El Colegio de México in Mexico City since 1977. He has also been a visiting professor at numerous universities in Mexico and abroad, including the New School for Social Research and the University of Chicago. His research focuses on security, U.S. foreign policy, U.S.–Mexican relations, and human rights. He has written or contributed to over twenty books, and he writes a weekly newspaper column which appears in Mexico's major newspapers.

Publication of important new research on Mexico and U.S.–Mexican relations is a major activity of the Center for U.S.–Mexican Studies. Statements of fact and opinion appearing in Center publications are the responsibility of the authors alone and do not imply endorsement by the Center for U.S.–Mexican Studies, the International Advisory Council, or the University of California.

For a list of all Center publications and ordering information, please contact:

Publications Sales Office
Center for U.S.–Mexican Studies
University of California, San Diego
9500 Gilman Drive, DEPT 0510
La Jolla, CA 92093-0510
Phone (619) 534-1160   Fax (619) 534-6447
e-mail: usmpubs@weber.ucsd.edu